D0208841

A History of Evil in Popular Culture

A History of Evil in Popular Culture

What Hannibal Lecter, Stephen King, and Vampires Reveal about America

Volume **2**: Evil in Words, Imagery, the News, Trials, Myths, and Religion

Sharon Packer and Jody Pennington, Editors

 PRAEGER

AN IMPRINT OF ABC-CLIO, LLC
Santa Barbara, California • Denver, Colorado • Oxford, England

Library of Congress Cataloging-in-Publication Data

A History of Evil in Popular Culture : What Hannibal Lecter, Stephen King,
and Vampires Reveal about America / Sharon Packer and Jody Pennington, editors.
 pages cm
 Includes index.
 ISBN 978-0-313-39770-7 (hardback) — ISBN 978-0-313-39771-4 (ebook)
1. Evil in literature. 2. Evil in motion pictures. 3. Evil—Social aspects.
I. Packer, Sharon, editor of compilation. II. Pennington, Jody W., 1959– editor of
compilation.
 PN56.E75H57 2014
 809'.93353—dc23 2014000164

ISBN: 978-0-313-39770-7
EISBN: 978-0-313-39771-4

18 17 16 15 14 1 2 3 4 5

This book is also available on the World Wide Web as an eBook.
Visit www.abc-clio.com for details.

Praeger
An Imprint of ABC-CLIO, LLC

ABC-CLIO, LLC
130 Cremona Drive, P.O. Box 1911
Santa Barbara, California 93116-1911

This book is printed on acid-free paper ∞

Manufactured in the United States of America

Contents

Introduction

Auschwitz. Treblinka. Dachau. Slave ships of the Middle Passage across the Atlantic. The Killing Fields of Cambodia. The Mai Lai Massacre, Vietnam. Columbine High School. Newton, Connecticut. Century 16 movie theater in a mall in Aurora, Colorado. Alfred P. Murrah Federal Building, Oklahoma City. The Twin Towers. Somalia. Bosnia, birthplace of ethnic cleansing. 16th Street Baptist Church bombing, Birmingham. The Rape of Nanking. The Boston Marathon bombing. The City of Sodom. These are places where evil occurred, unequivocally, even though places are not evil per se. Some of these places are American; all of them, or rather the evil that occurred, have had an impact on American society and culture.

Ted Bundy. Richard Speck. Leopold & Loeb. John Wayne Gacy. Jeffrey Dahmer. Charles Manson. Vlad the Impaler. Dr. Mengele. Adolf Hitler. Al Capone. Westley Allen Dodd. Rapists. Wife beaters. School shooters. Child molesters. Evil men, all of them, most Americans would strongly agree—yet there are countries and cultures where child brides are standard fare and where women expect to be beaten by their husbands. Where does evil begin and where does evil end? Is evil a social construction? Is it culturally relative? Can evil vary across jurisdictions? What about cannibals, for example? Are cannibals evil or not? Cannibalism is evil if done by Jeffrey Dahmer or Albert Fish. In 2013, New York City's "cannibal cop" was convicted of conspiring to kidnap, cook, kill, and cannibalize women. That was evil. Yet it was not thought to be evil by the Fore on New Guinea, who, until the 1950s, retained the rites of their ancestors and honored their dead by consuming their brains. Beyond the geography of evil, there is the cause of evil: what drives perpetrators? Consider Andrea Yates, the delusional mother of five who drowned her children because she hoped to save their souls from Satan's clutches and free hers: was she evil? Or was she psychotic? Does it even matter? News shows and press reports, judges and juries swung back and forth. It is not so clear, not even to the courts that overturned her earlier conviction and eventually found her not guilty by reason of insanity. What about other mothers who watch their sons die for reasons that are not so dissimilar to Yates's reasoning? Does the way we *explain* causes influence which acts and their perpetrators count as evil?

Hannah, fabled mother of the Maccabee warriors, and one of two heroines of the Chanukah story, watched her seven sons accept death over apostasy. (After their deaths, Hannah committed suicide.) Mary, mother of Jesus, witnessed the sacrifice of her son, supposedly for the salvation of humankind. Other mothers send their sons to war, knowing that the boys may die on the battlefield. The latter examples are deemed honorable, not evil, provided the spectator supports the same value system as the story's protagonist.

Questions about evil continue. As do explanations. Myth, religion, philosophy, sociology, and as in the case of Andrea Yates, psychology, have all weighed in. So too, the works of popular culture and critics' interpretations of them.

Tony Soprano, the fictional mobster that hires hit men, aids his psychiatrist when she is raped in a parking garage. Does his single act of kindness override his countless acts of evil? Michael Corleone renounces Satan and all of his works as his henchmen carry out a series of murders. Is he redeemed? What about real-life mobsters who care for their wives, children, and mothers, because they have "superegos lacunae" that function under certain circumstances but not others? That metapsychological "superego lacuna" has holes like Swiss cheese, so that it remains intact in some areas and imparts a circumscribed sense of morality, but has glaring gaping holes that relieve the person of remorse for many other acts.

Evil—and its cognates in other languages—is the term used to condemn deliberate acts by human beings, acting individually or collectively, that are beyond the moral pale. There is also a category called "natural evil," which includes acts of nature, such as typhoons, floods, famine, earthquakes, and even shark attacks. However, some philosophers attribute "natural evil" to human acts or moral choices. For instance, the Lisbon earthquake of 1755 seemed to be an act of nature, yet commentators of the stature of Jean-Jacques Rousseau linked the death and destruction that followed the earthquake to human choices. By escaping the countryside and moving to coastal cities (which carried the connotation of sin), more people and buildings were in harm's way, so suffering escalated after this natural disaster.[1]

In many instances, societies and their members reach a consensus as to what constitutes evil. But the complexity of human motivation, the variety of perspectives found in various cultures about a given behavior—the political disagreements over one person's terrorist and another's freedom fighter—raise as many questions as provide answers to what would on the surface seems to be cut-and-dried. Are suicide bombers who sacrifice their lives to commit mass murder evil? For almost all Americans, the answer is absolutely, unequivocally, emphatically, "yes"—but many fundamentalist adherents of their faith view them as martyrs and revere them as saints.

What about the Crusades during the Middle Ages, when Christians killed Muslims and other infidels? Or the judges at Salem in the 17th century, who drowned or burned women accused of witchcraft, because they believed that they were saving the greater society from the evils of Satan? Acts that most Americans consider the epitome of evil may amount to a guaranteed place in Paradise in some other societies. Again, is it relative and does it depend upon whom you ask?

Questions are raised and answers sought about which acts are evil, whether the person carrying out an act is evil, or if the society that condones it—even orders it—is evil. More than anything else, we ponder about the influences that catalyze those evil acts. In American history, we consider the case of Thomas Jefferson, who advocated equal political opportunity and opposed privilege, aristocracy, and corruption, yet was a slave owner himself. At the Nuremberg Trials of Nazis accused of war crimes, the world heard one Nazi after another deny responsibility for heinous deeds by claiming, "I was only following orders." Some were exonerated, and some were imprisoned, and several were sentenced to death. Another curious case is that of two-time Nobel Prize winner, Daniel Gajdusek. There is no doubt that Dr. Gajdusek advanced science and medicine through his discoveries, but the courts doubted his defense against pedophilic activities conducted with some of his adopted sons. Gajdusek remained unrepentant and argued that such activities are accepted in many of the societies he studied and in several now-extinct societies. In other words, Gajdusek, the medical scientist who functioned as both anthropologist and virologist, promoted cultural relativism.

Even if we agree that different societies disagree on the definition of evil, who is qualified to answer questions about evil? These are theological questions, moral questions, sociological questions, criminal justice questions, or possibly forensic psychiatry questions. Yet, again, there is no consensus among expert sources. Were there agreement, there would be no need for appeals of convictions, or for hung juries, or for theories of just war. If moral judgments remained the same from religion to religion, from culture to culture, then right and wrong, good and evil would remain the same, regardless of religion or culture. In a secularized world, the moral codes of religions might not even be relevant at all, although concern with evil has in many ways become restricted to specialists in the philosophy of religion, according to moral philosopher Susan Neiman, author of *Evil in Modern Thought: An Alternative History of Philosophy* (Princeton UP, 2004) and winner of books awards in both religion and philosophy, as general philosophers no longer seem interested in asking or answering these questions.

Speaking of theology, we encounter just as much confusion about the nature of evil in that sphere. It is older than the Abrahamic religions, if we search pre-Biblical sources. For believers in the Bible, evil begins in the Garden of Eden. Eve unleashed evil when she ate the apple and offered it to Adam. In Christianity, this act became "original sin," a concept that was revised over the millennia. In Judaism, Eve's tasting of the apple unleashed "the evil desire," or libido, which counters "the good inclination." Sex and sin are conflated, according to this interpretation, and remained so in America, from the time of the Puritans through the Motion Picture Production Code (The Hays Code) of the early 1930s. Not so long ago, then, sex was sin and banned from cinema. Today, censors are condemned for their evil, authoritarian intentions. "Censorious" is an adjective with negative connotations, one that implies that the possessor has a potential for evil. The same goes for sexual preference: in contemporary society, it is illegal to discriminate against someone who prefers same-sex partners, or who aspires to change genders. Yet some religions—and many regions—continue to view same-sex sex as evil, and link it to the intrinsically evil Biblical city Sodom (which, incidentally, bequeathed the name of its towns on such practitioners). Even within the same religion and the same culture, both perspectives can be found.

The interchangeability between sex and sin, and the equation of (unsanctified) sex with sin, persisted until the latter half of the 20th century, if not later. The AIDS epidemic, which began in earnest in 1981, highlights the conflicts between religious and secular interpretations of illness, sex, and sin. To AIDS sufferers and to most (but not all) members of the medical community, AIDS was a deadly and disfiguring disease and another example of "natural evil"—becausedisease is inherently evil. To the religious right, AIDS was not evil; rather, it was just retribution for behavior that defied normative sexual preferences and conservative religious (and often legal) codes. Like the Lisbon earthquake of the 18th century, the AIDS epidemic represented more than a lethal virus unleashed on society. In the 1980s, we had no Voltaire and Rousseau to argue with one another, yet we had other outspoken commentators.

The conflation of sexual behavior with sin is symptomatic of a larger trend during the 20th century: the turn from religious explanations for human misdeeds to the human sciences of psychology and sociology, a shift from notions of inherent evil as part of human failing, a human fall from the Garden of Evil, to ones governed by a different epistemology. The ancient Greeks acknowledged the existence of "divine possession." Hippocrates railed against the "sacred disease" (as epilepsy was called). Christian Europe attributed madness to satanic possession until the 18th century, and left neuropsychiatric symptoms to the purview of doctors of the church, rather than doctors of medicine.

Gradually, though, evil fell within the purview of human and medical sciences and an empiricist set of explanations rooted in physical or mental health or the role of society—or important actors in family such as abusive mothers or fathers—in inducing evil behavior, a medicalization of evil, a set of explanations—and often identity—with various pathologies.

Anyone who thinks that the courts or the criminal justice system or psychiatrists can identify evil when they see it (in the way that U.S. Supreme Court Justice Potter Stewart, and many after him, said he could identify hard-core pornography "when I see it") is mistaken. Most contemporary measures of evil are solipsistic, reflecting back on themselves and creating a virtual house of cards. Arbiters rely upon ambiguous assessments to make definitive determinations. Courts turn to psychiatric testimony to decide if a man or a woman who is charged with "evil" acts is mad or bad, or both. There is rarely a consensus among psychiatrists that testify about the presence or absence of evil—or mental illness. Both the defense and the prosecution can find professionals who espouse one side or the other.

To see what Americans think about the use of professional testimony to identify "evil" and distinguish "mad" from "bad," we can recall when forensic psychiatry dropped to its depths with the unforgettable "Hostess Twinkie" defense. An otherwise respectable psychiatrist hypothesized that blood sugar shifts, caused by excessive junk food consumption, catalyzed the murderous impulses and compromised the intellectual judgments that led to the killing of city supervisor Harvey Milk and San Francisco Mayor George Moscone in 1978. The ex-police officer, ex-firefighter, and current city supervisor, Dan White, admitted to pulling the trigger but was exculpated of first-degree murder charges and convicted of a lesser offense because of his "diminished capacity." White served time in Soledad until 1984 and committed suicide in 1985. Forensic psychiatry had made a mockery of itself in this instance. The jury accepted the "Twinkie defense" even though critics (and most psychiatrists) condemned it. The year was 1979.

We also look at the legacy of the fictional Dr. Hannibal Lecter, in both the novels and the films. The original Hannibal novels evolved soon after the "Twinkie defense" made its way into popular culture. Author Thomas Harris refuses to reveal the inspirations for his stories (be they about Hannibal or anyone else), yet the chronological correspondence between the Harvey Milk and Mayor Moscone murder trial and the publication of Harris's first Hannibal novel suggest that this highly publicized event registered in Harris's consciousness.

We know that the heinous acts of Ed Gein found their way into the best-selling Hannibal novels, which subsequently became a series of award-winning films and recent TV shows. Gein was a mentally compromised serial killer who sewed the skins of his victims into costumes used for his own cross-dressing. We know that Harris visited the FBI's recently formed psychology unit while researching his subject matter. While we cannot prove that Hannibal's creator deliberately spoofed the Twinkie defense when he fleshed out the flesh-eating character of Dr. Hannibal Lecter, the astute reader strongly suspects as much. We can sense his disdain for the moral authority enjoyed by forensic psychiatry, if we look at the character he has created, a character that has since become emblematic of evil.

Harris insinuates that Hannibal comprehends the most evil criminals because he himself is a "fellow traveler" who tours the netherworld of otherwise unimaginable evil. In other words, according to Harris (and his many devoted fans and the filmmakers who turned his novels into movies and TV shows), the professional who is authorized to identify evil is no different from the person who perpetuates evil.

Dr. Lecter is an aesthete with a European education. He has an enviable knowledge of culture in general and psychiatry in particular. He also possesses a criminal mind and lacks a conscience and acts on his atypical sexual preferences, which include cannibalism and mutilation. Hannibal Lecter went on to become America's best-recognized movie villain of the late 20th century. This brilliant but polymorphous perverse murderer advises the FBI about serial killers, and outwits wardens when he escapes prison after prison. In *The Silence of the Lambs* (1991), Lecter (Anthony Hopkins) also rescues an imperiled Agent Starling (Jodie Foster), proving that he can be a gentleman as well as a murderer.

Hannibal Lecter answers our questions about German Kultur that descended into the Nazi mass murderers; about Jefferson, the slave owner and the democracy advocate; and about a doctor like Gajdusek, who saved the world from certain dreaded diseases but preyed upon impoverished children (and sent some of them to college and medical school). Hannibal proves that a person can be both admirable and despicable at the same time, and that evil can coexist with good. Yet more questions pop up. How much good is needed to override evil? How much evil undoes a long legacy of goodness? Those are questions for the courts, for sentencing judges, for deliberating juries, and for the American public.

Even though Lecter represents Americans' imago of psychiatrists who possess professional insight into what and who are evil, psychiatry's Diagnostic & Statistical Manual of Mental Disorders does not list a diagnosis of "evil"—although it acknowledges the existence of an "antisocial personality disorder." Yet even this pronouncement may be premature and subject to change in the near future, as biological psychiatry advances, and identifies biological markers and brain abnormalities that transmit anti-social traits or correlate with it and thereby imply that these traits exist without free will, another example of the medicalization, augmented by a biologization, of evil. "The fault," as Cassius tells Brutus in *Julius Caesar*, is "not in our stars, But in ourselves." Does the fault lie in our genes and synaptic misfires?

Let us say a little more about such anti-social persons, since they by definition commit evil without conscience and do harm without apparent concern for the well-being of those that they harm.*

It used to be thought that "sociopathy" stood apart from ordinary mental illness. However, newer data shows that such traits can be inherited, and transmitted from generation to generation. Sometimes antisocial behavior follows from localized brain trauma or disease (rather than just emotional trauma). Half of all persons with alcohol use disorder meet the criteria for antisocial personality disorder (ASPD) but half do not. The data concerning persons with alcohol use disorder who are dependent upon illicit substances are even stronger, but the data that compare men and women with the same genetic profile is more confusing; certain types of monoamine amine oxidase (MAO) transmitters increase the odds of ASPD.[2] Persons with bipolar disorder (manic depression) can engage in sociopathic acts when manic, but show no such traits when their moods are level, and then manifest intense (possibly suicidal level) remorse when depressed.[3]

Specific brain injuries can increase the risk of antisocial behavior. This includes the highly publicized traumatic brain injury (TBI) that affects many veterans. The consequences depend upon which part of the brain is injured (and other factors, which may include premorbid personality and certainly substance use). Severing the corpus callosum that connects the brain's right and left hemisphere can produce such antisocial effects. Damage to the amygdala can result in automatic rage attacks. Some degenerative disorders produce antisocial behavior as well as dementia. For instance, deterioration of the frontal lobes of the brain can remove a preexisting sense of morality and social appropriateness. Is the grandfather who develops dementia—and subsequently sexually mistreats his grandchild—the same as the inveterate and unrepentant sociopath who chooses to live an evil life? The demented grandfather is just as much a danger, but does he deserve the same punishment that society reserves for volitional acts?

Similarly, alcohol is known as the great "superego solvent." Sometimes, intoxicated people engage in evil activity that they shun when sober. Bar

---

* The "antisocial personality traits" that we speak of here are *not* related in any way to the social avoidance exhibited by shy, socially phobic, schizoid or autism spectrum people. This "antisocial" behavior refers to behavior that goes *against* society and societal norms, without concern for other members of that society.

fights abound when drunk. Domestic violence soars. Sometimes, "vehicular homicide" results from driving while drunk. The courts decide if "vehicular homicide" is as evil as premeditated homicide or manslaughter. The public debates if the courts are correct and the courts solicit medical and psychiatric opinions to make their decisions. On a related note, habitué drug users typically engage in "evil" behavior to support their habits. They rob, steal, prostitute themselves, and some even sell their AIDS meds to earn extra cash for a fix. Are they victims of their biology, or are they evil when they refuse to seek treatment? Does it make a difference if they already undertook such treatment, complied with the current standards, but that recommended treatment was not effective in the past?

There are so many questions about evil, and so few absolute answers. Because America is both a melting pot and a democracy, we encounter many different opinions about evil, each one informed by different cultural, religious, and national backgrounds, and tempered by socioeconomic issues, political persuasion, and age and perhaps gender. Because America is a democracy, we value everyone's opinions, and strive to give equal weight to minorities as well as majorities (even though such efforts often fall short of goals).

That is where mass media comes in. Americans can dissect and debate the nuances of evil via the media. Popular culture is the greatest melting pot of all. Pop culture tackles thorny issues and sometimes draws conclusions. Each time we watch a movie about evil, we experience a personal reaction. We are free to reflect on our gut reactions and revise them. We can read about the opinions of others, via reviews, "cocktail party or school cafeteria conversations," or discussions with intimate partners or with complete strangers whom we encounter while standing in line to purchase popcorn. We can compare our personal response to the consensus—and we can see that there is rarely a consensus, and that there are many caveats to evil.

In short, in America, evil invades all forms of entertainment: movies, TV shows, novels, theme parks, video games, music, myth, and "murderabilia." Let me emphasize something, though. Saying that Americans turn evil into entertainment is not the same as saying that Americans trivialize evil. On the contrary, mass media and pop culture are the crossroads of American culture, a place where people of diverse backgrounds, different ages, races and genders, and national origins have a common meeting place and can ask themselves the same moral questions about the nature of evil.

This volume surveys the presence of evil in American society and in American culture. Evil is found in American homes and on unsafe streets. Domestic violence and serial killers, rape and murder—all too often—crimes that are agreed to be *malum in se* exist in the country.

Representations of evil are also found throughout popular and high culture. A fascination with that which we abhor seems to find an acceptable outlet in movies, literature, music, and other forms of cultural expression. At times, this fascination becomes eerily experiential, as when "fans" of serial killers emerge to shape a market for items associated with celebrity murderers. The very notion of celebrity murderer suggests a cultural ambivalence to the heinous, one captured in popular culture from Oliver Stone's *Natural Born Killers* (1994) to the Showtime TV series *Dexter* (2006–2013) and other works. How does one confront the dissonance of the popularity of representations of the moral abyss? Exactly what is it that we find entertaining?

If we consider film critic Parker Tyler's comments in his famed book, *Hollywood Hallucination* (1944), we can gain a better understanding of how popular culture refines our understanding of moral questions about good and evil. In *Hollywood Hallucination*, Tyler described movies as the "poor man's psychoanalysis," because the spectator observes the reactions of characters on-screen and compares them to his (or her) own reactions. Watching movies (or reading novels or playing video games or listening to lyrics) provides a point of comparison with the "common man" (or woman) and functions as a measuring stick for our personality traits, relationships, goals, values, fears, and conceits. Similarly, engaging in entertainment that employs themes of evil allows us to ask ourselves, "What is evil," "would we do evil, and under what circumstances," and "how would we react to evil, when we encounter it?"

Admittedly, it is unlikely that anyone consciously chooses to spend an evening on a Hitchcock film, in lieu of rereading Hannah Arendt's *Eichmann in Jerusalem: A Report on the Banality of Evil* (1963), and then expects cinema to produce the same results as assigned readings for college classes. That is the whole point.

While some students gravitate to courses on ethics, morality, and philosophy, most people choose entertainment over edification. College professors can confirm that the average student will readily watch a three-hour film—or play video games for hours on end—in lieu of completing a reading assignment on the very same topic, even when the textbook reading requires less time. Persons who choose entertainment about evil are rarely making an "either-or" choice. They are simply exercising their free will when they read or write poems or listen to lyrics about philosophical topics that sound too "heavy" or too foreboding on the surface.

Embedding tough topics in entertainment makes them more accessible to the average person. And, yes, some people enjoy identifying with the villain, if only for a few hours, and if only in fantasy, just to imagine how they might feel if given the opportunity to do evil. The thought *is not* the deed (except in some religions). Forensic psychiatrist Robert Simon elaborates on this phenomenon in his book with a self-explanatory title, *Bad Man Do What Good Men Dream*.[4]

More often than not, the average person indulges in fantasies about evil without serious intentions of carrying out those fantasies. Life can be frustrating, and fantasies can relieve tensions, and create distractions, without necessarily solving the problems.

Who does not have a fight with a boss, a spouse, a parent, a neighbor, a classmate, or a coworker? Some people fume, some people get depressed, some drink or drug, and some resort to reveries of revenge. In other words, they contemplate committing evil acts, or they gravitate to media with related motifs.

Through pop culture, they can imagine what would happen if they fulfilled those fantasies. When we watch *The Postman Always Rings Twice* (1946) (or read James M. Cain's novel that inspired director Tay Garnett), some of us identify with the bored hausfrau who lives with a caring but boring husband—but few seriously plot to murder their spouse, either before or after the film. Just in case we get carried away while watching the plot unfold, the film's denouement acts as the greatest deterrent, for it informs us that trivial details can foil the best-laid plans. The drama functions as a morality tale and warns us against engaging in evil, not merely because of the ethical implications, but because of the possibility of being discovered, arrested, imprisoned, and possibly executed.

Similarly, Poe's stories about beating hearts remind readers about pangs on conscience that plague potential evildoers after the fact. *Rear Window* (1954) or *Shock* (1946) tell us that witnesses are watching through the windows, and offer one more reason for avoiding murder during marital disputes, no matter how angry or annoyed we get with our spouses.

True, there are many forms of pop culture that condone evil acts or that inflict evil on innocent or unintended victims. First-person shooter games are obvious examples. Even third-person shooter games, such as the wildly popular Grand Theft Auto (1997–), and its many versions, are all about evil: rape, murder, pillage, and plunder for starters. That is where public controversy comes in and reins in our reactions to evil. Even when the censors do not have their way, the debates provoked by such media call more attention to the distinction between good and evil.

The works in the first volume of this collection examine a variety of manifestations of evil and attitudes toward evil. They examine evil in words and evil in deed and different fascinations with evil from the rhetorical framing by U.S. presidents of social problems, terrorism, and so-called rogue states to the fascination ranging from the aesthetic flirting with evil by rock musicians in the Southern California of the 1960s to the collection of trinkets and relics that are vestiges of horror, guilty by association of evil, but collected as mementos. From popular culture to real-life examples of evil, the volumes present different perspectives, understandings, and interpretations of evil.

Popular culture in the United States is immense, so there will invariably be topics and works these volumes do not treat. Films as different as *The Wizard of Oz* (1939), *The Abominable Dr. Phibes* (1971), *Se7en* (1995), *Charlie and the Chocolate Factory* (2005), and those that comprise the *Saw* franchise (2004–2010) have represented evil in different ways at different times in Hollywood's history. The list of serial killers, mobsters, and criminals is unfortunately long and many notorious Depression era bank robbers such as Bonnie Parker and Clyde Barrow have not made it onto these pages. The impact of the settlement of the New World on the indigenous peoples who did not survive the violent confrontations with settlers as they moved across the continent is likewise not treated. These are not oversights but merely a function of the limits of two volumes and a sad commentary on the extensiveness of evil.

As with so many other elements of our lives, film and television are two media that have represented evil profusely. This collection looks at a number of themes, including racism. It examines the complicity of small towns, whether a Mississippi community looking the other way while local rednecks violently enforce Jim Crow or a small Western community covering up the murderous misdeed of a local thug, the evil of murder being matched by that of the evil of passivity in the face of knowledge of evil. The evil of racism has become a staple of Hollywood film, although the mainstream American film industry has been complicit in that racism, not least in its representation of African American males.

It also concerns itself with a classic source of evil, authoritarianism, ranging from Nazis to Soviets to the emperor and the empire as oppressive from Rome to the distant galaxies of science fiction. Hollywood has portrayed the Holocaust as well as Nazis in various ways, including as zombies. Sometimes film has envisioned the empire taken down with a punch, the basic theme of many Hollywood films during the 1980s; other times the empire-to-be can be thwarted only with the aid of nonhuman beings.

Crime genres provide thrilling vicarious exposure to evil in its circadian commonality, as in the films of one of the most significant filmmakers to grapple with representations of criminal evil and its consequences, Martin Scorsese. This collection concerns itself with the criminal mastermind as an incarnation of sorts of the devil, the blurring of the boundaries between good and evil as a narrative device, the notion of finance as the root of all evil, the banker and investor as greed driven and barely human and perhaps infected with a bubble-fueled contagion. Violent crime is known through its association with mafia and the mob's henchmen paid to murder. At the other end of the spectrum of right and wrong, but circling back on itself to be another form of evil, is the violent vigilante. Hollywood has had audiences pulling for both the hit man and the vigilante. The criminal as predator is a common theme in numerous films, including postapocalyptic genres when the predation leads to cannibalism. Another form of predatory behavior is that of the psychotic killer in the horror genre and that genre's ability to raise questions in the mind of members of the audience about the extent of evil perpetrated by the mentally ill.

In less quotidian fictional universes, the threat of evil is from creatures not quite human but not unhuman either. Vampires and zombies have had a vogue over the last decade or so, bringing to the screen a variation on the cannibal theme. Their popularity raises questions of how representations on our screens reflect not so much reality but of collective notions of our perceptions of the world around us, including our fears. Those fears extend beyond earth to imagined threats from creatures from space or from spiritual spaces that demons leave to enter into human beings. Imagined worlds include evil incarnate in characters such as Lord Voldemort that have to be challenged by the cunning and guilelessness of a child.

While the collection does not examine the murder ballads of American folk music such as "The Story of the Knoxville Girl," it does look at some of the darker sides of popular music and its antecedent, the blues. Mid-century popular music examined the evil of lynching and racism. Various genres, not least heavy metal, have depicted evil in lyrics even as the musicians have struck various poses and adorned themselves with costumes to suggest an affinity with evil, even if staged. In some cases, as often with heavy metal and later with hip-hop, as with the blues and rock 'n'roll earlier, the genre itself is seen as being evil.

By the time the reader reaches the second volume of this series, something becomes apparent: although we organized these two volumes into five circumscribed sections, in reality, many essays do not fall into single discrete categories. Some essays could fit into at least one other category, or maybe more.

There is a good reason for this overlap: many topics and tropes cross into various forms of media, and one medium cross-pollinates another. Sometimes, works go back and forth, so that a Poe story is made into a film, and the film adaptation is subsequently retold in story form and sold as a book. In our section on novels, poems, and short stories, we find many films, video games—even puppet shows or costumed events, ballets, and operas—that are dedicated to the same subject matter or based on the same source material. For instance, Gothic is a literary form, as our essay explains, but it may be even more recognizable as a fashion trend.

For more examples, Stephen King and Edgar A. Poe both wrote short stories, novellas, and some full-length novels in the case of King, or poems of everlasting fame for Poe. Their ideas were too rich to restrict to the written word, even though they began with the written word. So film, TV, and video games tapped into their themes as did Halloween costumes or quill desk sets that recollect Poe's era.

The same can be said for Hannibal Lecter stories, which sprang from novels, but turned into a string of films and a TV series. While Thomas Harris has not yet gained the fame of a King or a Poe, he has made an enduring mark on American culture. For it is Harris who explores current social constructions of evil when he satirizes forensic psychiatry, the field that is responsible for filtering information for the courts and recommending who is mad, versus who is bad or evil, who has "diminished capacity" and who is NGRI (not guilty by reason of insanity) and who is "seriously and dangerously mentally ill," as opposed to being "seriously mentally ill" alone. Harris's character, Dr. Hannibal Lecter, became the best-recognized villain of late 20th-century America, outpacing old-time horror film and Halloween favorites, such as Count Dracula or Frankenstein's monster.

Speaking of vampires, we include a few essays on vampirism (and zombies) in this series. One essay is devoted to literature and another focuses on television. Theoretically, we could have included an essay on breakfast cereals (think of Count Chocula) or vampire clubs where members dress as the living dead and drink the guests' blood. The vampire themes in media live everlasting lives, and are as immortal as the vampires themselves. Different generations reinterpret vampires, reconstructing and reimagining them to reflect the realities of the day. In some cases, capitalistic vampires suck blood as if it were money. More recent vampire stories hint at the bloodborne AIDS epidemic, which claimed souls and bodies and turned socially ostracized victims into the living dead.

Hardboiled detective fiction is dramatically different from supernatural tales about vampires, but both tropes share something significant: like other examples above, evil themes in hard-boiled fiction may begin in books, pulps, and comics, but many end up on-screen, big and small, stationary or animated. Detective stories and other thrillers and dramas are often inspired by real-life events that are played out in newscasts and courtroom dramas. Hence, we have a separate section on political polemics and legal cases that are publicized by the press. In fact, many of the most evil events that are chronicled in fiction and nonfiction media have occurred in real time, and were woven into fictionalized forms after the fact. The boundaries blur, as do the categories that are demarcated in this book.

Essays on hit men, mobsters, and vigilantes draw from everyday events that make front-page news. Some inspire video games. Video games, with their action orientation and the need to stop villains in their tracks, are obvious vectors for riffs on evil. We wish we had space for more essays on this rapidly growing mass media, which attracts more males than females and more younger people. Our section on video games appears in our art and animations section, which also includes other visual imagery, such as murderabilia mementos. Fine art is rarely conceived of as "evil," per se (unless we count Goya's *Black Paintings*, but they are not American). There are notable exceptions, such as Francis Bacon's depictions of butchered bodies, which influenced far more films than we realize (until we read our essay). Bacon contrasts with Edward Hopper's sad and lonely cityscapes that are not evil but are simply lonely and that influenced film noir aesthetics.

Even happy-looking clowns can be evil, as John Wayne Gacy taught us in recent times, as medieval puppeteers knew long ago and as *Batman's* Joker shows. Children's entertainment often focuses on evil, not to encourage it but to convey morality tales and teach the consequences of evil. The essays on Walt Disney document the ways that Disney sanitized fearsome European fairy tales for young American audiences—even though Disney's lifestyle and political persuasions conflict with the wholesome, all-embracing image he parlayed. Comics also focus on evil, given that their action-oriented drama is driven by battles between heroes and villains. In our collection, we use *Batman's* villains as examples of evil. Batman began in comics, but has franchised into films, video games, lunchboxes, and innumerable academic studies.

The documented deeds of serial killers such as Ted Bundy, Ed Gein, and the Killer Clown, John Wayne Gacy, are more horrifying than our worst nightmares. True tales of these tragedies are blended into fiction, which can be easier to tolerate than pure documentary-style renditions or news shows. Still, our collection includes firsthand accounts of the prosecutor who finally convicted Bundy, the handsome ladies' man who continued to receive love letters and marriage proposals while behind bars.

Political events involving evil play themselves out in many ways, as our section on that subject shows. These events are commemorated in speeches, legal debates, newscasts, or public rallies. Topics include the Holocaust, which sent many refugees to the Americas, and left even more dead on European soil. Tales of internment of Japanese Americans during World War II, satanic panics, not just in the rural South but also in New York City, increased attention to sexual victimization of children, in pornography and in the personal arena, found their way into our essays. Civil Rights issues, and lack of rights, are represented.

Sadly, so many evil events occur on a regular basis, but most could not be included in this series, because of time and space constraints. Sexual trafficking, the criminalization of the mentally ill, racially disparate sentencing for drug-related offenses, sexually or racially motivated murders, and illicit medical experiments performed in America or by Americans outside of America are but a few of the "real evils" that deserve more mention than they received. Those omissions do not reflect the fact that they are less important than "killer clowns" or sensationalized serial murderers. Rather, their absence reflects publishing limitations, and our need to complete a project that will probably never have a real end.

As we close, let us go back to the basics, and look at our section on myth and religion. Before secular forces held sway, religion, in its many varieties, determined what is right and what is wrong, what is good and what is evil. As our essays show, sometimes those absolutes worked and sometimes they were twisted. Essays on the West Memphis Three and criminal trials for satanic cults prove that the religious preoccupations that catalyzed the colonization of America still hold sway in many religions, and can inspire contemporary witch hunts than are eerily reminiscent of Salem. An entire series could be devoted to myth and religious explanations for evil, but we must make do with a small section.

One glaring omission of our essay collection is our lack of attention to "natural evil," which has consistently been a concern for religion. We have chapters on evil animals in evolution (but not in fairy tales, where the "big bad wolf" is so persistent a presence and it almost escapes detection). There is not enough focus on the "killer animals" of the 1970s films, which began the blockbuster trends that have remained with us to this day. The good/bad news is that there is much to contemplate in the material that we did include. Good news, because this series contains extensive reading material and fresh ideas, but it is also bad news, because these two books document the ever-expanding existence of evil in real life, which, in turn, is transformed into entertainment, mass media, and pop culture.

Sharon Packer and
Jody Pennington

NOTES

1. Voltaire, "Poem on the Lisbon Disaster, Or: An Examination of That Axiom 'All Is Well'," in *Toleration and Other Essays*, translated, with an introduction, by Joseph McCabe (New York and London: G. P. Putnam's Sons, 1912). Jean-Jacques Rousseau, "Rousseau's Letter to Voltaire Regarding the Poem on the Lisbon Earthquake," http://www.indiana.edu/~enltnmt/texts/JJR%20letter .html (accessed November 23, 2013).

2. A. I. Herman et al., "Variation in the Gene Encoding the Serotonin Transporter Is Associated with a Measure of Sociopathy in Alcoholics," *Addiction Biology* 16, no. 1 (2011): 124–32.

3. Alan C. Swann et al., "Antisocial Personality Disorder and Borderline Symptoms Are Differentially Related to Impulsivity and Course of Illness in Bipolar Disorder," *Journal of Affective Disorders* 148, no. 2–3 (2013): 384–90.

4. Robert I. Simon, *Bad Men Do What Good Men Dream: A Forensic Psychiatrist Illuminates the Darker Side of Human Behavior* (Washington, DC: American Psychiatric Publishing, 2008).

PART I

Novels, Poems, and Short Stories

CHAPTER 1

Gender, Goth, and Gore: Evil in the Horror Fiction of Poppy Z. Brite

Aalya Ahmad

In renowned Lovecraft scholar S. T. Joshi's *The Evolution of the Weird Tale*, only one female-identified author—Poppy Z. Brite—gets a chapter of her own. Joshi scoffs that "Brite can write, but in many cases she has nothing to write about." Phrases such as "naïve and hyperventilated" litter Joshi's scathing essay on Brite; here the author is indulging in "owlish school-girl philosophy," there she is "not as good a writer as she thinks she is." Joshi's literary takedown of Brite may be, as he concedes, "a generational thing"[1]; it may also be a gender thing. No other author selected for Joshi's otherwise all-male pantheon of contemporary weird fiction writers gets such scornful treatment. At least Joshi has noticed Brite's work, which nowhere receives mention in any feminist discussion of contemporary fiction.

Since writing the fictions discussed here, Brite has transitioned and now goes by the name of Billy Martin. Such gender fluidity supports the idea that Brite's horror fiction best fits a Third Wave, rather than a Second Wave feminist horror paradigm. In what follows, I will discuss the early work of Brite *as* Brite, since Martin has consciously distanced himself from both the horror genre in general and his earlier work; however, the persona of Brite continues to exist on the World Wide Web and in authored works. This raises interesting questions about authorship and transgendered identities; unfortunately, such questions are beyond the scope of this essay, in which I will discuss Brite's fiction against the grain of much feminist scholarship that has traditionally been more concerned with the portrayal of women within horror, what Cynthia Freeland calls "a somewhat old-fashioned feminist approach . . . the 'images of women' approach."[2] Building on Freeland's important critique of much feminist horror criticism, especially psychoanalytic film theory, I will examine how Brite's characters, particularly in the novel *Exquisite Corpse*, struggle with concepts of evil that are no less compelling for being contemporary.

In fact, Brite's work in its entirety can be read to signify both a continuation of and a radical break with the older feminist concept of the "Female Gothic," where evil resides in patriarchal structures and authority figures plotting to exert ruthless control over women's bodies and lives.[3] In *Redefining the American Gothic*, Louis Gross remarks that "American gothicists do not remove their characters to Italy, Spain, France, or the other centers of English Gothic mystery; they shriek and faint in familiar surroundings and near the readers' own time."[4] In what follows, I will discuss Brite's novels *Lost Souls*, *Drawing Blood*, and *Exquisite Corpse*, and the stories in *Wormwood*, arguing that they present an American "Goth" rather than a Female Gothic sensibility—one that embodies American Third Wave feminist concepts of sex positivity, gender fluidity, and intersectionality through the lens of Goth youth subculture. In doing so, a radically different framing of evil can be discerned—one that challenges and "makes strange" the "familiar surroundings" of mainstream American patriarchal society.

By "Third Wave," I mean the complex, fragmentary, and often contested versions of American feminism emerging in the 1990s, operating both as a resistance to the postfeminist backlash against Second Wave or 1970s-era feminism and as a critique of that feminism, particularly in the areas of sexuality and gender identity. The differences between the waves have been overblown as part of the diatribe against feminist movement; still, undeniable fault lines appear. As Astrid Henry comments on the "sex wars," "Rejecting the so-called victim feminism of Catherine MacKinnon and Andrea Dworkin, with its danger of rape and women's lack of agency, third wave feminists have instead celebrated a woman's right to pleasure." In *Not My Mother's Sister*, Henry traces the popularization of the term "Third Wave" to a 1992 essay by Rebecca Walker in *Ms. Magazine*.[5] Brite's *Lost Souls* also debuted in 1992, around the same time that Susan Faludi publicized the backlash and Naomi Wolf exposed the beauty myth. As such, it is hardly surprising that the feminism of Brite's horror fictions is part of the Third Wave.

The trouble with conceptualizing Third Wave feminism in relation to cultural production is its tendency to evade definition: "Third Wave," writes Victoria Bromley, "is characterized as eclectic, humorous, nonmainstream, accessible, empowering, dynamic, hip and happening, and undefinable." Bromley further points out that Third Wave expands the Second Wave feminist axiom that "the personal is political" to render the political *personal*, making lifestyle and sexuality central to battling the unequal socioeconomic power structures articulated by earlier feminists. In addition to these intimate explorations, Third Wavers often also reject the Second Wave emphasis on patriarchy as the singular root of all evil, advocating instead for the recognition of multiple oppressions intersecting with patriarchy, such as racism, colonialism, class inequality, ableism, and homophobia.[6] As such, Third Wave feminisms resemble other "post-" movements in their antiessentialism. However, Third Wave feminist political engagement is often critiqued for individual rather than collective action. Much Third Wave cultural production prides itself on audaciously trespassing across boundaries that have historically cordoned off "unfeminine" territory, such as pornography or cyberspace.

Horror, therefore, would seem to be fertile ground for Third Wave feminist cultural production as it has been a masculinized area for Second Wave cultural critics. Elsewhere, I have discussed in detail feminism's struggle with horror, showing that where feminists have talked about horror, again, mainly in film studies, they have tended to feel obliged to judge and, more often than not, condemn it because it dishes up heaping platters full of terrorized and tortured women for the consumption of salivating male voyeurs. Integral to feminist definitions of horror has been an aversion to imagery of violence and pain, which I will discuss later.

Critics have argued that the filmic monster symbolizes what is repressed by society, opening up space for questioning normative ideologies; therefore, the radical potential of a given horror text rests on the definitions of normalcy and monstrosity contained therein. Thus, Robin Wood's formulation of the progressive horror film cautions us to watch out for narratives that rely upon the "designation of the monster as *simply evil*"—such narratives are, he argues, usually reactionary. Similarly, Freeland observes that horror can "often question the traditional values and gender roles associated with patriarchal institutions such as religion, science, the law and the nuclear family" even though "the feminist message seems qualified."[7] This sense that horror might contain feminist potential, but that women's pleasure in horror must needs be *qualified*, continues to haunt feminist horror criticism.

Carol Clover's Final Girl theory—perhaps the most influential articulation of this idea—was first advanced in 1991, also coinciding with the emergence of the Third Wave. Clover's Final Girl is a powerful argument that horror cannot be regarded as merely female victimization since, in many cases, slasher films conclude with a "Final Girl" who triumphs over the monster-killer. However, Clover argues that the Final Girl is "a kind of feint, a front through which the boy can simultaneously experience forbidden desires and disavow them on grounds that the visible actor is, after all, a girl." The implied male horror viewer therefore indulges in a sadomasochistic fantasy that Clover calls "an act of perhaps timeless dishonesty."[8]

The alternative scenario—that watching horror might be empowering rather than oppressive for some women—is fairly recent, surfacing in the work of Freeland, Isabel Cristina Pinedo, and Brigid Cherry's empirical studies of female horror fans as well as Linda Williams's revisitation of her earlier essay "When the Woman Looks." In short, a few feminist film scholars have revised their earlier positions and rather grudgingly admitted that the reigning psychoanalytic concept of Laura Mulvey's "male gaze" may be flawed and that female spectatorship should be taken into account. This shift in perspective may be characterized as part of the Third Wave reclamation of unconventional territory and masculinized pleasures.

When it comes to written horror, however, very different critical paradigms apply. Whereas in film a space has had to be staked out for women's participation in horror, such a field for horror fiction has long existed in the form of the literary Gothic, under which horror is usually subsumed in literary studies. Ellen Moers, the originator of the term "Female Gothic," traces its emergence in *Literary Women*, locating the Female Gothic in the period when "religious fears were on the wane, giving way to that vague paranoia of the modern spirit for which Gothic mechanisms seem to have provided welcome therapy." Moers writes, "As early as the 1790s, Ann Radcliffe firmly set the Gothic in one of the ways it would go ever after: a novel in which the central figure is a young woman who is simultaneously persecuted victim and courageous heroine."[9] Thus, Final Girls existed in literature long before the slasher films in which Clover situates them, with much less doubt as to both their femininity and that of their audiences. If the horror film viewer is always presumed male, the implied Gothic reader has always been female.

It has been a matter of some debate as to whether the Female Gothic is conservative or feminist, mirroring Woods's reactionary-versus-progressive formulation for horror film. Jeffrey Andrew Weinstock describes the debate as follows:

> ... the literature on the Female Gothic has developed into two camps: The first, derived from Moers, reads Gothic literature by women as generally conservative and expressive of internal female division. The second, which also develops out of Moers's work but more particularly out of Doody's proposition of feminine radical protest, reads Female Gothic literature as revolutionary in its critique of the oppressiveness of patriarchal constraints and, in some cases, its fantasization of a reordered, more egalitarian cultural distribution of power.[10]

Either way, women writers from Jane Austen in *Northanger Abbey* to Margaret Atwood in *Lady Oracle*, have played with the Female Gothic, wittily parodying major Gothic conventions such as the imperiled young heroine, the evil tyrant, and the mysterious ordeals to which the former is subjected by the latter in a haunted or fantastic space. Such narratives can be read as staging an ongoing struggle with patriarchy, akin to the grand battles of First and Second Wave feminism for enfranchisement, participation in the public sphere, and reproductive rights.

Second Wave feminist horror fictions, such as Ira Levin's 1967 *Rosemary's Baby* or the 1972 *The Stepford Wives*, were more explicit about the evils of patriarchy. Both Joanna Eberhart in *The Stepford Wives* and Rosemary Woodhouse in *Rosemary's Baby* are betrayed by their husbands into submission to patriarchy, one murdered and replaced by a domestic robot, the other surrendering to a maternal instinct to nurture her demonic baby. Both Joanna and Rosemary are sacrificed to the masculinity crises of their respective partners: Walter Eberhart and Guy Woodhouse are presented as weak characters, unworthy of their wives, and far too easily seduced by the prospect of a successful acting career in Guy's case and conformity with the old boys' network in Walter's. Third Wave feminist horror such as Brite's, though, does not entirely discard Second Wave concerns. For example, the discourses of reproduction and abortion frequently arise in Brite's stories, such as "Ashes to Ashes" in *Wormwood*. However, Brite also plays with the concept that evil originates from male monsters and the sense of marginality that such monstrosity conveys. Rather than placing an innocent young woman in peril at the heart of the narrative, Brite's fictions portray monstrous, often queer characters on the margins, yearning for relationship, connection, and community, with the societal evils of homophobia, racism, and prejudice in combination with sexism working against them. Under conditions of inequality, mere survival is the best that one can do and sexuality is gutted, de-romanticized, and stripped bare of its (gendered) pretensions.

In fact, the very notion of romantic love is queered, particularly through Brite's series of gay male relationships that, in the case of *Lost Souls*, may even be incestuous Nothing, a boy, falls in love with his vampiric father, the androgynous and omnisexual Zillah. In *Drawing Blood*, Brite's lovers, one of whom survives the trauma of familial abuse and murder, nearly kill each other. The potential sickness underlying the concept of romantic love becomes even more explicit in Brite's unlikely serial killer lovers in *Exquisite Corpse* (1996). Writing of the impact that HIV/AIDS had on late 20th-century art, Linda S. Kauffman reminds us that "the notion that those afflicted go on feeling sexual, or having sex, or being desirable to others is still wholly taboo." Brite's *Exquisite Corpse* breaks this taboo by

depicting not only gay serial killers with AIDS in love, but also the relationship between the Vietnamese American boy Tran and HIV-positive
Lucas Ransom. The tenderness and explicit imagery with which Brite depicts men loving men mirrors the mindset of romance writers. Kauffman
observes, "in my view, one of the virtues of porn is that it is anti-romantic,
for since women have been most subjected to the ideology of romantic
love, they may have the most to gain by endorsing an anti-aesthetic that
defies it."[11]

The Goth youth subculture of the 1980s and early 1990s provides such
an anti-aesthetic—a subculture that permeates Brite's fiction, with repeated references to the "Dachau children with blue-black hair and flickering, fishnetted hands" who were stereotyped in those decades as evil,
Satan-worshipping, and drug-addled perverts. Brite's fiction frequently
alludes to Gothic bands such as Bauhaus and the Cure, black eyeliner,
black clothing, and red lipstick, as well as vampirism, absinthe drinking,
and other Goth accoutrements. Following the escape of *Exquisite Corpse*'s
serial killer narrator Andrew from prison, he strolls through Leicester
Square, admiring the punks,

> painted children who of a Saturday might parade up and down the King's
> Road staring in the shop windows at zebra-striped vinyl raincoats, at
> Dr. Marten boots and at the gaudiest, prettiest things of all, their own re-
> flections in the glass. Below the neck these children wore black, gray and
> white garments of various materials and textures, held together with bits
> of metal. Above the neck they were like abstract paintings done in furi-
> ous rainbow hues. A technicolour scribble of tortured hair, great panda-
> smudges of azure or chartreuse round the eyes, a slash of vermilion across
> the soft young mouth, and off they went.

Upon coming to New Orleans, Andrew observes "a young Gothic crowd [. . .]
resplendent in their monochrome regalia, the myriad textures of teased
hair, torn lace, fishnet, and crushed velvet more fascinating to the eye than
colour."[12] In other stories, Brite returns again and again to sensuous descriptions of the Gothic aesthetic—in "A Georgia Story," another pair of
male lovers is described as "Gene with his vampire face, Sammy with long
tangled sparkles of hair as glossy as ravens." In "His Mouth Will Taste of
Wormwood," yet another Gothic nightclub crowd is "queerly beautiful in
their thrift shop rags, their leather and fishnet and cheap costume jewelry,
their pale faces and painted hair," while in "The Sixth Sentinel," the narrator describes Goth music as "alternately lush as a wreath of funeral roses
and dark as four A.M., composed in suicidal gloom by [. . .] androgynes."[13]

In his pioneering study of subcultures, Dick Hebdige discusses "the
tensions between dominant and subordinate groups" that

can be found reflected in the surfaces of subculture—in the styles made up of mundane objects which have a double meaning. On the one hand, they warn the "straight" world in advance of a sinister presence. . . . On the other hand, for those who erect them into icons, who use them as words or as curses, these objects become signs of forbidden identity, sources of value.[14]

Gothic style, which has always deliberately cultivated an air of "sinister presence" mingled with gender-queerness—as the target of a moral panic following the Columbine massacre, for example—surely invokes evil with its fascination with mortality, amorality, and both human and inhuman monstrosity. However, Brite's "deather-children" are portrayed tenderly by their author as "lost souls" who are "queerly beautiful" rather than wicked, who yearn, as I suggested earlier, only for connection. Like other subcultural figures, the extravagant clothes and tormented passions of Brite's characters can be interpreted as Hebdige's "gesture of defiance and contempt" against straight, mainstream culture; rather than outright speaking of an oppositional feminist politics, Brite's characters embody it through their insistence on resisting conventional standards of beauty, conformity, heterosexuality, and monogamy. Whereas the Female Gothic placed its beleaguered heroines in strange places or made domestic spaces strange, the queer characters of Brite's fictions inhabit spaces that are conspicuously marginal, from dark little nightclubs to pirate radio stations or decaying mansions in the New Orleans swamps, where Gothic dramas reach their bloody *dénouements.*

Judith Halberstam argues that the *visibility* of the monster signifies a particular recognition of the way in which evil is framed and represented. Freeland similarly suggests that horror stages a spectacular confrontation with evil in which monsters are

beings that raise the specter of evil by overturning the natural order, whether it be an order concerning death, the body, God's laws, natural laws, or ordinary human values. The spectacles of horror—the gruesome wounds, slimy beasts, undead vampires, or exploding heads—may be more central even than plot to forcing our confrontation with evil.[15]

The gory spectacles of horror often excoriated as "torture porn" have troubled Second Wave feminists. Discussing what she calls "the wet death," Pinedo reflects that contemporary horror portrays "a universe out of control where extreme violence is endemic and virtually unstoppable [. . .] familiar categories collapse" and the body is "the site of this collapse."[16] Brite's *Exquisite Corpse* is a strong example of this type of spectacular confrontation with evil, a "wet festival of scarlet," to use one of

Brite's metaphors for the sight of an eviscerated body. The novel features not one but two serial killers, one being a Jeffrey Dahmer–like American named Jay Byrne, wealthy scion of a corrupt old New Orleans family, who orchestrates the sadistic torture and consumption of boys in his secluded mansion. The other is a Dennis Nilsen–like, HIV-positive, British murderer named Andrew Compton, nicknamed "The Eternal Host" by the British tabloid press, who uses the fear engendered by his HIV-positive status to escape from jail by feigning death under the reluctant scrutiny of his jailers. Although they differ at first in their approaches to murder— Andrew sympathizes with at least one of his victims while Jay revels in torture—both killers' performances are occasions for horrific display. "I killed them by cutting," Andrew tells us early on in his narrative, "because I appreciated the beautiful objects that their bodies were, the bright ribbons of blood coursing over the velvet of their skin, the feel of their muscles parting like soft butter." Possibly one of the most unbearable scenes in the novel comes when our suspicions about Jay Byrne's proclivities are confirmed. In a prior chapter, we see him taking a young street kid home as a "pet," using his wealth to lure him, and in this passage, he casually strolls into the bathroom where his now-abject pet is tethered:

> The dazzle of light on black and white tile was relieved by glistening scrawls and blots of red, like handfuls of rubies thrown about. The boy was curled upon himself in the bathtub, trussed at the wrists and ankles and tightly around the skinny smooth thighs, his eyes bright with acid and hideous awareness. His body was scoured, scraped away to raw nerve. Over the sharpest points of his body, cheeks and knees and hips, Jay could see the blue-white gleam of bone. The bleach had raised angry chemical burns on what little skin he had left. His cock was as wet and shapeless as a spit-out mouthful of food. At some point his stomach had been partly slit open, the layers pulled apart and a shiny bubble of intestine exposed.

Michel Foucault famously claimed that "the disappearance of torture as a public spectacle [. . .] the gloomy festival of punishment" meant the disappearance of "the body as the major target of penal repression" in the 18th century; in Foucault's account, the "confused horror" emanating from the scaffold becomes "an additional shame that justice is ashamed to impose [. . .] so it keeps its distance from the act [. . .] This sense of shame is constantly growing: the psychologists and the minor civil servants of moral orthopaedics proliferate on the wound it leaves."[17] In the display of its tortured bodies, horror does not allow us to keep our distance from the shame of punishment. Much Third Wave feminism has been indebted to Judith Butler's theorizing of gender as performance, but Third Wave feminist horror might also be said to combine Butler's gender-queering with Antonin Artaud's influential concept of the theater of cruelty: "the urgent demand for a new type of corporeal speech: 'We need above all a theater that wakes us up: nerves and heart,'"[18] In Brite's gaudy, gory *tableaux* such as the above, a similar type of wake-up call might be discerned—one that refers back to the society that allows such killers to flourish.

In *Exquisite Corpse*, Jay initiates Andrew into the macabre pleasures of torture and cannibalism. At first, Andrew refuses but when he meets another protagonist, the young, beautiful Vietnamese American boy Tran, he persuades Jay, reluctant to touch the locals, to murder Tran, making that killing the condition of his foray into cannibalism. Tran—his name the sign of gender fluidity—is recovering from a breakup with his HIV-positive ex-lover, Lucas Ransom, the voice of a pirate radio station, WHIV, operating under the persona "Lush Rimbaud" from a boat in the New Orleans swamp. Lush Rimbaud's voice is a blistering, apocalyptic snarl, WHIV his source of "aural infection," denouncing the straight world's indifference to HIV/AIDS, the religious right and hypocritical "breeders": WHIV also reflects the subversive Third Wave feminist DIY political culture of zines, blogging, and campus radio shows.

At the novel's conclusion, Lucas, having heard that Tran is at Jay's house, seeks him out only to find that Tran has managed to escape the first attack by the killers, and has run bleeding into the street. Brite here retells the story of one of Jeffrey Dahmer's victims, the "bleeding fourteen-year-old Laotian boy, Konerak Sinthasomphone, [. . .] seen pursued by Dahmer on the street": "The intoxicated Asian naked male [*laughter heard in background*] was returned to sober boyfriend and we're ten-eight" . . . [*officers sent to a battery complaint*] . . . "Ten-four. It'll be a minute. My partner's gonna get deloused at the station [*laughter*]."[19] In *Exquisite Corpse*,

> The black cop bent to examine Tran more closely, then straightened up and pointed to the bite mark on the boy's nipple. "He did that to himself, too?"
>
> Jay shrugged. "I did that. I'm not responsible for his sexual proclivities, but I do try to indulge them."
>
> The cops glanced at each other. Utterly unlike in every other way, their faces bore twin expressions of distaste. The white cop handed Jay's license back, scissored gingerly between thumb and forefinger [. . .].
>
> "Mr Byrne, I suggest you take your, uh . . . friend home and keep him there until he sobers up. I see him on the street in this condition again, I'll arrest him."

Apart from Lucas, who is also treated roughly by the police when he attempts to intervene and rescue Tran, a black street musician is the only one who can see that Tran is in trouble, but the musician, in line with the racism endemic to police operations, is thrown up against the wall and threatened with arrest while the aristocratic Jay bribes the police to hand Tran back to him to die in terrible pain. According to Tithecott, North American society's construction of the serial killer myth, the police and the FBI often take "paternal control" of the sane and evil killer away from psychiatry:

> "Our dominant policing discourses [. . .] describe a world threatened more by inexplicable horror than by various forms of medically and legally defined insanity.
> The horror evoked is beyond the reach of psychiatry, is indicative of a madness which cannot be treated, and consequently imprisonment or execution [. . .] are perceived as the state's only suitable response. Central to such discourses is the idea of evil, the widespread acceptance of which [. . .] allows those who protect society from its monsters to once again assume an aura of priestly authority."

Exquisite Corpse resists this authoritarian concept of evil by failing to protect Tran from the monsters due to the intersectional homophobia and racism of the police who erroneously locate their mythology of evil in the queerness of the triangle facing them and the blackness of the musician who speaks up for Tran. As a result, they are easily bribed to tolerate the atrocities of a serial killer in their midst. No order is restored, no normalcy affirmed by this narrative; it does not fit Wood's formula for reactionary horror. Lucas does manage to break into Jay's mansion and dispatch him while the pair are ferociously mutilating Tran's dying body but it is too late to save Tran and a devastated Lucas begs Andrew to kill him next. The serial killer refuses and escapes yet again; Luke returns to his downward spiral of shooting heroin and drinking rotgut, juxtaposed with the floridly grotesque imagery of Tran's and Jay's bodies decomposing together. *Exquisite Corpse*'s theater of cruelty thus "wakes us up" spectacularly: the real monsters win due to the evil of the indifference of straight society to those perceived as abnormal and monstrous.

Such intersectional moments highlight the attention to oppressions other than solely sexism that mark Third Wave feminist horror. It must also be noted that Brite's spectacularly gory prose has also been historically *masculinized*. In claiming the authority to write so lovingly of guts and gore, to show the spectacle of the wet death and to queer both the monsters and their victims, Brite unsettles our assumptions about the

Female Gothic and gendered horror. Brite, therefore, refuses to shun the conventionally masculinized fictional style of explicitly graphic prose, even while continuing to explore the Female Gothic terrain of family, reproduction, relationships, and gender roles. In shifting representations of evil toward racist and homophobic practices in addition to patriarchal structures, as I have demonstrated, Third Wave feminist horror writers such as Brite have made important contributions, *contra* Joshi, to a submerged yet powerful version of the American nightmare.

NOTES

1. S. T. Joshi, *The Evolution of the Weird Tale* (New York: Hippocampus Press, 2004), 203–08.

2. Cynthia A. Freeland, *The Naked and the Undead: Evil and the Appeal of Horror, Thinking through Cinema* (Boulder, CO: Westview, 2000), 13. Freeland writes, "I seek to avoid universalizing assumptions about gender as I ask how a given film depicts gender in relation to its larger themes about good and evil [. . .] I consider psychoanalytic feminisms to be theoretically ill-grounded and too reductive" (4).

3. Ellen Moers, *Literary Women* (Garden City, NY: Doubleday, 1976).

4. Louis S. Gross, *Redefining the American Gothic: From Wieland to Day of the Dead, Studies in Speculative Fiction* (Ann Arbor, MI: UMI Research Press, 1989), 23.

5. Astrid Henry, *Not My Mother's Sister: Generational Conflict and Third-Wave Feminism* (Bloomington: Indiana University Press, 2004), 14–23.

6. Victoria L. Bromley, *Feminisms Matter: Debates, Theories, Activism* (North York, ON: University of Toronto Press, 2012), 145–48.

7. Robin Wood, "An Introduction to the Horror Film," in *American Nightmare: Essays on the Horror Film*, ed. Andrew Britton, et al. (Toronto: Festival of Festivals, 1979), 14–23; Freeland, *The Naked and the Undead: Evil and the Appeal of Horror*, 4.

8. Carol J. Clover, *Men, Women, and Chain Saws: Gender in the Modern Horror Film* (Princeton, NJ: Princeton University Press, 1992), 18, 53.

9. Moers, *Literary Women*, 91–92.

10. Jeffrey A. Weinstock, *Scare Tactics: Supernatural Fiction by American Women* (New York: Fordham University Press, 2008), 11.

11. Linda S. Kauffman, *Bad Girls and Sick Boys: Fantasies in Contemporary Art and Culture* (Berkeley: University of California Press, 1998), 33, 60.

12. Poppy Z. Brite, *Exquisite Corpse* (New York: Simon & Schuster, 1996).

13. Poppy Z. Brite, *Wormwood: A Collection of Short Stories* (New York: Dell, 1996).

14. Dick Hebdige, *Subculture, the Meaning of Style, New Accents* (London: Methuen, 1979), 3.

15. Freeland, *The Naked and the Undead: Evil and the Appeal of Horror*, 8.

16. Isabel C. Pinedo, *Recreational Terror: Women and the Pleasures of Horror Film Viewing, Suny Series, Interruptions—Border Testimony(ies) and Critical Discourse/s* (Albany: State University of New York Press, 1997), 9.

17. Michel Foucault, *Discipline and Punish: The Birth of the Prison* (New York: Vintage Books, 1979), 7–10.

18. Kauffman, *Bad Girls and Sick Boys: Fantasies in Contemporary Art and Culture*, 68.

19. Richard Tithecott, *Of Men and Monsters: Jeffrey Dahmer and the Construction of the Serial Killer* (Madison: University of Wisconsin Press, 1997), 76–77.

CHAPTER 2

Inviting the Devil to "Cross Over" the Threshold: The Short Stories of Joyce Carol Oates, Iteration, and American Fears of Precariousness in the 21st Century

Jennifer S. Carlberg

Once upon a time—or rather, once upon a few times—critics of Joyce Carol Oates's fiction have charged her with writing "the same story over and over" again.[1] Granted, at first the pronouncement seems to be a pithy one. But that pithiness, I'm afraid, encourages us to ignore the more productive query. That is, do we, as Americans of the 20th and now 21st centuries, enjoy *reading* the same story over and over again?

Of course, I do not mean to imply stories that are composed of exactly the same words, written in exactly the same order, over and over again. Save the bedtime stories of children, this surely cannot be the case. Instead, I refer to the many permutations that a somewhat predictable pattern might have. Encountered separately, each one *seems* to be a bit different. Yet at the bottom, all of them share a reliable, subterranean pattern.

Indeed, recent work regarding how the human brain encounters and orders the many stimuli in its environment suggests a preference for this sort of reliability. In fact, the brain imposes order upon its chaotic environment precisely by arranging the many fragmentary and inchoate stimuli accosting it into patterns that allow for the making and testing of predictions.[2] At times in its gusto, even, the brain discerns patterns where, objectively, they are not.

So it is within this context of an overarching preference for pattern, as well as the caution against its kneejerk acceptance, that I encounter Oates's recent short story, "Pumpkin-Head" (2009). Although part of her larger collection of stories, *Sourland* (2010), "Pumpkin-Head" first appeared separately in *The New Yorker* in January of 2009. I was struck by its uncanny resemblance to an earlier of Oates's texts, "Where Are You Going, Where Have You Been?" (1966). But rather than dismissing this resemblance peremptorily as more and mere repetition, with—no doubt—an exasperated sigh, it seems to me worth considering how these two narrative iterations shed light upon the changing contours of American fears as we enter the 21st century. For, if we take Oates at her word, that "her place is to dramatize the nightmares" of her time, then our comparison of two such "nightmares"—oddly similar yet separated by nearly half of a century—promises to speak also to what *precisely* makes our skin crawl—what did then, what does now, and what that difference might reveal.[3]

To date, "Where Are You Going? Where Have You Been?" remains Oates's most frequently anthologized work. Now canonical, the story reprises the rape and murder of 15-year-old Alleen Rowe in suburban Tucson, Arizona, in 1964, the nonfictional account that likely animated it. First published in *Epoch* in the fall of 1966, Oates's story followed closely on the heels of *Life* magazine's rendering of the crime's perpetrator, Charles Howard Schmid Jr., the so-called Pied Piper of Tucson.[4] Charles Schmid Jr., or "Smitty" as he was known, could have easily strolled out of the pages of fiction: At 23 years old, he stood only a few inches over five feet. Suspended from high school for stealing from a welding class, he nonetheless still haunted the teenage hangouts located all along the Speedway, where he cruised up and down in a number of eye-catching cars. The *Life* account notes his golden jalopy, as well as his caricature-like appearance, for "[H]e wore face make-up and dyed his hair. He habitually stuffed three or four inches of old rags and tin cans into the bottoms of his high-topped boots to make himself taller than his five-foot-three and stumbled about so awkwardly while walking that some people thought he had wooden feet."[5]

Further, the *Life* account does one better: It mentions his love of Elvis Presley, whom Schmid mimicked in his own affect, drooping his eyelids or curling his lips into that trademark sneer. As a result, then, his crimes provided to members of the American public who were uncomfortable with certain generational changes of the 1960s an apt rung upon which to hang their concerns regarding rock 'n' roll music and its seeming potential to lure adolescents into sexual exploits, experimentation with drugs, and fleeing home.[6] Indeed, Schmid's murder of Alleen Rowe, as well as his later murders of Gretchen and Wendy Fritz, were transcribed as cautionary tales. As such, the *Life* account ended, even, with twinned emphases: how in the tragedy's wake many Tucson parents had barred their children from hangouts along the Speedway, and yet how the lyrics of Bo Diddley's "Who Do You Love?" still spilled imperviously from those hangouts' doors.

Acknowledging the borders between nonfiction and fiction to be contingent and, at times, illusory ones, Oates often reworks and reimagines headlines torn directly from the violence-spattered American newspapers. In fact, she regards the fictional realm as a fitting space for working through the brutal and cruel things that happen outside of art and might otherwise (and often still do) remain recalcitrant to our understanding.[7] In her words, these are "riddlesome" experiences "that can only be contemplated in the solitude of art."[8] Within the boundaries of fiction, Oates can exercise at least a modicum of resistance: the ability to memorialize the attendant scenes and their persons, to "bear witness."[9]

As Oates tells it, the scene to which she bears witness in "Where Are You Going, Where Have You Been?" unfolded within her own imagination after listening to the Bob Dylan song "It's All Over Now, Baby Blue." And somewhat befittingly, she renders her tale in a sort of incandescent prose, one that is both opaque and luminous, much like the music that inspired it. But unlike *Life* magazine's version of events, Oates's account foregrounds the contents of the victim's own nascent psyche, laying bare the desires, needs, and fears of a main character that she calls "Connie."

Quite possibly, it is this privileging of her characters' psyches that has contributed to Oates being labeled a Gothic writer. Though the adjective "Gothic" hearkens back to Edgar Allan Poe, he was neither the only nor the first writer to work within the genre's broad contours. Rather, Poe famously honed certain stock-in-trade characteristics of Gothic writing. The broader genre, nonetheless, was a place where he and other writers, "transformed what had been essentially descriptive landscapes into a geography of the imagination," one whose "interior worlds were fraught with far more nightmares than comforting dreams."[10] And within contemporary American fiction, Oates negotiates certain traditionally Gothic plot devices, including the ways in which burgeoning sexuality can suddenly assume dangerous shapes, the impingement upon a naïve female, the loss of innocence, and the magic of signs, symbols, folk superstitions, and fairy tales. Drawing a distinction, however, Oates describes her own writing as "gothic with a small-letter 'g,'" suggesting "a work in which extremes of emotion are unleashed."[11]

It is both the unflinching accuracy with which Oates renders the cogitations of her main character as well as the rehearsal of certain plot devices that remind the reader of "Where Are You Going, Where Have You Been?" when reading "Pumpkin-Head." Both narratives make use of the same basic contrivance of plot: a visitor, at first seemingly benign, turns viciously upon an isolated female within her suburban home. But more, the way in which both stories underline evil's potential to exceed the boundaries of time and place—our parlance aimed at confining evil to and thereby containing it within discrete, distant "events"—provides an additional chilling parallel. For in both accounts, Oates's "evil" has a workaday quality that is capable of reaching her characters when they are billeted within their very homes, which they presume to be most secure.

Beyond this seeming "ordinariness" of evil, more nuanced parallels between the two iterations create something of a latticework, one whose correspondences suggest that careful consideration of these stories in light of one another might stand to tell us something about the changing shape of our own fears, especially those attending the recent crossing over from the 20th to the 21st centuries. Of course, in speaking of the writing process (as recently as 2001) Oates acknowledges that, "Writers . . . are very likely in the grip of powerful unconscious processes, that are recurring, obsessive, thrilling and filled with dread simultaneously, so that simply to write . . . will be to express linked material with no deliberate effort."[12] Indeed, the two short stories do share a rich assemblage of linkages. But the iterations also vary—and quite obtrusively so. Thus, I think that taking stock of the stories' similarities and dissimilarities might be an appropriate point of departure, one in which evaluating where we have been can provide us traction in where we are going.

In "Pumpkin-Head," Hadley, the recent widow of a professor, and in "Where Are You Going, Where Have You Been?," Connie, a 15-year-old girl, who remains at home in order to sunbathe and listen to the radio while her parents and sister attend a barbeque, are both startled from their respective reveries when vehicles turn into their driveways. "Pumpkin-Head," set in New Jersey, late within the month of October and near to sundown, includes a visual alarm, as "headlights turned into the driveway, some distance away at the road." These lights "startled [Hadley] into wakefulness—at first not sure where she was. Then she realized, Anton Kruppe was dropping by to see her at about this time" (3–4).[13] Analogously, "Where Are You Going, Where Have You Been?" includes an aural one: Connie hears a "car coming up the drive . . . gravel kept crunching all the way in from the road—the driveway was long—and Connie ran to the window" (31).[14] Perhaps if this repetition offered Oates *only* a convenient way to emphasize evil-as-a-trajectory, its ability to reach—quite literally—into the ordinary homes of her characters, then we might dismiss the gesture, again as more (and mere) coincidence. Yet, this is not the case. There is more.

Aside from rehearsing this "delivery apparatus" as a plot device for both stories, Oates conserves many similarities between her main characters, Hadley and Connie. For instance, both are self-absorbed. Hadley's is the more serious self-absorption, which follows upon the trauma of bereavement, while Connie's, simply a product of adolescence. Nevertheless, both states exert near-narcotic pulls. Since late March, Hadley—somewhat fittingly called Mrs. Schelle at the co-op—had been in a "trance of self-absorption that was like a narcotic to her—In fact, to get through the worst of her insomniac nights Hadley had to take sleeping pills which left her dazed and groggy through much of the day" (7). And "For long entranced minutes like one in a hypnotic state she found herself listening to a voice not her own yet couched in the cadences of her own most intimate speech" (7). Although of a less severe sort, Connie's stupor smacks of adolescent self-concern and stubbornness. She, too, sits "with her eyes closed in the sun, dreaming and dazed with the warmth about her as if this were a kind of love" (30). And as she listens closely to the radio, she feels "bathed in a glow of slow-pulsed joy that seemed to rise mysteriously out of the music itself" (31). In both cases, Oates's narrator blames this stupor in part for relaxing each character's vigilance, leaving her vulnerable to attack. Yet, so do both narrators note each character's desire to be liked as a compounding factor in the attack, a sort of comorbidity.

Quite possibly, it is because both characters are most concerned that others share in their self-absorption that they are anxious to be liked. In "Pumpkin-Head," even, Oates's narrator characterizes this trait as an explicitly American one: "so *American* was her nature, so female, she was anxious that he should like her, and admire her" (14). Not yet conjoined to nationality in "Where Are You Going, Where Have You Been?," the need to be liked nonetheless informs Connie's actions. Habitually, she checks "other people's faces to make sure her own was all right" or speaks in a "high, breathless, amused voice that made everything she said sound a little forced, whether it was sincere or not" (26). In the case of both characters, though, securing the affections of others becomes a tactic by which to gain superiority, rather than a means toward any empathic union.

For once liked, both characters relish the power that this sentiment accords them. Hence, when inside her home, "Hadley felt a *frisson* of power over her awkward visitor. . . . Her power, she thought, lay in her essential indifference to the man, to his very maleness: his sexuality clumsy as an odd-sized package he was obliged to carry, to proffer to strangers like herself" (8). More, Hadley is elated and exhilarated by the privilege that this dynamic awards her: ". . . *if I wanted a lover. A lover for whom I felt no love*" (16). Likewise, Connie recounts the nights that she and a friend, having been dropped off at the theatre, instead parade around the drive-in across the road. "One night in midsummer they ran across, breathless with daring, and right away someone leaned out a car window and invited them over, but it was just a boy from high school they didn't like. It made them feel good to be able to ignore him" (27).

And if Hadley favors an older Connie, Oates's Anton Kruppe also recalls Arnold Friend. Anton entreats Hadley, "You know this, I am your friend Anton—yes?" (16). In fact, the antagonists' likeness pervades their ways of moving, even. In particular, both assailants exit their vehicles obtrusively, in a fashion that warrants narrative comment. As Anton climbs down from the pick-up truck's high cab, he "lurched toward her on the shadowy path—a tall male scarecrow figure with a misshapen Halloween pumpkin for a head. . . . It's leering cut-out eyes not lighted from within, like a jack-o'-lantern, but dark, glassy" (4). Oates's narrator then underlines how the "uncanny pumpkin-head" had been "gutted" in order to form "a kind of pumpkin-mask" (6). And all of this talk of lurching and masks and pumpkins returns us to the descriptions of Arnold Friend. For Arnold, too, exits his car with extreme care, opening "the door . . . as if he were afraid it might fall off" and "planting his feet firmly on the ground," lest his stuffed boots give way (33). More explicitly, the "drawing of a round, grinning face" on the side of Arnold's car, which reminds Connie of "a pumpkin, except it wore sunglasses," pegs him to Anton (33). Just as Anton's eyes beneath the mask disconcert Hadley, so does Arnold's removal of his sunglasses, Connie: for "she saw how pale the skin around his eyes was, like holes that were not in shadow but instead in light. His eyes were like chips of broken glass" (35). When Arnold smiles, it was "awkward as if he were smiling from inside a mask. His whole face was a mask, she thought wildly, tanned down to his throat but then running out as if he had plastered makeup on his face but had forgotten about his throat" (41).

These uncanny parallels include the assailants' feet, as the boots of both become objects of wonder. Of course, Connie makes observations that would have concurred with the odd way Charles Schmid Jr. stuffed his boots in order to appear taller, such as, "one of his boots was at a strange angle, as if his foot wasn't in it. It pointed out to the left, bent at the ankle" (42). Yet Anton Kruppe, who is already tall, does not make such odd attempts at dissimulation. His boots nonetheless transfix Hadley. For instance, when she invites Anton into her house, he scrapes their muddied soles against the welcome mat, and then removes them "with a grunt and left them on the front step carefully placed side by side. What large boots they were, like a horse's hooves!" (11). Finally, both assailants make "slips of the tongue"—albeit unforked—that are similar in type and context.

Put more plainly, in climactic moments, both Arnold and Anton begin to confuse objective details. To illustrate, when commanding Connie to follow him from her home toward her eventual rape and murder, like "a brave, sweet little girl," Arnold Friend calls her, "My sweet little blue-eyed girl," although her eyes were brown (47). Likewise, Anton Kruppe recounts the ways in which the university had conspired to rob him of his scientific findings. The head of his former molecular biology laboratory connived, along with the university president, the provost, and the attorney, to cheat him of his findings, used campus security to remove him from the building, and at last threatened to have Homeland Security deport him. Conveniently, then, the federal grant that supported Anton's contract with the Institute was terminated prior to anyone helping him apply for U.S. citizenship. When Anton forces himself upon Hadley, in his emotion he refers to her former husband as the "Trustee," yoking him to this theft.

On their own, these parallels between Oates's two stories might prove interesting enough, but her musings about the nature of recurrence when communicating with psychoanalyst, Dale Boesky, suggest that we look even more closely at them. In her response to Boesky dated September 30, 1973, Oates pointedly explains the recurring images, themes, and plots that inhere in a writer's work: she says, these things "must have the analogous function of the recurring dream: something demands to be raised to consciousness, to be comprehended by the ego, but for some reason the ego resists or refuses to understand. And so he is fated to dream and re-dream the same paradoxical problem, and he can't be freed of it until he 'solves' it."[15]

At first these musings of Oates sit uneasily next to another of her more terse replies. In responding to a concern regarding the likelihood of writing the same story or lines over again, especially given her large body of work, Oates states, "If I thought I *had* written a scene before, or written the same lines before, I would simply look it up."[16] On the face of things, Oates's two remarks seem to openly contradict one another. But instead, they should give us pause. Indeed, when taken together, her comments suggest that we might consider her short stories of 1966 and 2009 as more than just mirror images of one another—even doppelgangers, to court melodrama—but rather as iterations—repetitions of something, for sure, but ones aimed at the continuous accretion of some understanding. Within an iterative context, then, the stories' distinctions—however slight—swell with importance. For if Oates so carefully reproduces the "nightmares" and savageries of American society in hopes of recuperating some shred of understanding in the doing so, or at least of memorializing those caught within and destroyed by its cruelties, her process also documents—however indirectly—the changing shape of American fears during the "crossing-over time" that was the last half century.

Certainly, in the case of both narratives, the salience of Oates's account derives in part from how adeptly she shapes evil into a liminal phenomenon, one that is ever capable of exceeding the specifics of times, places, and "events," the artificial verbiage by which we attempt futilely to forbid it enter our hermetically sealed homes, "impervious" to breach. In defiance, though, we see its headlights turn into our drives at dusk, or hear its car crunch along their gravel. And to Oates's contemporary readers, I will suggest, it is this liminality, or potential "crossing over," that most frightens (3). Indeed, this "crossing over," or liminality, is a fear,

I think, with which we are not finished. And that is how Oates carefully hones "Pumpkin-Head" (2009) in such a way as to distinguish the story from its precursor "Where Are You Going, Where Have You Been?" (1966).

Within the 2000s, consider briefly the upsurges in gated communities as well as the glut of both residential and personal security systems, like Life-Alert. When placed within a motor vehicle, even, these various security systems promise to summon emergency responders in the event that you are incapacitated by a motor vehicle crash and cannot do so independently, allowing one to yet exercise volition—agency—though incapacitated. Or what of the various types of software that are bent on safeguarding one's personal identity online, as well as the larger fascination with various predators lurking "there" (with "there" loosely defined as *anywhere* that the subject is not)? Indeed, for a nominal fee, one can now search instantly the backgrounds of potential suitors, employers, employees, physicians, teachers, ad infinitum, with only a few keystrokes and without ever leaving the "safety" of one's home. Additionally, we carry insurance policies of all kinds, against all things, and insist upon their portability, in an attempt to foreclose upon—or preempt—uncertainty and thereby to "blunt" evil's impact by presuming its menacing of us will occur along certain of our predetermined and defended pathways. Describing a tailored investment plan by Wells Fargo, the female model explains that, "Confidence comes from knowing I have a plan for my future." And Wells Fargo's Envision is "With you when you need clarity in an uncertain world."

In war, even, the "preemptive strike," which draws a sneer from Anton Kruppe in "Pumpkin-Head," aims to preserve the security of the homeland well before any opposing force might launch an attack upon it. And to be clear, I am debating neither the necessity nor the utility of these various policies and tactics. I am simply pointing out that, overall, these things condense to a longing at present for a place that is impervious to breach, as well as an agency incapable of curbing. More, these things anticipate the keen sense of horror that arises when these "supposedly" safe spaces are breached, when the familiar becomes uncanny. So perhaps, it is certain: Americans of the 21st century *do* prefer evils that are more predictable than precarious. We prefer to read something of the same stories over and over again—that is to say, evils of the Jack-in-the-Box variety: Americans all, and loving predictability every one.

But what happens, then, when the conditions that undergird such a story change? What happens when the subject is instead thrust into a state of precariousness, where the predictions that formerly founded her actions, her agency, no longer seem to hold? Precariousness, it would seem, is a horror that Oates's "Where Are You Going, Where Have You Been?" only hints at. To be sure, in the interim decades the 21st century world has become increasingly precarious. And it is noteworthy that to this day we attempt to exorcise this sense. For instance, consider Dateline TV's reality series, "To Catch a Predator" (airing from 2004 to 2007), which provided the network television-viewing American public with yet another iteration of Oates's calamitous scenario, training a hidden camera lens upon adults who attempted to lure underage youth into sexual liaisons over the Internet. Only this time, perhaps *most* telling is the way in which "To Catch a Predator" nullifies any feelings we might have of precariousness. After chatting luridly online with agents of *Perverted Justice* masquerading as the underage, these potential "Arnold Friends" are invited to an adolescent decoy's suburban home, where police are poised "at the ready" to arrest the would-be evildoer, safely foreclosing upon his intended crime. Then, after anchorman Chris Hansen informs the would-be predators that they have actually become entangled in a sting operation conducted by Dateline NBC, he emits this near-constant, cautionary refrain, "What do you think would have happened if we [the Dateline team and Perverted Justice] were not here, and there was truly a teenager home alone?"

But do appreciate how, if uncertainty has become an acute horror of the 21st century, and if Joyce Carol Oates acts to record the nightmares of her time, then her short story "Pumpkin-Head" resists the reader's ability to decipher what may be predicted, reliably so. And in this way, perhaps, it sharpens the peculiar horror that accompanies the instance when the familiar turns suddenly unreliable and uncanny. Of course, in "Where Are You Going, Where Have You Been?," Arnold Friend mimics those things most familiar to Connie—turns of phrase, the lyrics of popular music, kids' expressions—co-opting and redeploying them in order to rape and kill her, and the matter is a chilling one. Yet the story's ending also leaves us quite certain that Connie has followed Arnold toward her own rape and murder: "She put her hand against the screen. She watched herself push the door slowly open as if she were back safe somewhere in the other doorway, watching this body and this head of long hair moving out into the sunlight where Arnold Friend waited" (47). Connie muses, "so much land that Connie had never seen before and did not recognize except to know that she was going into it" (48). For certain Connie is a self-absorbed adolescent, whose mind is filled with trashy daydreams—but she is neither any more, nor less.[17] She did not invite Arnold Friend to her home; the screen door serves throughout as a makeshift prop delineating the inside, a place of safety and familiarity, from the outside, where Arnold first cajoles and then threatens; and finally, we—as readers—can *predict* how the story will end, without the very conditions that subtend such predictions eroding.

Not so, however, with "Pumpkin-Head" (2009). Here, Oates heightens the sense of liminality, allowing it to infuse even our sense of complicity between victim and offender. From the first lines of the story, when Hadley recounts March's sleet storm in north central New Jersey, she begins to elide concepts. Her rational mind knows that "there was no connection" between the sleet storm and her husband's premature death days before it, "Except." Certainly, this sort of elision indicates the fuzzy contours of posttraumatic thought, which often refuses discrete categories, but also this gestures toward much more, laying the groundwork for a consideration of this "crossing-over time." Befitting such questions of liminality, it is never clear whether or not Hadley had invited Anton Kruppe to her house. Of course, in no way does an invitation make it acceptable for him to molest and rape her, but it does draw a distinction between the events of "Where Are You Going, Where Have You Been?" (1966) and the later story. For unwittingly, Hadley becomes complicit in the conditions of the attack. When she attempts to parse events clearly, Hadley notes that this is Anton's second visit to the house, but muses: *Dropping by* he'd said. Or maybe she'd said *Why don't you drop by*" (4).

Likewise, the earlier story involves the screen door as a prop around which negotiations between Connie (clearly inside) and Arnold Friend (clearly outside) occur. At one point, Arnold makes clear, "I'm not coming in there but you are coming out here" (41). Yet in "Pumpkin-Head," Hadley shows Anton through the home that she formerly shared with her husband, inflecting matters almost as a sort of punishment, for "She had caused her husband to be burnt to ashes, and now other men would drop by." Nor is it an accident, I think, that Arnold Friend is a foreign postdoctoral student, in this case from the former Yugoslavia.

Certainly, his origin recalls NATO's military intervention into the conflict in the Balkans in 1999—itself something of a "crossing-over time" between the two centuries. But more precisely this detail unleashes a collision between the "privilege" accorded to Hadley, who was the wife of a professor "in her previous, protected life," and Anton, whose "back" is "prematurely rounded," a possible result of his formerly unprotected—even malnourished—one (3, 6). Indeed, oft repeated in articles concerning her work is Oates's quotation that appeared originally in *Harper's* (1972): "The greatest realities are physical and economic; all the subtleties of life come afterward."[18] Similarly emphasized is her preoccupation with guilt, especially with that of an 'American' variety. In her own words, Oates compares and contrasts her work with that of William Faulkner, who consistently raises the "unforgivable" specter of slavery in his own attempts to articulate the "impossible racial situation in the South."[19] Oates, too, sees "a historical 'guilt' in America . . . compounded by our involvement in Vietnam."[20] And of late—no doubt—America's own complicity with various other imperialistic military actions in the Middle East, among other locations.

It is this disparity of circumstance that occasions Anton's vehement derision, as well as certain of Hadley's own thoughts and comments of Oates's narrator, which together trace the contours of the gap of authority, power, and privilege between the two. For instance, trying "too hard," Hadley considers a "sign of the foreign-born" (5). Or upon removing the carved pumpkin mask from his head, Anton presents it to Hadley, "smiling in his shyly aggressive manner that was a plea for her, the rich American woman, to laugh at him, and with him; to laugh in the spontaneous way in which Americans laughed together, mysteriously bonded in their crude American humor" (6).

This privilege, according to Anton, allows also certain "ignorant" American prejudices to be maintained—for instance, against the "day-old" or against stem-cell research (90). It is this privilege, too, that tempts Hadley to disregard polite conventions: "Thinking possibly she didn't have to invite her awkward visitor into the house, a second time; maybe Anton wouldn't notice her rudeness—wouldn't know enough to interpret it as rudeness," or allows her to laugh when Anton asks naïvely if the impressionist New England pastel landscape was the work of Cezanne (10, 11). It is this privilege, also, that leaves Anton aghast: coming from the "minimal, cramped" living quarters provided by university housing, he prowls Hadley's house (15). In amazement, he stares at the "Artifacts from trips Hadley and her husband had taken over the years—Indonesian pottery, African masks, urns, wall hangings, Chinese wall scrolls and watercolors, beautifully carved wooden figures from Bali. A wall of brightly colored 'primitive' paintings from Mexico, Costa Rica, Guatemala" (14). That is to say, the artifacts that privilege allows one to poach without question and to display upon one's walls.

Indeed, as Anton explores the solarium of Hadley's home, Oates's narrator begins to inflect his manner as "admiring yet faintly sneering, taunting" (15). In particular, he begins to probe the sort of "luck that affords one such a large house, . . . so big, for one person. . . . On each acre of land, it may be one person" (15). Or when Hadley argues the semantics of receiving things by luck or earning them, Anton needles, "And you, Hedley? You have 'earned'—also?" (16). After recounting how the Institute's lab supervisor referred to him as "stoic," Anton explains these euphemisms pointedly: "what this means, this flattery of Americans, is how you can be used. To be *used*—that is our [the less-privileged, foreign postdoctoral students] purpose to the Institute. But you must not indicate, that you are *in the know*" (18). And then, the attack ensues.

At the risk, now, of assuming any hackneyed, one-to-one correspondence between Oates's iterative short stories and the international standing of America since Operation Iraqi Freedom, also savaged by Anton, I do believe it is nonetheless useful to appreciate just how Oates underscores—formally within "Pumpkin-Head"—the way in which the drastic altering of a character's agency compromises her ability to make predictions. For, if she—perhaps like others within her "chatty middle-class"[21]—mistakenly conceives *only* of evil in vectored terms, directed *always* toward her and her beautiful, spacious home from somewhere without, then she will no doubt remain unable to comprehend—let alone to anticipate—how deeply she, too, is imbricated with the political, ideological, economic, and social structures that generates its many shapes. Just another "human soul caught in the stampede of time, unable to gauge the profundity of what passes over it."[22]

In fact, looking closely at the final paragraph, we notice that the verb phrases, which aim to contain the subject's actions, begin to change as the conditions upon which her agency is founded erode, inexorably. Since it would be a curious sort of story, then, that might be founded upon shifting conditions, Oates's final paragraph proves most resistant to the reader's making and testing of predictions. After the attack, Anton "staggered away" while Hadley remained stunned and lying on the floor for 10 or 15 minutes (20). In the instant, she identifies the attack as "the *crossing over*" (20). After climbing to her feet, Hadley peers outside into the "near-to-fading light" and realizes that she must call for help quickly, "For badly she required help, she knew that Anton Kruppe would return" (21). However, the verb phrases that rigidly contain the whole of the tragedy—her "clothing . . . **had been torn** and **was spattered with blood**," or she "**wiped** at her mouth, **that was bleeding**"—as well as the future imperatives that she imagines contain and articulate her response to the attack—she "**would run** back into the house, she **would dial** 911. She **would report** an assault. She **would summon** help"—begin fluidly to ebb (21, bolding mine). Rather, the story ends with Hadley "staring toward the road," at the headlights of an unmoving vehicle. As she calls out, the reader is left with only, "Headlights on the roadway, where his vehicle was parked" (21). Upon finishing, we notice, too, that Oates has refused us even the safety and comfort here of a fully retrospective vantage point.

NOTES

1. These particular words belong to Walter Sullivan, from Walter Sullivan, "The Artificial Demon: Joyce Carol Oates and the Dimensions of the Real," in *Critical Essays on Joyce Carol Oates*, ed. Linda Wagner-Martin (Boston: G. K. Hall, 1979), 86. But see also Elizabeth Dalton, "Joyce Carol Oates: Violence in the Head," *Commentary* XLIX, no. June (1970): 75–77.

2. For a personable and approachable introduction to recent neurocognitive findings, see Sandra Blakeslee and Matthew Blakeslee, *The Body Has a Mind*

of Its Own: New Discoveries about How the Mind-Body Connection Helps Us Master the World (New York: Random House, 2008), especially page 41.

3. Eva Manske, "The Nightmare of Reality: Gothic Fantasies and Psychological Realism in the Fiction of Joyce Carol Oates," in *Neo-Realism in Contemporary American Fiction*, ed. Kristiaan Versluys (Amsterdam: Rodopi, 1992), 131–43.

4. Don Moser, "The Pied Piper of Tucson: He Cruised in a Golden Car, Looking for the Action," *Life*, March 4, 1966. Tom Quirk, "A Source for 'Where Are You Going, Where Have You Been?'," in *Where Are You Going, Where Have You Been?*, ed. Elaine Showalter (New Brunswick, NJ: Rutgers University Press), 81–89.

5. Moser, "The Pied Piper of Tucson: He Cruised in a Golden Car, Looking for the Action," 513.

6. Elaine Showalter, "Introduction," in *Where Are You Going, Where Have You Been?*, ed. Elaine Showalter (New Brunswick, NJ: Rutgers University Press, 1994), 8.

7. Gavin Cologne-Brookes, "Joyce Carol Oates," in *A Companion to Twentieth-Century United States Fiction*, ed. David Seed (Chichester, UK: Wiley-Blackwell, 2010), 446.

8. James Knudsen, "Where Are You Going, Where Have You Been?," *World Literature Today* 68, no. 2 (1994): 369. Knudsen reviews *Where Are You Going, Where Have You Been?: Selected Early Stories*, which includes an afterword in which Oates addresses her "motives" in writing stories.

9. Manske, "The Nightmare of Reality: Gothic Fantasies and Psychological Realism in the Fiction of Joyce Carol Oates," 2.

10. Benjamin F. Fisher, "Poe, Edgar Allan (1809–1849)," in *The Handbook to Gothic Literature*, ed. Marie Mulvey-Roberts (New York: New York University Press, 1998), 173.

11. Manske, "The Nightmare of Reality: Gothic Fantasies and Psychological Realism in the Fiction of Joyce Carol Oates," 3.

12. Greg Johnson, "Fictions of the New Millennium: An Interview with Joyce Carol Oates," *Michigan Quarterly Review* 45, no. 2 (2006): 389.

13. Joyce Carol Oates, "Pumpkin-Head," in *Sourland: Stories* (New York: Harper Collins, 2010), 3–4. This and all forthcoming quotations from this version of "Pumpkin-Head."

14. Joyce Carol Oates, "Where Are You Going, Where Have You Been?," in *Where Are You Going, Where Have You Been?*, ed. Elaine Showalter (New Brunswick, NJ: Rutgers University Press, 1994), 31. All quotations from *Where Are You Going, Where Have You Been?* are from this version.

15. Dale Boesky, "Correspondence with Miss Joyce Carol Oates," in *Joyce Carol Oates: Conversations, 1970–2006*, ed. Greg Johnson (Princeton, NJ: Ontario Review Press, 2006), 51.

16. Robert Phillips, "Joyce Carol Oates: The Art of Fiction," in *Joyce Carol Oates: Conversations, 1970–2006*, ed. Greg Johnson (PrincetonNJ: Ontario Review Press, 2006), 67.

17. A.R. Coulthard, "Joyce Carol Oates's 'Where Are You Going, Where Have You Been?' As Pure Realism," *Studies in Short Fiction* 26 (1989): 505–10. I highly recommend Coulthard, whose tone strikes me as appropriate.

18. Alfred Kazin, "Oates," in *Joyce Carol Oates: Conversations, 1970–2006*, ed. Greg Johnson (PrincetonNJ: Ontario Review Press, 2006), 13.

19. Boesky, "Correspondence with Miss Joyce Carol Oates," 55.

20. Boesky, "Correspondence with Miss Joyce Carol Oates," 55.

21. Kazin, "Oates," 14. ·

22. Kazin, "Oates," 10.

CHAPTER 3

Stephen King: Evil in Its Many Forms—Children Beware!

Laura Colmenero-Chilberg

INTRODUCTION

Stephen King's novels—what comes to mind? It might be the pseudo-Satanic Randall Flagg fighting against the power of community and friendship in *The Stand*. Or maybe it is our obsession with automobiles and one very special possessed car in *Christine*. How about the title character drenched in pig's blood in *Carrie*, or the ability to reanimate dead loved ones in *Pet Sematary*? Or maybe what comes to mind is Pennywise the Demonic Clown in *It*. Or do you remember how mobile phones turned people into zombie in *The Cell*? This handful of Stephen King's novels as well as all the rest of the many books he has written demonstrate King's ability to panic and delight us at the same time by skillfully pairing realism with terror. This has turned King into a literary phenomenon with broad public appeal, and it has skyrocketed him to global star status. King's books tell stories that resonate with his readers. Interestingly enough, we find this same kind of deep emotional response to the traditional fairy tales we know so well. From the child abuse, abandonment, and sibling bond that we see in *Hansel and Gretel* to the dangers of the wilderness in *Little Red Riding Hood* or *Cinderella*'s abusive and neglectful home situations to the dangers of beauty and the redemptive qualities of true love in *Snow White*, fairy tales also touch us at the deepest level of human reality with a popular appeal that has kept the stories alive, quite possibly in one version or another for millennia. What is both surprising and interesting, however, is that we can draw strong parallels between traditional fairy tales and the novels of Stephen King. This chapter will investigate where those parallels lie. To do so we will look at two of King's novels: *Carrie* and *It*.

FAIRY TALES AND HORROR STORIES—SIBLINGS IN THE LITERARY WORLD

Fairy tales—this word conjures up images of fairy princesses, flying carpets, poison apples, and glass slippers. These mental pictures and many others like them today have worked themselves into the nooks and crannies of our lives. Earlier generations sat transfixed in movie theaters at the animated Disney films, and they listened as their parents read the beloved stories to them in their traditional forms from authors such as the Grimm Brothers, Charles Perrault, and Joseph Jacobs. Their children and grandchildren today watch these same Disney movies, and some new ones, as their parents did in the theater, but they also view them at home, in the car, and at school. They too read books of fairy tales, but often they are the sanitized Disney versions of the stories and not so often the original tales. "... Disney's film is ... an attack on the literary tradition of the fairy tale. He robs the literary tale of its voice and changes its form and meaning. ... In fact, the fairy tale is practically infantilized."[1] Fairy tales permeate many areas of our lives, however, including in the products that represent them—on lunch boxes and as Halloween costumes, on stickers and folders, and in many other franchise-related products. Like the novels of Stephen King, fairy tales have become big business.

How could these delightful images of lightness and magic have anything at all to do with the evil and darkness found in the horror novels of Stephen King? For that we need to look not at the cleaned-up versions with their cotton candy fluffiness but instead to the original set of fairy tales.

The traditional fairy tales that we usually read can be traced to the 19th century where a small group of authors including the Brothers Grimm (Germany), Charles Perrault (France), and Joseph Jacobs (England) accumulated well-known stories, edited them where they thought appropriate, and published them under their own names. These well-known stories, however, had already been through multiple incarnations, likely beginning with oral versions. It is clear that the fairy tales we know today are not the original forms of the stories. As is usually found in oral literary traditions, these tales underwent changes that made them more relevant to a particular culture and time period. In fact, while we often think of our traditional fairy tales as originating in England, France, and Germany, we can find stories with an obvious common source in each of these countries as well as in many versions from other countries. A good example of this is found in Maria Tatar's *The Classic Fairy Tales*.[2] Consider the fairy tale *Cinderella*. Tatar's text provides side by side not only versions of this story from the Grimm Brothers, Perrault, and Jacobs, but also two versions from China and one each from Egypt and the Himalayas. Each of these versions clearly includes common elements of plot and message, but they are uniquely from a specific culture.

Another characteristic of the early traditional fairy tale that needs to be considered is its audience. Beginning in the 19th century and continuing today, fairy tales are usually seen as children's literature, but the original stories were meant for a much broader audience. Adults and children both enjoyed and passed on these tales. Children's literature as a separate genre is fairly new. Childhood as a distinct stage in the human life span is less than 200 years old. By the 19th century, however, childhood had become fully identified as unique stage in the life span requiring different treatment from adults including the need for a literature of its own. What today we call fairy tales until fairly recently has been the oral and written literature meant for people of all ages. That is clearly not the case with contemporary Disney and Disney-like stories.

What purpose have fairy tales served in the many cultures in which they are found? One of the clear goals of fairy tales has always been entertainment. At their foundation they really are good stories. They are scary, suspenseful, funny, and filled with engaging characters—but to reduce them to that function alone would be misguided. What else do fairy tales do?

Socialization into a culture is an obvious second major function—transmitting the culture of the society in which the story is told. Socialization helps answer important questions such as, "What are the values held dear in our society? What are the rules defining right behavior? What are the proper roles for members of my group? What happens to those who fail conform to our cultural rules?" As Carol Heilbrun clearly points out:

> Let us agree on this: that we live our lives through texts. These may be read, or chanted, or experienced electronically, or come to us, like the murmurings of our mothers, telling us of what conventions demand. Whatever their form or medium, these stories are what have formed us all, they are what me must use to make our new fictions. . . . Out of old tales, we must make new lives.[3]

Magistrale and Tatar identify these primal concerns found throughout fairy tales as disintegration of the family (like found in *Hansel and Gretel* and *Cinderella*), death (*Snow White*), isolation (*Rapunzel, Cinderella*), sex (depending on how they are interpreted, *Beauty and the Beast, Little Red Riding Hood*), and violence (*Little Red Riding Hood, Rumpelstiltskin*).[4] We also find some very specific messages transmitted in the stories including cautions to children to beware of strangers (*The Pied Piper of Hamelin*); warnings about venturing into the wild (*Little Red Riding Hood*); fears about blended families and child abuse (*Cinderella, Hansel and Gretel*); the difficulties of coming of age (*Jack and the Beanstalk*); and the power of beauty, love, and friendship (*Snow White*). As we read through these lists of cultural messages commonly found in fairy tales, we discover they are often the very same themes found in the work of Stephen King. At least in the work of King, the boundary between what is a fairy tale and a horror story blur together.

Consider the following short fairy tale "The Wilful Child" that comes from the work of the Brothers Grimm. The tone, the outright horror it creates in us, is no less effective than what can be found in the best novels of Stephen King:

> Once upon a time there was a child who was wilful, and would not do what her mother wished. For this reason God had no pleasure in her, and let her become ill, and no doctor could do her any good, and in a short time she lay on her death-bed. When she had been lowered into her grave, and the earth was spread over her, all at once her arm came out again, and stretched upwards, and when they had put it in and spread fresh earth over it, it was all to no purpose, for the arm always came out again. Then the mother herself was obliged to go to the grave, and strike the arm with a rod, and when she had done that, it was drawn in, and then at last the child had rest beneath the ground.[5]

The images and themes depicted in this short tale are horrifying, but are they so very different from what is found in the novels of contemporary horror writers? Stephen King clearly thinks they are not, "To my mind, the stories that I write are nothing more than fairy tales for adults."[6]

It is clear that King does not write for children, and his work does not have a lot in common with the contemporary Disney-style fairy tales. King's stories draw their inspiration from the earlier and bleaker tales in their plots, themes, and imagery. While children may not be part of King reading audience, however, children and adolescents clearly play key roles in many of his novels, as they also do in many of the traditional fairy tales. Over and over again, King returns to a single powerful thread—the innocence of childhood endangered and sometimes corrupted by evil. In his novels, King is able to "knock the adult props out from under us and tumble us back down the slide into childhood."[7] Whether it is the evil clown in *It*, the lost child in *The Girl Who Loved Tom Gordon*, or the deeply magnified teen angst of *Carrie*, themes of children and terror are solidly woven throughout King's writing. His sophisticated targeting of the frightened child hidden within each one of us continues a rich tradition usually relegated to children's literature where we find Little Red Riding Hood facing and being eaten by the vicious wolf and Hansel and Gretel abandoned by their parents in the woods and captured by a cannibalistic witch who puts them on her menu.

King has identified for us what he sees as the eight key elements of a horror story,[8] and they clearly parallel what is found in the traditional fairy tale. Both horror stories and fairy tales allow readers to (1) *Prove our bravery*. We can test our courage without risking our lives. We are sure we would act differently and with greater courage than those people in the novel or movie. (2) *Reestablish feelings of normality*. What we read in a horror novel or in a fairy tale is not what is happening in our life (for the most part), and so, usually we are able to set it aside and leave the horrors of the story and return to our normal lives. (3) *Confirm our positive feelings about the status quo*. Our lives sometimes might be boring, but there are no vampires or wolves to endanger us when we walk across town at night. We are comfortable and safe with our existing life. (4) *Feel we are part of the larger whole*. We are not alone. We are part of social groups that have a logic with rules that we all (more or less) follow. Life makes sense; our roles in that life also make sense. (5) *Penetrate the mystery of death*. We can consider the mystery and dread of death from a distance, and somewhat dispassionately. If we become too distressed, we can close the book and rejoin the world of the living. (6) *Indulge our darkest collective and social fears*. There may be no Hannibal Lector in the real world, but there is (or has been) Ed Gein and Jeffrey Dahmer and Casey Anthony. By reading about horrifying fictional people, we can more safely confront the horrors of the world without facing them in reality. (7) *Return to childhood*. Childhood is rarely a perfect place, but is sometimes fun to pretend to be children once again; however, when the horror story or fairy tale comes to an end, we can return to our safe adult lives where we at least believe we are in control of our world. (8) *Transcend the world of darkness and negation*. In the fairy tale or horror story we may read about being lost in the wilderness, be terrified by monsters (some that look monstrous and others that do not), face abusive and/or neglectful parents, or any other plot element that can be written, but in the end we can turn our backs on them all because they are not our reality.

In general, then, we find a series of common characteristics between traditional fairy tales and the novels of Stephen King, including that both (1) often use children as the focus of the action of the story; (2) socialize readers into the dominant culture's societal values, norms, and belief systems, including ideas and practices on family, death, isolation, sex, violence, friendship, and love; and (3) exhibit the elements of what we have come to call the horror genre.

Let's take a look at two novels by Stephen King—*Carrie* and *It*—to see if they really are "fairy tales for adults." How well do they fit into the three criteria we have identified? Let's also add one more element to our investigation of the parallels between King's novels and traditional fairy tales. Do we see specific fairy tale themes, plots, and character elements in the structure of King's two novels? In other words, do some of the stories that King tells fit into the category of a new generation of millennial old fairy tales?

STEPHEN KING'S MEMBERSHIP IN THE FAIRY TALE CLUB

Let's begin our analysis with *Carrie*, the first novel published by King. Its action follows a short period in the life of Carrie (Carrietta) White, a high school student from a small town in Chamberlain, Maine. The daughter of a mentally unbalanced Christian fundamentalist mother, Carrie has been abused and neglected at home by her mother. Her odd ways and old-fashioned appearance has held her up for ridicule at school, and she has suffered severe bullying at the hands of her classmates. Extremely naïve about issues of a sexual nature, Carrie begins menstruating for the first time while taking a shower at school, terrifying herself and also opening herself to derision from the other girls in the school. Carrie is an adolescent in chronological age, but she is also a child in experience, unaware of one of the most basic of bodily functions for women as well as lacking in normative social skills for a girl of her age. The incident in the shower room also provides Carrie with the knowledge that she has telekinetic powers. Sue, one of the girls who mocked her because of the shower incident has a change of heart, and ashamed at what she has done, she arranges for her boyfriend Tommy to accompany Carrie to the prom. Not everyone is so interested in being forgiven. Chris, another of the girls who ridiculed Carrie, instead plans to humiliate her by dropping pig's blood on her head at the prom. She stuffs the ballot box to make sure Carrie wins the election, and Tommy and Carrie are crowned prom king and queen. At the crowning, the moment of her greatest triumph, Carrie is doused in blood, becomes enraged and uses her telekinetic powers to kill those who have humiliated her and destroy most of the town. She goes home to her mother who tells her that she is the sinful child of a drunken rape and then knifes her in the shoulder. Carrie kills her mother and then bleeds to death.[9]

The book performs as a socializing agent with clear messages condemning child abuse, fanaticism, bullying, and uncontrolled violence. While we may understand why Carrie acts as she does, ultimately we do not support her revenge. When we look at the elements of horror fiction as defined by King, we can see that the novel very clearly correspond to many of them, but perhaps the most powerful element from the list deals with our ability to return to our own childhood through the action of the book.[10] Unable to fit into any of the social cliques at her high school, Carrie is a pariah, bullied and dismissed. While high school may be a time of great joy for some, it is also a time of great pain for many. Adolescence and with it our attempt to solidify our sense of self, maintain a healthy level of self-esteem and walk the rocky path to maturity is often difficult. In *Carrie*, we can reexperience this often-disturbing time and then return to our adult lives, safe in the knowledge that we need never physically return there.

Does *Carrie* parallel any specific fairy tales? *Cinderella* comes to mind immediately, although it can be argued that there are definitely differences in the stories. Carrie is the child of an abusive mother, while Cinderella is the stepdaughter of an abusive stepmother. Both of the characters are held back by the mother characters from fully joining their normal social environment. Carrie is restrained from participating in the normal life of a teenager, and Cinderella does not accompany her stepmother and stepsisters to the activities that are appropriate for her social station. Both girls gain the opportunity to attend a major social event, dressed in beautiful clothing and with the attention of the most handsome man at the party—Carrie attends the prom with the smart and handsome football player Tommy, and Cinderella attends the ball with the handsome and wealthy prince. While *Carrie* ends with almost all of the main characters dead, their deaths are caused by Carrie herself and her uncontrollable rage. *Cinderella* does not have this same type of bloody ending. However, in the Grimm Brothers version of the story, the stepsisters are directed by their mother to hack off their toes so they can fit their too large feet into the slippers, and they do so. A lesser remembered part of the Grimm Brothers version also includes blindness as the punishment for the stepmother and stepsisters for their "wickedness and malice." Other versions go in for a much bloodier revenge, including a Filipino version where the stepmother and stepsisters are pulled apart by horses and an Indonesian one where one stepsister is boiled, cut up and pickled, and then sent to her mother to eat.[11]

We find all four of our criteria in King's novel *Carrie*. The focus is on children; we undergo an element of socialization as we read the novel, learning what is right and wrong behavior, and the major themes of the book are those that are shared between fairy tales and horror fiction, in particular an ability to mentally return to childhood as we read the novel. What about the last characteristic; do we find plot and character elements from any specific fairy tale? We clearly see parallels between *Cinderella* and *Carrie*. While the stories are very different from each other, the basic story found in *Cinderella* seems quite clearly to provide part of the skeleton of King's novel.

Does *It* have these same elements demonstrating its close ties to traditional fairy tales? The novel is set in the town of Derry, Maine, in alternating time periods. The first, 1957–1958, follows the actions of a group of seven teenage outcasts (one girl and six boys) who have named themselves the Losers Club. An ancient and alien spider-monster has awakened and taken on the persona of the murderous Pennywise the Dancing Clown. Child abuse and neglect, violence against adults and other children, a clown in the sewer that pulls off arms and eats children—all of these provide the environment where an untried group of flawed young heroes take to the sewers to fight against an ancient evil. Most horrible is that the adults in the town have consciously made a bargain with the monster to allow it to prey upon and kill their children for about 1 year every 27 years. In return, they will receive an economically healthy community. In other words, their children are the coins that they pay for their financial security. The second period is 27 years later during 1984–1985 when the now adult members of the Loser's Club like heroes in a fairy tale quest choose to return to Derry to fight the evil monster that has once again awakened to feast on a new generation of children still abused and ignored by their parents.

Children also play a significant role in this novel as they did in *Carrie*, both as heroes and victims. Where in the *Carrie/Cinderella* story the fight is an individual one, in *It* there is a group/community component to the battle. In an environment where adults cannot be depended upon for even the simplest of protections, the Loser's Club, itself acting as a replacement for absent and abusive family members, attempts to provide both support and protection for its members, although not always successful. The number and gender division of the Loser's Club—one female and a group of six males who serve as a family for each other—reminds us somewhat of the characters found in *Snow White* with Snow White herself and her seven dwarf family members. In *Snow White* we see persecution by a stepmother (the Queen), while in Derry it is all parents that participate in the depravity of the bargain with *It*. Parallels can also be seen between the parents and children of Derry with the fairy tale *Hansel and Gretel* where the children's father and stepmother short of money intend to sacrifice the lives of the two children by abandoning them in the wilderness. Both King's novel and the fairy tales clearly deal with child abuse and parental ignorance and neglect. King identifies children as extremely important, and it is to them that he dedicates the book: "Kids, fiction is the truth inside the lie, and the truth of this fiction is simple enough: the magic exists."[12] The children of Derry, and in particular the members of the Loser's Club soon learn that there is a monster in their sewer, and that they can depend on no one but themselves, their family, to fight it.

Do we find the primal concerns that Magistrale and Tatar identify?[13] Most definitely there is ample evidence of disintegration of the family, death, isolation, sex, violence, fear of strangers and blended families, the dangers of venturing into the wilderness, coming of age, and the power of beauty, love, and friendship. This one novel includes all of them. King succeeds in, as he has said, "knock[ing] the adult props out from under us and tumble us back down the slide into childhood."[14]

Carrie and *It* both focus on children and the world of childhood, normatively held values and rules are identified as important, they display obvious characteristics that fit into the fairy tale/horror genre, and there are strong connections that can be drawn between specific fairy tales to each of the novels that seem to have provided support for the underlying structure of the novels. In these two novels, and arguably in most if not all of King's novels, we find definitive ties traditional fairy tales. It is clear that Stephen King does not mind being known as a 21st-century writer of fairy tales.

NOTES

1. Jack Zipes, "Breaking the Disney Spell," in *From Mouse to Mermaid: The Politics of Film, Gender, and Culture*, ed. Elizabeth Bell, Lynda Haas, and Laura Sells (Bloomington: Indiana University Press, 1995), 32.

2. Maria Tatar, *The Classic Fairy Tales: Texts, Criticism* (New York: Norton, 1999).

3. Carolyn G. Heilbrun, *Hamlet's Mother and Other Women*, Gender and Culture (New York: Columbia University Press, 1990), 128.

4. Tatar, *The Classic Fairy Tales: Texts, Criticism*; Tony Magistrale, *Hollywood's Stephen King*, 1st ed. (New York: Palgrave Macmillan, 2003). It is probably easier to identify those that do not fit here since violence is such a mainstay of the genre.

5. Jacob Grimm and Wilhelm Grimm, *Complete Fairy Tales* (London: Routledge, 2002), 469.

6. Quoted in Tony Magistrale, *Stephen King: The Second Decade, Danse Macabre to the Dark Half* (New York: Twayne Publishers, 1992), 4.

7. Stephen King, *Danse Macabre* (New York: Berkley Books, 1981), 99–101.

8. Magistrale, *Stephen King: The Second Decade, Danse Macabre to the Dark Half*, 22–23.

9. It is interesting to note that in the movie version of the novel, *Carrie* (Brian De Palma, 1976), in a nightmare Sue imagines that she stands on the property where Carrie's house had burned. A bloody hand reaches out to grab her, and then she wakes up. There seems a clear parallel of images between this story and that of "The Wilful Child," the Grimm fairy tale.

10. Magistrale, *Stephen King: The Second Decade, Danse Macabre to the Dark Half*, 22–23.

11. Tatar, *The Classic Fairy Tales: Texts, Criticism*, 101.

12. King, *It* (New York: Signet, 1986), vii.

13. Magistrale, *Stephen King: The Second Decade, Danse Macabre to the Dark Half*; Tatar, *The Classic Fairy Tales: Texts, Criticism*.

14. King, *Danse Macabre*, 99–101.

CHAPTER 4

Evil Monsters in Horror Fiction: An Evolutionary Perspective on Form and Function

Mathias Clasen

INTRODUCTION

Horror fiction teems with evil monsters. It would seem that audiences cannot get enough of stories about supernatural menaces and unequivocally antagonistic maniacs. The popular appetite for horror stories about scary and evil monsters is striking, partly because the fears that such stories depend on—chiefly the fear of predation—are vastly disproportionate to real-life mortality hazards, and partly because social psychologists insist that evil, in any literal sense, does not exist in the real world. "The face of evil is no one's real face," writes Roy Baumeister. Nobody in the real world considers himself or herself evil. Evil is a psychological artifact, a "false image" that is projected onto an antagonistic out-group or a member of an antagonistic out-group, probably because characterizing an opponent as evil tends to dissolve painful self-blame. In the perspective of social psychology, evil is a moralizing and distorting concept that emerges from a psychological need to de-rationalize the behavior of antagonistic others, attributing to them a pure and unmotivated desire to inflict suffering. That is why Baumeister uses the phrase "the *myth* of pure evil." Nonetheless, "the image of evil is familiar to everyone today, just as it has been familiar to everyone for thousands of years. How," asks Baumeister, "can we be so familiar with something that doesn't exist? How can so many different cultures and peoples all over the world come up with roughly the same image of evil, if it is not founded in reality?"[1] Moreover, why is the idea of supernatural evil so imaginatively compelling? If the evil monsters in horror stories do not straightforwardly reflect real-world entities, they must reflect psychological propensities. I argue that adopting an evolutionary perspective can help us make sense of such propensities, and by extension, explain the form and function of evil monsters in horror fiction.

Not all horror monsters can be rightly characterized as evil. Zombies, for example, are usually portrayed as merely following zombie nature in their relentless pursuit of sustenance. Likewise, the alien monster in *The Thing* (John Carpenter, 1982) is represented as an efficient parasitic organism following its biological programming. Even so, such horror monsters are cast as antagonistic threats to the protagonists. They are designed to cause fear, anxiety, dread, and/or disgust, and they do so by effectively targeting domain-specific cognitive adaptations that have evolved to handle danger from lethal agents in the environment. The cues that trigger such adaptations are nonrandom and our species' phylogeny explains why.

In the following, I briefly introduce evolutionary psychology and outline the main features of cognitive danger-management adaptations, explaining, that is, how a process of evolution by natural selection has fine-tuned the human central nervous system to let us respond adaptively to threats emanating from the environment. I then analyze a few representative horror monsters to substantiate the idea that such monsters reflect ancestral threats and are well engineered as cues to target cognitive danger-management adaptations. I invoke research on adaptations for cooperative social behavior to explain why evil characters are typically portrayed as profoundly antisocial. Finally, I discuss the psychological function of horror stories featuring evil monsters.

EVOLUTIONARY PSYCHOLOGY AND THE NATURE OF NEGATIVE EMOTION

Evolutionary psychology (EP) is not a subfield within psychology, like developmental or social psychology. It is an approach to the study of the human mind, and as such encompasses all subfields of psychology. EP is strongly interdisciplinary and builds on findings from evolutionary biology, genetics, anthropology, cognitive science, primatology, archaeology, and several other disciplines. EP grows out of Darwin's discovery of natural selection as the primary mechanism of organic evolution. Given that minds are products of brains and brains evolved like any other organ, the mind must be the product of an evolutionary process. Evolutionary psychologists thus view the mind as an "organ" shaped by natural selection, like the heart or the eyes, encompassing a vast amount of evolved, domain-specific programs. "Each [program] is functionally specialized for solving a different adaptive problem that arose during hominid evolutionary history . . . and each is activated by a different set of cues from the environment," according to founders of the field Leda Cosmides and John Tooby.[2]

A pertinent adaptive problem in hominid evolutionary history was staying alive in dangerous environments. Without negative emotion, the function of which is to protect the organism from harm, we would not have lasted long. Thus, the mental structures that produce negative emotions such as fear and anxiety, known collectively as the fear module, are good examples of "evolved, domain-specific programs." The human fear module is "preferentially activated . . . by stimuli that are fear relevant in an evolutionary perspective."[3] In other words, humans are born with a tendency to acquire quickly and effortlessly fear of objects that have posed a danger to our ancestors over evolutionary time. These tendencies explain why the objects of phobia are nonrandomly distributed. People typically develop phobia of such evolutionarily relevant fear objects as snakes, spiders, darkness, heights, deep-water, and other people. They do not typically develop phobia of cigarettes, deep-fried chicken, handguns, or lawnmowers, since such hazardous objects have not been around long enough to select for domain-specific defense mechanisms. In contrast, mammals have coevolved with dangerous reptiles for millions of years. Although it makes little rational sense to be afraid of the dark, reptiles, or large terrestrial predators in the contemporary world, ancient, evolved dispositions guide awareness and cue emotions. The fight-or-flight machinery in our brains is preprogrammed to disregard probability. The odds of meeting a hungry feline during a twilight stroll in the woods are very slim, but the rule of thumb etched into our neurological hardware is "better safe than sorry." In the logic of survival, a false positive is vastly better than a false negative, that is, better to jump at shadows than to shrug off the sound of what turns out to be a predator getting ready to pounce.[4] Hyper-reactivity is a functional feature of the fear module.

The human fear module is deeply embedded within highly conserved neurological structures and relatively impenetrable to conscious control. If a person with arachnophobia finds a hairy spider the size of a quarter under his or her bed cover, that discovery is likely to cause a strong negative emotional response, even though the person realizes that the spider is harmless. Even a rubber replica or a dust bunny can do the trick. Conscious knowledge that the spider or spider-like object is harmless does not immediately extinguish the instinctive fear response. We tend to react strongly even to ambiguous cues of danger, because that is the safer, hence adaptive, strategy. Thus, conserved dispositions in human cognitive architecture explain why people are captivated by even implausible, fictional monsters. Humans are biologically designed to be hyperaware of dangers in the environment, and our evolutionary history explains why certain cues of danger are more likely than others to catch our attention and activate our fear responses. The negative emotions aroused by fictional representations of dangerous agents are modulated by higher cognitive functions located in the evolutionarily younger prefrontal cortex, which is why we do not run screaming from the movie theater. Fear blends with fascination when there is no real danger. Our attention is preferentially captured by evolutionarily relevant threats, whether truly dangerous or not, and the monsters of horror fiction capitalize on this tendency.

Memorable and emotionally engaging fictional monsters match the input specifications of cognitive adaptations for danger management. Thus, rather than signifying "the monstrous oral-sadistic mother," as Barbara Creed would have it, the "huge razor-sharp teeth"[5] of the monsters in *Alien* (Ridley Scott, 1979) can more plausibly be analyzed as reflections of an evolutionarily recurrent danger. The alien monsters are well designed to activate defensive cognitive mechanisms, and that is why they provoke strongly negative emotions in audiences. Likewise, the parasitic monster of *The Thing* targets cognitive adaptations designed to protect humans against infectious disease. The "thing" is disgusting and infectious, even predatory. In the climax of the movie, the monster is depicted with giant, sharp teeth and reptilian tentacles. The audience is never invited to share the perspective of the "thing," only the perspective of the good guys whose lives the monster threatens to take and whose community it destroys. The monster is solitary, predatory, infectious, and antisocial—and a good example of what I mean by a *reflection* of evolutionarily recurrent dangers. There were, of course, no such organisms in ancestral environments, but this famous movie monster is an imaginative, supernormal amalgamation of various threats that *did* exist in prehistoric times: mammalian predators with sharp teeth, dangerous reptiles, and infectious microorganisms.

KIDS FIGHTING MONSTERS, #1: PENNYWISE VERSUS THE LOSERS' CLUB

Pennywise the Dancing Clown from the TV miniseries *It* (Tommy Lee Wallace, 1990) has become one of the most iconic embodiments of evil in American popular culture. Pennywise (Tim Curry), who resides mainly in the sewers of fictional Derry, has been around for centuries and wakes up from hibernation every 30 years to feed. The protagonists, the troubled, bullied children making up the "Losers' Club" temporarily defeat Pennywise in the summer of 1960. When 1990 rolls around, Pennywise comes back and the now-grown protagonists must resume the fight against evil.

Pennywise is only one incarnation of the evil that exists under Derry. He is described by Ben Hanscom (Brandon Crane, age 12; John Ritter, age 42) as "some kind of evil being that can read our minds and take the shape of whatever we're afraid of." While the series makes it perfectly clear what Pennywise wants—to kill, maim, and eat children—we are never told *why* Pennywise wants what he wants. The series does not give us access to his point of view, which is characteristic of stories about pure evil. Whenever we see things from the perspective of the perpetrator, his or her evilness begins to crumble. In accordance with the myth of pure evil, Pennywise is portrayed as a monster who thoroughly enjoys his vocation and spouts vaguely ominous catchphrases such as "They *all* float down here," which underscore his lack of intelligible motivation. He has no sympathetic character traits, no positive motives, no exculpatory rough childhood. Conversely, we are given abundant access to the protagonists' lives and hardships.

Pennywise is represented as a clown, creepy enough in its own right. Clowns obscure their facial expressions with face paint, making it impossible to read their emotional state and intentions. They behave unpredictably, erratically. Pennywise is several times shown with claws, fangs—"a mouth full of razor-sharp teeth"—and distorted features. He is a predator masquerading as a happy trooper. Within the logic of the story, this incarnation probably functions to attract the children who become prey. Aesthetically, however, a clown with "a mouth full of razor-sharp teeth" and homicidal intent is a powerful concept because it invokes the kind of psychologically potent stimuli discussed above and sets them in tension with the manic joie de vivre embodied by this particular figure. The evil in *It* also takes the shape of an animated, decomposing corpse and, ultimately, a giant spider-like creature. Decomposing corpses activate evolved defense mechanisms designed to protect the organism from infectious disease, and *animated* decomposing corpses upset intuitive ontological boundaries. (These two factors together—invoking infectious disease and upsetting ontological distinctions—also make the zombie an attention-demanding, viscerally repulsive figure.) The oversized spider likewise taps into evolved defense mechanisms. Theoretically, the filmmakers could have chosen any of literally countless shapes with which to represent evil. But in an evolutionary perspective it is unsurprising that they would settle on a spider. Poisonous spiders have exerted a strong selection pressure on hominids over evolutionary time. Our ancestors acquired fear of spiders because such fear was adaptive in environments where spiders posed a mortal danger, and the giant spider of *It* plays on such biologically constrained fear.[6]

The evil represented by Pennywise has nonsupernatural counterparts in *It*. Dysfunctional families, abusive parents, and mean-spirited bullies serve as naturalistic (and relatively manageable) parallels to the monstrous evil residing in the sewer system, and also emphasize that one need not look evil to be evil. Antisocial, destructive behavior suffices. All this evil is offset by the group of preadolescent protagonists. When the protagonists meet as adults, Mike Hanlon (Marlon Taylor, age 12; Tim Reid, age 42) refers to the summer of 1960 when "we found each other." He speculates that "our togetherness made us strong. Otherwise, 'It' would have picked us off one by one." Negligent parents, insensitive bullies, and homicidal clowns from Hell are juxtaposed to the positive values of social affiliation and prosociality embodied by the Losers' Club. This distribution of values reflects the egalitarian ethos found in hunter-gatherer communities. Humans have evolved dispositions to form cooperative social groups and to monitor and stigmatize dominance behavior in others,[7] and *It* elevates the happy buzz of friendship, the pleasure of social affiliation, to a spiritual Force of Good. This force is contrasted to the solitary, domination-seeking, destructive force of evil, as well as to the antisocial human antagonists in the series.

An evolutionary perspective can explain why Pennywise the Dancing Clown has achieved iconic status in contemporary popular culture. The figure is well designed to capture and hold the attention of a prey species. It has the physical attributes of a predator, is clearly characterized as dangerous, has the intent to do harm, and is even able to transcend the laws of physics. Such a figure taps into cognitive danger-management mechanisms and evokes predictably negative emotions in viewers. Moreover, the moral universe of *It* strongly privileges prosocial behavior and constructive effort over antisocial, destructive behavior. It thus reflects an evolved egalitarian ethos, presented as a moralized battle between the forces of good versus the forces of evil. As the embodiment of evil, Pennywise is aptly characterized as a dangerous predator with no redeeming qualities and a distinctly antagonistic profile.

KIDS FIGHTING MONSTERS, #2: EVIL VERSUS THE BIKE PATROL

The evil in Dan Simmons's novel *Summer of Night* (1991) is derived from Egyptian mythology. Occult forces of darkness, tied to Osiris, god of the underworld, have somehow been concentrated in a bell and transported from Italy to Elm Haven, Illinois. When a black man is unjustly condemned of murder and hanged from the bell by an angry lynch mob at the turn of the 19th century, the forces slumbering in the bell are roused. In 1960, they are finally wide awake, ready to wreak havoc on Elm Haven and usher in a new Age of Darkness.

Summer of Night is structurally and thematically similar to *It*. *Summer of Night* takes place over the course of a few weeks in the summer of 1960, in a sleepy Midwestern town. It also pits a group of preadolescents—the Bike Patrol—against ancient forces of evil. In both works, children are endowed with powers of perception denied to the oblivious grown-ups. The protagonists are up against not only evil monsters, but the malice of psychotic peers and the indifference of adults who fail to acknowledge the existence of supernatural evil. The moral universe of *Summer of Night* is likewise starkly polarized in terms of the egalitarian ethos. Prosocial behavior and social affiliation are at the positive pole, and a gratuitous desire to do harm (embodied by the supernatural forces of evil) and selfish ambition (embodied by psychotic Congden and his crooked father) are at the negative pole.

In *It*, the one protagonist to die is Stanley Uris (Ben Heller, age 12; Richard Masur, age 42). In 1960, Stanley responds to supernatural evil with the line "That's not empirically possible." As an adult, he refuses to believe that "It" has returned and refuses to join his childhood friends in the communal effort to vanquish Pennywise. By committing suicide, he escapes unbearable cognitive dissonance and irrevocably opts out of the Losers' Club. In *Summer of Night*, the one protagonist to die is Duane McBride, the bookish loner and least socially attuned character. As Duane's ghost tells his friend Dale: "If you guys try to keep fighting this thing by yourselves . . . you're going to end up like me."[8] Collective action is required to defeat evil.

The force of evil in *Summer of Night* enlists corrupt humans as well as wicked "agents from the Dark World"[9]—presumably some occult, spiritual dimension—in its apocalyptic mission. When darkness falls, rotting corpses stumble to life and 35-foot-long serpents with 6-inch teeth and homicidal intent emerge. The evolutionary perspective puts into sharp focus why Simmons would come up with giant snakes as embodiments of evil or "agents from the Dark World." Snakes have posed a mortal danger to mammals for about 100 million years. The coevolutionary arms race between reptiles and mammals has profoundly shaped our genome. When snakes developed venom, mammals developed sharper eyesight and bigger brains.[10] Humans today retain the mammalian instinct to pay preferential attention to snakes, regardless of whether poisonous snakes actually exist in their local environments. Serpents play a prominent role in mythologies, legends, and religions around the world. Snakes provoke strong visceral responses from humans, ranging from awestricken fascination to wide-eyed terror. There is no ignoring a snake, let alone a 35-foot one, and our evolutionary heritage explains why.

Simmons pits his protagonists against ancient, supernatural evil in an epic battle. The novel is less about creepy serpents and rotting zombies, though, than it is about strong bonds between preadolescent boys and the golden glow of childhood in mid-century small-town United States. Simmons uses evil and the monstrous embodiments of evil as dramatic catalysts to tell a nostalgic, engaging story about friendship, loyalty, and the sanctity of childhood. The attention-catching monsters become dramatic foils, narrative devices that allow Simmons to put his protagonists in extreme situations and to tell a story that is more imaginatively and emotionally compelling than it would have been without outlandish monsters and occult evil.

CONCLUSION: THE ALLURE AND FUNCTION OF EVIL MONSTERS

Monsters command attention. In *The Descent of Man*, Darwin described how monkeys raised in captivity exhibited strong instinctual fear toward a snake in a bag. An aversive behavioral response to an ancient enemy was etched into the nature of those monkeys, even though they had never personally met a snake. Darwin observed how the monkeys recoiled in terror at the sight of the snake, but interestingly, could not resist "taking momentary peeps into the upright bag, at the dreadful object lying quiet at the bottom."[11] The monkeys were overwhelmed by curiosity, much as humans are drawn toward the horrible as long as the horrible is safely distanced—for example, within fiction.

Supernatural horror stories feature patently unrealistic monsters and outlandish forces of darkness, but the psychological responses that such stories engender are real enough. Horror stories are playgrounds of the mind, occasions for vicariously living through the worst and for exercising and getting experience with our own negative emotions. Horror stories furnish us with imaginatively compelling images of evil. They allow for emotional engagement, and they can provoke reflection on and intellectual engagement with such issues as the nature of evil. The most psychologically engaging horror stories are those that effectively target adaptive cognitive mechanisms. The human fear module is one such mechanism targeted by horror stories, and the nature of the human fear module explains why the monsters of horror fiction are nonrandomly distributed and conceptualized to match the input specifications of danger-management circuitry in the central nervous system.

In response to Baumeister's question—"How can so many different cultures and peoples all over the world come up with roughly the same image of evil, if it is not founded in reality?"—we can offer an evolutionary explanation. Universal images of evil—the snakes, the spiders, the fearsome beasts with sharp teeth and claws—are founded in real dangers, just not the reality of urban dwellers in the modern age. Such images mirror a distant, prehistoric reality: the reality of our ancestors anxiously hoping to make it through another dark night fraught with danger. For that danger to register not merely as frightening but morally reprehensible—evil—we must set it in the social context that is Baumeister's primary concern. Our sense of evil is a perspectival bias in which our motives are essentially good—prosocial, reasonable, decent—and in which the creatures that threaten us, whether human, animal, or monster, are animated by motiveless malignancy. That kind of illusion helps us resist danger and do whatever is necessary to others as long as it benefits ourselves or our groups. It also provides a crucial element in the aesthetic *frisson* that is the peculiar province of horror stories.

NOTES

1. Roy F. Baumeister, *Evil: Inside Human Cruelty and Violence* (New York: W.H. Freeman, 1997), 62.

2. Leda Cosmides and John Tooby, "Evolutionary Psychology and the Emotions," in *Handbook of Emotions*, ed. Michael Lewis and Jeannette M. Haviland-Jones (New York: Guilford, 2000), 91.

3. Arne Öhman and Susan Mineka, "Fears, Phobias, and Preparedness: Toward an Evolved Module of Fear and Fear Learning," *Psychological Review* 108, no. 3 (2001): 483.

4. Isaac M. Marks and Randolph M. Nesse, "Fear and Fitness: An Evolutionary Analysis of Anxiety Disorders," *Ethology and Sociobiology* 15, no. 5–6 (1994): 247–61.

5. Barbara Creed, "Horror and the Monstrous-Feminine: An Imaginary Abjection," *Screen* 27, no. 1 (1986): 66.

6. David H. Rakison and Jaime Derringer, "Do Infants Possess an Evolved Spider-Detection Mechanism?," *Cognition* 107, no. 1 (2008): 381–93.

7. Joseph Carroll et al., "Human Nature in Nineteenth-Century British Novels: Doing the Math," *Philosophy and Literature* 33, no. 1 (2009): 50–72.

8. Dan Simmons, *Summer of Night* (Headline, 1991), 358.

9. Simmons, *Summer of Night*, 281.

10. Lynne A. Isbell, "Snakes as Agents of Evolutionary Change in Primate Brains," *Journal of Human Evolution* 51, no. 1 (2006): 1–35.

11. Charles Darwin, *The Descent of Man, and Selection in Relation to Sex*, 2 vols., vol. 1 (London: John Murray, 1871), 43.

CHAPTER 5

The Evils of Slavery and Their Legacy in American Literature

Carol Colatrella

In a *Saturday Night Live* skit titled "White People Problems," which first aired on January 7, 2012, African American professional basketball player Charles Barkley acts the role of a reporter filing a news story about a white woman buying fast food. Two African American restaurant employees explain to the reporter that this woman asked whether the chicken on the menu is free range, that is, whether "it could come and go as it pleased" while it was raised. Aghast, Barkley sputters his commentary to the restaurant employee: "She was worried about that? This woman ever heard about slavery?!" One among a series of white-black interactions revealing whites whining about aspects of privilege, the skit prompts viewers to consider the long reach of slavery as a continuing legacy in America.[1]

The topic of slavery in American literature encompasses considerations of racial abuse, putative biological differences, discrimination, and identity, issues revealing sociopolitical interests and representing historical events and contexts. The first published African American writer, Phillis Wheatley, was a slave whose literary talent was encouraged by her owners. Her *Poems on Various Subjects, Religious and Moral* appeared in 1773 as a result of her visit with relatives of her owner to London; her poetry "uses her own experience of oppression" as a slave to criticize "racial inequity." Arguments against slavery and racial inequality also appear in other literary genres such as drama, nonfictional prose, fiction, and memoir. Political treatises identify "our peculiar institution," a phrase employed by Southerner John C. Calhoun and others during the antebellum era, while the distinct majority of texts representing the appalling conditions of slavery and its many injustices are accounts by former slaves.[2] Many literary works explore issues of slavery and race by highlighting issues of identity and social justice, noting the physical torments inflicted by masters and overseers on slaves, their resistance, escaping from these conditions, and discrimination and abuse African Americans experienced before and after emancipation. Contemporary U.S. literary, televisual, and cinematic texts continue to explore this difficult history, while suggesting possibilities of recuperation and reparation.

Despite laws forbidding the importation of slaves, slave ownership expanded in the United States between the American Revolution and the Civil War as regional investments in the institution threatened to divide the country and as slave owners continued to breed, buy, and sell slaves. Eric Sundquist points to instability in the period between wars that affected literary production:

> A time of new revolutions in Europe, it was in America a time during which the national memory of Revolution took on a particularly fragile cast and during which the forces of social and sexual reform, an accelerating market economy, and the crisis over territorial acquisition and the extension of slavery that were to produce the major issues for the writers of the American Renaissance first become tangible.

Identifying "the contradiction between liberty and slavery" in the early republic, Sundquist notes that "Revolutionary pamphlets often cast Americans as slaves of king and parliament, suggesting at times that chattel slavery was but an extreme form of a more pervasive political oppression."[3]

The United States outlawed importing slaves in 1808, while still allowing ownership, breeding, and trading of slaves in many states until the end of the Civil War (1861–1865). As political divisions over slavery persisted in the antebellum era, the rhetorical association of rebels and slaves, the depiction of oppression, and the plea for social justice, particularly regarding the sexual abuse of female slaves and the breaking apart of families, became mainstays of the abolitionist argument against slavery. Conservatives countered abolitionist claims with arguments lobbying for owners and traders who pressed politicians to protect and to expand slavery, sometimes arguing that free wage laborers in the north suffered more than slaves working for genial masters on Southern plantations. The antebellum paradox of whether slaves were property or citizens prompted Major General Benjamin Butler to claim fugitive slaves contraband in 1861, yet a number of former slaves enlisted in the Union Army. President Abraham Lincoln issued the Emancipation Proclamation in 1863, and the ownership and trading of slaves was declared illegal with the passage of the Thirteenth Amendment to the U.S. Constitution in 1865 at the end of the war.

Questions concerning the supposed inferiority of blacks pervaded so-ciopolitical arguments about slavery. Many Americans and Europeans voiced opinions about "natural" inferiority that seemed to account for the persistence of inequality. Stephen Jay Gould reports in *The Mismea-sure of Man* that "All American culture heroes embraced racial attitudes that would embarrass public-school mythmakers," quoting Benjamin Franklin's desire to exclude "all blacks and tawneys" so as to increase "the lovely white and red." Philosophical and moral views expressed by other Americans, including founding father Thomas Jefferson and Abraham Lincoln (in the Douglass debates), also identified blacks as in-feriors. European visitors seeking to understand democratic reforms in the United States observed persistent inequalities between races in vari-ous regions of the country. Alexis de Tocqueville referenced tensions regarding racial difference that he observed during the visit he made in 1831–1832 to the United States. In *Democracy in America* (1835), he predicts that abolishing slavery would not eliminate these challenges: "I plainly see that in some parts of the country the legal barrier between the two races is tending to come down, but not that of mores: I see that slavery is in retreat, but the prejudice from which it arose is immov-able." Later in the passage, he writes, "Race prejudice seems stronger in those states that have abolished slavery than in those where it still exists, and nowhere is it more intolerant than in those state where slavery was never known."[4]

Other European visitors also weighed in on the subject of slavery, largely to criticize its physical abuses and legal inequities. Tocqueville's companion on his visit to the United States, Gustave de Beaumont, wrote *Marie or, Slavery in the United States* (1835), a novel about slavery that de-scribes the love affair of a Frenchman and an American young woman of African ancestry and their persecution by whites. Also in the antebellum period, British novelist Charles Dickens, in a chapter of *American Notes for General Circulation* (1842) about slavery, listed phrases from approxi-mately 60 advertisements seeking return of fugitive slaves document tor-tures such as "collar with one prong turned down," "iron bar on her right leg," and "much marked with irons," and "iron band about her neck." Dickens was appalled by the numerous advertisements noting cuts, bites, marks left by whippings, burns, missing fingers and toes, ears partially bit-ten off, and brands among the scars that identify particular escaped slaves. He asserts that the notices "might be made for every year, and month, and week, and day; and which are coolly read in families as things of course, and as a part of the current news and small-talk; will serve to show how very much the slaves profit by public opinion, and how tender it is in their behalf."[5] Speculating about behaviors of those identifying with slave owners, Dickens follows the horrors of slavery with newspaper excerpts

showing the violent actions of Americans, who employ guns and other
weapons to resolve social and political disputes.

Powerful arguments against slavery as an evil dominate many slave narratives. Escaped slaves shared their histories, at first to document injustices and to shore up abolitionist arguments against slavery, and later to
pass down their observations and experiences of discrimination to descendants and other citizens. By 1944, according to Marion Wilson Starling's
count, *"six thousand and six ex-slaves* had narrated the stories of their captivity, through interviews, essays, and books," including many who provided
their testimony in the context of the Roosevelt era Works Progress Administration (WPA) oral history project. Henry Louis Gates argues that
slave "narratives provided the basic paradigm for virtually all later fiction
and biography by black Americans."[6] The "paradigm," as texts discussed
in this essay illustrate, includes representations of torture, violent physical
punishments, and sexual abuse; social injustices; economic inequalities; discrimination based on race and/or color; anxieties regarding racial identity
and mixing; and religious hypocrisy rationalizing slavery and punishments.

Like captivity narratives and accounts of religious transformation, the
paradigmatic slave narrative promises redemption, often linked to learning to read and write and to escape. In the introduction to *The Classic
Slave Narratives*—a collection consisting of *The Interesting Narrative of
the Life of Olaudah Equiano, Or Gustavus Vassa, The African* (1789), *The
History of Mary Prince, Narrative of the Life of Frederick Douglass* (1845),
and Harriet Jacobs's *Incidents in the Life of a Slave Girl* (1861), Henry
Louis Gates points out that "there is an inextricable link in the Afro-
American tradition between literacy and freedom. . . . In literacy lay true
freedom for the black slave." For many slaves, literacy and freedom are
often represented as the necessary steps to eliminate the unjust oppression endured by a slave, including the breaking up of the family. Equiano's memoir begins with his and his sister's kidnapping, moving from
"African freedom, through European enslavement, to Anglican freedom," a transformation that becomes a model for subsequent narratives.
Douglass acknowledges his witnessing of horrific scenes of torture, including his aunt's whipping, and his own later punishments as motivating
his desire to escape, which he enables by learning to read. Mary Prince
begins her account by describing her master's selling Mary (at age 12)
and her sisters to separate owners and continues by describing what she
learned from her next mistress:

> She taught me to do all sorts of household work; to wash and bake, pick
> cotton and wool, and wash floors and cook. And she taught me (how can
> I ever forget it!) more things than these: she caused me to know the exact
> difference between the smart of the rope, the cart-whip, and the cow-skin,
> when applied to my naked body by her own cruel hand.

Prince's narrative is the first by a woman and dwells particularly on the sadistic, indecent punishments endured by female slaves, even sick or pregnant ones. Harriet Jacobs's incredible story describes the relentless attentions of Dr. Flint, her owner's father. He had refused to let her marry a free black man so that he could continue what the narrator calls his "base proposals," and he sends her to the family plantation. The narrator acknowledges that she was protected from Dr. Flint "by trading sexual favors for the protection of another white man, Mr. Sands, by whom she bears two children."[7] Linda Brent, as Jacobs styles herself in the narrative, runs away to hide with accommodating friends before sneaking into her grandmother's attic, spending nearly seven years in hiding. Jacobs's account was long assumed to be written by a white abolitionist before Jean Fagan Yellin pieced together archival evidence that documents the true author's identity.

Now canonical American authors also incorporated references to slavery and race in their works. Herman Melville acknowledged the problem of slavery and racial discrimination in a number of works, leading Cornel West to call him "America's greatest writer."[8] For example, the first-person narrator of Melville's *Moby-Dick* (1852), Ishmael, a sailor forced to accept little wages for backbreaking work on a whaling ship, describes the lowliness of his situation on the whaling ship by asking "Who ain't a slave?" Melville's "Benito Cereno" (1855) goes further in pressing readers to understand that all touched by slavery are implicated in its evils: as it responds "to the dilemma of slavery as a continuing problem outlined by Tocqueville, 'Benito Cereno' pinpoints the failings of an ideology that persists in equating amoral behavior with racial difference."[9] Adapting American captain Amasa Delano's *A Narrative of Voyages and Travels in the Northern and Southern Hemispheres* (1817), Melville's story includes perspectives of the slave owner, the Spanish captain who trades in slaves, and the American captain who saves the Spanish from the rebellious slaves who have mutinied, but the fiction omits any account from the slaves of their kidnapping, rebellion, and masquerade. The gap caused by their silence in the fiction forces readers to speculate on how the horrors of slavery led slaves to commit bloody murder as the best means of their own escape. Uruguayan author Tomás de Mattos's *La fragata de las máscaras* (*The Frigate of Masks*), a novel published in Spanish in 1996 and in 2008 in expanded form, presents multiple perspectives, including those of the slaves who rebelled, within a narrative that reconfigures elements of two previous accounts of this historical incident by Delano and Melville.

Questions of narrative authenticity, like those related to the publication of Jacobs's *Incidents in the Life of a Slave Girl*, have been raised with regard to other slave narratives such as that by the illiterate Josiah Henson, who dictated his story to an abolitionist. *The Life of Josiah Henson* (1849) highlights the slave's trustworthiness, revealing that Henson resisted the temptation to run away while doing business for his master in Ohio, a free state. He later escaped with his wife and children. Henson's was among the accounts that inspired Harriet Beecher Stowe to write the influential novel *Uncle Tom's Cabin or, Life Among the Lowly* (1852), which was serialized between June 5, 1851, and April 1, 1852, in the *National Era*, a Washington, D.C., antislavery paper. In Stowe's novel, Mr. Shelby's debt to the slave trader Haley initiates the sale of the faithful Tom, who accepts that he is being sold so other slaves may not be, and the escape of Eliza and her son, assisted by abolitionists, to Canada. Before dying from abuse inflicted by the vicious slave owner Simon Legree, Tom's struggles include being owned at one point by a New Orleans gentleman, Augustus St. Clare, who hates the institution but who cannot manage to free his own slaves. Stowe's appeal in the novel focused on the ideals of Christian love and motherhood, idealizing St. Clare's daughter Eva, whose life and death serves as an inspiration to others to abolish slavery.

The vivid scenes of Stowe's *Uncle Tom's Cabin* inspired countless adaptations, which variously mixed racist stereotypes and progressive messages, including stage plays, vaudeville, and "Tom shows" that toured around the world and early films. Fearful that the illustration of slavery's horrors in *Uncle Tom's Cabin* would influence Americans to abolish the institution, numerous writers penned fictional works depicting "the benign and patriarchal slavemaster" and only the most reasonable, nonviolent punishments for slaves. Anti-Tom literature such as Caroline Rush's *The North and South* (1852) contrasts the protected lives of Southern plantation slaves with the abusive treatment of Northern laborers. D. W. Griffith's 1915 silent film *The Birth of a Nation* imaged corrupt black and Yankee politicians dominating Reconstruction era politics, adapting Thomas Dixon's fictions, which incorporated turn of the century, racist "ethnological pseudoscience."[10]

Seeking to explain the poor treatment of blacks in the north, Harriet E. Wilson's *Our Nig; or, Sketches from the Life of a Free Black* was published in 1859 as the first novel by an African American woman. *Our Nig* relates the story of Frado, an orphaned mulatto tortured by Southern-inspired members of a Northern family who provide her with a poor home while requiring her to labor incessantly. Frado survives the physical and emotional abuse heaped on her, drawing strength from her religious training and her interest in books. Near the end of the novel, Frado unwittingly marries a man who earns a living as a lecturer on the abolitionist circuit by purporting to be an escaped slave. Henry Louis Gates, in his preface to *Our Nig*, identifies the novel's intermediate status between autobiographical slave narrative and sentimental fiction in that its silences and gaps point to its tensions between these literary genres.[11]

Elizabeth Keckley's autobiography *Behind the Scenes, or Thirty Years a Slave, and Four Years in the White House* (1868) describes the author's working as a seamstress for the Lincolns during the period 1861–1865. Keckley reveals her friendly relationship with Abraham and Mary Lincoln, acknowledging that she hopes her book will be a defense of Mrs. Lincoln. Among the anecdotes of life in the White House she reports, Keckley mentions that Frederick Douglass was not permitted to attend the reception at the second inauguration of President Lincoln in 1865 until "a gentleman, a member of Congress" intervened on behalf of Douglass, who entered the event despite the initial prohibition that blacks might not be invited. The president's inaugural address affirmed that "American slavery is one of those offenses which, in the providence of God, must needs come, but which, having continued through His appointed time, He now wills to remove."[12]

Post–Civil War fictions such as Frances Ellen Watkins Harper's *Iola Leroy* (1892) recognize the Negros' contributions to the Union victory and sketch the problems and prospects for former slaves during Reconstruction. Iola's white father and her black mother, who was manumitted by her husband before marrying him, do not tell their children the truth about their race, instead raising their son and two daughters as white. Unfortunately, the father's untimely death places his wife and children in jeopardy when the widow and her older daughter are forced by the father's legal heir into slavery. Harper's novel combines a sentimental plot, political debate, and religious affirmation to tell Iola's story as one of a number of accounts of heroism and bravery of the formerly enslaved. Iola is rescued to become an army nurse during the Civil War, while her brother Harry enlists in a black regiment. After the war, she and her brother manage to reunite with their mother. Refusing a marriage proposal from the Northern white doctor she worked with during the war, Iola identifies herself as black but confronts discriminatory attitudes of many employers and peers when she works as a clerk. Her brother Harry marries a woman of unadulterated African heritage who is a teacher and a role model for her race. Iola also becomes a teacher of black children and later marries a man of mixed race who joins her in working for the racial uplift of the formerly enslaved. A temperance advocate, Harper interweaves the sentimental plot with personal and political conversations among the family members and their acquaintances and discussions in churches. The former slaves debating their economic and social prospects recognize positive and negative outcomes depending on hard work, temperance, moral integrity, and religious faith.

Pauline Hopkins's *Contending Forces* (1900) makes use of sentimental and sensationalist features in its two plots. The first plot details an antebellum narrative about "community" violence enacted on the Montfort family: the white father is murdered, the mixed race mother is forced to become the concubine of the primary murderer, and her two sons are separated. The elder, Charles Montfort, goes to England as a slave, and the younger, Jesse Montfort, is enslaved until he escapes to New Hampshire, where he marries the daughter of the African American family taking him in. The second plot reveals a mystery concerning the secret of a mixed race young woman trying to make her way in the world. Under the identity Sappho Clark, she moves in with the Smith family and becomes friend with the daughter, Dora, who is engaged to John Pollock Langley, while the son Will, a philosophy student at Harvard, falls in love with Sappho. John interferes by figuring out Sappho's secret: she was raped and bore an out-of-wedlock son. Dora gives up John, and Sappho and Will separately leave the Smith household. Later, Will finds Sappho, and they reunite and marry. Dora marries Dr. Lewis. On the novel's title page, Hopkins quotes Ralph Waldo Emerson: "The civility of no race can be perfect whilst another race is degraded."[13] The political argument in the fiction opposes the historical violence enacted upon the slaves, also finding troublesome the continuing discrimination and injustice that former slaves face because whites covet and rape black and mixed race women.

Plots mixing races and the appearance of mixed race characters appear in a number of other works in the late 19th century. Mark Twain's *The Tragedy of Pudd'nhead Wilson* (1894) tells of two boys switched at birth: Chambers, the nearly white baby born by the slave Roxy, and Tom, the young master of an affluent household. Roxy makes this change when the babies are quite small, so that her son might have a better chance at life and avoid the oppression and dangers of slavery. Unfortunately, the outcome of this switch has her son (in the guise of the affluent heir) amassing debt, getting into fights, disguising himself as a woman to elude surveillance, and committing murder and theft. After identities are revealed by checking fingerprints collected by Wilson, Roxy's son is sold south, and the true heir is reinstated. Outcomes for the true heir are also negative, for this young man has not been educated to be part of his social class:

> He could neither read nor write, and his speech was the basest dialect of the negro quarter. His gait, his attitudes, his gestures, his bearing, his laugh—all were vulgar and uncouth; his manners were the manners of a slave. Money and fine clothes could not mend these defects or cover them up, they only made them the more glaring and the more pathetic. The poor fellow could not endure the terrors of the white man's parlour, and felt at home and at peace nowhere but in the kitchen.[14]

Charles Chesnutt's novel *The House behind the Cedars* (1900) considers the trials of a mixed race family bearing "the taint of black blood as unpardonable sin."[15] The novel tells of the star-crossed romance between their daughter Rena and the white George Tryon, who struggles to overcome his bias so he can marry his true love. When they part, Rena is pressed by an African American suitor to leave town to take a job teaching formerly enslaved black children, a situation that makes her vulnerable to his attentions. The suitor Mr. Wain deceives Rena and attacks her when she is unprotected. George and Wain separately attempt to meet Rena one afternoon in a wood; she escapes both only to collapse near a swamp, where she is found the next morning suffering from exposure. As Rena dies of brain fever, she is cared for by her childhood friend Frank. Rena is delirious, blaming Wain and hoping that George can love her. Attempting to find her, George decides to ignore convention and to ask again for Rena's hand in marriage, but his decision comes too late. Chesnutt's novel explores how treating former slaves and their descendants as inferior beings results in a tragedy.

Chesnutt's *The Marrow of Tradition* (1901) contrasts the differing outcomes of whites and blacks in the post–Reconstruction era when provisions to ensure enfranchisement and opportunity were rolled back, particularly in the South Focusing on the Wilmington (fictionalized as Wellington), North Carolina, Massacre of 1898, which affected members of Chesnutt's family, the novel offers a sentimental plot that acknowledges dramatically differing outcomes for descendants of the same leading family. Half sisters Olivia Carteret and Janet Miller have been raised separately but greatly resemble each other. After Olivia's mother dies, her father married their black maid, who gives birth to Janet. Evidence of this second marriage and Janet's rightful claim to her inheritance is long withheld from Olivia by Polly Ochiltree, her mother's sister. The wealthy Olivia marries Major Philip Carteret, newspaper editor and white supremacist, while Janet marries the successful African American physician William Miller. Other doubles in the novel include old Mr. Delamare's grandson Tom and the Delamare family servant Sandy. Tom also compares unfavorably with newspaper reporter Mr. Ellis as both men vie for the hand of Olivia's niece Clara.

The novel employs doubles in a mystery subplot to question racial inequality as the white Tom disguises himself as the black servant Sandy to steal from Polly Ochiltree; discovering the robbery causes her heart to fail, Mrs. Ochiltree's corpse is found the next day, and she is presumed murdered. In the Jim Crow era "Suspicion was at once directed toward the negroes, as it always is when an unexplained crime is committed in a Southern community," for "the American habit of lynching had so whetted the thirst for black blood that a negro suspected of crime had to face at least the possibility of a short shrift and a long rope, not to mention more gruesome horrors, without the intervention of judge or jury."[16] Major Carteret, Captain McBane, and General Belmont conspire against blacks, aiming to restore "white supremacy" of pre-Reconstruction. Polly

Ochiltree's death resulted from a crime, in Carteret's speculation, that "is a murderous and fatal assault upon a woman of our race," which, to him, justifies punishing blacks as a race for the crime presumably committed by one of their own, an opinion that his newspaper endorses (182). Mr. Ellis, who is against lynching, recognizes the signs of the town preparing to execute Sandy without a trial: a T-rail is erected, chains and wood appear nearby, and someone builds bleachers for viewers. Mr. Ellis hears that the burning will take place in early evening so that children can attend and that the railroad will run excursions for spectators from other towns. Old Mr. Delamare believes in Sandy's innocence and investigates the murder to find the real criminal, learning that it is his own grandson Tom, who was in desperate need of money to pay gambling debts. Disinheriting Tom, Mr. Delamare makes a will to leave his money to Sandy and Dr. Miller's hospital, but General Belmont hides the legal document to cheat the blacks from their due. Carteret uses his newspaper to fan the flames of white rage against the black newspaper's editorial against lynching, a debate that leads to violence in the streets as whites arm to attack and blacks to defend themselves and their families. During the riot, Carteret's son is taken ill, and Carteret and Olivia plead with Dr. Miller, who was not formerly allowed to treat the boy, to attend their son. Dr. Miller refuses and points out that the riot fomented by Carteret's newspaper has killed Miller's child. Only after Olivia recognizes Janet as her sister, promises to restore her inheritance, and appeals as a mother to Janet is Janet moved by Olivia's plea. Janet refuses the inheritance, but, in memory of her own departed son, she asks her husband to treat the Carteret boy. *The Marrow of Tradition* thus uses a fictional plot to identify white bigotry and black moral courage and integrity as key factors in African Americans reaching equality.

Literary works from different genres in the 20th century also illustrate the long-standing harm of slavery and of the pseudoscientific and racist social theories that blamed and punished the Negro. Post-Reconstruction authorities in the outh used peonage and lynching to control blacks, many of whom took part in the Great Migration to Northern cities to find release from intimidation, oppression, and murder. Many fictions, among them James Weldon Johnson's *Autobiography of an Ex-Colored Man* (1912), Nell Larsen's *Quicksand* (1928) and *Passing* (1929), and Zora Neale Hurston's *Their Eyes Were Watching God* (1937), consider the color line, passing, and, in the latter, the prospect of African American communities. William Faulkner's *Absalom, Absalom* (1936) explores the life of slave owner Thomas Sutpen, whose early marriage to a mixed race woman results in the birth of a son who comes to court Sutpen's daughter from his second marriage to a white woman. Willa Cather's *Sapphira and the Slave Girl* (1940) points to the cruelty of the white slave owner who masquerades as a genial matriarch. Octavia Butler's fantasy *Kindred* (1979) imaginatively sends Dana, a black female writer of the 20th century, back in time to confront her antebellum ancestors, a white slave owner, and a once-free African American woman he enslaves. Also incorporating supernatural elements, Toni Morrison's *Beloved* (1987) investigates the history of slavery by telling the life history of a mother, Sethe, who suffers, witnesses, and experiences its abuses. Sethe kills her child to save the girl from slavery, but she is forgiven by her community after the dead child returns as a ghost to haunt her mother and surviving sister. Sherley Anne Williams's novel *Dessa Rose* (1986) describes what Deborah McDowell summarizes as "a well-oiled scam," as escaped slaves "sell themselves back into slavery only to escape again," a scheme that turns the "'authoritative' texts of slavery back on themselves."[17] David Feldshuh's play *Miss Evers' Boys* (1997) portrays the legacy of slavery embedded in the medical practices of the Tuskegee syphilis study, which enrolled hundreds of African American men, mostly tenant farmers, from 1932 to 1972 to study the consequences of untreated syphilis. After the public learned of the study from newspaper accounts, which pointed to its significant lapses in medical ethics, the Belmont report created the field of bioethics and laws were enacted to regulate the use of human subjects in medical research.

Depictions of slavery in American literature represent critical aspects of history and culture. Two of the greatest American novels, Mark Twain's *Huckleberry Finn* (1885) and William Faulkner's *Absalom, Absalom,* "are in significant ways meditations by their authors on the meaning of this institution to American life," according to Deborah McDowell and Arnold Rampersad. They cite Willie Lee Rose, who "remarked on the intriguing fact that the three most spectacularly successful publishing events in American history" were three texts highlighting slavery: Harriet Beecher Stowe's *Uncle Tom's Cabin,* Margaret Mitchell's *Gone with the Wind* (1939), and Alex Haley's *Roots: The Saga of an American Family* (1976), which was quickly adapted into a television miniseries.[18]

Although the texts mentioned in this essay highlight slavery, the presence of African Americans in literature remains underacknowledged and, therefore, constrains majority understanding of the historical legacy of slavery. *Playing in the Dark: Whiteness and the Imagination* collects three lectures by Toni Morrison ("Race Matters," "Romancing the Shadow," and "Disturbing Nurses and the Kindness of Sharks") that track the diverse ways that American literary texts treat race and that point to how many majority writers do not adequately include the perspective of blacks in their works. Morrison's conclusion recognizes the need for critics and scholars to continue exploring Africanism in America and American literature, for "All of us, readers and writers, are bereft when criticism remains too polite or too fearful to notice a disrupting darkness before its eyes."[19]

NOTES

1. The phrase "white people problems" inspires a range of YouTube and other fan-produced videos. The SNL skit parodies this genre along with white privilege.

2. Helen Burke, "Problematizing American Dissent: The Subject of Phillis Wheatley," in *Cohesion and Dissent in America*, ed. Carol Colatrella and Joseph Alkana (Albany: State University of New York Press, 1994), 198; John C. Calhoun, *Remarks of Mr. Calhoun, of South Carolina, on the Reception of Abolition Petitions, Delivered in the Senate of the United States, February 1837* (Washington, DC: W.W. Moore & Co., 1837), 3.

3. Eric J. Sundquist, "Slavery, Revolution, and the American Renaissance," in *The American Renaissance Reconsidered*, ed. Walter Benn Michaels and Donald E. Pease (Baltimore: Johns Hopkins University Press, 1985), 7–9.

4. Stephen Jay Gould, *The Mismeasure of Man*, rev. and expanded ed. (New York: Norton, 1996), 64, 66; Alexis de Tocqueville and J. P. Mayer, eds. *Democracy in America*, 2 vols., vol. 1 (Garden City, NY: Doubleday, 1969), 342–43.

5. Charles Dickens, *American Notes for General Circulation*, ed. John S. Whitley and Arnold Goldman, Penguin Classics (London: Penguin, 2000), 274–75, 77.

6. Cited by Henry Louis Gates, "Introduction," in *The Classic Slave Narratives*, ed. Henry Louis Gates (New York: New American Library, 1987), ix; Deborah E. McDowell, "Negotiating between Tenses: Witnessing Slavery after Freedom—Dessa Rose," in *Slavery and the Literary Imagination*, ed. Deborah E. McDowell and Arnold Rampersad (Baltimore: John Hopkins University Press, 1989), ix, citing Henry Louis Gates.

7. McDowell, "Negotiating between Tenses: Witnessing Slavery after Freedom—Dessa Rose," ix, xvi, citing Henry Louis Gates; Mary Prince, "The History of Mary Prince, a West Indian Slave," in *The Classic Slave Narratives*, ed. Henry Louis Gates (New York: New American Library, 1987), 194; Harriet A. Jacobs, "Incidents in the Life of a Slave Girl, Written by Herself," in *The Classic Slave Narratives*, ed. Henry Louis Gates (New York: New American Library, 1987), 372; Frances S. Foster, *Written by Herself: Literary Production by African American Women, 1746–1892*, Blacks in the Diaspora (Bloomington: Indiana University Press, 1993), 102.

8. Cornel West, "Dr. King Weeps from His Grave," *New York Times*, August 26, 2011, A27.

9. Carol Colatrella, *Literature and Moral Reform: Melville and the Discipline of Reading* (Gainesville: University Press of Florida, 2002), 81.

10. Thomas F. Gossett, "Anti-Uncle Tom Literature," in *Uncle Tom's Cabin: Authoritative Text, Backgrounds and Contexts, Criticism* (New York: W. W. Norton, 1994), 442–53; David S. Reynolds, *Mightier Than the Sword: Uncle Tom's Cabin and the Battle for America* (New York: W. W. Norton, 2011), 213–73.

11. Harriet E. Wilson, *Our Nig, or, Sketches from the Life of a Free Black, in a Two-Story White House, North, Showing That Slavery's Shadows Fall Even There*, 2nd ed. (New York: Vintage Books, 1983), xxxvi.

12. Elizabeth Keckley, *Behind the Scenes: Or, Thirty Years a Slave and Four Years in the White House*, The Schomburg Library of Nineteenth-Century Black Women Writers (New York: Oxford University Press, 1988), 158–59; Abraham Lincoln, "Second Inaugural Address." March 4, 1865; Bartleby.com, http://www.bartleby.com/124/pres32.html.

13. Emerson, Address at Concord, 1844, quoted in George W. Cooke, *Ralph Waldo Emerson: His Life, Writings, and Philosophy* (Honolulu: University Press of the Pacific, 2003), 135.

14. Mark Twain, *Pudd'nhead Wilson and Other Tales* (Oxford: Oxford University Press, 1992), 144.

15. Charles W. Chesnutt, *The House behind the Cedars* (Boston: Houghton Mifflin, 1900), 86.

16. Charles W. Chesnutt, ed. *The Marrow of Tradition*, Penguin Twentieth-Century Classics (New York: Penguin Books, 1993), 178–79.

17. McDowell, "Negotiating between Tenses: Witnessing Slavery after Freedom—Dessa Rose," 158.

18. Deborah E. McDowell and Arnold Rampersad, "Introduction," in *Slavery and the Literary Imagination*, ed. Deborah E. McDowell and Arnold Rampersad (Baltimore: John Hopkins University Press, 1989), vii.

19. Toni Morrison, *Playing in the Dark: Whiteness and the Literary Imagination*, The William E Massey, Sr. Lectures in the History of American Civilization (Cambridge, MA: Harvard University Press, 1992), 91.

CHAPTER 6

Hannibal: His History and His Heirs

Sharon Packer

Hannibal Lecter, MD, is a fictional forensic psychiatrist.[1] He epitomizes evil, but he is also charming, cunning, and clever. Anthony Hopkins's Oscar-winning Hannibal character is among the most recognized movie villains of our times.[2] Dr. Lecter pushed Dr. Frankenstein to the sidelines and eclipsed old-time favorites, including Drs. Moreau, Jekyll, and Fu Manchu.

Dr. Lecter was not invented for film, although he gained the most fame from film. Rather, he was born on the pages of Thomas Harris's best-selling novel, *Red Dragon* (1981). Five feature films followed, based on Harris's four Hannibal books. Given the fact that Hannibal lives dual literary and cinematic lives, it seems fitting to trace Hannibal's origins to both venues. Ideally, we would start with Harris's personal inspirations, which the notoriously publicity-shy Harris is reluctant to reveal. Before we go further, we should mention that the historic Hannibal (the one who crossed the Alps) was a favorite of Freud, who was also an MD before turning to psychoanalysis. Again, Harris refuses to acknowledge the reasons behind his choice of names, although we are free to reflect.

It is equally fitting to examine Hannibal's cinematic career on its own merit, apart from its literary precursors. That way, we can see how Hannibal fits into the well-established mold of sinister cinema psychiatrists that appears repeatedly in films and dates to the early evolution of cinema.[3]

Those evil screen shrinks follow fairly predictable patterns. They are sicker than their patients, more brilliant (or more conniving) than their peers, and as evil as the devil. Sometimes they are indeed the devil in disguise. Dr. Lecter shares much with Dr. Caligari of the 1919 German

Expressionist classic, but has even more in common with Dr. Mabuse, who also began as a literary character, before inspiring 12 films over 50 years.

Hannibal himself has spawned several filmic heirs to date, apart from the direct sequels and prequels. *Gothika* (Kassovitz, 2003) came on *Hannibal's* heels chronologically, but it is a throwback to 1970s-era Blaxploitation. As we will discuss in detail later, *Gothika* can be seen as a black rendition of the malevolent and psychosexually sick Dr. Lecter. It is peppered with occult touches that recollect séances from Fritz Lang's 1922 *Doktor Mabuse* and millennial-era intrigue with mysticism.

Dr. Lecter's influence extends beyond film. His forensic skills spearheaded a new television genre: the forensic procedural. Forensic procedurals assure audiences that forensic science can explain evil after the fact, even if laws cannot stop evil in its tracks. As an example, *CSI* (Crime Scene Investigation) enjoyed years on prime time TV before inspiring its own heirs, such as *Dexter* and *Bones*.

It would be nice if we could reconstruct the day when Dr. Lecter was "born" in Harris's imagination. That way, we might understand how Hannibal came to personify evil and function as a latter-day version of the devil. However, the Southern-born, -bred, and -educated Harris has not permitted public interviews since 1976. Harris refuses to reveal sources or inspirations. Like a good mystery writer, he cloaks his own motivations and methodology in secrecy. By default, he forces his followers to dig for clues, which is what we will do. Without definitive data, it is difficult, if not impossible, to get a firm grasp of what went on in Tom Harris's mind when he created the cannibalistic Hannibal character. So we will make do with educated guesses and clinical-style hypotheses.

It is known that Harris visited the Federal Bureau of Investigation's (FBI) new Behavioral Science Unit prior to writing *Red Dragon*. To catch serial killers, the FBI staffed the unit with PhD-level psychologists. Remnants of that research appear in the Hannibal novels. For instance, *Red Dragon* revolves around a fictional FBI agent named Will Graham, who is the first of several imaginary FBI agents.

For film fans, Agent Graham is barely a blip on the radar. He cannot compete with Jody Foster's Agent Starling in *Silence of the Lambs* (Demme, 1991). Yet Graham's character is critical to the storyline because he introduces us to Hannibal the Cannibal, the cultured killer and skilled psychiatrist.

Silence of the Lambs, the film is particularly important, not just because of its striking commercial success, but because of its timing. *Silence* was released in February 1991. Notorious serial killer Jeffrey Dahmer was arrested in the summer of 1991. Dahmer was a real-life cannibal and necrophiliac, who abducted, raped, tortured, and ate dozens of young men, keeping some skulls for souvenirs. This strange coincidence added credibility to the over-the-top fictional film.

Dr. Lecter's larger-than-life persona dwarfs the FBI agent who narrates the story and drives the plot. When played by Anthony Hopkins in *Silence of the Lambs*, Dr. Lecter oozes with Old World aplomb. He drinks fine wines, cooks with chef-style copper-bottomed pots, and then serves sautéed human brains, all the while dining by candelabra light. Sometimes, he uses his teeth to gnaw human flesh, dispensing with his elegant accoutrements altogether.

Dr. Lecter glistens with brilliance, even when locked in a cell, or when his face is encased in his now iconic mask. His diction radiates refinement and European erudition. He asks probing questions and makes astute observations.

Film versions of Hannibal remain etched in our memories, but it is worth speculating about the possible influence played by other films from the early 1980s, when *Red Dragon* (the novel) was still in the mental incubator. *Dressed to Kill* (De Palma, 1980) focuses on sexually deviant, morally bankrupt psychiatrists, although Michael Caine's character pales in comparison to Dr. Lecter, in spite of some superficial similarities.

In *Dressed to Kill*, a superficially successful Upper East Side psychiatrist (Caine) kills his patient (Angie Dickenson) as she rides the elevator in his Manhattan skyscraper. Caine dresses as a woman when he wields his knife. The sole witness to the murder is a prostitute who works the high rise that houses Caine's professional office.

Two years after *Dressed to Kill*, and a year after *Red Dragon's* release, Barbara Carerra plays a psychiatrist who runs a swanky but kinky sex clinic. She collaborates with the CIA, murders as needed, and meets her end while trying to shoot Mike Hammer as they lock in passionate embrace. *I, the Jury* (Heffron, 1982) is an ode to sex, violence, and the gross violation of professional propriety. Still, it lacks cannibalism.

It is unclear if the bizarre behavior of these two contemporaneous cinema psychiatrists influenced the development of the even more twisted Dr. Hannibal Lecter. Perhaps this string of extremely strange screen psychiatrists simply reflects audience preferences of that era, or comments on the wavering state of psychiatry at a time when the reigning princes of psychoanalysis were being cast aside, as newer approaches to biological psychiatry moved forward, before gaining firm footing. Alternatively, this triad may be nothing more than a nod to the decadence of the 1980s, with its "nothing can shock me now" attitude.

Neither the cross-dressing, knife-wielding killer psychiatrist of *Dressed to Kill* nor *Jury's* sexually seductive Park Avenue doctor who engineers threesomes with twins approaches the depravity and inhumanity of Dr. Lecter. Lecter eats human flesh (but not exclusively). He feeds enemies to wild boars. To his credit, he unravels clues about serial killers, when not pontificating about fine art, hanging crystal chandeliers from his townhouse ceiling, or lobotomizing sexist FBI agents seated at his banquet table.

In both the book and the film, Dr. Lecter claims to understand people like Buffalo Bill because he treated similar patients before leaving his private psychiatric practice (and becoming a full-time prisoner). Like the real-life killer, Ed Gein, Harris's fictional Buffalo Bill skins his victims.

Still, no one understands Dr. Lecter's odd dietary preferences—and the reasons behind his infatuation with human flesh—until the prequel, *Hannibal Rising* (Webber, 2007). This film connects Hannibal's bizarre behavior to an even stranger traumatic experience in his childhood home in war-torn Europe, when an itinerant band of Nazi sympathizers cooks his little sister and serves her as soup, after admiring her chubby cheeks. The preposterous prequel implies that Hannibal is not inherently evil, but has been made evil by those who are pure evil: Nazis and their collaborators.

In the interim, *Red Dragon* became a best seller and turned into a film called *Manhunter* (Mann, 1986). Michael Mann's *Manhunter* attracted little fanfare. Harris's second Hannibal book was a different matter. The film based on that book—*Silence of the Lambs* (1991)—boasts a magnetic cast and a different director: Jonathan Demme. *Silence* won eight Academy Awards, including one for Anthony Hopkins's Dr. Lecter.

With that accolade, public demand for all living evidence of the Hannibal character skyrocketed. *Red Dragon* was eventually remade into a film by the same name. Hannibal fans, hungry for more, retrieved the original *Manhunter*, to ensure that they consumed every known morsel about Hannibal the Cannibal.

Michael Mann's original *Manhunter* (1986) film grossed only $8,620,929, a pittance compared to *Hannibal*'s gross of $165,092,268 in 2001. *The Silence of the Lambs* (1991) earned $130,742,922. Some say that Brian Cox's Hannibal performance did not scintillate the way Anthony Hopkins's did. Many attributed the appeal of *Silence of the Lambs* (1991) to the special chemistry between Hopkins as Dr. Lecter and Jody Foster as the unassuming Agent Starling.

We learn more about Dr. Lecter in 2001, after Jody Foster is replaced by Julianne Moore, who is anemic as Agent Starling when compared to Foster's original. Hopkins returns as Dr. Lecter. Hopkins's Dr. Lecter is now a familiar face; he has become America's most recognized movie villain, as per the American Film Institute. *Hannibal* broke box office records. Via the character of Mason Verger, it adds another kink to Dr. Lecter's overall polymorphous perverse personality.

Ten years have passed, and only one of Hannibal's original victims still lives. That victim is a despicable person himself and a pedophile at that.

Played by Gary Oldman, Mason Verger's face is scarred beyond recognition. His hidden visage reminds us of Hannibal's muzzle.

Mason Verger is wheelchair-bound because of self-inflicted injuries acquired at Hannibal's urging. When Mason was under the influence (of both drugs and Hannibal), Hannibal directed him to cut off his own flesh and feed it to his animals. Mason was too infatuated with Dr. Lecter, and too disoriented from drugs, to resist Hannibal's hypnotic-like hold. The parallels between Mason's restrictions of movements, and Hannibal's movement restrictions, when tied to his prison hand truck, are obvious to the viewer.

It is clear that Mason Verger is immensely wealthy—as is Hannibal, albeit to a lesser degree. However, Hannibal is a cultured consumer who admires fine art, fine food, and fine wine. Mason, on the other hand, is consumed by hatred. Mason makes no secret of his same-sex preference (which once included Dr. Lecter). This fact makes us wonder if Dr. Lecter's libidinal urges are more pluralistic than previously revealed.

The crippled Verger has but one reason left to live: to avenge the injuries inflicted by Dr. Lecter. Yet Mason never gets to wreak the revenge that he so desperately desires. Instead, Verger is thrown to the boars that he acquired with Hannibal in mind. He is fatally dismembered and dies one of the worst deaths of all of Hannibal's victims.

Box office stats do not lie. They prove that Dr. Lecter appeals to audiences, for reasons that elude us. In response to the successes of *Silence of the Lambs* and *Hannibal,* both of which starred Anthony Hopkins, a remake of the *Manhunter* was undertaken, with Hopkins cast as Hannibal. This time, the film retains the title of Harris's book: *Red Dragon.*

Red Dragon's story takes place before the events chronicled in *Silence* and *Hannibal. Red Dragon* returns to Baltimore, Hannibal's hometown, and to his townhouse. The year is 1980. The city of Baltimore is also home to Johns Hopkins, the famed medical center. The action precedes Dr. Lecter's capture and incarceration, and begins during his dinner party, where guests dine in elegant surroundings. The omniscient audience realizes that the menu of the cannibalistic Dr. Lecter may be more complicated than his guests expect.

High-profile stars grace *Red Dragon.* Ralph Fiennes, Phillip Seymour Hoffman, Mary-Louise Parker, Ed Norton, Emily Watson, and Harvey Keitel pump up the bill—but Jody Foster is missing. Ed Norton plays Agent Graham, the G-man who substitutes for Jody's Agent Starling.

Agent Graham is not an invited guest. Rather, he visits Dr. Lecter after the party, hoping to glean facts from the doctor's vast fund of knowledge. Graham wants to learn why livers and kidneys were removed from recently recovered dead bodies. Agent Graham suspects that the murderer is a cannibal who retrieves edible organ meat for personal consumption.

He shares his hunch with Dr. Lecter, but soon starts to suspect Dr. Lecter himself. The agent confronts the doctor, only to find himself partially disemboweled—by Hannibal, of course.

Dr. Lecter is shot by the felled agent whom he presumed dead. Agent Graham's injuries, and Dr. Lecter's subsequent incarceration, could easily end each of their careers, but, luckily for audience members, the story is just starting.

The FBI's hunt for a new killer, known as "The Tooth Fairy," forces an uneasy reunion and an even more complex alliance between Lecter and Graham. Ralph Fiennes appears as the psychotic destroyer who leaves characteristic teeth marks on his victims. His torso is tattooed with images taken from William Blake's paintings. In an oral rage, he eats priceless Blake lithographs housed at the Brooklyn Museum. He calls his alter ego "The Great Red Dragon," in homage to his Blake tattoo on his back. However, the media demeans him and dubs him, "Tooth Fairy."

The Tooth Fairy shares some similarities with Dr. Lecter. Both show knowledge of art, affinity for continental culture, and uncontrolled oral urges. Again, Dr. Lecter alone is equipped to unravel the mystery of the Tooth Fairy. Even though Lecter is permanently confined to a hospital for the criminally insane, FBI agents track him down and plead for his expertise. His narcissism overtakes him, and Hannibal obliges.

For those who wonder how Hannibal developed his unusual proclivities, Harris writes another book. *Hannibal Rising* (2006) comes to the rescue and addresses those questions. *Hannibal Rising* portrays a young Hannibal, while he and his beloved young sister struggle to survive after their parents are murdered by Lithuanian marauders. The war is almost over, and hungry Nazi sympathizers overtake the family estate. They kill the Jewish cook (and thereby inform us that they are vicious and that Hannibal is not Jewish).

We learn of Hannibal's noble lineage. His family was targeted by scraggly soldiers who pillage their palace before tracking down the few survivors who hide in a lodge in the woods. Unable to find sufficient food, the soldiers turn his sister into soup.

Hannibal's compulsion to eat human flesh is born out of this tragedy. He identifies with the aggressor, in the classic psychoanalytic sense, and lives out his life reliving this trauma. The explanation is too pat to be entertaining, but it is plausible, as plausible as analytic explanations come. This film lacks the adult Anthony Hopkins, and was not as popular as its predecessors were.

Even though *Hannibal Rising* offers a rational explanation that makes sense to Dr. Lecter's psychiatric colleagues, we the audience cannot make sense of our reactions to Hannibal. We like Hannibal. Why else would we watch films about him or read books about him? We wonder why we crave more novels and films about this man-eating killer who should turn our stomachs, were he not the epitome of civility on other occasions.

We strive to explain our own attraction to this man-beast, and that is part of the appeal. We realize that Hannibal's knowledge and expertise are coveted by the most skilled government agents, in spite of the fact that he is not just sociopathic and unscrupulous, but that he engages in the most heinous activities known to humans. What a brilliant man he must be, to be able to attract FBI agents at the same time that he repulses them so!

Even his relationship with the FBI's Agent Starling is ambiguous. Hannibal is ready to cut off his own hand, if that buys freedom for this young female. He protects her and carries her to safety, while wearing his muzzle-mask. The depth of his affection exceeds ordinary understanding. Hannibal interfaces with artists, curators, and opera singers—but also eats their innards. How versatile and multifaceted he is!

We can say that Hannibal's dual nature helps us deal with evil, both in our own paths, and in the course of history. Those who studied Nazi Germany's history know that Germany was the cradle of civility before it was overtaken by the Nazi disease. Even German Jews who escaped the hands of Hitler still reminisce about the Weimar Republic that they toasted just before the Third Reich took hold in 1933.[4]

Hannibal's dual nature assures us that we can easily be taken in by pure evil or by the proverbial devil, simply because evil can be cloaked in fine clothes, with impeccable speech, advanced education, and lofty professional standing. By watching Hannibal films or reading Harris's novels, we are exculpated for our gullibility and we understand the ease with which we respond to superficial charm that can encase evil intentions.

Some might argue that Hannibal does not appeal at all. Perhaps he simply acts as a conduit for our anxieties about serial killers such as Ted Bundy, Jeffrey Dahmer, John Wayne Gacy, Son of Sam, or the Boston Strangler. Serial killers became prominent in the decades leading to Harris's Hannibal. Until historians proved otherwise, many journalists suggested that such serial killers were recent inventions, and a sign of our times.

Hannibal is unique, however. Not only is he the best-known movie monster of our times, but he is also the most popular *human* monster of 20th-century pop culture. Universal horror films of the 1930s started the movie monster trend, with Frankenstein's monsters, vampires, and werewolves, none of which were fully human. The gap between the supernatural and the natural closed. Universal films appeared just before the Holocaust began. During the Holocaust, the magnitude of evil surpassed any evil previously known, proving that humans are capable of committing the worst horrors. World War II, with its Nazi sympathizers, also molded Hannibal's mind-set.

By the late 20th century, classic horror monsters were supplanted by newer incarnations of evil: Freddy from *Nightmare on Elm Street* (Craven, 1984), Jason from *Friday the Thirteenth* (Cunningham, 1980), and Michael Myers of *Halloween* (Carpenter, 1978). Each of these villains starts as human, but none remains fully human, for each lives eternal lives, reappearing after death, like vampires of old.

Hannibal has no supernatural links (to date). He connects to the Holocaust, and shows that post-Holocaust culture can turn victims into victimizers as they identify with the aggressor.

Hannibal is different in another important way. He is a doctor, and a psychiatrist no less, and a forensic psychiatrist who knows even more about evil and how it is punished (or how evil evades detection). He is not a janitor, like Freddy. Nor is he intellectually deficient, like Jason's "Mongoloid" character.

We can ask ourselves if Dr. Lecter's professional status as a psychiatrist makes a statement about society's attitude toward psychiatry—or if it comments on forensic psychiatry in particular, and on its use (and misuse) as a courtroom tool. It is worth considering this aspect, even though such specialized social commentary alone cannot account for the enduring success of Hannibal books and films.

Psychiatry was in a state of flux in the early 1980s. It is and always was a medical specialty, and its practitioners sport MD credentials (like Hannibal's). Yet it became bastardized because of its link to psychoanalysis, which severed its medical roots in the early 20th century, at Freud's urging. Even before psychoanalysis was invented in 1896, it was unclear if clerics or medics claimed control over aberrations of behavior.

By the mid-1980s, the sun that once shined so brightly over American psychoanalysis was about to set. Psychoanalysts were forced out of academic medical centers. Neuropsychiatry and psychopharmacology were rising stars, replacing older therapeutic models.

Neuropsychiatry had not fully eclipsed the psychoanalytic model in the early 1980s, when Dr. Lecter surfaced. The glow of psychoanalysis was fading fast, like the setting sun of midwinter. Still, the "Decade of the Brain" would not start until 1990, to signal that the tides finally turned. Hannibal the Cannibal was created when psychiatry was in a state of flux: no longer synonymous with psychoanalysis, but not yet fully scientific.

During states of transition, membranes that separate one state from another become porous and easy to penetrate. It is easy to poke bigger holes in porous barriers, and parody both sides. Psychiatry was a divided specialty in the 1980s, with both factions warring with the other, and with neither side equipped to defend the specialty as a whole.

The problems that emerged in forensic psychiatry are easy to pinpoint. Psychiatrists who testify in court have historically been accused of selling opinions to the highest bidder. Public respect for forensic psychiatry reached its nadir in 1979, with the "Hostess Twinkie" defense, which preceded Thomas Harris's first Hannibal book by a mere two years.

The "Twinkie Defense" began when psychiatrist Martin Blinder testified at the murder trial of Dan White, one-time San Francisco Police Officer and Firefighter who became a District Supervisor. White stood accused of assassinating San Francisco's Mayor George Moscone and Supervisor Harvey Milk in 1978. White never denied that he himself pulled the trigger.

Because Harvey Milk was openly gay, his assassination became a cause célèbre for gay activists. These events were re-excavated in *Milk* (Van Sant, 2008), with Sean Penn starring as the martyred Harvey Milk.

At the trial, Dr. Blinder claimed that White had been depressed when he committed his crime. Because this one-time fitness fanatic and health food advocate began to consume junk food and sugary soft drinks, Dr. Blinder attributed White's volatile mood swings to blood sugar fluctuations.

Judge and jury agreed that White had "diminished capacity" because of his sugar rush. He was convicted of voluntary manslaughter, acquitted of premeditated murder charges, and spared the death penalty. Riots followed, as did accusations of homophobia. Faith in forensic psychiatry plummeted.

It is entirely conceivable that Harris was influenced by this trial, and that his Hannibal character parodies a profession that seemed capable of self-parody. Because Harris refuses interviews, we cannot say with certainty that a cannibalistic psychiatrist with the lowest moral character imaginable is impugning the morale caliber and professional credibility of psychiatrists who testified in the Harvey Milk trial.

We can confirm that Hannibal is one of a long line of sinister cinema psychiatrists who graced—or disgraced—the silver screen, almost since the start of cinema. In the earliest years of film, evil hypnotists were popular subjects. Movies were mesmerizing, and spectators stared at the screen as if staring at the proverbial hypnotic eye. Since the media is the message, hypnotists enjoyed extra prominence in early film. Some hypnotists were doctors, some are showmen. Some were family members. Few if any were psychoanalysts (since psychoanalysis was born within a year of cinema and was nowhere as well known to the public as hypnosis).

By 1919, the Great War had ended, but memories of the war dead and wounded remained. So did revulsion at military psychiatrists who forced shell-shocked soldiers back to the front, accused them of malingering or pension seeking. Worse yet, they subjected soldiers to painful treatments known as "Kaufmannization." They shocked hysterical men until their symptoms subsided or until they succumbed to heart attacks, absconded, or committed suicide. Hypnosis was sometimes used to treat shell-shocked soldiers, but proved to be insufficient for those who did not speak German or suffered from hysterical (or organic) hearing loss.[5]

Thus, the granddaddy of all sinister psychiatrists was born: Dr. Caligari. Co-written by Czech and German screenwriters, the character of Dr. Caligari represents the reviled military psychiatrists of the Great War who hypnotized their charges, turning them into murder machines.

The Cabinet of Dr. Caligari (Weine, 1919) is the story of a charlatan psychiatrist who performs at sideshows during his off-hours—and when he is not coercing his confederate, Cesare, to murder those who offend him. Cesare will die of stress after Caligari commands him to kill a woman he loves.

Later, when Dr. Caligari becomes psychotic, he is stuffed into a straightjacket and committed to his own asylum. This scenario recurs repeatedly throughout cinema history.

There are clear parallels between Dr. Caligari and Dr. Lecter. Both are psychiatrists, or pretend to be, and both are sicker than their patients. Both condone, cause or commit murder. Dr. Caligari is tame compared to Dr. Lecter, given that he orders Cesare to strangle his victims, whereas Dr. Lecter eats their cheeks or lobotomizes his victims, or sautés their brains and serves them as dinner fare.

Apart from the simplicity of his murders, as opposed to Hannibal's complicated cannibalistic rituals, Dr. Caligari is one-dimensional, whereas Dr. Lecter is very versatile. Caligari functions in his own sphere, be it the fairgrounds or the asylum. In fact, the claustrophobic stage where *Caligari*'s action takes place instills a sense of constriction rather than expansiveness.

Dr. Lecter, on the other hand, is expansive and covers vast terrain. Even after he is captured and incarcerated, Dr. Lecter escapes and crosses continents. He takes us with him on excursions to Italy, where he lectures on art to admiring audiences. It is there that he hangs the curator by his intestines (which are still attached to his insides). Hannibal dangles his victim over a museum-quality, public piazza.

Because of these traits, Dr. Lecter is much more reminiscent of Dr. Mabuse, who arrived on the silver screen two years after Dr. Caligari's debut. Dr. Mabuse premiered in novels and in serialized sections of tabloid pages, thanks to his literary creator, Norbert Jacques. Jacques strived to imitate the pulps. He was inspired by Fantômas, the master of disguises.

Dr. Mabuse is not that well known to Americans, but he remains recognizable to most Europeans, who consider him a horror figure on par with Dr. Frankenstein. Fritz Lang's first Mabuse film is *Dr. Mabuse, the Gambler (Shpeiler)* (1922). Dr. Mabuse starred in 12 films over 50 years. He began in Europe but moved to America, following Fritz Lang in his exile from Europe. Hannibal has appeared in a mere five films. Of course,

Hannibal's career is nowhere near complete, even though Harris has not produced new novels.

Like Dr. Lecter, Dr. Mabuse is suave, sophisticated, and attractive to women. He is a master of disguise (as was Fantômas). He is adept at telepathic hypnosis, not unlike the hypnotist Dr. Caligari, and somewhat similar to the charming antisocial Hannibal, who enthralls both women and men.

Dr. Lecter departs from Dr. Mabuse's examples in other ways. Hannibal Lecter acts alone, and enjoys his sadistic deeds with perverse satisfaction, whereas Mabuse orchestrates conspiracies. Hannibal often acts on impulse, and leaves his trademark teeth marks. Yet he manages to evade his pursuers and kill again, and again, and again.

Lest it seem that there is a direct line between Dr. Mabuse and Dr. Lecter, uninterrupted by other intervening variables, I must mention that sinister psychiatrists have been staples of 20th-century cinema, and persist into the 21st century. With the exception of a short six-year span between 1957 and 1963, screen psychiatrists have been portrayed badly, more often than not. For reasons that we cannot delve into here, the "Golden Years" of cinema psychiatry idealized mind doctors, and showed them accomplishing feats that could not be replicated by their real life peers.

Yet none of the dozens upon dozens of sinister screen psychiatrists could compete with Hannibal the Cannibal's crimes. Interestingly, few of those sinister psychiatrists earned a remake or a sequel. *Manchurian Candidate* (Condon, 1962; Demme, 2004), *House on Haunted Hill* (Castle, 1959; Malone, 1999), *The Cabinet of Dr. Caligari* (Weine, 1919), and *The Cabinet of Caligari* (Kay, 1962) are the rare exceptions to this rule.

As we know, Hannibal has had five films, and one of them is a remake of the first. He even merited a psychoanalytic-style prequel, with a return-to-youth, to help us understand how he became the monster that he is.

There is one recent film whose sadism approaches the sadism seen in the Hannibal series. That film is *Gothika* (2003), an exploitative film that rides on the heels of Hannibal's success, and still does not succeed.

Gothika revolves around two African American psychiatrists, husband and wife. Dr. Miranda Grey (Halle Berry) works at a mental hospital. She is married to another psychiatrist (Charles Dutton). His sadistic sideline is exposed after he is murdered, well into the film, when his home torture chamber is uncovered.

The action starts with Miranda. While driving from work on a stormy night, Dr. Miranda Grey sees a girl standing on the road. To avoid the girl, she swerves and has an accident. She later learns that the girl is the ghost of her supervisor's deceased daughter.

After the accident, Miranda awakens in the hospital, this time as patient, not as psychiatrist. Her arms are carved with letters that she insists are communications from the girl's ghost. Not surprisingly, she is presumed to be psychotic. Her former coworker, Dr. Peter Graham, is played by Robert Downey Jr., whose dabbling with drugs and repeated attempts at rehab are well known. Dr. Graham shows sympathy for her claims about supernatural contacts, and for her contention that she did not murder her sadistic husband. Like Agent Graham in Harris's novels, Dr. Graham functions as a foil.

This film exemplifies many things. Like *The Exorcist* (Friedkin, 1975), it reminds us of psychiatry's historical connections with the supernatural, and the long-standing battle between doctors of the church and doctors of medicine. Like *Hannibal*, it contends that psychiatrists are capable of committing stranger, more sinister, and more secret deeds than other people.

Hannibal left behind another, less occult, legacy. His filmic success paved the path to a new genre of prime time TV shows that feature "forensic procedurals," such as *CSI, Dexter,* and *Bones.* As of 2013, sanitized television shows about forensic investigations come full circle, when *Hannibal* turns into a television serial.

It is curious that the last Hannibal film, the prequel, connects Hannibal's twisted evolution from a loving brother to a bestial murderer to the greatest moral evil that ever occurred: the Holocaust and the Nazi era that begot it. Perhaps the only way to make such a character credible is to link him to history's worst episode of evil. In forging this connection, author Harris pushes our hypothesized social commentary into a sidebar, and cements his now iconic character to the History of Evil itself, making us wonder if this is a personal political statement, or if this characterization is simply a way to drive the plot and make readers "suspend disbelief" as they absorb his over-the-top stories.

NOTES

1. Thomas Harris, *Red Dragon* (New York: Dell, 1981). Harris's novel makes a point of referring to Dr. Lecter as Hannibal Lecter, MD, as if to alert us to the distinction between psychiatrists, who are medical doctors, and doctoral-level psychologists, who have PhDs and are addressed as "Dr." but are not physicians.

2. American Film Institute, "Afi's 100 Years . . . 100 Heroes & Villains," American Film Institute, http://www.afi.com/100years/handv.aspx (accessed February 10, 2013). Paul, "10 Most Recognizable Movie Villains," 10 Awesome, http://10awesome.com/10-most-recognizable-movie-villains/ (accessed February 10, 2013); David Steinsdoerfer, "The Best Movie Villains of All Time," *Ranker.com*, http://www.ranker.com/crowdranked-list/the-best-movie-villains-of-all-time (accessed February 10, 2013); John McCarty, *Movie Psychos and Madmen: Film Psychopaths from Jekyll and Hyde to Hannibal Lecter* (Secaucus, NJ: Carol Publishing Group, 1993).

3. Sharon Packer, *Movies and the Modern Psyche* (Westport, CT: Praeger, 2007); Sharon Packer, *Cinema's Sinister Psychiatrists: From Caligari to Hannibal* (Jefferson, NC: McFarland, 2012); Glen O. Gabbard and Krin Gabbard, *Psychiatry and the Cinema*, 2nd ed. (Washington, DC: American Psychiatric Press, 1999).

4. Amos Elon, *The Pity of It All: A Portrait of the German-Jewish Epoch, 1743–1933* (New York: Picador, 2003).

5. Anton Kaes, *Shell Shock Cinema: Weimar Culture and the Wounds of War* (Princeton, NJ: Princeton University Press, 2009); Andreas Killen, *Berlin Electropolis: Shock, Nerves, and German Modernity*, Weimar and Now (Berkeley: University of California Press, 2006); Paul F. Lerner, *Hysterical Men: War, Psychiatry, and the Politics of Trauma in Germany, 1890–1930*, Cornell Studies in the History of Psychiatry (Ithaca, NY: Cornell University Press, 2003).

CHAPTER 7

The Man of the Crowd: Following Poe and Finding Evil in Popular Culture

Caleb Puckett

For over 150 years, the writings of Edgar Allan Poe have transcended countless trends in literary and popular culture. Poe's resilient body of work has, in fact, secured him a position among the most widely read and most influential authors in the history of the United States. Interestingly, Poe has also achieved another rare distinction among his peers: his strange and fascinating life has become an established part of the American mythos. Over time, numerous writers, musicians, filmmakers, and other artists have been drawn not only to Poe's work, but also to the image of Poe himself in the role of the shadowy, artistic genius who is tortured by his awareness of evil and his own vices. This image has proven so compelling that Poe's life has been fictionalized in many works in popular culture, ranging from cartoon episodes to an entire series of novels. These representations of Poe provide both creator and audience an opportunity to engage with the archetypes of outsider and artist, and examine all manner of iniquity and misery from a highly distinctive perspective.

Fictionalized representations of Poe were first promulgated during the author's own time. Indeed, Poe is himself responsible for some of these earliest and most durable depictions. Poe's self-representations, which blur fact, wishful thinking, and out-and-out deception, were often a matter of conscious image-making, self-promotion, and defensiveness. At various times in his life, Poe refashioned his identity in order to suit some specific end. Starting in his late teens, Poe appropriated events from his adventurous brother's life and presented himself as the aristocratic "Henri Le Rennet" to both confuse his creditors and effect a dashing, Byronic image of himself. Poe's tendency toward self-mythologizing and engaging in what he called the art of "diddling" became a persistent pattern in his life, even after the "real" Edgar Allan Poe achieved recognition for his writing, criticism, and lectures. Others also did their best to make or remake Poe's image for their own purposes, be they artistic, political, or personal in nature. Poe had no shortage of defamers and apologists. By the end of his life, his public identity had undergone many striking alterations. Poe's proclivities coupled with the spate of representations and outright misrepresentations created by others have made it difficult to stably situate his image, particularly in the context of popular culture.

Perhaps the most calculated self-portrait Poe created was his biography in the *Saturday Museum* (February 25, 1843). At the age of 34, Poe had long struggled with poverty, rejection, and failure, but his imagination would never allow him to be defined by such indignities—especially in a widely read magazine. Over the years, Poe had refined his desired public image and he readily supplied the *Saturday Museum* with his finest stock of personal attributes and accomplishments. The biographical portrait Poe crafted presents him as a worldly and gifted artist who is nobly struggling against the shoddy art and mournful affairs of the day. While there is little question that Poe sincerely wished to perfect his writing, advertise his redoubtable talent, and strengthen America's reputation abroad, the Byronic posture he exudes is riddled with self-serving falsehoods. Indeed, Poe's self-aggrandizing details are meant to provoke admiration and sympathy in readers more than provide them with any genuine insight into who he is as a person. As Jonathan H. Hartmann shows, this effort "attracted readers ready to identify with his struggles" and continues to do so to this very day.[1] In short, Poe produced a compelling image of himself that has seemingly secured him the reputation for vision, sophistication, and selfless martyrdom he felt he deserved.

Poe's biography would ultimately be challenged by an underhanded man bent on destroying the reputation of the writer—Rufus Wilmot Griswold. Unlike Poe's admirers and supporters, including a very fervent Charles Baudelaire, Griswold saw Poe as a duplicitous and quarrelsome drunkard who had estranged himself from good society and frittered away his one endowment. A former friend of Poe's, Griswold had come to despise the author and chose to carry out a grudge that would haunt Poe well into the future. After Poe's death, Griswold exposed the author to further condemnation by repeatedly demonizing him in print. Hiding behind a pseudonym, Griswold published a withering obituary of Poe. Griswold followed this piece with a more sustained and savage attack on the author's life and works. Under the auspices of Poe's literary executor, Griswold prefaced a three-part Poe anthology with the spiteful and wholly defamatory "Memoir of the Author." Although Griswold's "Memoir" was a clear case of attempted character assassination, it has succeeded in continually insinuating itself into the public image of Poe. Indeed, as Mark Neimeyer notes, popular culture "presentations of the author's life cannot seem to resist perpetuating it, even when ostensibly striving for historical accuracy."[2] Indeed, it seems that some artists find even the most specious scandals involving Poe far too laden with dramatic potential to resist repeating them in some form or another.

Poe and Griswold created two clearly conflicting images of the author which have colored all of his subsequent biographical treatments. The author is at turns grand and sordid, sympathetic and despicable—an endlessly fascinating outsider seeking surcease. Since Poe's death, scholars have turned to these characterizations and a range of other accounts in order to untangle the factual aspects of Poe's life from those which were invented. Suffice it to say, the distortions and slippage that affect any definition of Poe can prove troublesome for scholars, but they can be an absolute boon for artists. Most artists who have created treatments of Poe's life and person for popular consumption have inevitably tended to be less fastidious than Poe's serious biographers when it comes to presenting a facsimile of Poe to their audiences. Curiously enough, while many of the claims in Poe's and Griswold's biographical treatments have long been discredited, the aggregate likeness they convey and the collective narrative they establish have remained a vital part of the Poe legend. As John E. Reilly explains, this "dominant popular image" of the author "was cultivated not only by admirers of Poe but by his detractors . . . who, in their determination to assassinate his character, unwittingly rendered the image more fascinating and thereby assured it a long and hardy life."[3] The lasting power of both Poe's and Griswold's representations are indeed due in large part to their treatment of one of fiction's most enduring types—the brilliant but tortured antihero. The intriguingly personal nature of Poe's work and the tragic actualities of his life appear to be enhanced by such a self-sustaining mythos, for this mythos makes him an infinitely malleable character and symbol from an artistic perspective.

Starting with Poe's traumatic childhood and ending with his shocking, mysterious death, the author's life has always been rife with bizarre and sensationalistic circumstances which have become a conspicuous part of America's cultural consciousness. These circumstances have provided no shortage of material for artists who wish to explore the darker sides of the American experience. In this respect, "Poe has largely been taken up by popular culture because of its ability to exploit his personal suffering and the sad, and sometimes strange, realities of his life as well as the even more fantastic myths that have grown up around him."[4] Indeed, many artists have found his life and works suitable for a range of enterprises, be they surrealistic tone poems or more conventional thrillers. Typically, works that utilize Poe's biography and myth fall into one or more of two major genres: fantasy and mystery. As a notable influence on the fantasy genre and the father of the detective story, Poe's works and life are quite naturally matters of interest for artists working in these areas.

Many artists involved in creating horror and science fiction works for children and young adults have chosen to depict Poe in their works. In most cases, these works feature amusing caricatures of Poe and make no pretense to accuracy. In television shows, we often see Poe depicted in a lovingly irreverent fashion. The "Poe Pourri" episode of Tim Burton's animated *Beetlejuice* series (1989–1991) is an excellent example of this approach, for it is a raucous, allusion-filled engagement with Poe's life and works. In the episode, a maudlin Poe shows up at Beetlejuice's house in search of his lost Lenore. As part of a wry commentary on the overlap of Poe's personal and professional lives, Poe literally dispenses money each time he goes into one of his self-pitying fits of sobbing. This phenomenon piques Beetlejuice's interest, as he sees an opportunity to collect a fortune from the writer's suffering. Consequently, an avaricious Beetlejuice invites Poe to stay with him, but he soon regrets the decision, as all of his dreams quickly turn into Poesque nightmares.

"The Legion of Super Writers" episode of *Histeria!* (1998) and "Every Poe Has a Silver Lining" episode of *Time Squad* (2001–2002) provide outlandish versions of Poe to a young audience. In the two-part episode of *Histeria!*, a melodramatically sinister Poe and his gang of literary stylists battle a heroic Ernest Hemingway and his crew of fellow Super Writers for control over the books in the Library of Congress. In "Every Poe Has a Silver Lining," Poe is presented as the cloying author of bad greeting card verse. From his pastel pink suit to his sickly sweet voice, Poe is a disappointment and irritant to the members of Time Squad who have traveled back in time to meet the miserable master of the horror story. Their mission is to prompt him to write once again in the manner that made him famous. Much of the comedic effect of the episode comes from the situational irony involved with Poe's radically altered personality and verse. This same situational irony is used in a more superficial fashion in the "Phantom Menace" episode of *Sabrina, the Teenage Witch*, wherein a "sissy-pants" Poe character reads his awful inspirational poetry at a Halloween party to the chagrin of a once adoring audience. On the whole, these caricatures make two points quite clear: America finds Poe's dark world and maladjusted perspective infinitely more satisfying than the sunny platitudes of conventional society.

DC Comics has produced two works focused on Poe's life for a young adult audience: *The Shadow of Edgar Allan Poe* and *Batman: Nevermore*. *The Shadow of Edgar Allan Poe* is a disquieting, Griswoldian graphic novel that exposes a purportedly lost secret diary Poe kept during his final days and explores the unreliable narrator's related existential dilemmas. The diary consists of Poe's confessions, which revolve around two sordid plot points: Poe's agonizing incestuous relationship with his aunt, Maria Clemm, and his Faust-like bargain for fame with a group of malevolent spirits who are masquerading as his father. Throughout the graphic novel, readers are confronted with a tangle of delusions and regrets perpetuated by Poe and the narrator/audience surrogate. These erratic perceptions and feelings problematize the audience's ability to distinguish between moral and immoral actions and real and unreal consequences.

Len Wein and Guy Davis's five issue *Batman: Nevermore* series is notable for bringing together one of America's darkest and most popular comic book heroes, Batman, with one of its darkest and most popular literary figures, Poe, in a seemingly inevitable alternate universe partnership. The "Dark Knight Detective" and the father of the detective story team up to investigate the so-called Raven Murders which have been troubling the well-heeled members of The Gotham Club. The plot of *Batman: Nevermore* consists of creatively repurposed vignettes from Poe's tales, such as "The Pit and Pendulum" and "Masque of the Red Death," and utilizes a farrago of characters from both the Poe and Batman universes. In fact, Poe's Roderick Usher and Batman's Jonathon Crane (otherwise known as Scarecrow) are the main protagonists in the story. From the standpoint of characterization, Poe is, in effect, the Robin to this iteration of Batman, as he serves as a sidekick to the titular character. As the classic sidekick, Poe is a naive, loyal, and often ineffectual character compared to the hero. However, like many sidekicks, Poe does have unique characteristics and abilities which make him an invaluable companion. Poe is an intrepid investigator of evil and utilizes his analytical skills—which Batman terms "ratiocination"—to help solve the mystery and restart his faltering writing career. In the bargain, Batman confers a newfound level of cool confidence to a writer better known for his anxiety and misery.

Adult audiences also have a wealth of Poe-centric fantasy works at their disposal. George Higham's *Annabel Lee* stands out among the newer works in the medium of film, as his short employs striking, surrealistic stop-motion animation to examine Poe's poetry and personal suffering. Higham's harrowing yet ultimately hopeful interpretation of the poem "Annabel Lee" creates an empathetic and memorable portrait of a writer who has been physically deprived of his love by the cruel machinations of fate. Mark Redfield's *The Death of Poe* is a more realistic, less symbolic cinematic portrayal of the author than *Annabel Lee*. Nonetheless, the black and white film is an atmospheric, hallucinatory rendering of Poe's last days. In the work, Poe is presented as an abject failure verging on complete derangement as he struggles to generate financial support for his writing and editing and to remain sober. Curiously, the film begins and ends with Griswold's contemptuous obituary and, on the whole, presents Poe in a manner that fails to give viewers much fresh insight into the writer. Indeed, as Redfield acknowledges, the film is a "sketch" of Poe—one that relies heavily on its audience's familiarity with preexisting narratives and the mythos surrounding the author in order to flesh out its characterization.

While depictions of Poe appear in a range of film and television productions, the author is most frequently represented in short stories and novels. Unsurprisingly, we find Poe appearing in works as diverse as Seth Grahame-Smith's campy horror novel *Abraham Lincoln, Vampire Hunter,* Angela Carter's surrealistic, psychoanalytical short story "The Cabinet of Edgar Allan Poe" and Ray Bradbury's allegorical science fiction short story "The Exiles." Bradbury's story provides readers with a unique characterization of Poe. In the short story, the audience is thrust into the space age—a time where factuality, rationality, and self-control are valued above all other characteristics. Readers soon discover that Poe and other famous authors have exiled themselves to Mars because modern man has accused them of the apparent offense of promulgating morbid, superstitious, and imaginative works of literature. As hostile rocket men from Earth descend upon Mars to hunt down this band of creative miscreants, a heroic Poe tries to rally his colleagues into a unified resistance. Bradbury uses this dramatic situation to draw a parallel between genocidal behavior and censorship practices.

Roger Zelazny and Fred Saberhagen's science fiction novel, *The Black Throne,* utilizes a doppelganger conceit to explore Poe's life and writings. While this approach appears in a number of works involving Poe characters, Roger Zelazny and Fred Saberhagen employ it in a manner both particularly suited to the conventions of the science fiction genre and to paying clear homage to Poe. In the novel, two contemporaneous versions of Poe—the soldier Edgar Perry and the writer Edgar Allan Poe—must trade places in their respective universes. Edgar Perry, who hails from a universe like our own, goes in search of his love, Annabel Lee, and finds himself inhabiting an extraordinary universe animated by characters from Poe's ostensibly imaginary works. Poe, in turn, now inhabits our mundane world and quickly discovers that he is psychologically and physiologically ill suited for it. The authors use this situation as a means to rationalize the historical Poe's misery and irrationality and to explain away his intemperance. Of course, readers who feel misunderstood or exiled from mainstream society can easily identify with this iteration of Poe.

As one might expect, many treatments of Poe involve otherworldly or speculative elements. Whether Poe is being haunted or doing the haunting, one of his important functions in popular culture is to foreground psychic dissonance and spiritual unrest. The short stories "Richmond,

Late September, 1849" and "A Revenant" are standouts among those ghost stories which feature Poe as a central character. Like many works examining Poe's life, Fritz Leiber's "Richmond, Late September, 1849" takes place during the writer's final days. Leiber characterizes Poe as a Byronic visionary who is tormented by his powerlessness, loneliness, and self-destructive tendencies. Poe discusses art and philosophy over drinks with a responsive French woman who calls herself Berenice. Fancying himself in love, Poe desperately pursues a relationship with Berenice, only to discover that the mysterious and alluring woman he courts is actually Death itself.

Walter de la Mare's "A Revenant" is at once a straightforward ghost story and a nuanced indictment of those people who misrepresent Poe to suit their own purposes. In the piece, Professor Monk delivers a reductive and needlessly trenchant lecture on Poe, only to discover that Poe's ghost is a member of his audience. Poe subsequently challenges Professor Monk's Griswoldian claims and lazy interpretations. Suffice it to say, Professor Monk is shaken by Poe's unassailable assertions and terribly frightened by such vengeance from beyond the grave. The primary attraction of this story is that it employs Poe's popular approach to storytelling as a way to combat those popular conceptions regarding the author's life. In essence, de la Mare effectively uses one fiction to deconstruct another fiction, leaving readers with an ironic commentary on the crude shield of self-serving myths and suppositions culture creates in order to ward off complex truths.

Characterizations of Poe have been presented in many works classified as historical fiction over the past 50 years. An excellent example of this type of work is the short story "No Spot of Ground" by Walter John Williams. The tale is a somber and engrossing piece of alternative history featuring Poe as a gifted but querulous Confederate general tasked with defending Richmond from a Union onslaught. The story is interesting for the manner in which it selectively intensifies Poe's worst attributes and identification with the South, and uses them to cast Poe as an embittered elitist and rampant racist. On the whole, the representation is as fantastical and repulsive as any portrait of Poe that Griswold might have dreamt up, while maintaining enough plausibility to give the story a sense of historicity.

Poe's influence on the development of the mystery genre is well documented in literary scholarship. What is not well documented, though, is how frequently and fully Poe has been depicted in modern works of detective fiction which also fit into the category of historical fiction. Within the context of popular culture, such a natural amalgamation of his works and life appears quite attractive, for it allows the audience to enjoy two of its favorite subjects at once: the pursuit of criminals and the exposure of a celebrity's private life (however fabricated). Tellingly, the usual portrayal of Poe in these historical novels does not stray far from the conventions of modern detective novels even when it acknowledges his historical context and personal idiosyncrasies, such as the writing of poetry. Like many stock detective characters, these Poe characters operate on the periphery of mainstream society, but provide the services necessary to maintain its norms. Poe is often characterized as having an intuitive and nuanced understanding of evil, a grasp of scientific developments and tools, a working knowledge of the city's unseemly elements, and a defiantly unconventional approach to his life and work.

The young adult novel, *The Man Who Was Poe* by Avi, and the children's book, *Eddie: The Lost Youth of Edgar Allan Poe* by Scott Gustafson, present imaginative renderings of Poe's life in a mystery story format. *The Man Who Was Poe* depicts Poe as a selfish, jaded but insightful amateur detective who reluctantly helps an abandoned boy search for his kidnapped sister and solve the mystery behind his mother's death. Avi appears to have taken cues from Griswold and film noir antiheroes, for Poe's drinking and acts of duplicity make him a morally reprehensible burnout. However, Poe's young companion discovers that there are degrees of culpability in life and Poe, for all of his faults, is by no means the most egregious reprobate in the world. In order to appeal to children, *Eddie* features a youthful Poe in a page-turning adventure. In the work, Poe is presented as a proud, precocious, but isolated boy who has been wrongfully accused of engaging in a destructive prank that he is said to have committed while sleepwalking. Along with his companions, the reasonable Raven and the troublesome imp McCobber, a heroic Poe sets out to clear his name before his surly father, John Allan, punishes him for the act. Along the way, Poe learns about the fundamentals of "ratiocination," the secret to successful magic tricks, and the value of loyalty. As a suspect and detective, Poe also learns that people have a tendency to hastily attach terms like "wicked" or "evil" to what is strange or misunderstood.

Louis Bayard's darkly comic thriller *The Pale Blue Eye* and, to a lesser extent, Andrew Taylor's *American Boy* (*An Unpardonable Crime*) also place a youthful version of Poe at the heart of their mysteries. *The Pale Blue Eye* follows Poe during his brief stint at West Point. Poe is presented as a gifted, quirky, and downright virginal cadet more interested in pursuing love and poetry than making an officer out of himself. After a suspicious suicide and mutilation occur on campus, Poe is enlisted by a mordant retired constable, Gus Landor, to assist with the investigation. During their investigation, a naively innocent but suspicious-acting Poe becomes the prime suspect in a series of related murder cases. Poe's idealistic beliefs about the nature of love, friendship, purity, and corruption undergo substantial changes as he becomes an effective investigator in his own right.

Bayard uses Poe's revelations as a means to comment on the abuse of authority and vengeful side of justice in American society.

A significant number of historical detective stories take liberties with Poe's life in order to exploit interesting possibilities or otherwise develop a compelling storyline. John Carr Dickson's short story pastiche "The Gentleman from Paris" features Poe as a Dupin-like amateur detective solving a case very much like the "Purloined Letter." Barry Perowne's *A Singular Conspiracy* is a caper story based around a blackmail scheme the Poe character concocts in order to assist his nearly penniless, wastrel friend—Charles Baudelaire. Joel Rose's novel *The Blackest Bird* takes the fictionalization even further by not only changing events in Poe's life, but by also appropriating and altering Poe's writing in order to work out potential discrepancies in the narrative. Rose discloses his manifold inventions in the "Author's Note and Acknowledgements" section of the book and asserts that they are necessary for the sake of the story. In the novel, Poe is presented as a dubious intellectual and down on his luck opportunist who just happens to possess some of the essential skills necessary to solving a murder mystery. Rose assigns historical figures, such as a sinister Samuel Colt, prominent roles in his thesis-driven examination of class privilege, political intrigue, and media manipulation.

Harold Schechter's series of "Edgar Allan Poe Mysteries" also take great liberties with Poe's life and the actualities of history. Schechter's four novels, *Nevermore, The Hum Bug, Mask of the Red Death*, and *The Tell-Tale Corpse*, feature Poe as an eccentric, pedantic, slightly ridiculous, but nonetheless effective amateur detective. Per Schechter's buddy comedy formula, Poe is always partnered with another notable figure from history, including Davy Crockett, P. T. Barnum, Kit Carson, and Louisa May Alcott. Frequently, these characters first seek out Poe after he has published a scathing review of their work and they ultimately find themselves requiring his assistance. The characters then serve as pragmatic foils for the dandified and cerebral Poe, with whom they collaborate during his investigations and sundry adventures. Schechter uses Poe's experiences to explore fundamental taboos, such as cannibalism, and a range of topics central to the American experience. Schechter's use of the latter topics, which include the ethos of frontier individualism, the development of media manipulation, and the implications of miscegenation in the early to mid-19th century, gives what would otherwise be considered light reading some sense of historical heft.

A number of historical detective novels use Poe's famous fictional detective C. Auguste Dupin as their primary investigator. Matthew Pearl's *The Poe Shadow* concentrates on the mystery surrounding Poe's final days and employs the standard elements of the mystery genre to heighten tension and forward the investigation. However, the novel does have a curious and surprising element to it that should leave readers wondering at the author's intentions. Despite conspicuous fabrications throughout the novel, Pearl uses his "Historical Note" to claim his work is based on previously undiscovered facts regarding Poe's actual life and that the novel should be viewed as more historical than fictional in nature. Although George Egon Hatvary makes no such claims of scholarly authority in *The Murder of Edgar Allan Poe*, his novel does share a similarity with Pearl's work in that readers again see Dupin traveling to America to investigate the circumstances which led to Poe's death. Throughout *The Murder of Edgar Allan Poe*, Dupin feels a great affinity for Poe, owing in part to their striking commonalities. Indeed, Hatvary clearly insinuates that Dupin may constitute the other half of Poe's "bi-part soul." Such gestures push his seemingly straightforward detective novel into the realm of "metaphysical detection."[5]

Stephen Marlowe's *A Lighthouse at the End of the World* is a fascinating and at times bewildering novel that juggles a variety of genres and narratives while remaining at heart a mystery story with a metaphysical turn. While the narrative approach to the novel is decidedly nonlinear, it focuses on the mysterious events surrounding Poe's final days. On the whole, Marlowe presents Poe as an alienated genius beset with poverty and grief. However, Poe is also highly unstable, which is to say that his intentions, actions, and identity in the novel are subject to almost constant flux. Indeed, while Marlowe grounds the events of the story and characterization of Poe in a considerable amount of historical fact, both aspects of the novel are predominantly guided by a dream logic that Poe can only hope to understand by employing the assistance of Dupin. While determining the actual circumstances behind the mysterious death of the historical Poe is a significant part of the novel, readers discover that much of the detection focuses on making sense of Poe's identity as a temporal and nontemporal entity. In this way, *A Lighthouse at the End of the World* utilizes many elements from Poe's works to frame an essential and altogether self-reflexive question to readers. The question is not ultimately about why or how Poe died; rather the question is "Who is this man we believe to have died but lives on in so many forms?" This question might appear entirely academic; however, it is one that most audience members must consider when engaging with these depictions of Poe in popular culture.

As each of these works show, Poe's incongruous life has maintained a lively mass appeal. Hartmann correctly observes that part of this appeal can be attributed to Poe's "play[ing] on readers' tendency to link author and storyteller-protagonist to build sympathetic interest in his life and works."[6] This appeal can also be attributed to the ease with which artists can use Poe to expose a variety of evils, ranging from cannibalism to fraud and from media manipulation to incest. In such roles, he provides us with a means to confront our suspicions, terrors and taboos, and temporarily inhabit a world where the space between madness and sanity is often quite nebulous. The seemingly inexhaustible manifestations of Poe in popular culture ultimately give both artist and audience the opportunity to experience grief, terror, alienation, self-destruction, love, and creative brilliance without great risk. Approaching Poe in this visceral manner can be cathartic, enlightening, and truly entertaining.

As Neimeyer points out, these manifold mutations of Poe have now become such a fixture in American society that the author can longer be contained within the once generous confines of popular culture: indeed, his image has now spilled over into "meta-popular culture."[7] Regardless of how fitting or strained Poe's wide-ranging representations might appear to us, the growing body of work containing links to his life will find a ready audience among those people searching for a reference point to the dark, uncanny, or wretched spaces they must inhabit in life. In the near future, audiences can expect to encounter more works treating Poe's life, including an episode of the animated series *Frankenhole* and a wide release movie, *The Raven*, starring John Cusack as Poe. Suffice it to say, these works and others will continue to add to Poe's already considerable mystique and function in the public conscious, and they will ensure him a position of incomparable relevance in American culture. Neither Poe nor Griswold could have imagined such a singular fate when they penned those fictionalized portraits over 150 years ago.

NOTES

1. Jonathan H. Hartmann, *The Marketing of Edgar Allan Poe*, Studies in American Popular History and Culture (New York: Routledge, 2008), 14.

2. Mark Neimeyer, "Poe and Popular Culture," in *The Cambridge Companion to Edgar Allan Poe*, ed. Kevin J. Hayes (Cambridge: Cambridge University Press, 2002), 210.

3. John E. Reilly, "Poe in Literature and Popular Culture," in *A Companion to Poe Studies*, ed. Eric W. Carlson (Westport, CT: Greenwood Press, 1996), 472.

4. Neimeyer, "Poe and Popular Culture," 209.

5. Patricia Merivale and Susan E. Sweeney, "The Game's Afoot: On the Trail of the Metaphysical Detective Story," in *Detecting Texts: The Metaphysical Detective Story from Poe to Postmodernism*, ed. Patricia Merivale and Susan Elizabeth Sweeney (Philadelphia: University of Pennsylvania Press, 1999), 2–4.

6. Hartmann, *The Marketing of Edgar Allan Poe*, 34.

7. Neimeyer, "Poe and Popular Culture," 206–07.

CHAPTER 8

"Like Rats behind the Wainscoting": Evil in American Hardboiled Fiction

Eric Sandberg

American fiction has long been fascinated by the many forms and diverse manifestations of evil. From colonial era tales of native savagery to contemporary fantasies of the vampiric, writers have attempted to understand and represent the nature of evil. One of the most notable and persistent forms of this literary exploration has occurred in the quintessentially American hardboiled crime novel, a genre that since its birth in the 1920s has repeatedly and insistently scrutinized depravity, iniquity, and corruption.

In his 1944 essay "The Simple Art of Murder," Raymond Chandler claimed literary realists including Ernest Hemingway and Sherwood Anderson as hardboiled fiction's predecessors, defining the genre as the application of the principles of realism to the detective story. Part of the enduring and widespread appeal of this genre, from its earliest appearances in pulp magazines like *Black Mask* to more recent incarnations in a huge range of novels, movies, and even video games, arises from this sense of reality. Hardboiled, Chandler argued, took murder out of the detective story's drawing room, and "dropped" it back "in the alley" where it belonged. In these stories people kill not as a pretext for investigation, "to provide a corpse," but for a reason; murder is not an opportunity for intellectual display, but an act of evil.[1] The key point in understanding hardboiled evil, however, is to realize that the metaphoric alley is not simply more realistic, but that it is also crowded with dirty politicians, shady businessmen, hypocritical judges, corrupt policemen, venal lawyers, and apathetic citizens who, given a chance, will always look the other way. This genre is fascinated by evil, but its crimes of omission and commission, its betrayals and depravities, its rapes and murders, are not safely relegated to a clearly demarcated criminal sphere. Instead, they are part of the fabric of society, an illicit weft to the licit warp: quite simply part of the way things are. Alleys connect to streets, and streets to all types of houses and buildings: the squalid apartments of the poor, the luxurious mansions of the rich, dens of vice and prostitution, police offices, and town halls.

The idea that evil links different parts of society appeals to our sense of the real—we know, however much we might like to deny it, that evil over there is not so very different from evil over here. This hardboiled idea of evil arose from the Prohibition-era crime wave from which the genre drew much of its inspiration. One of the unintended side effects of the attempt to ban America's intoxicant of choice was to create, or reveal, systematic connections between organized crime, big business, and the political world. It also involved normal citizens, through their bottle of smuggled liquor or their surreptitious visit to the speakeasy, in a criminal enterprise. Thus, hardboiled evil is both extremely social and extremely personal, a phenomenon of the society that surrounds and shapes normal individuals and of the individuals themselves. The history of the hardboiled genre can be seen as a prolonged meditation on this theme, a deepening and spreading exploration of a type of evil that connects levels of society and individuals in a network of iniquity.

Dashiell Hammett was one of the first hardboiled writers, and his seminal novels, published between 1929 and 1934, focus on the capacity of evil to connect different parts of society. In *Red Harvest*, the town of Personville is known as "Poisonville" for good reason: it is a thoroughly corrupt place in which competing gang bosses—Pete the Finn, Lew Yard, and "Whisper" Max Thaler—collude with mining-mogul, banker, and newspaper owner Ellihu Willsson and the chief of police Noonan to control and despoil the town. There is, in fact, no difference between the gang and the government. Ellihu, for instance, is a legitimate businessman, but he brought the gangsters to Personville in the first place, using them as "hired thugs" to break a miners strike. Pete the Finn's "specials" are deputized toughs, while uniformed police officers take payoffs to help Max Thaler escape arrest. Ultimately, martial law and the National Guard are needed to restore order. This solution leaves the corrupt Ellihu untouched, although the novel's investigator, the Continental Op, wants nothing more than to "top off the job" by seeing him hung.[2] The nameless city of *The Glass Key* reveals a similar intertwining of legal and illegal authorities, linking gangsters, businessmen, and politicians in a dense and tangled network of criminal complicity. In *The Maltese Falcon*, evil also ramifies through disparate levels of society. The motley crew of small-time hoods so memorably portrayed in John Huston's 1941 film, who betray each other so assiduously, are connected not only to a Russian general but also, if only distantly, to Emperor Charles V and the Knights of Malta for whom the "Holy Wars . . . were largely a matter of loot."[3] In Hammett's hardboiled vision everyone, high and low, is out for what they can get.

But Hammett's novels explore only one-half of hardboiled evil. They delineate a corrupt social world, but have little to say about personal evil. *The Maltese Falcon*'s Joe Cairo, Gutman, and Brigid O'Shaughnessy are crooks, cheats, and killers, but they do not radiate individual malice. Gutman, for instance, is a positively cheerful, even comic figure, both in the novel and as portrayed by Sydney Greenstreet in Huston's film. The ineffectual Cairo is a study in petty avarice. How else could a slimily ingratiating Peter Lorre have played him so successfully? Similarly, Hammett never implies that Brigid O'Shaughnessy is more than dishonest, manipulative, and untrustworthy. Even her murder of Sam Spade's partner Miles Archer is strangely innocent, the result of an intricate plot gone wrong rather than a manifestation of personal evil. Similarly, the world of *Red Harvest* is certainly evil, but in spite of the novel's tremendous body count only in a disengaged and impersonal fashion. The deaths mount up without ever seeming to be individually attributable: they are simply the type of thing that happens in a town like Personville. Even a gangster like Max Thaler is not personally evil: dangerous certainly, and as a participant in the novel's networks of crime complicit in the social evil that *Red Harvest* so carefully depicts. However, there is nothing malicious about him: he will kill you if he has to, but it will not be personal.

Hammett's investigators display a similar sort of detachment. Part of the cool and unemotional atmosphere of *Red Harvest* arises from the Op's laconic first-person narration. He presents the woes of Personville as a set of abstract problems regarding justice, law enforcement, and corruption that seldom challenge his own disengagement. The Op has "hard skin all over what's left" of his soul due to his years of association with crime and criminals, but "getting a rear out of planning deaths," or enjoying the process of organizing the gang wars that are sweeping the town clean, worries him. This is the town's particular poison. The risk of personal infection by evil is made clear in the rather labored plotting of the murder of Dinah Brand, a "big-league gold-digger" used by the Op as part of his plan.[4] The Op wakes up after a bender to find his hand clasped around an ice pick buried in her breast, and for several chapters the reader is left in rather tenuous doubt as to whether he has in fact killed her. But this is really no more than a muddying of the waters as the novel approaches its conclusion: the Op is protected by his employer's strict rules, his own sense of professional responsibility, and a toughness deeper than a simple layer of moral scar tissue from any real personal entanglement with the evil he confronts.[5] The same is true of Spade, who for much of *The*

Maltese Falcon seems to be walking dangerously close to the line that separates an investigator from the object of his investigation. This turns out, however, to be no more than a pose: "Don't be too sure I'm as crooked as I'm supposed to be," he says. His apparent corruptibility brings in "high-priced jobs" and makes "it easier to deal with the enemy."[6] Combined with an investigative ethic similar to the Op's, this act insulates Spade from the evil he faces. Thus, in Hammett's work evil is a social and exterior phenomenon which does not implicate individuals.

The same cannot be said of Raymond Chandler's novels, which are arguably more central to the hardboiled genre: his particular combination of "romance and realism" has been described as characterizing it as a whole.[7] However, if Chandler is seen by many as the definitive hardboiled writer, both due to his own literary success and that of movie adaptations of his work, most notably Howard Hawkes's 1946 version of *The Big Sleep*, he has also been seen as comparatively light, less explicitly and seriously concerned with evil than someone like Hammett.[8] This is evident in Hawkes's film, a romantic vehicle for Humphrey Bogart and Lauren Bacall that adds love scenes and a morally edifying ending while removing references to drug use and homosexuality. Someone familiar with *The Big Sleep* only through this film might think that hardboiled evil was an oxymoron. Yet Chandler's novel—his first and best—in fact reveals an evil that is more individual and insidious than any in Hammett's work.

This sense of evil develops gradually, as private eye Philip Marlowe moves through intensifying circles of "nastiness" toward a hardboiled heart of darkness. The novel begins as Marlowe arrives for a meeting with the elderly General Sternwood, who is trapped in the midst of something very nasty indeed. On one level, this concerns his family: two wild daughters, Carmen and Vivian, one vanished son-in-law, and a genteelly phrased blackmailing attempt are rather more than a man of the general's years can be expected to deal with. Sternwood is a man out of place: someone who likes his champagne "as cold as Valley Forge" can hardly be comfortable with the "thick, wet, steamy" air of the greenhouse in which he meets Marlowe, nor with what he thinks of as the sexual degeneracy of his "nasty" orchids.[9] The general is associated with a romanticized version of American history and its martial past, yet he sits immobile and helpless amidst what the novel characterizes as a sexualized corruption. Many readers have noted the relevance of the stained glass window in the Sternwood mansion, its image of a knight rescuing a naked woman foreshadowing Marlowe's quest "to rescue the damsel-in-distress" Carmen.[10] But this is peculiar: Carmen is the source of the nastiness that menaces Sternwood. Instead, the general as a representation of a lost America is the endangered object of Marlowe's quest, an innocent America now surrounded by the rank decay of evil.

Carmen is central to *The Big Sleep*'s exploration of evil, and more broadly to the development of hardboiled fiction's vision of evil as a personal as well as social phenomenon. Firstly, the interconnected social evil of the novel originates from what it characterizes as her sexual misconduct. Soon after Marlowe begins his investigation, he finds her drugged and naked next to the corpse of the pornographer Geiger. The photographic plates are missing, and Marlowe's attempts to retrieve them involve him in a network of death. Geiger has been shot by Owen Taylor, the Sternwood's chauffeur, who is himself soon found dead. Next, the blackmailer Joe Brody survives an attempted murder by Carmen only to be shot minutes later by Geiger's lover Carol Lundgren. Turned over to the police by Marlowe, Lundgren will inevitably end up in the "deathhouse." Harry Jones, an associate of Brody's, is forced to drink cyanide by gangster Eddie Mars's enforcer Canino, who in turn becomes the novel's final corpse, deservedly gunned down by Marlowe. All of these deaths are preceded by the off-stage murder that sets the sequence in motion: Vivian's husband, Rusty, has been murdered by Carmen for declining her sexual favors, and Marlowe's investigation merely returns him to the Sternwood mansion where the body is concealed. Hardboiled evil inhabits not only the social spaces of Los Angeles, but also the domestic sphere of the American home, and arises from a single person.

Marlowe's descriptions of Carmen make it clear that there is something fundamentally wrong with her. Her eyes are like "a couple of bottle tops," a description that registers of her lack of empathy. She has "predatory sharp teeth" and a "curiously shaped thumb, thin and narrow like a extra finger, with no curve in the first joint." When she is angry, her face is "like scraped bone." These elaborately rhetorical descriptions label Carmen as something less than human, a monster: Ironically, the damsel in distress becomes herself distressing. Yet she is also nacreously beautiful: "her skin . . . had the shimmering luster of a pearl." Another metaphor that is repeatedly applied to Carmen may indicate what is going on here: her laughter is compared to the sound of "rats behind the wainscoting."[11] This indicates how "apparent respectability . . . masks a fundamental core of horror: corruption, perversity, death."[12] The pearl metaphor reinforces this; pearls are objects of beauty that accrete around foreign contaminants. By implication, Carmen is herself structured around a corrupt core, just as she herself is a corrupt core around which her society deposits the protective shroud of its wealth and power. She will not, after all, be executed for her crime like the hapless Lundgren.

Carmen's infantilism, corruption, and degeneracy ultimately illuminate the social evil that surrounds her, for Chandler's hardboiled evil explicitly connects the personal to the social and political. In Chandler, as in Hammett, society is depicted as an interconnected network of corruption. Carmen's personal sexual profligacy is mirrored in the publicity of Geiger's pornographic lending library that peddles books of "indescribable filth" beneath the benignly neglectful eyes of the police. Geiger may have arranged his protection through Eddie Mars, gambler and gangster, who has the local police in his pocket. The obverse of this official corruption is the superficial respectability of the criminal world represented by Mars, whose pleasant appearance, fine clothes, and polite mannerisms mask a genuine evil. Mars uses Canino to kill by proxy, runs a gambling den with official collusion, and intends to blackmail Vivian with his knowledge of her sister's crime. He is "a pornographer, a blackmailer, a hot car broker, a killer by remote control, and a suborner of crooked cops" yet he is untouchable. The fact that gangster-businessmen like Mars are able to blend into society and thus go unpunished is an indictment of the society that allows them to do so: it is itself infected by the evil of men like Mars.

Chandler thus portrays two forms of evil in *The Big Sleep*, the social and the personal, and indicates that they are intimately connected. When Marlowe has followed the path of this evil outward from the Sternwood mansion, through the social world of Los Angeles, and back to the abandoned oil sump on the mansion's grounds which holds its rotting secret, the dead body of Vivian's husband, he realizes that "it all ties together—everything." Captain Gregory, "a plain ordinary copper" summarizes the situation: he and Marlowe may want to see "flashy well-dressed mugs like Eddie Mars spoiling their manicures in the rock quarry at Folsom, alongside of the poor little slum-bred hard guys," but this is simply not possible "in any part of this wide, green, and beautiful U.S.A. We just don't run our country that way." Personal evil in the novel is embodied by Carmen and Mars, whose polished surfaces conceal their interior corruption. This evil is not, however, limited to criminals; in a world where everything is connected, this would be impossible. It affects even Marlowe, who set out on his investigation as a knight-errant, but realizes by its conclusion that he is "part of the nastiness now."[13] When he allows Carmen to avoid jail, he protects General Sternwood, but also becomes complicit with the corruption that runs through the novel. Chandler's hardboiled evil is not only all around us, but also within us.

This vision of an evil that is at once social and personal has been extended by James Ellroy, a more recent hardboiled novelist whose work both draws evil closer to the investigator and extends it further into the social and political world. In Ellroy's 1987 breakthrough novel *The Black Dahlia*, the personal evil that is one of the poles of Chandler's classic hardboiled world is relocated directly onto the investigator. This is accomplished in part by making the investigator a police officer, thus aligning him with official corruption. While a private investigator can criticize formal structures of power, Ellroy's investigator Bucky Bleichert only gradually earns and embraces his status as an outsider able to resist official corruption and brutality, and this despite the fact that he recognizes early on that "the good guys were really the bad guys." For instance, Bleichert initially uses his position to start a sexual relationship with Madeleine Sprague, and protects her from the investigation of Betty Short's murder, a clear example of hardboiled corruption. Also significant is officially sanctioned violence. In Marlowe's last appearance in *The Long Goodbye*, he is the victim of police brutality; his status as outsider guarantees him moral protection, but attracts physical danger. Bleichert, on the other hand, calmly watches an interrogation that leaves a suspect dribbling "blood and spittle into his lap," and himself attacks a recent parolee while "wondering how hard you had to squeeze a dog's throat to make its eyeballs pop out." Bleichert eventually rejects the systematic brutality of the police force, but only after he participates in a savage interrogation of four suspects suspended from meat hooks. His story is thus as much one of recognizing and rejecting the potential for evil within himself as it is of revealing the evil behind the murder of Betty Short. This is a point that Brian De Palma's ambitious 2006 film adaptation signally fails to develop, another example of the apparent inability of cinema to deal effectively with hardboiled evil.

Ultimately, Bleichert resists the evil of the world surrounding him, and, ironically fired from the police force "on grounds of moral turpitude and conduct unbecoming of an officer," is given a chance to live an upright life. However, Ellroy uses another technique to superimpose evil on the investigator. Bleichert has a double, his partner Lee Blanchard, "Mr. Fire" to Bleichert's "Mr. Ice." These two are superficially as different as "oil and water," but the novel brings them so close together that they become, in effect, two facets of the same individual. The partners are both in love with Kay Lake, and the temporary domestic trio they establish only works because Bleichert and Blanchard share one role. The murder of Betty Short unravels this peculiar version of domestic bliss, but after Blanchard's disappearance, Bleichert simply takes over more and more of his life, eventually reducing the "Blanchard/Bleichert/Lake triad" to a duo, with Bleichert living Blanchard's life. The problem is that Blanchard is "the most audacious rogue cop in history," his career a saga of corruption culminating in his betrayal of the Short murder investigation.[14] Instead of doing his duty as a police officer, he blackmails the wealthy Sprague and flees with the money. This mirrors Bleichert's own initial betrayal of the investigation. In the terms established by the novel, Betty Short is the sign and symbol of all victims, an innocent betrayed, tortured, and killed, essentially a female Christ-figure, and to betray the investigation of her death as Bleichert/Blanchard does, is as evil an act as is imaginable. While Marlowe recognizes that he is not immune to evil, in *The Black Dahlia* as much evil radiates outward from the investigators as penetrates into them.

In the same way that Ellroy has extended the range of hardboiled evil to encompass the investigator, he has also pushed it into new social territory, describing "the realities of American power during a brutal, expansionist century."[15] Literary critic F. R. Jameson has argued that Chandler's hardboiled depends upon a conceptual bifurcation of American politics into a local realm of corruption, sleaze, and materialistic nihilism, and a national realm of idealistic abstraction.[16] The traditional hardboiled world is evil to its core, but this is the local evil of a corrupt police station and a dirty town hall. Ellroy's *American Tabloid* breaks with this tradition, and extends hardboiled evil to its logical conclusion. The investigator, who gradually reveals the illicit links between seemingly irreconcilable levels of society, uncovering networks of corruption, no longer exists: instead, we have players in the construction of these networks who operate simultaneously for the Central Intelligence Agency (CIA) and the mob, and sell heroin to finance shadowy government operations. Beyond these antiheroes, evil exists as always in the hardboiled world. It is a combination of money, power, and sex that circulates through the body politic, but this corrosive fluid does not stop at the Mayor's office. Instead, it penetrates all the way to the Kennedy White House, connecting on its way the KKK, Cuban revolutionaries, teamsters, the Mafia, big business, and the CIA in a seamless network of interlinked corruption. This is a world without innocence, in which Camelot, a product of "mass seduction" financed by Joe Kennedy's illegal slush fund of "cancerous money," is no more than an extension of the networks of sex, power, and money to include, through their votes, all Americans.[17] Kennedy, the white knight of American politics is portrayed as being no more than a step away from drug dealers, hit men, and torturers, and this step is no more than the fancy footwork of a smooth operator. The actual distance, Ellroy wants us to believe, is far less than the apparent. This is an evil that makes literally true Chandler's contention that hardboiled represents "a world in which gangsters can rule nations."[18]

Ellroy thus represents a culminating point in the development of hardboiled fiction's exploration of evil. While the genre as a whole is certainly capable of dealing with other issues—other recent practitioners of hardboiled have, for instance, focused on questions of race and gender—a preoccupation with the nature of evil is a defining feature of the genre as a whole. Early hardboiled fiction, such as Hammett's novels of social corruption, tended to explore an external evil largely characterized by its multifaceted social interconnections, offering a realistic, unromantic depiction of a world in which the police, business, government, and crime were, at least at the local level, simply different players in the same racket. In Chandler's classic hardboiled novels, this external evil persists, but it is more clearly related to personal corruption, to an evil that resides within the individual, which is indeed a part of the individual, however well it may be concealed behind a veneer of respectability. Social and personal evil are related phenomena. However, it is in the work of Ellroy that these hardboiled versions of evil achieve their apotheosis, stretching from the investigator himself, who is revealed to be, at least potentially, as brutal and murderous as any villain, to the highest levels of government. His novels manifest at its fullest the evil of the hardboiled genre, an evil that has resonated with American audiences for decades as readers seek fictions that seem to offer an explanation, however unpalatable it may be, of their world. The hardboiled novel undermines conventional pieties, peeling back layers of superficial decency from both social structures and individuals to reveal the inevitable leer of the skull beneath the skin. Reading hardboiled allows us to hear, however faintly, the scuttling of the rats behind the wainscoting.

NOTES

1. Raymond Chandler, "The Simple Art of Murder," *Atlantic Monthly*, December 1944, 57–58.

2. Dashiell Hammett, "Red Harvest," in *Complete Novels* (New York: Library of America, 1999; reprint, 1929), 5, 10, 169, 77.

3. Dashiell Hammett, "The Maltese Falcon," in *Complete Novels* (New York: Library of America, 1999; reprint, 1930), 498.

4. Hammett, "Red Harvest," 137, 22.

5. Steven Marcus, "Dashiell Hammett," in *The Poetics of Murder: Detective Fiction and Literary Theory*, ed. Glenn W. Most and William W. Stowe (San Diego: Harcourt Brace Jovanovich, 1983; reprint), 206–08.

6. Hammett, "The Maltese Falcon," 583.

7. John Scaggs, *Crime Fiction*, The New Critical Idiom (London, New York: Routledge, 2005), 62.

8. Lee Horsley, *The Noir Thriller*, Crime Files (Houndmills, Basingstoke, Hampshire, England: Palgrave Macmillan, 2009), 35.

9. Raymond Chandler, *The Big Sleep*, 1st Vintage Crime/Black Lizard ed., Vintage Crime/Black Lizard (New York: Vintage Books, 1992), 230, 7–8.

10. Garrison Kristen, "Hard-Boiled Rhetoric: The 'Fearless Speech' of Philip Marlowe," *South Central Review* 27, no. 1 (2010): 115.

11. Chandler, *The Big Sleep*, 5–6, 36, 66, 104, 158, 217.

12. Peter J. Rabinowitz, "Rats behind the Wainscoting: Politics, Convention, and Chandler's 'the Big Sleep,'" *Texas Studies in Literature and Language* 22 (1980): 231.

13. Chandler, *The Big Sleep*, 04, 30, 194, 223.

14. James Ellroy, *The Black Dahlia* (New York: Vintage, 1995), 4, 5, 23, 62, 117, 228–29, 319.

15. Horsley, *The Noir Thriller*, 255.

16. Fredric Jameson, "On Raymond Chandler," in *The Poetics of Murder: Detective Fiction and Literary Theory*, ed. Glenn W. Most and William W. Stowe (San Diego: Harcourt Brace Jovanovich, 1983; reprint), 129–30.

17. James Ellroy, *American Tabloid: A Novel* (New York: Vintage, 1995), 355.

18. Chandler, "The Simple Art of Murder," 59.

CHAPTER 9

"Is It Safe?": Evil and the Escaped Nazi War Criminal in American Novels in the 1970s

Christoph Schiessl

The escaped Nazi war criminal appeared as a theme in American novels for the first time in the 1970s. Since the capture and trial in the early 1960s of Adolf Eichmann, who notoriously had planned the train schedules to Auschwitz, a public awareness that Nazi war criminals were still living in safety in the United States, South America, and Europe had developed. This developing Holocaust consciousness inspired U.S. authors to include Nazi war criminals as villains in their works. This type of evil first emerged in the form of Christian Szell, the sadistic Nazi dentist in William Goldman's *Marathon Man* in 1974. Szell clearly is meant as a reference to the infamous Nazi doctor Josef Mengele. Two years later, Mengele himself appeared in Ira Levin's novel *The Boys from Brazil*. Here the infamous Auschwitz doctor is at the heart of a plan to clone another Adolf Hitler. Finally, in 1978, M. E. Kerr, an author of novels for young adults, included a suspected Nazi war criminal, called Frank Trenker, in her novel *Gentlehands*. All three characters have committed undoubtedly evil acts of extortion, torture, and murder of helpless Jewish victims during the Holocaust. All three appear cultured and refined, but only Szell and Mengele are still capable of heinous, cold-blooded murder. The motivation for their crimes also differs. While Szell seems to have been merely an opportunist trying to amass a fortune, the megalomaniac Mengele has never given up his dreams of an Aryan race dominating the rest of the world. Szell and Mengele are in many ways caricatures and the authors do not explore their evil in any meaningful way. Only Trenker's motivation remains in the dark and an easy explanation for his evil deeds is not obvious.

In William Goldman's *Marathon Man*, evil comes in the form of Christian Szell.[1] Goldman made a career as a novelist and screenwriter since the late 1950s. Among others, he wrote the Oscar-winning screenplays to *Butch Cassidy and the Sundance Kid* and *All the President's Men*. He also penned the novel *The Princess Bride* and the screenplay for the movie based on it. Clearly inspired by the real-life Josef Mengele, Goldman portrays the fictitious Szell as a German dentist who served at Auschwitz alongside Mengele. Since his hair had turned prematurely gray at age 25, inmates called him "The White Angel" (131). Jews in the camp referred to Mengele as the "Angel of Death." Therefore, both together were known as the "angel twins" (213). Goldman portrays Szell as imbued with a superior intellect. After all, "Mengele had a Ph.D. plus an M.D., and he was considered the dummy of the two," as a close associate of Szell, explains (213). As Mengele's protégé in the experimental block, Szell was able to extract bribes from Jewish inmates especially in the form of diamonds. After he took all valuables, he had them killed. In addition, he stole gold fillings from prisoners, often knocking them out of the Jews' teeth (214–216). After the war, he escaped to Argentina, which issued him an identity card, and he eventually settled in Paraguay. The stolen diamonds, however, remain in a safe deposit box in a Manhattan bank. Szell's father had access to it and periodically transferred some to Paraguay.

Surprisingly little historical research is available on the role of dentists at Auschwitz. The SS did establish a dental station at Auschwitz and allowed Jewish and German dentists to operate there. According to one of these Jewish dentists, Benjamin Jacobs, German patients obviously received better treatment than Jewish ones. In addition, under the supervision of the German dentists, Jacobs had to pull gold fillings from dead inmates. At least some of this gold ended up in new fillings for German SS men.[2] The gold teeth from the gassed individuals had to be dropped in a special security container. The German dentists then supervised the melting and safekeeping of the dental gold, before it was sent on to the correct SS branch. Moreover, from the spring of 1944 on, with a large number of Hungarian Jews arriving, German dentists (and also pharmacists) had to participate in the selection process at Auschwitz's train station.[3] There, doctors usually decided who was allowed to survive and go to the labor camp, and who was scheduled to die almost immediately in the gas chambers.

As Szell did in *Marathon Man*, numerous Nazi war criminals managed to escape in particular to South America after World War II through the help of so-called ratlines. These were unofficial networks often run by Catholic clerics, which operated either via Spain or via Rome and Genoa leading mostly to Argentina. One of the most important men running these networks was Bishop Alois Hudal, rector of an Austrian German church and seminary called Santa Maria dell'Anima in Rome. Hudal helped individuals such as Franz Stangl, commanding officer at the Treblinka death camp, and Adolf Eichmann, who was responsible for facilitating and managing the logistics of the mass extermination of Jews and others, find a safe haven in Argentina. Another individual instrumental in operating the ratlines was Monsignor Krunoslav Draganovic, a Croatian supporter of the Ustasha, a group which led the Nazi puppet regime in Croatia during the war and which was responsible for the murder of hundreds of thousands of Jews, Serbs, Roma, and political opponents. Draganovic's most prominent "client" was Croatian wartime dictator Ante Pavelic.[4]

Argentina opened its gates to escaped Nazi war criminals for a variety of reasons. While serving as military attaché in Mussolini's Italy in 1938, Juan Domingo Peron had become obsessed with fascism. As president of Argentina from 1943 to 1945 and again from 1946 to 1955, he instituted a series of reforms modeled after the Fascist corporate state he had seen in action in Italy earlier. With Nazi Germany clearly losing the war, he set aside 10,000 blank Argentine passports and identity cards in 1945 for high-ranking Nazi refugees. Peron also sought to benefit financially from the incoming Nazi refugees. After all, Nazi officials had smuggled large amounts of gold, diamonds, and hard currency into Argentina during the war. Argentina also had a lot to offer to German refugees. It was the most advanced of all nations in South America, and its capital Buenos Aires was the most culturally advanced and sophisticated city of the continent, as it featured plenty of newspapers, theaters, and universities. In addition, it already gave home to a large German community. At the same time, the country was dominated by a conservative brand of Roman Catholicism and a close-knit group of quasi-aristocratic families; both were conditions, which appealed to Mengele and others like him.[5]

In *Marathon Man*, Goldman portrays Christian Szell as pure evil, anti-Semitic, but also cold blooded and calculating. Szell is not a Nazi who is foaming at the mouth with vitriol and hatred, but he remains cool and composed almost until the end. However, at the same time, Szell is capable of incredible cruelty and violence. In the torture scene, made famous by the Hollywood movie based on the book, starring Dustin Hoffman and Sir Laurence Olivier, Szell is trying to find out if it is *safe* to pick up the diamonds that he stole from Jews at Auschwitz. The diamonds are now in a safety deposit box in New York.

He suspects that the main character called Babe, who is also Jewish, knows about the diamonds from his brother, who it turns out was secretly a contract killer and occasional courier for Szell called Scylla. After being mortally wounded by Szell's associate, Scylla manages to make it back to Babe's apartment and die in his brother's arms. To find out what exactly

Babe knows, Szell uses dental tools to torture him, asking repeatedly "Is it safe?"

From Babe's point of view, Szell with his bright blue eyes seems obviously brilliant (200). He never raises his voice during the whole ordeal and remains completely calm the whole time. At first, Szell just cleans out a cavity, but that alone begins to instill terror in his victim. As Babe ruminates, "Dentists were frightening, no matter how much music they piped into their offices or the number of Novocain shots they offered. It was all very primitive. It went beyond pain" (202). Babe still does not know what Szell's question refers to and says so. Then Szell shoves a needle pointed instrument into the cavity repeatedly until he hits the nerve, which understandably causes indescribable pain to Babe. In between, the dentist offers relief in the form of oil of cloves rubbed on the tooth, but he does this just to prolong the torture and renew the suffering until Babe falls into unconsciousness (203–206).

But Babe's agony is not over yet. After pretending to save him and so get Babe to confess freely what he knows, a close associate of Szell called Janeway brings him back to the dentist's chair. In this scene, Szell meticulously and fastidiously prepares for the second round of dental probing. Again he uses the tactic to explain in great detail beforehand what he is planning to do to Babe in order to instill fear and get him to confess faster (225–230). While working on Babe, Szell also vigorously rejects the accusation of being mentally unstable. He compares himself positively to Mengele, who he describes as being "involved in lunatic fancies," while he claims that "every [test person] . . . under my care was there for a sound, viable reason" (227). Finally, he drills into a healthy tooth's nerve, which causes even greater pain than before, but Babe still does not know anything about the diamonds. Szell finally gives up and orders Babe killed (231–233).

Szell remains calm and composed almost until he meets his end in Manhattan's Central Park. In addition, he shows that despite his seemingly rational approach to his situation, he still has deeply ingrained anti-Semitic stereotypes, especially about Jews and their relationship to money and wealth. While torturing Babe, Szell declares that the only thing Jews can be trusted with is money (227). That apparently is the reason why he plans to sell the diamonds in the Jewish-dominated diamond market in Manhattan. Here he thinks of Jews as "the Chosen People . . . [who spend] their days in exhaustive haggling" (284). When a Jewish store owner does not give him a straight answer after being asked what a one-carat stone was worth, he has a hard time controlling himself and he thinks that "the insolence of the kike was simply not to be tolerated" (287). Despite his belief in these stereotypes, Szell resorts to pretending to be Jewish in order to avoid being recognized (289). Despite his disguise, a Jewish Holocaust survivor finally identifies him on the street and several Jewish individuals follow him to Central Park. After Szell brutally stabs one of the Jews pursuing him, Babe, who managed to escape Szell's henchmen, catches up with him and executes him by firing several shots slowly and deliberately. Before Szell finally dies, Babe gets his revenge by telling him that all people after their death go to "this way station, [where] innocent people wait, and then when their savager comes, they get to exact a little portion of revenge. . . . Do you know who's waiting for you, Mr. Szell? All the Jews. They're all there, and you know what else? They've got drills, like you used on me. . . . [A]nd they're waiting, and I don't know about you, but I think it's gonna be terrific" (305).

In comparison, Ira Levin's *Boys from Brazil* features the real Josef Mengele.[6] Levin began writing plays and novels in the 1950s, of which many were turned into Hollywood movies. His most famous works include *Rosemary's Baby* and *The Stepford Wives*. As in *Marathon Man*, the Nazi criminal is hiding out in South America, in this case in Brazil. But unlike Szell, who only is interested in continuing his comfortable life, Mengele has farther reaching plans. In a very complicated and truly evil scheme, he is trying to clone another Adolf Hitler to finally fulfill the promise of a 1,000-year Reich. He does not shy away from multiple murders to achieve this goal. However, a well-known Nazi hunter, named Yakov Liebermann, obviously modeled after real-life Nazi hunter Simon Wiesenthal, is on his trail.

The real-life Josef Mengele conducted heinous medical experiments in Auschwitz, especially ones involving twins. Coming from a well-to-do Bavarian industrialist's family, he was raised in a strict Catholic family. He joined the SS in 1938 and at about the same time finished his PhD and MD. He came to Auschwitz in 1943 and served in several capacities there. Mengele conducted many of the selections at the train stations, where he decided with the flick of a riding crop who was allowed to live at least for a while longer and who went directly to the gas chamber. He also decided in the Auschwitz hospital blocks who was healthy enough to return to work or who should be gassed. Doing this, he was usually calm, highly efficient, and gentlemanly, but at times he erupted in rage and violence. He shot women and children at the railroad ramp if they did not obey his orders quickly enough.[7]

Mengele's name is most closely associated with medical experiments on twins. His interest in twins and what they could tell him about heredity began in his student days and continued with fervor at Auschwitz. He was instrumental in selecting twins, especially identical twins, at the camp's railroad station. They were then kept in special blocks together with dwarfs and inmates with other abnormalities. Mengele's specific motivations in researching twins remain unclear. He might have tried to find a way to accelerate Germany's population growth by ascertaining the secret to multiple births. Or he might have wanted to understand how to improve the genetic makeup of the German people. No matter his motivation, as part of his activities, he frequently had inmates killed, often through phenol injections, just to dissect their bodies and determine the causes for their special abnormalities. Moreover, he conducted experiments on live individuals. The most infamous included his attempt to change eye color from brown to blue by injecting methylene blue directly into the eyes.[8]

The fictitious Mengele in *Boys from Brazil* is living in Brazil and still part of a network of former Nazis, called the *Kameradenwerk* (in English "comrades' organization"). Its members are planning and scheming to bring about finally the dream of a 1,000-year Reich in which the Aryan race dominates the rest of the world. As it turns out, Mengele by taking Hitler's blood right before his death in Berlin in 1945 created 94 Hitler clones. He managed to place them with specific families in Europe and North America as orphans. All these families share features with Hitler's family in order to as closely as possible re-create Hitler's upbringing. As with the actual Hitler, all fathers are older and low-level civil servants and domineering, while all mothers are quite a bit younger than the fathers and overindulging. As part of the plan, Mengele orders all the 94 fathers killed at about the same time in the boys' lives Hitler's father would have died. When Nazi assassins begin the killings, all engineered to look like accidents. Yakov Liebermann, the renowned Nazi hunter, gets suspicious and begins investigating. In the dramatic finale, Liebermann personally stops Mengele from going through with his plan and one of the Hitler clones kills Mengele.

Levin portrays Mengele as cultured, polite, and efficient, but at the same time prone to violent outbursts of anger and violence. In his early 60s, Mengele is dressed all in white and impresses his fellow members of the *Kameradenwerk* with his charm, youthfulness, and lively persona (18). Even after he finds out that a conversation about his plan at a restaurant has been audiotaped by a young American college student, he remains calm and methodically traces the tape and has the student killed (27–43). Minutes before being stabbed to death, the student manages to call Liebermann and share some crucial details. Liebermann is still on the phone line when Mengele picks it up and tells the famous Nazi hunter: "The Fourth Reich is coming. . . . See you at the door of the gas chamber" (44). Even though Mengele does not identify himself, Liebermann is convinced it was him. Mengele just radiates evil as Liebermann explains: "[H]ate came over the phone. . . . Hate like I never felt before" (53). Under the thin surface of Mengele's gentility, therefore, lurks an evil character that is willing to do anything to put his sinister plan into reality.

Mengele meticulously plans the assassinations of the 94 fathers. He even creates a chart covering one whole wall of his office in the Brazilian jungle outlining all names of his intended victims and the places and dates where and when they are supposed to be killed. He systematically begins checking off several names of individuals already killed (85). The Brazilian painter who comes in to draw the chart on the wall is casually thrown off the plane on his flight back to the capital (80). Mengele's admiration for Hitler is as strong as it was decades before. Looking and smiling at a Führer portrait in his office, he thinks to himself: "You don't mind being moved to the side for this, do you, my Führer? Of course not; how could you?" (78). Further drifting into caricature, Mengele later looks up at the sky at night believing Hitler was watching him and promises him, "I won't fail you" (121).

Furthermore, Mengele is prone to strong physical reactions whenever he sees his plan in danger. After hearing that Liebermann is on his trail and is investigating some suspicious deaths in Germany, Mengele violently throws up his dinner in the bathroom (119). He is also given to violent outbursts which quickly shatter his usually genteel demeanor. At a Nazi-sponsored fund-raiser in Brazil, while charming a young, blonde former Ms. Nazi, Mengele finds out that one of the killers who is supposed to be on assignment in Sweden is in attendance. Believing that this man has shirked his duties, Mengele suddenly flings himself at him and strangles him. He yells, "This man is a traitor! . . . He betrayed me, he betrayed you! He betrayed the race! He betrayed the Aryan race!" (167). For fear of being detected the *Kameradenwerk* eventually calls off the operation so that Mengele decides to finish the mission alone. He abandons his villa, but before his departure destroys the chart of assassination targets in a fit of rage. "Slashes like red blood tore down through the boxes in the third and second columns. The first column's boxes held neat red checks halfway down, then larger and wilder checks, stabbing beyond the boxes." Upon seeing this, one of the members of the *Kameradenwerk* observes amazed: "He went outside the lines" (173).

In contrast to his sudden fits of rage, later he is also able to cold-bloodedly plan and execute the murder of another one of the Hitler clone's fathers. He deliberately disguises himself in public and despite his personal distaste tries to blend into a neighborhood which features blacks, Jews, and Asians (193–197). He then personally kills one of the boys' fathers in cold blood. He pretends to be Liebermann, even deliberately retaining a slight German accent, and convinces the father to look for an item in the basement before he shoots him in the back (220). Finally, he assumes the dead father's identity, again carefully practicing his American English accent, to get a chance to kill the arriving Liebermann—a task at which he finally fails.

Levin contrasts Mengele's evil intentions and behavior with the character of Yakov Liebermann, the elderly Nazi hunter who apparently has his best days behind him. Liebermann admits that originally he began hunting down escaped Nazis out of revenge, but with time realized educating especially young people was the best way to prevent genocide like the Holocaust (65). In the end, it is not even Liebermann who kills Mengele, but vicious Dobermans tear him apart, as ordered by one of the cloned boys (244–245).

In contrast to both Szell and Mengele, the Nazi war criminal in M. E. Kerr's *Gentlehands* is quite different.[9] M. E. Kerr, the pen name of Marijane Meaker, began writing mystery novels and nonfiction books in the 1950s. In the early 1970s, she switched to writing novels for young adults. In *Gentlehands*, Frank Trenker, the grandfather of the main protagonist named Buddy, served not as a doctor but allegedly as an SS guard in Auschwitz. Unlike neither Szell nor Mengele, he has never been involved in another crime since World War II. He came to the United States because he had married an American woman after getting her pregnant. He is not hatching any evil schemes, but just wants to be left alone until a Jewish journalist, whose sister was killed as Auschwitz uncovers the truth. In the end, Trenker goes into hiding.

Kerr's idea of incorporating an escaped Nazi camp guard into one of her novels was inspired by the actual search for such individuals in the United States, which began in earnest in the early 1970s. Into the early 1960s, most Americans remained relatively unconcerned with the Holocaust and instead, after the long years of the Great Depression and World War II, exhibited a forward-looking attitude with a focus on job and family. The capture and subsequent trial of Adolf Eichmann, who, for example, was responsible for the planning of train schedules to Auschwitz, in Argentina in the early 1960s, changed the dynamic. Through the publicity the Israeli trial created, many started to realize that the Holocaust survivors and perpetrators were aging and that time began to run out to bring Nazi war criminals to justice. A Holocaust consciousness and awareness developed, which culminated in 1979 in the founding of the Office of Special Investigations (OSI), a U.S. government agency which was solely responsible for locating and trying to deport or extradite suspected Nazi war criminals. Since the end of World War II, an estimated 10,000 Nazi war criminals have entered the United States through a variety of channels.[10] Most came as so-called displaced persons in the late 1940s and 1950s through generous immigration legislation passed by Congress. Often they served as camp guards or auxiliary policemen in the Nazi-occupied territories in Eastern Europe. As a result, a good percentage were not ethnic Germans but collaborators from Ukraine or Lithuania. As such, they participated in the mass murder of Jews and others.[11]

In *Gentlehands*, Trenker is the grandfather of Buddy, a 16-year-old teenager from a lower-middle-class background, who falls in love with a slightly older, attractive girl from a very well-to-do family. On a whim, maybe to impress his girlfriend, Buddy and his girlfriend visit his grandfather, who he has only seen once in his life. His mother and his grandfather are estranged. Trenker married Buddy's grandmother only because he had gotten her pregnant. Apparently, a sense of duty and responsibility played a role in this decision, as Trenker says: "When you got a girl pregnant in those days, you married her." Later he admits to Buddy, "I had no feeling for your grandmother" (95).

Trenker and Buddy quickly develop a closer relationship, and Buddy seems quite impressed with his grandfather's quiet, poised, but determined nature. After a fight with his parents, Buddy even moves in with his grandfather for a while. Kerr portrays Trenker as a lover of dogs and other animals. His beloved dog obeys instantly when ordered by him (24). He provides food for birds and other animals in his backyard, and when a raccoon gets hurt by a neighbor's trap, he nurses it back to health (120–121). Buddy is struck by his grandfather's dignity, confidence, and sophistication. Trenker listens to opera; his house features many books, paintings, and antique furniture (25–26). He is always well dressed, smokes an expensive pipe, and shows Buddy how to properly pour wine (85–87).

Trenker also is trying to build up Buddy's self-confidence, especially in relation to his girlfriend. He claims that Buddy could develop a little polish if pointed in the right direction by his grandfather. Buddy seems reluctant to believe him, but Trenker explains, "Obstacles are challenges for winners, and excuses for losers" (32). Later, he accuses Buddy of being too content with his admittedly boring lower-middle-class life. He challenges Buddy to take matters into his own hands:

> You're lazy, too, Buddy. If you're going to drink wine, you should learn how to drink it and how to pour it. If you want fresh orange juice in the morning, you should squeeze it yourself and not blame your mother because she has only Minute Maid. You should learn about opera, and that a lady always has to be escorted home after a date . . . and you should always own up to where you've been (97).

In the end, Buddy's relationship with his grandfather shatters under the pressure of the revelations about Trenker's Nazi past. A Jewish journalist named De Lucca publishes an article in the local newspaper accusing him of having served as an SS guard officer at Auschwitz. Ironically nicknamed Gentlehands, he allegedly ordered the playing of the aria *O dolce mani* ("Oh gentle hands") from Giacomo Puccini's opera *Tosca* to taunt Italian inmates on their way to the gas chamber. He frequently set dogs on helpless inmates as well (152–154). Moreover, he, together with a character named Werner Renner, who was chief physician at Auschwitz (an allusion to Mengele again), conducted selections at the railroad station (162–163). He escaped to Argentina after the end of the war and travelled all around the world for a while before meeting Buddy's grandmother.

In Trenker's case, the evil acts he allegedly committed seem hard to believe and Kerr deliberately never even attempts an explanation for why he carried them out. Indeed, the sophisticated and caring grandfather seems to be the complete antithesis to the young and sadistic SS officer. For the longest time, Buddy and many of his neighbors refuse to believe the accusations against his grandfather. "Not that man—he wouldn't hurt a fly!" (154). However, when Trenker goes into hiding, it becomes clear to Buddy that he indeed is guilty of these crimes. He takes his grandfather's previous advice to heart to take responsibility and goes to the police and tells them what he knows. He admits to his girlfriend, "My grandfather is Gentlehands. . . . I think I know where he is" (190–191). At the conclusion of the novel, however, the police still have not located him.

As these three novels clearly show, the evil Nazi exerts a tremendous fascination. In general, though, the escaped Nazi war criminal has been turned into a caricature; at once seemingly genteel and composed but also capable of murderous behavior and just plain sadism. None of these novels seriously try to explain and critically grapple with the issue of evil in an allegedly enlightened and sophisticated society. More recent treatments of this subject matter, like Stan Pottinger's *The Last Nazi* or Alan Elsner's *The Nazi Hunter*, do not go any farther and remain in the safe territory of science fiction and cheap thrills.[12]

NOTES

1. William Goldman, *Marathon Man*, 1st Ballantine Books ed. (New York: Ballantine Books, 2001). The following page references come from this edition.

2. Benjamin Jacobs, *The Dentist of Auschwitz* (1995–1997), The Nizkor Project, http://www.nizkor.org/features/dentist/chapter-14.html (accessed May 28, 2013).

3. Rudolf Höss, *Death Dealer: The Memoirs of the SS Kommandant at Auschwitz*, trans. Andrew Pollinger (New York: Da Capo Press, 1996), 223–24; Robert J. Lifton, *The Nazi Doctors: Medical Killing and the Psychology of Genocide* (New York: Basic Books, 1986), 196.

4. Michael Phayer, *The Catholic Church and the Holocaust, 1930–1965* (Bloomington: Indiana University Press, 2000), 165–75.

5. Gerald L. Posner and John Ware, *Mengele: The Complete Story*, 1st Cooper Square Press ed. (New York: Cooper Square Press, 2000), 96–100.

6. Ira Levin, *The Boys from Brazil: A Novel* (New York: Dell, 1976). The following page references come from this edition.

7. Lifton, *The Nazi Doctors: Medical Killing and the Psychology of Genocide*, 43, 338–39.

8. Lifton, *The Nazi Doctors: Medical Killing and the Psychology of Genocide*, 59, 62, 348.

9. M. E. Kerr, *Gentlehands* (New York: Harper Trophy, 2001). The following page references come from this edition.

10. Allan A. Ryan, *Quiet Neighbors: Prosecuting Nazi War Criminals in America* (San Diego: Harcourt Brace Jovanovich, 1984), 26.

11. For an example of a low-level camp guard see Eric C. Steinhart, "The Chameleon of Trawniki: Jack Reimer, Soviet Volksdeutsche, and the Holocaust," *Holocaust and Genocide Studies* 23, no. 2 (2009): 239–62.

12. Alan Elsner, *The Nazi Hunter: A Novel* (New York: Arcade Publishing: Distributed by Hachette Book Group USA, 2007); Stanley Pottinger, *The Last Nazi* (New York: St. Martin's Press, 2003).

CHAPTER 10

What American Vampire Literature Teaches Us about Dangerous Consumption

Andrea Siegel

INTRODUCTION

A recent Pew Center report finds that 47 percent of Americans believe that either the climate is not changing, or, if the climate is changing, humans are not at fault.[1] A large-scale poll of climate scientists found that 97 percent believe the climate is changing and we are at fault.[2] Polls show that the number of people who believe in human-caused climate change is *decreasing*.[3] While there is plenty of debate in the climate change community about the small details, the large hard science questions are relatively settled. The climate is changing. We are at fault. The critical issue facing us a planet, human ravenous overconsumption causing climate change, is no longer a matter of real scientific debate. Those who deny this change base their arguments not on evidence but on belief.

The key question now is sociological and psychological. How do we get folks to face hard facts and change behavior to save life as we know it?

The arts often lead the way in matters of sociological, psychological, and even technological change. Artists explore and articulate permutations of popular belief and visions of social progress that can open the ground for discussion of change, and even influence real necessary change. American utopian literature of the 19th century provided visions of human racial and sexual equality that were largely initially scoffed at by the Christian Caucasian male hegemonic power. Technological visions, such as the helicopter drawn by Leonardo da Vinci, or even cartoon detective Dick Tracy's videophone, were once largely seen as absurd fantasies. Writers of fantasy literature, historically, have contributed to these explorations and discussions in a specific way, according to Rosemary Jackson, "The fantastic traces the unsaid and unseen of culture: that which has been silenced, made invisible, covered over and made 'absent.'"[4]

I argue that in contemporary best-selling American vampire literature, we are seeing artists wrestle with ways of dealing with and eventually conquering the obsessive overconsumption that plagues our planet. These writers are discussing degrees of and varieties of resistance to the consumption issue, how minds and hearts are changed, and how resulting behavioral changes help to preserve life as we know it.

This chapter discusses vampires' issues in the two recent American best-selling series—the 11-books-and-growing Charlaine Harris's *True Blood* Southern vampire novels[5] and the 4-plus books of the Stephenie Meyers's *Twilight* saga[6]—in which the vampires' reactions to and struggles with radical behavioral change in their consumption habits (necessary to reduce their mass-murderous impact) reflects the ambivalences and difficulties humans are facing today in recognizing the impact of and changing our own habits in our genocidal and ultimately suicidal natural resources consumption.

VAMPIRE LITERARY HISTORY

Historically, in European culture, vampires have symbolized and reflected various perceived social evils. It is often assumed that Bram Stoker's *Dracula* is the originator of the vampire genre. However, well-known writers such as Voltaire in 1764, Goethe in 1797, Keats in 1819, and Karl Marx in 1867, among many others, wrote of vampires prior to Stoker.[7] For social scientists, the most familiar is Marx's characterization of bloodsucking capitalists as vampires.

The 19th-century vampires, including the later Dracula, often drank their victims into a consuming fever that usually led to death, also reflecting the public experience at that time of tuberculosis, which was also called consumption.

Closer to the time of the publication of Bram Stoker's *Dracula* in 1897, vampires were popular political metaphors: political commentators penned cartoons in Irish papers of the British as vampires, and likewise the British characterized the Irish as vampires in their popular press.[8] Similarly, Germanic nationalist Georg Ritter von Schönerer characterized Jewish people as vampires in his tirades and "thuggish demonstrations" claiming the victims were German farmers and craftsmen.[9] Given the much later German Nazi officer's uniforms, so similar in color and collar to those favored by Dracula, and, infinitely more important, the Nazi's mass murder of Jews, Roma, homosexuals, and activists, among others, it seems the vampire appellation would have been far better suited the Nazis themselves.

Our American "movie idol" *Dracula* (1931) originated in Bram Stoker's eponymous novel and the 1922 German Expressionist film *Nosferatu,* the heightened and exaggerated drama of which reflected a political climate of near panic. During this period, political instability and exponentially increasing inflation wrought increasing desperation in German society. As Eisner notes in *The Haunted Screen:*

> One can picture those excited minds. It was a period of inflation when everybody wanted to live at any cost, to drink the cup of pleasure to the dregs, to keep his balance somehow and anyhow on the debris of normal life. But no one could free himself from the anguish of the morrow. The cost of pleasure went up from minute to minute, billions of marks becoming mere scraps of paper.[10]

Our *Dracula* is also based on Bram Stoker's work. He drew inspiration from the Victorian vampire literature that starts with John Polidori's 1819 story, "The Vampyre." Polidori was Lord Byron's personal physician, and was present in that cold, wet, dreary summer in Switzerland, when Byron, Shelley, and Mary Wollstonecraft challenged each other to write horror stories to bide the time. Wollstonecraft wrote *Frankenstein.* Polidori wrote "The Vampyre," basing his lead character's seductiveness and misanthropy upon Byron. Because he both resented and admired Byron, he named the vampire Ruthven, which was the name on Byron's dumped mistresses.[11] From its onset, the Victorian vampire is a creature who focuses on seducing and destroying innocent women. The literature served to voice concerns about the misuses of sexuality in an era when women's ignorance of sex, called purity, was considered a virtue, and frank discussion of sexuality was suppressed. Sex was bad, and vampire stories allowed that suppressed desire to bubble up. It is a period when evil and good are clearly defined.

In the modern vampire tales I am discussing here, the lines between good and evil are blurrier, and sexuality is simply a part of life. Anne Rice's books are full of largely homoerotic friendship (her vampires do not have working equipment for intercourse). In the *True Blood* series, the heroine Sookie Stackhouse dates vampires and sleeps with them, but the sexual descriptions are no warmer than other chick lit of the period. In the *Twilight* series (originally written for teens and tweens), the lead characters do not have sex until after they are married, late in the concluding superlarge final volume.

Instead, a significant issue for the modern vampires is their changing patterns of consumption. For the purpose of this chapter, we must fast-forward through the plentiful vampire literature to the late 1970s. Up until that point, according to Suzie McKee Charnas, vampires largely exemplified part of the problem, "vampires, old or new, [were] cannibals feeding on the world around them, acting out in their own persons the bloody support system that sustains our lives—my shoes made by sweated labor in Brazil, my meat from castrated and constrained animals."[12]

During the 1970s, the first of Anne Rice's series of books marked a turning point in the literature. She wrote eight plus vampire books (she also wrote short stories and other books in which vampires appeared, but were largely about witches or mummies). Rice's first vampire book, *Interview with a Vampire* came out in 1976, but the many that followed took place from the 1980s on, when AIDS was still lethal, and when the erotic exchange of blood led to infection and eventual death (just like many humans' experience of vampires in Rice's novels). These postmodern vampire novels, told for the first time from the vampire's point of view, emphasized their humanity, and saw the first early vampire struggles to face and deal with their consumption.

For example, to slake their hunger, vampire law restricted their consumption, demanding they feast only on "evildoers." The killing of bad people was judged a less evil. Rice's coven also agonized over their choices and the impact of their acts even as they were powerless to stop choosing to drink blood. In *The Vampire Armand*, the eponymous narrator talks about vampires in this way:

> the tragedy of all of us, those who kill to live, and thrive on death even as the very Earth decrees it, and are cursed with consciousness to know it, and know by what inches all things that feed us slowly anguish and at last are no more. Sorrow. Sorrow so much greater than guilt, and so much more ready for accounting, sorrow too great for the wide world.[13]

If we were to draw connections with human emotional response to overconsumption, we could see us all shaking our heads and saying, yes, it is a tragedy we cannot stop destroying our own world. Isn't it sad?

And then we take no action about it, and continue to do the things that destroy our world. Maybe the really older folks cut down a bit. Maybe they buy very little. Maybe they occasionally slip.

TRUE BLOOD

The *True Blood* series is the first best-selling vampire literature that changes the consumption paradigm. Charlaine Harris's first novel in the series, *Dead Until Dark*, published in 2001, presents the new vampire consumption model. A vampire walks into a bar in the opening scene, and orders a bottle of what is called "True Blood," a synthetic product developed by the Japanese, the existence of which allows vampires to come out of the closet, or the coffin, and begin to function as part of the regular community. Thus begins the now-12-volume-and-growing series.

Here, the vampires really prefer live human blood to the synthetic stuff, but they quaff fake blood in order to be able "mainstream," to rejoin the human community and to publicly participate in human goings-on, specifically so they can be in business and profit from human commerce legitimately. Here, characters in the books draw large-scale comparisons between vampire behavior and human behavior, what Rosemary Jackson has called, "the relative insignificance of vampire predation when it is considered within the context of what human beings are capable of achieving all on our own."[14]

On a small scale, in *Dead until Dark*, Sookie's first boyfriend Bill's consumption patterns are basically changing because he wants to conform to social norms in order to be a regular member of the community. He is tired of being a hidden outcast. He wants to live in the family home, go to the local bar, and hang out with Sookie.

We'll skip over the were-panther Sookie dates next and go right to her second vampire boyfriend Eric. For Eric, drinking True Blood is a business decision. He is extremely interested in profiting from his ownership in a bar. As an out-of-the-coffin new member of the visible community, he has a professional reputation to maintain. So, in public, he drinks True Blood. He is fully cognizant that humans come into a vampire bar seeking the thrill or having a death wish and wanting to find a vampire who will suck their blood. He exploits this interest for commercial gain, and turns a blind eye to the goings-on in the bathrooms, and the goings-on after hours of humans and vampires who leave together.

In these books, some vampires in the series simply mock the "main-streamers" and remain true to the voracious human-killing, bloodsucking origins.

If we were to draw parallels with the human condition, we might see that by the early 2000s there are alternatives available. They do not taste good. We do not like them. We may perform a show of being frugal livers, and reformed consumers, but it is largely a token public performance, and only to the extent that the neighbors can see us do it, or because it is good for business. After dark, when no one can see us, we are the same old ravenous, destructive overconsumers. By the flickering light of the TV screen, we are sucking food down and getting obese.

TWILIGHT

The best-selling *Twilight* series (first published in 2005) presents a different model, and in a significant way a more progressive model of consumption. This series tells the story of Bella Swan, a child of divorced parents, who, when she moves back in with her dad, and moves back to his town, falls in love with Edward Cullen, who happens to be a vampire, and who is also part of a family of vampires, all of whom have sworn off drinking human blood.

In this series, the Cullens are part of a tiny minority of the vampire population who curtail their wanton destruction/consumption and re-channel it, sublimate their destructive urges in creative past times (one person is a doctor, another restores houses, another is a musician, etc.).

In this series, the majority of vampires still ruthlessly hunt and feed on humans. These are largely connected to a group called the Volturi. Like those human beings today who gleefully wallow in conspicuous consumption (often seen in so-called reality television shows), the Volturi wallow in gluttony, staging human-feeding sprees. And they mock vampires (like the Cullens) who do not want to gorge themselves in orgies of mass murder.

The Volturi are concerned with power, and the smaller Cullen group, somehow because they change their diet, form more powerful bonds based on love. The Cullen's bonds and growing power are viewed as a threat by the majority. And the majority is trying to discredit and destroy the Cullens. The majority vampires will stop at nothing in their efforts to destroy the Cullen's ethical model. The only thing that makes the majority pause in their destructive efforts is public opinion. They care about public opinion.

There are parallels to our current political climate, where corporate-funded think tanks spend millions to convince the public that overconsumption is not an issue. Their success in promulgating this false belief extends to the highest political office in the United States. For example, then president Bush saying that the appropriate response to the September 11, 2001 attacks on the World Trade Center and the Pentagon is to defend our freedom by going out and spending money. Soon after the attacks, the president said,

> When they struck, they wanted to create an atmosphere of fear. And one of the great goals of this Nation's war is to restore public confidence in the airline industry. It is to tell the traveling public: Get on board; do your business around the country; fly and enjoy America's great destination spots; get down to Disney World in Florida; take your families and enjoy life the way we want it to be enjoyed.[15]

In the *Twilight* series, the Cullens are successful in preventing the Volturi from destroying them, because with allies who support their cause, they form a democratic rabble of disparate free thinkers, and they stand together in defense in a public gathering that includes the Volturi and an enormous number of outside vampire witnesses. With the public viewing this through the mass media, especially through the Internet, we are seeing signs of an emerging Democratic movement in the present-day United States, #OCCUPYWALLSTREET.[16] Whether their tactics will help produce democratic social change remains to be seen, but some of those tactics worked for the Cullens.

On a more personal level in these books, each major Cullen character struggles with his or her inheritance of the desire to drink human blood to the point of human death in different ways. Each of these individual struggles is emblematic of a larger social struggle overconsumption in contemporary life.

Carlyle, the founder and father of this group, hunted vampires when he was mortal. He believed vampires are evil, and it was therefore his right and duty to slaughter them all. He believed himself a soldier of God. Once he was turned into a vampire, he did not see things in such absolute terms. Feeling the overwhelming desire to drink human blood, he grew in empathy for vampire creatures. With great difficulty, he consciously chose not to feed on people, and tried to simply die rather than do so. He found dying impossible, and reached for a passing deer once almost by accident, discovered it slaked his thirst, and thus found a way to conserve human life, and to thrive himself. He then got himself a medical education and now works among people saving lives, not taking them.

We might see parallels in Carlisle's story to folks who base their overconsumption on God-given right. They see their resulting prosperity as a sign of God's blessing, and their "fruitful" multiplication of people as part of God's plan. Today, we can see parallels to Carlisle's story in small groups fighting for changes in the Christian community, such as Eco-Justice Ministries, who see science as an ally, and see their role, as Carlisle sees his, as preserving stewards of God's creation.[17]

Carlisle's firstborn vampire son Edward, in his adolescent rebellion from his human-blood-abstaining vampire parents, went out on a killing spree. In his understanding parents' view, he was a wild, acting-out adolescent. During this period, Edward, who is telepathic, limited his kills to people with evil intentions. Thus, Edward hoped to mitigate his own guilt over murder. Eventually Edward returned to the fold of abstinence. His change of heart occurred because he was consciously sick of the overconsumption, sick of killing. He sees the animal-eating lifestyle as more humane and good. He wants to be a better person/vampire. Like Carlisle, Edward is trying to make a better world because of his sense of ethics. For him, though, this is not a spiritual decision. Edward is largely agnostic.

Jasper, Edward's brother, does not fundamentally believe stopping human consumption is possible, and has a great deal of difficulty with the Cullen family lifestyle. He only abstains because of his love for Alice, another vampire in the coven. Jasper provides an example that it is possible to stop even when it is terribly hard. His problems are presented not as physiological, but as psychological: his belief, not his digestive system, makes it difficult. It might also be useful to take note that it seems easier for people to stop overconsuming for ethical reasons than it is to stop destroying simply because you love someone else who has stopped. Ethics also seem to be a more powerful motivator than the desire to fit in with others.

In the *Twilight* series, Rosalie and Alice, characters in the Cullen family with a sense of entitlement about overconsumption, base this on the justification that their childhood or earlier-in-life traumas make this okay. Edward's sister Rosalie thinks it is fine to cause horrific mass murder only in the case where she herself was harmed (as a human). In other words, vengeance is a justifiable cause for rampant resource destruction. Edward's other sister Alice is good about not hunting people, but she has a serious overconsumption problem that is viewed with tolerant amusement by her family. The rationale that Alice had a lousy childhood (she spent her human childhood in a dark box in a madhouse) is justification for a kind of rampant consumerism that surpasses understanding. She dresses the entire family in extremely expensive designer clothes, and insists they wear them only once before discarding them. She joyfully drives gas-guzzling cars, and demands one of her own. Alice sulks if refused her desire to create mad spectacles of overconsumption. And she always wins. When she throws a party, a wedding, for example, she runs electric lights for hundreds of feet to get people to an event that is filled to the rafters with flowers and every manner of wedding stuff. Alice is similar to many consumers today. As Rob Latham says, "the individual laborer has been irreversibly penetrated by and infected with consumerist desire, an unquenchable, acquisitive lust."[18]

How do we address the public who, like Alice and Rosalie, view their overconsumption as part of their psychological right, necessary as a way to heal wounds they experienced earlier in life? Theorist Frederic Jameson asks, "Who is to break the news to them [consumers] that their conscious experience of leisure products—their conscious 'pleasure' in consumption—is in reality *nothing* but false consciousness . . . in other words, who is to drive the stake of critique through the vile undead heart of consumerist desire."[19] Meyers's books indicate that sense of entitlement might be a serious obstacle to making meaningful changes. Granted, both Alice and Rosalie have made a commitment to not murder humans. There has been some progress. The two women have changed their most primary damaging behavior, but clearly there's more work to do. This book provides no clues whether or how that work could happen.

Bella, the newest vampire, perhaps is a prototype of the possibility of what we could be. Bella came to the vampire life choosing it freely. Unlike the others, she knew what she would become, and that she would crave human blood. She asked a lot of questions beforehand, and was as prepared as a human can be. On her first hunt, just after she woke up as a vampire, her husband Edward took her to the woods to hunt animals. She caught the scent of humans in the woods, and took off like the wind to find them. Once she realized what she was doing, she stopped and covered her nose so she would not have to smell the delicious human aroma, and ran in the other direction. Thereafter, she does not go toward humans for food. There is an argument to be made, based on this, that if we educate our people fully, we can be people who choose not to murderously overconsume. However, there are obstacles: There is a huge movement in this country not to allow people to even teach that the climate is changing. This is closely linked with legislative efforts to prevent schoolteachers from teaching evolution science.[20] Our global population has reached 7 billion, and there is a huge movement to deny women access to healthcare education and birth control.[21]

We know of at least one premodern vampire with a conscience: Luella in Mary E. Wilkins-Freeman's 1902 story, "Luella Miller." When Luella realizes what she is, she dies rather than continue to kill. I would suggest that mass suicide is not our best response. Later in the literature, the first known modern conscientious vampire, George Smith in Theodore Sturgeon's 1961 book, *Some of Your Blood*, says "Everything that is alive in the whole world keeps taking things in and then working them over and then throwing out what it could not use . . . the first part, taking-in, gives you satisfaction and the second part, throwing out, gives you relief."[22] We have, perhaps, taken in as much as the world can bear, perhaps it is time to start, not throwing out, but really and sincerely, reducing, reusing, and recycling. The vampire Smith is incarcerated for madness: his worldview does not catch on and Sturgeon's book was not a blockbuster best seller.

These new vampires are different. The books in which they appear are massively best-selling. Perhaps, if we pay attention to these books we are so passionately consuming, these vampire stories can teach us something. Perhaps, as Suzy Lee Charnas has said, "we love and honor our monsters for bringing us to that place in ourselves, the place from which we continually create humanity in a brutal fearful world."[23] We do not have much time to learn, and to act.

With thanks to Jacob Tanenbaum and the North East Popular Culture Association at whose annual meeting elements of this paper were first presented in 2011.

NOTES

1. Pew Research Center for the People & the Press, *Public Praises Science; Scientists Fault Public, Media: Scientific Achievements Less Prominent Than a Decade Ago* (Washington, DC: 2009), http://www.people-press.org/2009/07/09/section-5-evolution-climate-change-and-other-issues/ (accessed December 21, 2011).

2. "Scientists Agree Human-Induced Global Warming Is Real, Survey Says," *Science Daily*, January 19, 2009, http://www.sciencedaily.com/releases/2009/01/090119210532.htm (accessed May 12, 2013).

3. Pew Research Center for the People & the Press, *Beyond Red vs. Blue Political Typology* (Washington, DC: 2011), http://www.people-press.org/2011/05/04/section-8-domestic-issues-and-social-policy (accessed December 21, 2011).

4. Quoted in Veronica Hollinger, "Fantasies of Absence: The Postmodern Vampire," in *Blood Read: The Vampire as Metaphor in Contemporary Culture*, ed. Joan Gordon and Veronica Hollinger (Philadelphia: University of Pennsylvania Press, 1997), 200.

5. Charlaine Harris and Copyright Paperback Collection (Library of Congress), *Dead until Dark*, Ace mass-market ed. (New York: Ace Books; Berkley Publishing Group, 2001); Charlaine Harris and Copyright Paperback Collection (Library of Congress), *Living Dead in Dallas* (New York: Ace Books; Berkley Publishing Group, 2002); Charlaine Harris and Copyright Paperback Collection (Library of Congress), *Club Dead*, Ace mass-market ed. (New York: Ace Books, 2003); Charlaine Harris, *Dead to the World* (New York: Ace Books, 2004); Charlaine Harris, *Dead as a Doornail* (New York: Ace Books, 2005); Charlaine Harris, *Definitely Dead* (New York: Ace Books, 2006); Charlaine Harris, *All Together Dead* (New York: Ace Books, 2007); Charlaine Harris, *From Dead to Worse* (New York: Ace Books, 2008); Charlaine Harris, *Dead and Gone* (New York: Ace Books, 2009); Charlaine Harris, *Dead in the Family* (New York: Ace Books, 2010); Charlaine Harris, *Dead Reckoning*, Sookie Stackhouse Novel/True Blood (New York: Ace Hardcover, 2011).

6. Stephenie Meyer, *The Short Second Life of Bree Tanner*, Large print ed., The Twilight Saga (New York: Little, Brown and Co., 2010); Stephenie Meyer, "Midnight Sun (Draft)," http://www.stepheniemeyer.com/pdf/midnightsun_partial_draft4.pdf (accessed December 21, 2011); Stephenie Meyer, *Twilight* (New York: Little, Brown Books for Young Readers, 2006); Stephenie Meyer, *Eclipse* (New York: Little, Brown Books for Young Readers, 2007); Stephenie Meyer, *New Moon* (New York: Little, Brown Books for Young Readers, 2006); Stephenie Meyer, *Breaking Dawn*, Second media tie-in edition. ed., The Twilight Saga (New York: Little, Brown Books for Young Readers, 2008), text.

7. Bram Stoker and John P. Riquelme, *Dracula: Complete, Authoritative Text with Biographical, Historical, and Cultural Contexts, Critical History, and Essays from*

Contemporary Critical Perspectives, Case Studies in Contemporary Criticism (New York: Palgrave, 2002); Voltaire, "Philosophical Dictionary Part 5," in *The Works of Voltaire: A Contemporary Version* (New York: E.R. DuMont, 1901); Johann W. von Goethe, "The Bride of Corinth," http://www.simplysupernatural-vampire .com/ (accessed December 21, 2013); John Keats, "Lamia," http://www.simply supernatural-vampire.com/ (accessed December 21, 2013); Karl Marx, "Capital: A Critique of Political Economy," http://www.marxists.org/archive/marx/ works/1867-c1/ch10.htm (accessed December 21, 2013).

8. Riquelme in Stoker and Riquelme, *Dracula: Complete, Authoritative Text with Biographical, Historical, and Cultural Contexts, Critical History, and Essays from Contemporary Critical Perspectives*, 376–79.

9. Edmund De Waal, *The Hare with Amber Eyes: A Family's Century of Art and Loss*, 1st American ed. (New York: Farrar, Straus and Giroux, 2010), 128.

10. Lotte H. Eisner, *The Haunted Screen: Expressionism in the German Cinema and the Influence of Max Reinhardt* (Berkeley: University of California Press, 1969), 140.

11. Leslie S. Klinger, Jeff Conner, and Mike Manomivibul, *In the Shadow of Dracula: Classic Vampire Fiction 1816–1914* (San Diego: IDW, 2011).

12. Jules Zanger, "Metaphor into Metonymy: The Vampire Next Door," in *Blood Read: The Vampire as Metaphor in Contemporary Culture*, ed. Joan Gordon and Veronica Hollinger (Philadelphia: University of Pennsylvania Press, 1997), 26.

13. Anne Rice, *The Vampire Armand*, The Vampire Chronicles (New York: Alfred A. Knopf; Distributed by Random House, 1998), 435.

14. Joan Gordon and Veronica Hollinger, *Blood Read: The Vampire as Metaphor in Contemporary Culture* (Philadelphia: University of Pennsylvania Press, 1997).

15. George W. Bush, "Remarks to Airline Employees in Chicago, Illinois," Speech, September 27, 2001. The American Presidency Project, http://www .presidency.ucsb.edu/ws/index.php?pid=65084#ixzz1hHQCnoQD (accessed December 21, 2011).

16. For more information, see http://www.occupywallst.org.

17. For more information, see http://www.eco-justice.org.

18. Rob Latham, "Consuming Youth: The Lost Boys Cruise Mallworld," in *Blood Read: The Vampire as Metaphor in Contemporary Culture*, ed. Joan Gordon and Veronica Hollinger (Philadelphia: University of Pennsylvania Press, 1997), 131.

19. Latham, "Consuming Youth: The Lost Boys Cruise Mallworld," 132.

20. American Institute of Biological Sciences, "Aibs State News on Teaching Evolution," http://www.aibs.org/public-policy/evolution_state_news.html (accessed December 21, 2011).

21. Andrew C. Revkin, "7 Billion and Beyond," *New York Times*, October 31, 2011, http://dotearth.blogs.nytimes.com/2011/10/31/7-billion-and-bey ond/?gwh=79B85B89A89383985C9962841D4C1D4C (accessed December 21, 2011); National Right to Life Committee, "National Right to Life Federal Legislation Issues and Legislation," http://www.capwiz.com/nrlc/issues/ (accessed December 21, 2011).

22. Mary E. Wilkins-Freeman, "Luella Miller," in *In the Shadow of Dracula: Classic Vampire Fiction 1816–1914*, ed. Leslie S. Klinger, Jeff Conner, and Mike

Manomivibul (San Diego: IDW, 2011); Theodore Sturgeon, *Some of Your Blood* (New York: Ballantine Books, 1961), 42.

23. Suzy M. Charnas, "Meditations in Red: On Writing the Vampire Tapestry," in *Blood Read: The Vampire as Metaphor in Contemporary Culture*, ed. Joan Gordon and Veronica Hollinger (Philadelphia: University of Pennsylvania Press, 1997), 67.

PART II

Comics, Animation, Video Games, Murderabilia, and Art

CHAPTER 11

"The Sanitation Man": Erasing Evil in Walt Disney

Li Cornfeld

"I know you," sings Sleeping Beauty in Walt Disney's 1959 film, "I walked with you once upon a dream." The lyrics, set to Tchaikovsky's *Sleeping Beauty Ballet*, are directed at Prince Charming, but the sentiment of dream-like knowledge, and of reencounter, could also be addressed to the story's wicked fairy. In his seminal work *The Uses of Enchantment*, Bruno Bettelheim argues that fairy tales' use of fantastic, dream-like narratives teaches children to negotiate their own impulses between goodness and monstrosity. Folkloric villainy thus functions not merely as pedagogical instruction but as an entry point of reader identification, one that suggests the potential of children and adults alike to master base instincts.

In transforming fairy tales into full-length feature films, Disney harnesses the haunting power of the Brothers Grimm while simultaneously branding each film with a uniquely American sensibility. The resulting films craft animated villains at once culturally familiar and commercially shrewd. To what extent do Disney fairy-tale films sanitize the ferocity of their folkloric predecessors? Given Bettelheim's theories regarding the psychological significance of villainy, what impact might such a whitewashing have on audiences, and on the stories themselves?

In her thorough 2006 study of Disney's feature-length animation, Amy Davis terms Walt Disney's "Classic Period" as lasting from 1937 to 1961, during which time the Studio cemented its dominance in the field of fairy-tale film. Although fairy-tale film adaptations made by other studios, both domestic and international, constitute significant contributions to the genre, Disney's impact is gigantic. Indeed, the reach of Disney's fairy-tale footprint is perhaps no place as palpable as in non-Disney fairy-tale adaptations produced after Disney's golden era. Such films contend with Disney's legacy both through reactionary devices and by interpolating Disney's films as de facto original source material with presumed audience familiarity.

Focusing on *Snow White and the Seven Dwarfs*, the Disney fairy-tale film that set the standard for all of the films to follow, I will examine, first, the significance of the Grimm material excised by Disney, and, subsequently, what Disney animates instead. Close readings of the Grimm Brothers' and Disney's versions of the story illuminate tensions regarding cultural understandings of girlhood, villainy, and desire.

Snow White and the Seven Dwarfs (1937) opens to a gold-embossed book that flips open to a page of extravagantly lettered text, as if to imply fidelity to literary source material. The Walt Disney Studio's innovative integration of animation, score, and moralistic plot, already evident in its animated shorts, reached new levels of technical mastery with the world's first full-length animated feature. Like its contemporary dramatic interpretations of *Snow White*, Disney's tale is based heavily on the text by the Brothers Grimm; that subsequent adaptations draw inspiration from both the Grimms and Walt Disney alike itself suggests the enormity of the Disney Studio's footprint in the fairy-tale genre, and the unparalleled success of its first feature.[1]

In adapting the story for the screen, Disney changed the title from the Grimms's title, *Snow White*, to the lengthier *Snow White and the Seven Dwarfs*. The shift is significant: whereas the Grimms's text focuses on the titular heroine's struggles to break free of her powerful, jealous stepmother, Disney's movie focuses on the refugee princess's woodsy interlude with a band of diminutive miners. In his multifaceted examination of Disney, Richard Schickel writes that the decision to emphasize the role of the dwarfs over that of the evil Queen arose out of concern that the original tale would be too bleak for popular entertainment. In response to the "grisly problems" posed by source text, writes Schickel, Disney found a happy solution in its decision to grant more screen time "to the funny little men."[2]

Whereas Disney's treatment gives the dwarfs names, personalities, and dance numbers, the Grimms's text is squarely a story of mother-daughter tension. The Grimms literally frame the tale with a maternal perspective: a queen sits sewing beside an ebony window frame, watching the snow. When she pricks herself with her needle, and sees the blood fall upon the snow outside, she wishes for a child red as blood, white as snow, and black as the window frame's wood.[3] As would be expected of a follower of Freud, Bettelheim imputes sexual significance to this description and reads the Queen's bloodletting as symbolic of both menstruation and loss of virginity. Without detailed explanation, he surmises, "the child learns that without bleeding no child—not even he—could have been born." Bettelheim finds the story comforting to children in that it informs them of an otherwise "upsetting event" (sexual bleeding) even as it explains how the anxiety-ridden event yields happy results (his own birth).[4]

If we accept Bettelheim's reading of the Queen's blood as sex symbolism, we might wonder that he inscribes the imaginary child receiving the lesson as male. Might a female child understand the bloody symbolism as betraying not merely biological fact but physiological trauma? Bettelheim connects sexual bleeding to menstruation and the breaking of the hymen that occurs during the loss of female virginity. Assault, a third version of injury commonly associated with sex, is conspicuously omitted from Bettelheim's reading. Yet Disney's film treatment skips over the tale's bloody beginning entirely: not for nothing has fairy-tale scholar Jack Zipes labeled Disney "that twentieth century sanitation man."[5] Doing so not only sanitizes the blood (symbolic or otherwise), but it also disrupts the foundation of the ensuing tale. Rather than starting with Snow White's biological mother, Disney's version begins well after her death; indeed, it begins even years after the arrival of her successor, Snow White's stepmother, the wicked Queen. At first glance, this may seem to be merely a directorial decision: to simplify the film's character. Yet this economy essentially dissolves the essence of the Grimms's tale: there is no primary mother, no wish for a child, and no suggestions of sexual bleeding, whether healthy or horrific, symbolic or straightforward.

According to the Grimms, Snow White's second mother arrives a year after the death of the first queen. From a child development standpoint, Bettelheim's claim that the stepmother represents a young child's belief that an angry, disagreeable parent is a magical substitute for his actual mother (who magically returns when mother is kind again), would perhaps be better supported if the Grimms's stepmother arrived after Snow White's infancy. In any case, Walt Disney famously categorized his audience segments not according to age brackets, but according to gender.[6] Perhaps as a result, the gendered implications of Disney's version, particularly as they relate to the film's central themes of goodness and evil, possess rich significations. In place of maternal desire, Disney's tale begins with maternal jealousy. The wicked Queen stands before her magic mirror, regally demanding that it provide testimony of her beauty. Instead, the soothsayer mirror, which we are meant to understand always tells the truth (and which feminist critics have read as the male gaze personified), dutifully informs her that her stepdaughter, Snow White, is more beautiful than she is.

Perhaps because Disney assumed an audience already familiar with pre-existing versions of the tale or perhaps because the Studio aimed quickly to get to the comedy of the dwarfs in the woods, minimal exposition sets the narrative in motion. Indeed, fewer than 10 minutes of screen time is devoted to depicting life at the palace. Minutes after the magic mirror establishes the Queen's rivalry with her stepdaughter, Snow White meets the prince whom she is destined to marry (a character not present in the Grimm text until the story's end). Although Disney introduces Prince Charming early on, however, the brawny tenor lacks the evil Queen's commanding cool or Snow White's bubbly optimism; his monotony is no match for the female characters' rich characterization. ("I have but one song," he croons, in the film's most aptly titled musical number, "One Song.")[7]

The Grimms published over 200 tales, including a vast collection of stories, which feature young male protagonists, as well as villains of all sorts. With *Snow White*, however, Disney began an American canonization of fairy tales focused exclusively on young women—and the evil fairies, witches, and stepmothers whose cruelties the young heroines endure. Disney essentially excises the Grimm's young male protagonists from the American canon.[8] All of Disney's subsequent heroines, over the next half century, would be modeled on the titular heroine of *Snow White*.

Zipes has noted the internal inconsistencies in the claims made by the magic mirror. Specifically, Snow White is drawn as a cheery, round-faced pubescent girl, while the Queen is a cool, devilishly sexy beauty, making it unlikely that the mirror really shows the Queen as less beautiful than her youthful competitor.

Although Bettelheim explicitly disavows Disney's adaptation of the tale as useful to childhood psychological development, the incongruity of the Queen's jealousy is nonetheless in keeping with Bettelheim's Freudian interpretation of the tale. Recognizing that young girls will be Disney's intended audience, Bettelheim reads the mirror's voice as the daughter's voice, for it is the daughter who initially believes her mother to be "the most beautiful person in the world." Then, as the daughter reaches puberty, writes Bettelheim:

> A mother may be dismayed when looking into the mirror; she compares herself to her daughter and thinks to herself, "My daughter is more beautiful than I am." But the mirror says, "she is a thousand times more beautiful,"—a statement much more akin to an adolescent's exaggeration.

Yet in the Disney version, the mirror's responses to the Queen are in formal couplets that are decidedly unchildlike, undoing a reading of the tale that interpolates the mirror's voices as the child's. Moreover, by the initial stage, in which the mirror affirms the Queen's beauty, the Disney version of Snow White occludes reading the tale's symbolism as a natural progression of filial feeling. Snow White is deemed more beautiful from the start.

Snow White's character may represent the urges and inclinations of girl children in general, but the wicked Queen is hardly an every-mother. Bettelheim considers her a cautionary tale unto herself, a warning to would-be maladjusted mothers against competing with their daughters "in looks, dress, and behavior," citing the disastrous consequences of such actions for mother and daughter alike. As in *Snow White*, Bettelheim contends, competitive mother-daughter relationships lead to arrested development on the part of the daughter (Snow White regresses to the woods and lives with miniature men) and to the mother's self-destruction. More comments on the Queen's death will follow.

In the Grimm tale, as interpreted by Bettelheim, the Queen and Snow White alike are tempted by narcissism and duly punished. After the Queen's first failed attempt on Snow White's life, the Grimms's version of the tale tells of the Queen making three subsequent attempts to incapacitate the princess. First, she approaches Snow White in the woods while disguised as a peddler, selling stay laces. She uses the ruse to tie the princess's corset so tightly that Snow White passes out, and remains unconscious until the dwarfs come to her rescue. For Bettelheim, the laces suggest the pubescent princess's wish to be sexually desirable, and her inability to remain conscious while wearing them indicates, "that she became overwhelmed by the conflict between her sexual desires and her anxiety about them." Later, the scene virtually repeats itself, with the stay laces replaced by a poisoned comb that the disguised Queen sticks in Snow White's hair and that the dwarfs remove upon their return home. For Bettelheim, the narcissistic missteps on the part of the princess lead not to her damnation (as does the stepmother's narcissistic cruelty), but to her successful negotiation of adult urges, and to a happily-ever-after ending with the prince. Here again, Disney's authorial excisions remove indications of life cycle events (Snow White's maturation) and sanitize the tale of its sexual suggestiveness (however oblique the suggestion). Further, it removes the cyclical pattern of the Queen's aggression. Might we consider the trifecta of objects with which the Queen threatens Snow White in the context of how they harm her? The laces take her breath away and the comb poisons her head, but only by eating the Queen's poisoned apple (a version, perhaps, of unwittingly "drinking the Kool-Aid"), does Snow White succumb to her stepmother's plot.

Bettelheim pays special attention to the color symbolism of the Grimms's apple: Snow White eats the red (poisoned) half, while the disguised Queen eats the unpoisoned white (healthy) half. Recalling the red drops of blood from the beginning of the story, Bettelheim reads Snow White's acceptance of the red half of the apple as her acceptance of sexual maturation. Her childhood, he argues, dies when she collapses, so that she may emerge from her coffin a woman. Curiously, Bettelheim devotes little attention to the shift in the object of Snow White's desire: rather than an object of adornment, the Queen's ultimate trap for Snow White is one of nourishment. From the perspective of psychological development, does Snow White's eating the apple suggest a Freudian oral fixation, or her acceptance of the carnal cravings that underscore her failed attempts to appear glamorous?

Make no mistake: for all the psychological symbolism with which Bettelheim recuperates the fairy tale, the evil Queen of the Grimms's text is unfathomably cruel, and her ensuing punishment is grisly. Perhaps the most significant element of the Grimms's text, which the Disney version cut—and certainly the easiest to identify—is the tale's ending. At Snow White's wedding, heated iron shoes are forced onto the Queen's feet. "She had to put on the red hot slippers," explains the Grimms, "and dance until she fell down dead." If, as Bettelheim argues, *Snow White* cautions women against becoming "the mother who tries . . . to be as youthfully attractive as her daughter," the Queen's demise illustrates the pointlessness of priding oneself on good looks: her beauty literally goes up in smoke. Perhaps, then, the hot slippers serve as a reminder that youthful beauty does not last forever, and that attempting to stay young too long can result in fast burnout. Additionally, there is a sense of communal justice surrounding the Queen's death. In the Grimms story, there is no specific character charged with forcing the Queen's feet into the treacherous slippers. Instead, the entire community steps forward, restoring order by punishing the Queen's evildoing, in a manner at once whimsical and gruesome.

Whimsically gruesome punishment of villains is a near staple of the Grimms's fairy tales. While the tales contain countless nondescript executions, the most memorable retributions are tinged with the fantastic. Pigeons peck out the eyes of Cinderella's stepsisters. Birds likewise meet out justice to the murderous stepmother of *The Juniper Tree;* they drop a millstone on her skull. *Rumpelstiltskin* concludes with the titular villain becoming so angry that he rips himself in half. In contrast, retribution, grisly or otherwise, is seldom meted out to Disney villains.

Without the bloody, maternal beginning of the Grimms's story, without the Queen's multiple attempts on the life of the protagonist, and without the gruesome death of the Queen to conclude the tale, Disney's inaugural fairy-tale film nearly negates *Snow White*'s interrogation of maternal desire and sexual maturation, ugliness and grace, goodness and evil.

Bettelheim made no secret of his distaste for Disney's adaptations. In his analysis of *Snow White*, he does not reference the entertainment Studio by name, but singles out the title of its movie for derision:

"Snow White and the Seven Dwarfs," the name by which [the tale] is now widely known, is a bowdlerization which unfortunately emphasizes the dwarfs, who, failing to develop into mature humanity, are permanently arrested on a pre-oedipal level (dwarfs have no parents, nor do they marry and have children) and are but foils to set off the important developments taking place in Snow White.[9]

What would happen if we take seriously Disney's shift in the story's emphasis, rather than merely writing off the dwarfs as a distraction? Let us keep Schickel's explanation of the shift in mind—that the Disney Studio actively sought a film with a lighter atmosphere than that of the Grimms's—and then see what can we glean from Disney's Americanized depiction of good and evil, as found in Disney's first animated feature.

In the Disney version, we meet Disney's dwarfs through their home in the woods, which Snow White finds after she is cast out by the wicked Queen. Examining the home full of tiny furniture and unwashed dishes, she surmises that the house must belong to motherless children. With her own mother long dead and a second who just tried to have her murdered, one might expect the plight of motherless children to have a special resonance with Snow White. At the very least, one expects the audience to make such a connection, even if Snow White herself never articulates it. Yet Disney's film shies away from such a psychological reading; Snow White is as indiscriminately kind to the dwarfs as she is to the animals of the forest. "They're orphans!" she coos, "that's too baa-aaad."

When at last the dwarfs appear onscreen, we find them cheerily digging in a sparkly diamond mine, after which they sing their way home from work. Once they arrive home, however, they are dismayed to discover their house has been invaded. Significantly, this first segment with the dwarfs situates the notion of evil as a joke. Afraid a monster has broken into their home, they putter about, struggling to appear brave, and to concoct a plan to chase out the intruder. The scene contains numerous gags (Doc stutters! Sneezy sneezes! Everyone tiptoes about!). This not only simultaneously establishes the dwarfs as a band of fools, but also burlesques the notion of evildoing that is so central to the plot. Further, by positioning Snow White as a potential threat, it briefly confuses the film's villain/protagonist dichotomy, even though it mocks the dwarfs for imagining that someone as kind and gentle as Snow White could be monstrous.

Although Bettelheim is not terrifically concerned with the dwarfs' presence in the Grimm tale, he nonetheless notes that, while living with them, "Snow White becomes a good housekeeper, as is true of many a young girl who, with mother away, takes care of her father, the house, and even her siblings." On this point, Disney and Bettelheim appear to see eye to eye. (In spite of all the motherless children that populate Disney and the Grimms, it should be noted that both Disney and Bettelheim were strongly invested in the sanctity of a traditional nuclear family.)

In Disney's version, Snow White has long served as a maid, even in her own palace, yet only when she lives with the dwarfs does she have an opportunity to exercise real authority, and to express maternal affection. In one of the film's most protracted gags, Snow White insists the dwarfs wash their hands. Smitten, they comply, as if they were bathing for the first time. The scene bolsters the dwarfs' role as both low-class fools and as Snow White's willing subjects, even as she proves herself worthy of their subjugation. Disney's woods thus retain the safe space of maturation denoted by the Grimms. Evil—personified by the wicked Queen—is far away in the castle.

"Nearly destroyed by the early pubertal conflict and competition with her stepmother, Snow White tries to escape into a conflict-free latency period," writes Bettelheim, and it is in this space that the Disney movie dwells. Significantly, a musical number in which the jolly dwarfs sing, dance, and play homemade instruments while Snow White sits in a chair and claps along would be duplicated nearly exactly by Walt Disney a decade and a half later, when the Studio released *Peter Pan* (1953). In that film, which focuses more explicitly on children's refusal to grow up, the lost boys assume the position of the dwarfs, while Wendy substitutes for Snow White. For both female protagonists, the goofy, gag-filled space among foolish, miniature male company provides them an opportunity to practice running a domestic environment, like the wives that both they (and their young female audience members) are expected to become, one day in the future. With their silly gags, the dwarfs steal the show, while Snow White's noble presence "elevates" the film from gag-filled cartoon to serious motion picture.

In spite of the many differences in their approaches to fairy tales, Bettelheim and Disney share a crucial similarity: both men championed nuclear family life, with traditional gender roles. It is therefore especially interesting that neither man succeeded in investing *Snow White* with a strong male presence. Although Disney's Prince Charming is responsible for awakening the comatose Snow White at the end of the story, he is hardly a strong male protector. He is not a Lancelot who arrives to slay the dragons. Yet the ineffectual Prince Charming of the Disney film is actually consistent with Bettelheim's reading of the tale, for Bettelheim's interpretation pays little attention to the story's would-be hero.

The male character that most concerns Bettelheim is the wicked Queen's huntsman, who is commanded by the Queen to kill the princess. Bettelheim reads this huntsman as the tale's father figure. In nearly every version of the story, the huntsman kills an animal in the princess's stead, yet he nonetheless fails to protect his charge from banishment. This prompts Bettelheim's quip, "wife-dominated husbands are not exactly new to this world." Bettelheim's certitude about the necessity of a father figure causes him to inflate the role of the huntsman, in much the same way that he accuses Disney of overemphasizing the role of the dwarfs. While Bettelheim therefore perceives *Snow White* as a cautionary tale that warns against destabilizing the patriarchy, feminist critics offer readings that elude a strictly Freudian interpretation of the tale.

Marina Warner, writing from a historical perspective, examines the contentious conditions that patriarchal society produced for women of different families, made to compete for limited domestic resources. Far from Bettelheim's psychological interpretation of a child who fantasies that his mother consists of two separate people, Warner's reading suggests that women who are related by marriage pose real-life threats to one another.[10] Such a reading both explains the female rivalry that forms the crux of the story, as well as the minimal role played by male characters. Similarly, in *The Madwoman in the Attic*, Sandra Gilbert and Susan Gubar identify the tale as a quintessential example of the antagonism between the "angel-woman" and the "monster-woman" of the Victorian literary canon.[11] In fact, Gilbert and Gubar open their investigation of feminist literary criticism with an analysis of *Snow White*, suggesting the enduring power of the tale, and alluding to the continued prominence of the tale in the Western fairy-tale canon.

In her examination of women in Walt Disney, Davis notes the striking similarities of Disney heroines. Though produced in different decades, *Cinderella* (1951), *Sleeping Beauty* (1959), and *Snow White* (1937) feature titular heroines who are remarkably alike. Although their clothing is distinctive and reflects the fashions of the films' respective decades, the personalities of each of these characters are eerily similar (kind, graceful, good-natured, beautiful, musical, innocent).[12] Further, the subsequent fairy-tale films pose few differences to the chaste, bland relationships between the female heroines and their male princes, nor to the considerably more dramatic, embittered relationships between the young female protagonists and the older women who seek their undoing.

Snow White's sexy evil Queen may be a scene-stealer, but Disney's movie chooses instead to develop the "conflict-free latency period" in which Snow White seeks refuge. Doing so establishes a sturdy foundation on which Disney set the stage for future decades of animated fairy-tale films. Unlike the Grimm folkloric tradition, where protagonists learn to negotiate evil and wickedness lurking at every turn, Disney films (to say nothing of its theme parks, its toys, and its line of princess paraphernalia) celebrate willful escapism. In place of the Grimms's grisly struggles and dark whimsy, Disney offers wholesome pleasantness and Technicolor glee. Good may triumph over evil in the end, but for Disney, pleasure is tied to latency: escapism for the whole family.

On a final note, we must connect Disney and Bettelheim's approaches to the significance of evil inherent in fairy tales to the real-life, albeit posthumous, accusations of that Bettelheim himself engaged in evil behavior. Both a celebrated and a controversial figure, Bettelheim's biographers revealed that he held a PhD in aesthetics, rather than in psychology—even though he presented himself as an authority on autism and behavior and many members of the public were led to believe that he headed the Orthogenic School for severely disturbed children at University of Chicago, when, in fact, he functioned as the administrative director who held no clinical responsibilities.[13] That revelation does not impugn his insights into fairy tales. On the contrary, that revelation affirms his knowledge of folkloric source material, even as it raises huge questions about the practical validity of his psychological claims.

More significantly, accusations about Bettelheim's use of violent control and coercion at the Orthogenic School lead to still more disturbing revelations: it is tempting to see Bettelheim as *Snow White*'s evil Queen corporealized. A figure obsessed with her own image who exercises cruelty as a means of maintaining social relevancy, the evil Queen's most important folkloric function (at least as interpreted by Bettelheim) is to compel the psychological maturation of its protagonist. Is that how Bettelheim saw the violence that he allegedly committed against students at the Orthogenic School? Or is his error more a theoretical miscalculation, with violent real-world consequences? We might consider his scholarly elision of distinctions between natural and exceptional injury, for example, as having disastrous practical repercussions. While this essay cannot confirm or refute the accusations against Bettelheim, the suggestion that Bettelheim himself practiced violence as a means of psychological correction points to dangerous real-world consequences of overly literal interpretations of folkloric symbolism of evil.

NOTES

1. Jack Zipes, *The Enchanted Screen: The Unknown History of Fairy-Tale Films* (New York: Routledge, 2011).

2. Richard Schickel, *The Disney Version; the Life, Times, Art, and Commerce of Walt Disney* (New York: Simon and Schuster, 1968).

3. Jacob Grimm and Wilhelm Grimm, *The Complete Fairy Tales of the Brothers Grimm*, trans. Jack Zipes (New York: Bantam, 1987).

4. Bruno Bettelheim, *The Uses of Enchantment: The Meaning and Importance of Fairy Tales* (New York: Vintage Books, 1989), 202.

5. Jack Zipes, *Fairy Tales and the Art of Subversion: The Classical Genre for Children and the Process of Civilization* (New York: Methuen, 1988).

6. Amy M. Davis, *Good Girls and Wicked Witches: Women in Disney's Feature Animation* (Eastleigh, UK: John Libbey, 2006).

7. An interesting counterpart to the one-note prince arguably exists in the characterization of the film's other primary male characters, the dwarfs, who are distinguishable precisely by their personalities.

8. In the early part of the 21st century, Disney further cemented its fairy-tale heroines with its "Princess Line," a loose collection of products that suggests Disney's assorted fairy-tale film heroines are bonded in female friendship.

9. Bettelheim, *The Uses of Enchantment: The Meaning and Importance of Fairy Tales*, 199–200.

10. Marina Warner, *From the Beast to the Blonde: On Fairy Tales and Their Tellers* (London: Chatto & Windus, 1994).

11. Sandra M. Gilbert and Susan Gubar, *The Madwoman in the Attic: The Woman Writer and the Nineteenth-Century Literary Imagination*, 2nd ed. (New Haven, CT: Yale University Press, 2000).

12. Davis, *Good Girls and Wicked Witches: Women in Disney's Feature Animation*, 101.

13. Ann R. Epstein, "Bettelheim: A Life and a Legacy," *The New England Journal of Medicine* 335, no. 19 (1996): 1468.

CHAPTER 12

From Pogo to Pennywise: The Rise of the Evil Clown in American Pop Culture since 1978 ∾

Adam W. Darlage

SEND IN THE EVIL CLOWNS

Most American clowns before the 1980s hailed from several different sources: the court jester or fool, miming, commedia dell'arte, and the Trickster of native cultures. Throughout most of its history, the clown was a live performer. When the first circus came to Philadelphia in 1793 under John Bill Ricketts, Americans enjoyed the Whiteface, Auguste, and character clown. The hobo, tramp, or bum clown eventually became the dominant character clown. Over time, circus clowns added elements from vaudeville and American burlesque, in addition to their visual, situational, and slapstick comedy. The popularity of the circus clown peaked in America during the career of Dan Rice (1823–1900), but began to decline in the wake of the Industrial Revolution and, later, the Great Depression.

Even with the advent of the new media technologies of radio and film and the growing popularity of the "Little Tramp" Charlie Chaplin, Buster Keaton, and television acts such as Abbot & Costello that co-opted the clown roles of straight man (Whiteface) and comic (Auguste), clowning remained the preserve of live performers for much of the 20th century. Emmett Kelly performed as the tramp clown Weary Willie for the Ringling Brothers and Barnum & Bailey Circus from 1942 to 1956. Other famous 20th-century American circus clowns include Felix Adler (1895–1960), Otto Griebling (1896–1972), Red Skelton (1913–1997), and Glen "Frosty" Little (1925–2010). These and other clowns are memorialized in the International Clown Hall of Fame and Research Center

(ICHOF) at Baraboo, Wisconsin, which serves as a national archive for the history of clowning.

Today, however, the evil clown is the preeminent clown within American pop culture, a culture dominated by prerecorded media in the form of movies, television, comics, blogs, YouTube videos, and video games. More Americans are familiar with the Joker than with live performers, and the Joker's rise in popularity since his first appearance as the "Clown Prince of Crime" in *Batman #1* (Bob Kane and Bill Finger, 1940) is undisputed. One of the most recognized villains in popular media, the Joker is no longer Cesar Romero's laughable villain in the *Batman* television series (Kane, Finger, and William Dozier, 1966–1968). Rather, he is Heath Ledger's psychotic character in *The Dark Knight* (2008), the second movie in Christopher Nolan's reset of the Batman mythology. The darkness of Ledger's drug-induced death, prior to the release of the film, and prior to his posthumous Academy Award for his performance, adds to the evil aura.

Most Americans' recent exposure to the harlequin character of commedia dell'arte has come through the Joker's popular sidekick Harley Quinn, who first appeared in Paul Dini's *Batman: The Animated Series* in 1992. Dini and Bruce Timm's one-shot comic *The Batman Adventures: Mad Love* (1994) later revealed that Harley Quinn was once a psychiatrist, Dr. Harleen Frances Quinzel, who treated the Joker in Arkham Asylum for the Criminally Insane. Soon after she began treating him, he seduced her and she fell in love with him. She then set the Joker free, abandoned her professional career and ethics, and became a villain herself. Mardi Gras fans and New Orleans residents, however, may recognize the harlequin face from the floats that glide through the city's drunken and debauched celebrations each February.

While the Joker may be the elder statesman of American evil clowns, the evil clown has been well represented in merchandise, state fairs, traveling carnivals, and popular media since the 1980s. Like the Joker, the evil clown is often the monster or force of chaos within a horror story that must be overcome by the hero, the one charged with restoring order and resolving the narrative. Evil clowns may be aliens, demons, or monsters in disguise, as in the case of Pennywise the Dancing Clown from Stephen King's *It* (novel, 1986; movie, Tommy Lee Wallace, 1990), Violator from the comic *Spawn* (Todd McFarlane, 1992–), the revenge demon Killjoy from the movie series (Craig Ross Jr., 2000; Tammi Sutton, 2002; John Lechago, 2010, 2012), or the alien clowns in the cult classic *Killer Klowns from Outer Space* (The Chiodo Brothers, 1988). Evil clowns may be human psychopaths, as in the case of young Michael Myers from *Halloween* (John Carpenter, 1978; Rob Zombie, 2007), Sweet Tooth from the *Twisted Metal* video game series (David Jaffe, Scott Campbell, 1995–), the escapees from the insane asylum in *Clownhouse* (Victor Salva, 1989), Captain Spaulding from Rob Zombie's *House of 1000 Corpses* (2003) and *The Devil's Rejects* (2005), or John Wayne Gacy, the "Killer Clown" himself, in Ford Austin's *Dahmer vs. Gacy*, a comedy horror that won the Audience Award at the Bare Bones International Film Festival in 2010.

Evil clowns may be humanoid dolls or clown-like puppets, thus overlapping with another popular monster in the horror genre. Examples include the possessed clown doll from *Poltergeist* (Tobe Hooper, 1982; screenplay by Steven Spielberg), Jester from the *Puppet Master* series (David Schmoeller, 1989; Dave Allen, 1991; David DeCoteau, 1991, 1998, 1999, 2010; Jeff Burr, 1993, 1994; Ted Nicolaou, 2004; Charles Band, 2003, 2012), and Billy, Jigsaw's ventriloquist doll in the *Saw* franchise (James Wan, 2004–2005; Darren Lynn Bousman, 2006–2007; David Hackl, 2008; Kevin Greutert, 2009–2010). The evil clown has inspired musical acts such as Insane Clown Posse, Mr. Bungle, and Shawn "Clown" Crahan of Slipknot, as well as the heel character Doink the Clown, who performed in World Wrestling Entertainment from 1992 to 1994. The category of the evil clown also includes the popular variant that I call the "bad clown." These clowns are bad people who seek to gratify their own selfish desires, which may include food, drink, and sex. Examples include Frenchy the Clown from "Evil Clown Comics" (Nick Bakay and Alan Kupperberg) in *National Lampoon* during the late 1980s and early 1990s, *Shakes the Clown* (Bobcat Goldthwait, 1992), Homey D. Clown from *In Living Color* (Keenen and Damon Wayans, 1990–1994), and Krusty the Clown from the *Simpsons* (Matt Groening, 1989–).

Intriguing evidence for the rise of the evil clown in American pop culture is the invention of the term *coulrophobia* sometime in the 1980s or 1990s to describe the fear of clowns. The term literally means "fear of stilt-walkers," the closest ancient Greek equivalent. Coulrophobia is a specific phobia, like arachnophobia or agoraphobia, and it often manifests after a traumatic experience with a clown in childhood. Its sufferers generally find the makeup, "frozen" facial features, and asymmetrical and lumpy appearance of clowns unnerving and threatening. Carlin Flora observes, "because reading facial expressions has long been a key to survival, our inability to discern a clown's expressions (and true intentions) underneath the accoutrements raises automatic suspicions."[1] The "uncanny valley" hypothesis in the fields of robotics and 3-D animation—that near-humanoid faces cause revulsion in human observers—also applies to clowns.[2] Finally, there are numerous websites and blogs devoted to the fear of clowns, including www.clownz.com and www.ihateclowns.com.

Research on clown images bears on the phenomenon of coulrophobia. Child psychologist Patricia Doorbar notes, "very few children like clowns. They are unfamiliar and come from a different era."[3] Doorbar's observation that clowns come from a "different era" reflects the steady decline of live clown performances and the growing unfamiliarity of younger generations with traditional clown acts and character types. Silent film actor Lon Chaney (1883–1930) made an eerily prescient comment that speaks to this unfamiliarity: "there's nothing funny about a clown in the moonlight."[4] Chaney hints at the shock that we might experience if we encountered a clown outside the familiar confines of the circus ring. For both the children and for Chaney, the clown frightens when it appears out of context.

Writer Joseph Durwin wonders about the "cultural phenomenon" of the evil clown and the rise of coulrophobia: "did it arise out of the phobia or the phobia out of it?"[5] In other words, did producers of pop culture media deftly transform the fear of clowns into Hollywood gold, as has been done with other phobias, including pediophobia with Chucky in the *Child's Play* franchise (Don Mancini, Tom Holland, 1988; John Lafia, 1990; Jack Bender, 1991; Ronny Yu, 1998; Don Mancini, 2004, 2013)? Or, did coulrophobia arise because people watched movies that featured evil clowns? Recent movies have certainly played on the fear of clowns. The comedy horror *Zombieland* (Ruben Fleischer, 2009) features a protagonist, Columbus, who hates and fears clowns even more than zombies.

Durwin's causality dilemma, while suggestive, is ultimately not very productive for a historical and theoretical explanation of the decline of the traditional clown and the rise of the evil clown in American pop culture. Here I argue that the media coverage devoted to the "Killer Clown" John Wayne Gacy and his clown personas, "Pogo" and "Patches," accelerated—if not initiated—the evil clown's gradual colonization of the American consciousness after 1978. This is not to say that the evil clown did not lurk before Gacy. Trickster characters, such as the Native American Coyote, are often both sympathetic culture heroes and cruel, self-serving rogues. Precursors of the evil clown may be found in the medieval clown devils that threatened to pull spectators into Hell. Some regard Pulcinella of the commedia dell'arte as a forerunner to contemporary evil clowns, and both Edgar Allan Poe's crippled dwarf jester Hop-Frog and Alfred Jarry's despicable Ubu Roi share certain characteristics with the evil clown. Die-hard comic book reader's aside, however, even the Joker could not capture the sustained attention of the American public until the media aftermath of Gacy's arrest and trial.

The popularity of the American circus clown was waning before Gacy, both within the circus and in other media. While the live television incarnations of Bozo the Clown (Ron Weiner, 1960–2001), the Town Clown in *Captain Kangaroo* (Bob Keeshan and Howard Friedlander, 1955–1984), and Ronald McDonald have forestalled its demise somewhat, the circus clown is now an endangered species in the United States outside of the

Big Apple Circus in New York and the Ringling Brothers and Barnum & Bailey Circus. "The Greatest Show on Earth" closed its Clown College in 1997, and very few pursue clowning through small programs such as the Ohio College of Clowning Arts in Akron, Ohio. Jane Bovary argues that ever since Willard Scott first portrayed Ronald McDonald in television commercials for McDonald's in 1963, "there has been a slow decline in the popularity of the circus, in large part due to competition from a diverse range of entertainment along with a growing public aversion toward animal acts, once a mainstay of the circus."[6] If, as Bovary argues, "the circus now carries an air of shabbiness and decay," so too does the traditional clown in other media.

In addition to these historical observations, I engage theoretical considerations as to why the evil clown has become so versatile to producers and so attractive to consumers of American pop culture over the last 30 years. I argue that the incongruity between the received historical and cultural content of the clown and its deployment as a monster within horror narratives has made the evil clown a highly adaptive pop cultural meme. This meme is represented and re-presented in various media every year, not to mention in other products, such as the scary clown mask and the evil clown of the Halloween haunted house. Numerous musical acts play on the meme in both their performances and their lyrics. The obvious example is Insane Clown Posse, who performs "horror-core" hip-hop for their legion of clown-faced "juggalos."

Finally, I follow Noël Carroll in his seminal article "Horror and Humor" on the place of the evil clown within horror fiction, and dissent from Mark Dery's position in "Cotton Candy Autopsy: Deconstructing Psycho-Killer Clowns" that the evil clown serves as the poster child for the postmodern modes of subversion, inversion, and transgression. In my analysis, the evil clown of American pop culture is certainly transgressive and "other," yet also predictable, precisely because it is nearly always imbedded in a story line that ends with its defeat by the hero. Finally, while Mikhail Bakhtin has focused on the clown or fool as a site of "carnivalesque inversion," challenge, and dissent in his classic *Rabelais and His World*, I point to the evil clown as a fusion between elements both human and monstrous. This creature represents deception, disorder, and chaos, and works through a plot by terrifying protagonists and wreaking havoc through special powers and abilities.

"CLOWNS CAN GET AWAY WITH MURDER . . ."

John Wayne Gacy murdered at least 33 teenage boys between 1972 and 1978 and buried most of them in the crawl space beneath his house in Des Plaines, Illinois. The nation was shocked to learn that someone apparently so normal could be one of the most prolific serial killers in American history. Gacy made a respectable living as an independent contractor, served a member of the Junior Chamber of Commerce in Des Plaines, and volunteered as the precinct captain for the local Democratic Party. Gacy joined the local Moose Club and their "Jolly Joker" clown club in 1975 so that he could perform as a clown at local parties, parades, and charity events. He learned to apply clown makeup, make his own costumes, and created the character clowns of "Pogo" and "Patches" for use in various settings. Gacy was an active member of his community, and he even served as the director of Chicago's annual Polish Constitution Day Parade in 1975.

The incongruity between his public respectability and his hidden life as a rapist and killer was not lost on Gacy. During the police investigation, he commented, "clowns can get away with murder," an allusion to the fact that he raped and killed boys for seven years and expected to continue to do so in the future.[7] This statement suggests that Gacy may have already embraced his identity as the "Killer Clown" long before the media explosion that followed in the months and years after his arrest in December 1978. Other evidence supports this conclusion; Gacy admitted to police that a clown routine inspired his practice of switching the toy handcuffs on his victims for real ones when their backs were turned.[8]

The media coverage of Gacy as the "Killer Clown" reached a fever pitch across Chicago and the rest of America between December 1978 and April 1979, when his last victim was found in the Illinois River. According to Christopher S. Kudlac, Gacy dominated Chicago news "for years on end. . . . The Chicago newspapers had multiple stories about the case every day for a month after the discovery of the bodies." Kudlac adds that the coverage of Gacy focused especially on the incongruity of his appearance with his private life. To this end, he cites an article in the *Chicago Tribune*, "Danger Cited: Killers Don't Always Look the Part," and a picture of Gacy as Pogo that appeared on the front page of the *Tribune* on December 27, 1978.[9] The media coverage reinforced Gacy's own contention that "clowns can get away with murder" by focusing on the terror inspired by the contradiction between Gacy the civic hero and Gacy the killer. Whether intentional or not, the media played on the widespread fear that anyone—even a clown—could be another Gacy underneath the metaphorical makeup and clown costume of public life.

Most accounts of Gacy's story that have appeared in the years after 1978 focus on the horror of this incongruity. Terry Sullivan and coauthor Peter T. Maiken's *Killer Clown: The John Wayne Gacy Murders* exemplifies this trend. First published in 1983, the back cover blurb presents the following questions:

WHO WAS JOHN WAYNE GACY?

The model citizen whose business skills were admired by his peers?

The hospital volunteer whose sweet-faced clowning lightened the patients' days?

The member of the Jaycees who was a civic-minded friend of the community?

The depraved maniac who sodomized, tortured, and killed 33 young men and boys?

While Gacy is not the only serial killer for whom the media has employed the incongruity angle (witness the coverage of Ted Bundy, Jeffrey Dahmer, and Dennis Rader, The BTK Killer), his volunteer work as a clown makes the incongruity that much more horrific and therefore more tantalizing to the public.

By the date of his execution on May 10, 1994, Gacy had played to his "Killer Clown" persona for over 15 years. He had taken up oil painting, and clowns were his favorite subject. In at least one instance, Gacy signed a piece of his clown art "John Wayne Gacy AKA 'Pogo,'" and added his infamous quote, "clowns can get away with murder." Gacy's execution itself was a media circus. By midnight of May 10, 1994, a crowd of nearly 2,000 had gathered outside Stateville Correctional Center in Crest Hill, Illinois. While some were there to protest the death penalty, most of the people in attendance were in their teens or early 20s and wanted to make a party of his death. Vendors sold T-shirts that read "no tears for the clown," and crowd members eagerly initiated clown-themed chants such as "put the clown in the ground!" Josh Emanuel, a teenager from Downers Grove, wore a rainbow clown wig and a shirt that read, "My parents went to Gacy's execution and all I got was this stupid T-shirt." Scott Koeneman observed, "one wonders if John Wayne Gacy's alter ego, Pogo the clown, would have appreciated the circus atmosphere created for his execution."[10] The crowd feasted on the contradiction between Gacy's clown persona and the serial killer who finally died from a botched lethal injection just after midnight. Most of them had no connection to Gacy's victims; they knew him as the "Killer Clown."

To be sure, observers of the human condition have studied John Wayne Gacy, and not all have focused on his "Killer Clown" persona. Nevertheless, most media representations of Gacy embrace it, precisely because the incongruity between the killer and the clown sells products. This incongruity terrifies and therefore fascinates the American public, who consume it again and again, especially because the threat is not real. As Talitha Ebrite observes, "once society feels it has rid itself of the potential danger from the individual, it can enthusiastically explore the life, crimes, and motivations of the serial murderer. As the facts become more bizarre, the exploration becomes more exciting." The immensely popular "Killer Clown" narrative has met and continues to meet the rising demand of the American public, for, as Ebrite adds, "the public interest in Gacy has not waned since his death."[11]

THE CLOWN AS MONSTER

I have argued for the rise of the evil clown in American pop culture over the past 30 years on the basis of two related observations. The first is that the popularity of the live performance clown began its steady decline in the wake of the Industrial Revolution and is now an endangered species despite efforts to deploy the clown in new media. Fans of Bozo, an international sensation for decades, may disagree, but WGN-TV Chicago still cancelled the show in 2001. The second is that the meme of the clown was and continues to be transformed by the enduring media coverage focused on the incongruity between the public and private faces of the "Killer Clown" John Wayne Gacy. As such, the evil clown and the concomitant fear and distrust of clowns have become commonplace in American pop culture, especially when more examples of clown-related evil are near at hand. Victor Salva, director of *Clownhouse*, was indicted for sexually abusing 12-year-old actor Nathan Forrest Winters during the filming of the movie, and juggalos have attracted media attention for a variety of criminal acts, including murder. In addition, James Holmes identified himself as the "Joker" to police after wounding 71 and killing 12 people in a horrific massacre at the midnight showing of Nolan's *The Dark Night Rises* in Aurora, Colorado, on July 20, 2012. Holmes dyed his hair red before his court appearance and looked very much the part of the evil clown.

Now I turn to why the clown works so well as a monster in horror and comedy horror narratives. To this end, I turn to the work of Noël Carroll on the link between horror and humor. Carroll notes that horror fiction may be distinguished from other forms of narrative fiction in that the genre of horror employs the monster, after whom the stories often take their names (e.g., Dracula and Godzilla). He comments on the emotions that monsters are designed to elicit: "we are horrified when the monsters who are the particular objects of our emotional state are thought of as harmful or threatening (i.e., they are fearsome) and they are also thought of as impure (i.e., they are revolting or disgusting)." Monsters inspire fear and revulsion by transgressing cultural categories and norms of thought, by presenting forms of being that are "interstitial, categorically contradictory, incomplete, or formless," as in the character of the werewolf, which is half-man and half-wolf, or zombies, who are both alive and dead.[12]

Next, Carroll turns to the "leading type of comic theory," the incongruity theory, for clues about the relationship between horror and comedy. Drawing on years of scholarship since the concept was first articulated by Frances Hutcheson in *Thoughts of Laughter* (1725), Carroll observes that the incongruity theory of humor is "the bringing together of disparate and contrasting ideas or concepts." Carroll presents a particularly relevant example for my purposes here: "European clown performances are frequently comprised of an immaculately clean, sartorially fastidious white clown—the epitome of orderliness and civilization—and an unruly, disheveled, hairy, and smudged clown—the lord of disorder and mischief."[13] The crowd's amusement comes from the interaction between the ordered Whiteface and the hopelessly chaotic Auguste. Of course, incongruity humor may be far more basic than Carroll's example. Surprise is the most elementary form of incongruity humor, and the game of Peekaboo amuses infants precisely because they expect their parents to disappear behind their hands and are surprised to find them still there. In both cases, conflicting expectations and concepts induce laughter in their resolution.

The connection between horror fiction and comedy born of incongruity is apparent when we consider that both involve a categorical transgression: "on the incongruity theory of humor, one explanation of the affinity of horror and humor might be that these two states, despite their differences, share an overlapping necessary condition insofar as an appropriate object of both states involves the transgression of a category, a concept, a norm, or a commonplace expectation." The clown is an ideal connection between humor and horror because the clown is both a historically fecund object of incongruity humor and, as anthropologists and historians have demonstrated, a "categorically transgressive" being. The clown may serve both humor and horror equally well, as it does in the comedy horror *Killer Klowns from Outer Space*. We both fear the Killer Klowns and laugh at them, because while they are revolting evil aliens who kill people, they do so by acting like clowns.[14]

Carroll points to the biology of the clown as that which makes it a monster and therefore a strong candidate for horror fiction: "it is a fantastic being, one possessed of an alternate biology, a biology that can withstand blows to the head by hammers and bricks that would be deadly for any mere human, and the clown can sustain falls that would result in serious injury for the rest of us."[15] As consumers of evil clowns in American media can attest, it is precisely this "alternate biology" that makes the clown so versatile and viable as a monster, for the evil clown can absorb an enormous amount of punishment from the hero and keep coming back for more. This attribute has allowed the Joker to survive for over 70 years, and numerous other evil clowns have yet to be completely killed off. Fans of Pennywise point to the Loser's Club plaque in Stephen King's *Dreamcatcher* (2001) that reads "Pennywise Lives" as evidence that it survives.

There are numerous examples of the clown's "alternate biology." Violator has superhuman strength, longevity, and several other special powers, Killjoy is able to craft illusions and absorb bullets in order to refire them from his mouth, the doll clown in *Poltergeist* uses its terrifying long arms to choke Robbie, and the Killer Klowns possess a number of unique gifts. They create living balloon animals, wield popcorn guns, create killer shadow puppets, and entomb their victims in cotton candy cocoons. Despite its humanoid appearance, then, the evil clown may just as easily be an alien or a demon as a psychotic human. It may even be a zombie, as in *Zombieland*, or a giant such as Rudy the Clown in the Super Mario Nintendo video game *Wario Land 3* (Takehiko Hosokawa, 2000). The clown is both human and "other," which makes it both a terrifying and revolting monster within the context of plotlines designed to induce visceral emotional responses in the audience.

Finally, clowns can be easily equipped with facial features and other cosmetic changes that render them inhuman and therefore fearsome and revolting. For their part, circus and hospital clowns seek to avoid scary features in their clown characters, lest they terrify their audience. John Wayne Gacy transgressed the traditional clown practice of painting rounded borders around the mouth in his character clowns "Pogo" and "Patches," whose mouths are notable for their sharp edges. Carroll cites the razor sharp teeth of Pennywise and the ugly misshapen teeth of the Killer Klowns, but countless other examples are near at hand. These include the sharp lines and grotesque shapes of scary clown masks, Devil's horns, glowing eyes, and, of course, menacing laughter from behind the smile. Indeed, the Joker's rictus grin, inspired by that of the tortured hero clown Gwynplaine (Conrad Veidt) in the silent film *The Man Who Laughs* (Paul Leni, 1928), is the classic example of evil clown cosmetic disfigurement.

Carroll's analysis of horror and humor attempts more than I do here, but it is clear that the clown serves horror and comedy horror narratives quite well. The evil clown may be as terrifying as Pennywise, or as funny as the Killer Klowns, who make us laugh by playing to almost every clown and circus stereotype imaginable: the popcorn, the cotton candy, the clown car, the tiny tricycle, and the carnival Big Top. The evil clown thrives in these narratives because of the incongruity between the historically received cultural content of the clown and its role as the monster within the story. As the monster, the evil clown is also malleable with respect to its appearance and abilities. As an interstitial and hybrid being to begin with, the simultaneously human and inhuman clown possesses an "alternate biology" that allows producers of evil clown media to imagine the bodies and powers of clowns in countless ways.

THE JOKER GETS AWAY

As both producers and consumers of pop culture, Americans draw from a deep historical and cultural well of clown associations with which to work. We are fascinated by the biology and liminality of the clown, which is somehow superhuman in its abilities. If we believe Lon Chaney, we may not want to meet the clown under the light of the moon, because clowns are garishly made-up, lumpy creatures with frozen facial features that often make us uncomfortable, even fearful. Americans have been ever more transfixed by the possibility that the clown may be evil since the media portrayal of John Wayne Gacy as the "Killer Clown," whose clown persona masked his murderous intent as a rapist and a killer. For over three decades now, the media has sold the terrible incongruity of Gacy's story, which has inspired countless others to market evil clown products to an insatiable public.

As the sustained popular success and cult followings of notable comic book and cinematic evil clowns suggest, the matrix of historical and cultural phenomena articulated above has produced an ever-adapting evil clown meme that works remarkably well in the typical horror or comedy horror narrative, stories in which the hero finally subdues the fearsome or funny (or both) monster. But that story is only the beginning, because the Joker gets away until the next episode of *Batman*, the Killer Klowns fly off into space (surely to return someday), and Killjoy waits impatiently for his next victim out looking for revenge. Like so many other monster types, evil clown biology allows for the serialization of the narrative into countless sequels and revisions. After all, what we really want as consumers of pop culture is another titillating story about how evil is finally vanquished and goodness is restored. Then we can sleep easy—at least until a clown knocks on the door in the dead of night.

NOTES

1. Carlin Flora, "No Laughing Matter: Coulrophobia, a Debilitating Fear of Clowns, Is a Fairly Common Phobia amongst Children and Adults," July 1,

2006, http://www.psychologytoday.com/articles/200610/no-laughing-matter (accessed March 5, 2012).

2. Elizabeth Landau, "Why Zombies, Robots, Clowns Freak Us Out," *Cable News Network (CNN)*, Video, 2:35, http://www.cnn.com/2012/07/11/health/uncanny-valley-robots/index.html (accessed July 30, 2012).

3. "Hospital Clown Images 'Too Scary,'" *British Broadcasting Corporation (BBC) News*, December 12, 2011, http://news.bbc.co.uk/2/hi/health/7189401.stm (accessed December 12, 2011).

4. Mark Dery, *The Pyrotechnic Insanitarium: American Culture on the Brink* (New York: Grove Press, 1999), 65.

5. Joseph Durwin, "Coulrophobia and the Trickster," *Trickster's Way* 3, no. 1 (2004), http://www.trinity.edu/org/tricksters/trixway/current/vol%203/vol3_1/Durwin.htm (accessed March 27, 2012).

6. Jane Bovary, "Clowns in the Moonlight," *HubPages*, http://janebovary.hubpages.com/hub/A-Clown-in-my-Nightmares (accessed March 15, 2012).

7. Terry Sullivan and Peter T. Maiken, *Killer Clown* (New York: Grosset & Dunlap, 1983), 94.

8. Dery, *The Pyrotechnic Insanitarium: American Culture on the Brink*, 72.

9. Christopher S. Kudlac, *Public Executions: The Death Penalty and the Media. Crime, Media, and Popular Culture* (Westport, CT: Praeger, 2007), 43.

10. Noël Carroll, *The Philosophy of Horror, or, Paradoxes of the Heart* (New York: Routledge, 1990), 32.

11. Talitha Ebrite, "Toward a Balanced Equation: Advocating Consistency in the Sentencing of Serial Killers," *Oklahoma Law Review* 58, no. 4 (2005): 688–89.

12. Noël Carroll, "Horror and Humor," *The Journal of Aesthetics and Art Criticism* 57, no. 2 (1999): 150–52.

13. Carroll, "Horror and Humor," 152–53.

14. Carroll, "Horror and Humor," 151–56.

15. Carroll, "Horror and Humor," 155.

CHAPTER 13

Marks of Cain: Physical Manifestations of Human Evil in Virtual Narratives

The introduction of the iconic Edward Hyde in Robert Louis Stevenson's *The Strange Case of Dr. Jekyll and Mr. Hyde* is accompanied by a physical description meant to inform the reader, in no uncertain terms, as to the nature of Hyde's character:

> God bless me, the man seems hardly human! Something troglodytic, shall we say? or can it be the old story of Dr. Fell? or is it the mere radiance of a foul soul that thus transpires through, and transfigures, its clay continent? The last, I think; for, O my poor old Harry Jekyll, if ever I read Satan's signature upon a face, it is on that of your new friend.[1]

Utterson, who serves as focalizer in this section of the novel, is explicit in his revulsion toward Hyde's appearance; this extreme reaction is then borne out by the events of the novel, which confirm Utterson's initial impression that Hyde is an evil man. But the correlation between deformities of the body and deformities of the mind/soul is not unique to Stevenson; indeed, this literary convention is commonplace in Victorian and pre-Victorian literature. Whether realistic (Shakespeare's hunchbacked Richard III) or fantastic (Bram Stoker's Dracula), the monstrosity of these fictional characters is inscribed on their bodies: evil is depicted as a physical manifestation, visible to the naked eye.

It is no coincidence that this association of appearance and personality is prominent in pre-20th-century literature; according to Noel Carroll's *The Philosophy of Horror*, evil is typically represented as a force of ideological and social transgression: "These monsters fit neither the conceptual scheme of the characters nor, more importantly, that of the reader . . . they are un-natural relative to a culture's conceptual scheme of nature. They do not fit the scheme; they violate it."[2] In realistic fiction, these breaches of cultural perception are often the result of characters' actions—a corrupt monarch, a serial killer, a thief—whereas fantastic creatures violate the scheme of nature by the mere fact of their existence (i.e., zombies, vampires). However, both categories of transgressors are marked in specific physical ways—their position outside the natural order marks them in such a way that they can be identified easily.

Over the past 50 years, most modes and genres of fiction have moved away from this convention. With the rise of cinema and television as platforms for visual narratives, the external and the internal have become dissociated; the appearance of a character is no longer conveyed exclusively through words, and psychological complexity has replaced moral absolutes as sources of motivations for narrative actants. As a result, evil is depicted as an invisible element for human and humanoid monsters; these become objects of fear not only because of what they do, but because they no longer carry any physical signifiers of their actions and are therefore indistinguishable from their potential victims. Contemporary descriptions of popular serial killers are particularly useful in demonstrating how this paradigm has shifted over time: where the 1846 penny dreadful *The String of Pearls* describes Sweeney Todd as a "long, low-jointed, ill-put-together sort of fellow, with an immense mouth, and such huge hands and feet, that he was, in his way, quite a natural curiosity," Bret Easton Ellis's *American Psycho* has protagonist Patrick Bateman describing himself thusly: "I had all the characteristics of a human being—flesh, blood, skin, hair—but my depersonalization was so intense, had gone so deep, that the normal ability to feel compassion had been eradicated, the victim of a slow, purposeful erasure."[3] The same holds true for supernatural entities that emulate human appearance: the figure of the vampire, for example, has become increasingly familiarized and humanized, to the extent that modern narratives such as *Buffy the Vampire Slayer* and *Fright Night* stress the ease with which such creatures are able to prey upon society with little fear of discovery. Of course, nonhumanoid entities such as the eponymous Alien evoke fear exclusively through their unnatural bodies, and as such are not included in this move toward undetectable monstrosity. In "The Devil Made Me Do It!" Matt Hills and Steven Jay Schneider discuss the significance of this increasingly common representation of human/humanoid evil, where subjects lack physical indicators of their "nature":

> This [depiction of evil] most directly links the figure of the serial killer to a "metaphysical evil" which dualistically, or even theologically, transcends the body. Such a device allows this representational type of serial killer to be

wholly othered from human identification, as well as becoming both threat-eningly "invisible" to those diegetically enforcing the law, and dualistically splitting into possessed body shells and an essential self or "soul/force" that is innately evil. Where realist serial killer films at least make some effort to engage with theories of psychological dysfunction, these films displace psy-chology with metaphysics.[4]

Evident in Hill's and Schneider's analysis is the concept of evil and mon-strosity as innate traits—albeit traits that have become so internalized as to be invisible to other characters (and, in some cases, to the reader/viewer as well). Many genres, such as fantasy, romance, science fiction, and detective stories, now stress the dissonance between the external and the internal, discouraging the assumption that the body is in any way an accurate symbol of the self.

However, while the invisibility of human/humanoid evil remains a dominant trend in literature, one medium has distinguished itself by gen-erating fiction that adheres to the previous convention: over the past de-cade, video games have produced many texts that maintain a relationship of causality between body and moral alignment. These games deliberately deploy an outdated trope as a narrative strategy, a process made possible by the very mechanism that enables video games to tell stories: the pres-ence of the avatar, key to any virtual experience. The avatar is a digital embodiment of the player that is projected into the fictional world, and that carries out the player's will within the ontological framework of the game. In "Understanding Video Games as Emotional Experiences," Aki Järvinen notes that most games encourage an emotional bond between players and their digital alter egos: "The aesthetic nature of play experi-ences—whether it involves performing, appreciating the design and com-position of game characters and environments, or being fascinated with the simulated minds of game characters—is an important aspect of the antecedents of pleasure and eliciting conditions for emotions as games."[5] Without discounting the many ways in which a novel may compel its readers, Järvinen argues that the player's active participation in the virtual narrative produces a much more heightened emotional response: "The difference is due to the interactive nature of gameplay: in other media forms, individual interpretations are seldom channeled back, via playful behavior, to the media content with which the audience interacts."[6]

Much like textual and cinematic literature, video game narratives are subject to classification by genre and subgenre; the Role-Playing Game (colloquially referred to as RPG) is perhaps the category which best ex-emplifies how the link between player and character is formed and nur-tured. Eastern RPGs, such as Square-Enix's *Final Fantasy* series, cast the player in the role of an already-established character—these avatars have

names, backgrounds, and predefined storylines, and the player is tasked
with a linear exploration of the plot. In doing so, they experience the stories of the characters they control. Western RPGs typically offer a more
flexible method for the player to project into the virtual world: the narrative protagonist/focalizer is *tabula rasa*, with its name and appearance
subject to alteration by the player. This malleability also extends to the
diegetic level, as many contemporary games are structured in such a way
that the player is granted a limited ability to manipulate the narrative sequence of events. Grant Tavinor's *The Art of Videogames* uses *Mass Effect*
(BioWare, 2008) to demonstrate how the multiplicity of potential choices
can affect the player's experience:

> The player chooses a general attitude to a previous sentence from a range
> of negative or positive responses, which is then concretely verbalized, al-
> lowing the player to express their attitude to the events that occur in the
> game world and narrative, knowing that the response they make may have
> an impact on the dialogue. As such, the dialogue is further personalized, in
> giving the impression that it is the *player's attitude* that is being expressed by
> the character.[7]

The options offered to the player typically extend not only to dialogue
but to action as well, and are situated on a moral spectrum: the avatar
may act in a heroic and selfless way (i.e., refusing a reward after aiding an
impoverished family), or the player may prefer a more villainous and self-
serving approach (i.e., stealing from an impoverished family). Choice has
become increasingly prevalent as a narrative factor in video games, and
more often than not the moral outcome of the protagonist's actions are
inscribed on the avatar's virtual skin—as in Victorian and pre-Victorian
literature, monstrosity manifests itself in physical ways and is visible to
the naked eye.

The following three games provide notable examples of how this inscription of evil is achieved: *Black & White 2* (Lionhead Studios, 2005),
Overlord (Codemasters, 2007), and *Mass Effect 2* (BioWare, 2010). *Black &
White 2* casts the player as an anonymous god-like entity, represented by
a disembodied hand and charged with cultivating a village populated by
the deity's worshippers. The *Black & White 2 Official Game Guide* makes
note of the player's ability to role-play a malevolent god and how this is
reflected within the game: "The way in which you play *Black & White
2* determines your alignment. Punishing or killing your people, driving
them to work harder, and attacking the towns of nonbelievers is a perfectly acceptable strategy."[8] If the player is consistent in performing evil
actions, the hand gradually turns red and its nails lengthen into talons,
creating a stereotypical "devilish" appearance. The game also provides

a similar moral spectrum and physical reaction for the player's Creature, a giant animal enforcer that acts in accordance with its master's wishes: "Like you, your creature has an alignment. His alignment is independent of your own, though—you can be a malevolent god and have a sweet, tender creature. Likewise, you can be a god of pure goodness, while your creature is a terrifying killing machine." *Black & White 2* demonstrates the principle of evil as a bodily indicator in a straightforward manner, despite the lack of complete embodiment on the part of the avatar: the "God Hand" serves as a metonym, and its appearance gradually shifts depending on the consistency of the player's moral choices. As the guide notes, there is no real penalty to discourage the player from immoral actions such as sacrificing villagers and conquering peaceful towns; role-playing an abusive god is simply one of several possible metanarratives to emerge from the way the player participates in the game.

Overlord is more complex in its depiction and conceptual exploration of evil: set in a Tolkienesque fantasy world populated by halflings, dwarves, and elves, the protagonist is the titular Overlord, a fallen villain seeking to rebuild his empire and crush the heroes of the land. Unlike *Black & White 2*, in which benevolence and malevolence can be pursued with equal ease by the player, the premise of *Overlord* requires the enactment of a villainous role—the mechanism of choice is in deciding how evil the Overlord will be: "During your adventures your choices and actions are reflected in how your Tower appears and how people react to you. . . . Whenever you commit a particularly Evil act you will hear and see your Overlord become darker."[9] In one scenario, the Overlord and his minions ransack a village and come across a large quantity of food; the player is then asked to choose whether to distribute the food to starving peasants or transfer the excess to the Overlord's army. Where *Black & White 2* offers no impetus to prefer one possible course of action to another—allowing the performance of evil acts only at the player's whim—*Overlord* subverts the generic formula of the heroic fantasy by awarding the protagonist for choosing the more corrupt path. The Overlord's body changes accordingly: black spikes emerge from his armor plates, an ominous red aura surrounds him, and even his Tower—the player's headquarters—becomes darker and more foreboding.

Mass Effect 2 serves as an example of how narrative structures and storytelling tools in video games have evolved in recent years. Rather than present the player with the traditional binary spectrum of "good versus evil" (i.e., choices based on morality), the game offers a more sophisticated and complex set of options, as per *Mass Effect 2 Official Game Guide:*

> Paragon and Renegade sound like absolutes, but as you know, life is never quite that black and white. So many choices deal in the gray area between

the absolutes. Paragons charm. They flatter. They may not choose the most expedient way to complete a task if the alternative is ethically questionable. Renegades are not wicked, but they could be considered intimidating or selfish. Renegades look out for themselves and are not always considerate of the feelings of other people, especially when such consideration stands between them and getting the job done.[10]

The protagonist and avatar of *Mass Effect 2* is Commander Shepard, whose gender, appearance, prenarrative background, and sexual preference is entirely at the player's discretion. Within the game narrative, Shepard is tasked with investigating an unknown, hostile alien species; though all players are bound to the same overall objective, there are multiple ways of experiencing the story. To prevent an oversimplification of the role-playing performance, the player's choices are framed not in terms of morality but as a conflict of idealism versus pragmatism. In an early section of the game, Shepard is confronted by a gang of armed thugs; as the enemy leader speaks, the player is presented with the possibility of triggering a surprise attack which kills some of the gang members—their deaths are violent and painful, but this course of action also reduces the number of hostiles Shepard must then engage in battle. If, on the other hand, the player prefers honorable tactics, Shepard can pass on the opportunity, though this will result in an initial disadvantage when combat begins.

As with many of its contemporaries, *Mass Effect 2* marks the body of the avatar in accordance with the role adopted by the player; unlike *Black & White 2* and *Overlord*, however, this particular game provides a diegetic rationale for the connection between body and personality. The game begins with Shepard recovering from major physical trauma and subsequent reconstructive surgery; regardless of the avatar's customized appearance, the character's face will bear the scars of that experience. The cybernetic implants and skin grafts are explicitly said to be related to the character's "mood"—pursuing the role of a Paragon will result in the scars eventually fading away. The *Official Game Guide* indicates that the reverse is also true: "If you walk the path of the Renegade, expect to see the effects of these decisions physically manifest on Shepard's face. Deep scars and red eyes are the marks of Renegades." Despite the shift away from morality-based gameplay, actions that favor expediency over ethics (i.e., killing a defeated enemy rather than allow it to surrender) result in Shepard adopting an increasingly severe appearance, to the point where the body of the avatar borders on the inhuman.

Having established the resurgence of external/internal correlation in video games, the question remains: why does this medium make use of a convention, which has largely been discarded in text-based and cinematic narratives? Why is the inscription of evil on the virtual body viewed as necessary when cultural representations of human monstrosity stress the invisibility of evil? Judith Halberstam's *Skin Shows* makes a compelling argument for the expression of monstrosity via physical representation:

> The monster's body, indeed, is a machine that, in its Gothic mode, produces meaning and can represent any horrible trait that the reader feeds into the narrative. The monster functions as a monster, in other words, when it is able to condense as many fear-producing traits as possible into one body . . . monsters and the Gothic fiction that creates them are therefore technologies, narrative technologies that produce the perfect figure for negative identity. Monsters have to be everything the human is not and, in producing the negative of human . . . make way for the invention of human.[11]

For Halberstam, the monstrous body serves as a way to differentiate these "evils" from that which is identified as human and "good"; this is broadly consistent with the way in which avatars are marked by the player's actions. However, where this differentiation is not inherently necessary in other media, the fact that many games make use of this strategy suggests that it is the nature of the avatar itself—and the relationship between players and the characters serving as their projections into the fictional world—which requires this physical manifestation.

As with cinematic figures, video game characters are defined in part by their visual appearance (of course, avatars grow increasingly detailed as the technology to render human expression advances). But where the film adaptation of *American Psycho* contains scenes where actor Christian Bale is covered in blood, signifying Patrick Bateman's violent actions despite the lack of any visible indicators, such temporary markers of brutality and evil are largely impossible for digital bodies; these remain static and unchanging simply due to the nature and limits of the technology responsible for creating and maintaining the digital world.

Barring specific story-based instances, the player's agent within the virtual environment does not change, age, or scar—they have singular bodies, and the player's experience in the game does not affect these bodies in any way. Even death, a fundamental force of alteration, is rendered impermanent by the very nature of gameplay; Grant Tavinor notes that death "almost always plays the function of failure to meet the challenges set by gameplay. Once the player-character dies, the game almost always sets the player back to an earlier stage in the game so that they can retry the section."[12] For linear, preplotted games, this is broadly acceptable; the player is tasked with completing specific objectives in a specific way, and failure—of the type that "kills" the avatar—is merely a setback, a result of the player being unable to meet those particular requirements, whether they are reflexive or logistical. There are no lasting consequences to the player's narrative experience, nor does the string of deaths and resurrections have any effect on the avatar's virtual body.

Nearly a century prior to the advent of video games, Oscar Wilde's *The Picture of Dorian Gray* provides an interesting literary precursor to this scenario: Dorian's descent into depravity is partly fueled by his discovery that the painting gifted to him by Basil (the portrait's creator) seems to age and change while he remains the same. However, in keeping with the literary conventions of the time, Dorian's evil actions leave immediate physical marks on the painting:

> A sense of infinite pity, not for himself, but for the painted image of himself, came over him. It had altered already, and would alter more. Its gold would wither into grey. Its red and white roses would die. For every sin that he committed, a stain would fleck and wreck its fairness. But he would not sin. The picture, changed or unchanged, would be to him the visible emblem of conscience.[13]

This transference of guilt to the simulacrum of Dorian's body allows the character to commit heinous criminal and sexual misdeeds, including murder, without fear of consequences. When Dorian—wracked at last by guilt—destroys the painting, the novel concludes with the revelation that the physical effects of his actions ultimately catch up with him: "Lying on the floor was a dead man, in evening dress, with a knife in his heart. He was withered, wrinkled, and loathsome of visage. It was not till they had examined the rings that they recognized who it was."[14]

As with Dorian Gray, the majority of virtual avatars are bound to a peculiar state of physical stasis, in which the player's experience has no effect on their "body." T. L. Taylor's *Play Between Worlds* notes the problematic nature of this immutability:

> Bodies are not simply neutral objects that have no bearing on our experience but act as central artifacts through which our identities and social connections are shaped. . . . Avatars are crucial in producing a sense of presence, of 'worldness.' Just as corporeal bodies are integral to our personal and social lives, avatars are central to our experience in digital environments.[15]

This underscores the fact that, unlike textual or cinematic characters, players are projecting themselves into static, unchanging objects that are unaffected by potentially cataclysmic events unfolding around them. The implementation of choice as a narratological and ludological (gameplay) tool necessitates the use of markers—indicators of the particular role the player has chosen to enact. These indicators manifest physically, inscribed onto the digital body in such a way that the player is constantly made aware of past choices and the moral/ethical alignment of their protagonist. *Black & White 2*, *Overlord*, and *Mass Effect 2* are only three examples of this growing phenomenon: in each instance, the use of scars, abnormal eye coloring or even foreboding alterations to the immediate landscape connote evil. Without these manifestations, the avatar would remain static regardless of the player's choices. Instead, the performance of monstrosity brings about the appearance of monstrosity; the player's choices are reflected in the face and body of their digital representative, and this serves to strengthen the emotional and narratological connections Taylor describes as linking player to avatar: "As each user encounters an avatar (their own or another's) he makes sense of it through a variety of social and personal 'stories.' Those stories help form the structure through which avatars act as agents for users." By generating gradual, consistent reminders of the player's past actions, these games reinforce the narrative power of choice and causality: the performance of evil acts leaves a stamp upon the body of the avatar, and as the narrative draws to a close, players who have acted out the role of a monster will find a scarred, red-eyed avatar staring back at them.

NOTES

1. Robert L. Stevenson, *The Strange Case of Dr. Jekyll and Mr Hyde*, Authorized ed. (New York: C. Scribner's sons, 1992).

2. Noël Carroll, *The Philosophy of Horror, or, Paradoxes of the Heart* (New York: Routledge, 1990), 33–34.

3. Bret E. Ellis, *American Psycho: A Novel*, Vintage Contemporaries (New York: Vintage Books, 1991), 265.

4. Matt Hills and Steven Jay Schneider, "'The Devil Made Me Do It!': Representing Evil and Disarticulating Mind/Body in the Supernatural Serial Killer Film," in *The Changing Face of Evil in Film and Television*, ed. Martin F. Norden (Amsterdam: Rodopi, 2007), 80.

5. Aki Järvinen, "Understanding Video Games as Emotional Experiences," in *The Video Game Theory Reader 2*, ed. Bernard Perron and Mark J. P. Wolf (New York: Routledge, 2009), 94.

6. Järvinen, "Understanding Video Games as Emotional Experiences," 88.

7. Grant Tavinor, *The Art of Videogames*, New Directions in Aesthetics (Malden, MA: Wiley-Blackwell, 2009), 122.

8. Ron Dulin, *Black & White 2 (Prima Official Game Guide)* (Roseville, CA: Prima Games, 2005), 34.

9. *Overlord* game manual, 10. Codemasters, 2007.

10. Catherine Browne, *Mass Effect 2: Prima Official Game Guide (Prima Official Game Guides)* (Roseville, CA: Prima Games, 2010), 19.

11. Judith Halberstam, *Skin Shows: Gothic Horror and the Technology of Monsters* (Durham, NC: Duke University Press, 1995), 21–22.

12. Tavinor, *The Art of Videogames*, 118.

13. Oscar Wilde, *The Picture of Dorian Gray* (London: Ward Lock and Co., 2008); Project Gutenberg, http://www.gutenberg.org/ebooks/174 (accessed May 28, 2013).

14. Wilde, *The Picture of Dorian Gray*, 174.

15. T. L. Taylor, *Play between Worlds: Exploring Online Game Culture* (Cambridge, MA: MIT, 2006), 117–18.

CHAPTER 14

Pictures of Evil: Francis Bacon's Painting in American Popular Culture

Monika Keska

In 1945, the art critic John Russell described Francis Bacon's first mature work, *The Triptych 1944: Three Figures at the Base of the Crucifixion*, after seeing it at the Lefevre Gallery, as "images so unrelievedly awful, that the mind shut snap at the sight of them. Their anatomy was half-human, half-animal, and they were confined in a low-ceilinged and oddly proportioned space. They could bite, probe and suck, and they had very long eel-like necks, but their functioning in other aspects was mysterious (. . .) Common to all three figures was a mindless voracity, an automatic unregulated gluttony, a ravening undifferentiated capacity for hatred. Each was cornered and only waiting for the chance to drag the observer down to their level."[1]

This frequently cited fragment of Russell's review is an early example of the association of Bacon's art with the idea of evil. Throughout his career he employed subjects and iconographic motifs such as blood drops, suggestive of a possible crime scene, bullfighting, scream, and crucifixions that carry the idea of violence. They are dissociated from their habitual religious or cultural context and are deliberately theatrical. The figures, isolated in circular, arena-like spaces and cages, resemble actors on stage. In Bacon's paintings, violence is often allied with eroticism, as he represented violent sexual acts, inspired by Mobridge's photographs of nude wrestlers, and violated nudes lying on sheets sunk in blood.

In addition, his screaming figures can be associated with brutality and pain, but that motif also has sexual connotations of an orgasmic scream. Bacon believed that painting is essentially a visual medium and is not meant to tell stories; therefore his images do not depict a violent situation or action, but an abstract idea of evil, a sensation of violence. Possibly, the only example of storytelling in his art is the *Triptych May-June* (1972), which represents the suicide of his lover, George Dyer. In many aspects, Bacon's painting had been a distorted mirror of his tormented life, the historical and political context of the post–World War II Britain, his sexuality, his family relations, and the tragic deaths of his lovers.

The deformed figures from Bacon's paintings have been predominantly inspired by a vast amount of source material found in the artist's studio that comprise medical and forensic photography, religious painting and images of war disasters, among others. The sexual connotations of violent images in Bacon's work are frequently employed in cinema to depict brutal or graphic sexual content, for example, in Bertolucci's *Last Tango in Paris* and *Intimacy* by Patrice Chereau (2001).

Bacon, who even described his triptychs as "a way of making a film," often sought inspiration and films stills, which he used as source material for his painting.[2] He was interested in silent cinema, Abel Gance's *Napoleon* (1927), surrealist works of Luis Buñuel, and especially the films of Sergei Eisenstein. The famous still of the nurse with broken glasses, who was just shot on Odessa steps, was the model for his screaming figures and the painting *Study for the Nurse from Battleship Potemkin* (1957). Emotionally intense and often visually violent works of the masters of the French *nouvelle vague* had a great impact on his work. He admired *Hiroshima Mon Amour* (1959) by Alain Resnais and films of Jean-Luc Godard, *Pierrot-le-Fou* (1965) and *Alphaville* (1965). He esteemed Ingmar Bergman's *Persona* (1966), as well as some films of Michelangelo Antonioni, *Eclipse* (1962) and *The Night* (1961), which in his opinion had a similar atmosphere to his paintings.[3]

At least since the 1960s, Bacon's paintings have been extensively quoted and emulated in art-house cinema, in the films of directors such as Pier Paolo Pasolini, David Cronenberg, and Derek Jarman, who were inspired by his representation of human body and the links between violence and sexuality. Bacon's rejection of storytelling in painting was a narrative model for David Lynch surreal films and Peter Greenaway's *cinema of ideas not plots*, while Bertolucci referred to the scream in the dramatic opening sequence of the *Last Tango in Paris* (1972) and Jerzy Skolimowski based his film *The Shout* (1978) on that sonic aspect of Bacon's painting.

Since the 1980s, Bacon's works progressively started to make its way to popular culture. His paintings are commonly associated with brutality, even when he is shown as one of the greatest painters of the century. This idea is brilliantly expressed in Roman Polanski's *Carnage* (2011), where the character played by Kate Winslet describes Bacon's painting as "cruelty and splendour," just before she throws up over the catalogue of his works, ruining a collection of pricey coffee-table books, strategically displayed as evidence of the host's intellectual concerns. In *Entrapment*, directed by Jon Amiel (1999), the protagonists, two art thieves, arrive at MacDougal's Scottish castle, where he keeps his exquisite collection. The canvas that hangs in the center place of a large room, alongside with masterpieces of Modigliani and other masters of 20th-century art, is Bacon's *Figure in Movement* (1978). Asked by his companion whether he paid for all those paintings, "Mac" (Sean Connery) answers that "they were all paid for with blood," making allusion to the brutality inherent in Bacon's painting.

Bacon's works are frequently employed to illustrate the idea of evil. George Dyer's portrait shown in Christopher Nolan's *Inception* (2010) reminds to Dom Cobb about his involvement in his wife's death. In *Jacob's Ladder* (1990), the protagonist experiences horrific hallucinations of regression from human to a cruel predator. Bacon's paintings were admired and imitated by some of the most vicious villains in cinema, Hannibal Lecter and Joker, and the monsters from John Carpenter's *The Thing* (1982) and Ridley Scott's *Alien* (1979) resemble the figures from his triptychs.

Hannibal Lecter from Jonathan Demme's *Silence of the Lambs* (1991) is a sadistic serial killer and a cannibal; manipulative and extremely intelligent, he trespasses all boundaries of human behaviour and taboos. He acts almost as an animal in the way he murders his victims, often mauling them to death and devouring them, following his lowest instincts. His animal side contrasts with his polished appearance, tastes, and erudition; he is well read and a skillful draftsman; he enjoys renaissance painting and classical music.

He is interned in a top-security prison, in a glass cage, just like some of the screaming popes from Bacon's paintings. Lecter is extremely dangerous, not only physically but also mentally. He is able to kill even from his confinement, as he proves by inciting one of his fellow inmates to commit suicide. After a senator's daughter is captured by a deranged serial killer called Buffalo Bill, he agrees to collaborate with the authorities in order to help them capture the criminal. He is transferred to a Tennessee courthouse, where he is kept in a cage in the middle of a large room and guarded by two police officers. Lecter manages to escape and he kills both guards. He severely disfigures one of them, erasing his features from his face, and he crucifies the other man on the cage, in which he was imprisoned. The result resembles one of Bacon's early intakes on this subject painted in 1933 that represents a ghostly eviscerated creature crucified in a dark unidentified space. In this act of unnecessary cruelty, Lecter dehumanizes his victims, a sign of his absolute lack of empathy and moral convictions. The disembowelled body of the crucified guard, a grotesque homage to Bacon's art, reminds us of a carcass in a slaughterhouse and not human remains. Bacon's crucifixions, often staged in abattoirs like a primitive ritual sacrifice, are expression of an ultimate act of violence, but they lack its original Christian symbolism.

Evil needs to be contrasted with good to be recognized as such; as a result, infinitely evil characters are often paired with immaculate heroes. Without moral norms, it is not possible to distinguish between evil and good. Georges Bataille observed in the preface to *Literature and Evil* (1957) that "the Evil, an acute form of Evil—which it expresses, has a sovereign value for us. But this concept does not exclude morality: on the contrary, it demands hypermorality."[4] In the series of adaptations of *Batman*, Joker is paired with Bruce Wayne/Batman, who never abandons his moral convictions.

Joker is the incarnation of pure evil, he is disguised as a clown, but his smile is in reality a scar (*Dark Knight*, 2008) or a spasmodic grin (*Batman*, 1989). In both films, the figure of the ultimate villain alludes to Francis Bacon. Joker's evil is contagious; it spreads like a virus and infects decent citizens. In *Batman*, he contaminates cosmetics with acid and his victims die with a grin on their faces. In *Dark Knight*, he tries to encourage criminal behaviour in law-abiding citizens and spread the fear. In one of the final scenes, he places bombs on two ferries, one filled with ordinary citizens and the other with convicts, and gives each the opportunity to blow up the other boat. If not, he would detonate both bombs. His plan eventually fails, even though many of the passengers from both boats were eager to commit a massive murder.

Joker succeeds though instigating police officers to betray the city and turning the attorney, Harvey Dent, into a revenge-seeking killer. Harvey's conversion to evil is marked by his physical transformation; he suffers terrible burns to half of his face, while the other half remains intact, as he did not completely abandon his moral values. After his death, Gordon and Batman decide to preserve Dent's memory as a heroic attorney as it would be demoralizing for the people of Gotham and they would possibly lose their faith in the forces of good.

The physical appearance of the protagonists fits into the old aesthetic concept that defines beauty as the sensory embodiment of moral goodness, while ugliness is associated with evil. Joker, interpreted by the late Heath Ledger and the members of his gang, wear grotesque clown masques that resemble faces of the characters from the paintings of Peter Brueghel the Elder (ca. 1525–1569); their scruffiness is matched by their moral decay; while the characters that represent the forces of good, Bruce Wayne (Christian Bale) and Harvey (Aaron Eckhart) are good looking and well dressed.

As Christopher Nolan said in an interview, Joker's looks were inspired by the works of Francis Bacon: "It's really a lot of different things mixed together. Certainly visually, with the makeup, I always had the idea of Francis Bacon paintings and I showed those to Heath and showed those to John Caglione who did the makeup. We were looking at smearing and smudging and caking the makeup on him, doing it in ways that we could degrade the look through the film. There are other influences there as well, but I wanted to point out the Bacon reference here."

In *Dark Knight*, there are other images possibly inspired by Bacon's imagery: the scene when Joker tortures a phoney Batman takes place in an ice-truck full of beef carcasses. This scene recalls a painting of Francis Bacon referred in *Batman*, directed by Tim Burton (1986), and associated with the vicious clown. Joker, played by Jack Nicholson, and his gang rush into the fictitious Fluegelheim Museum in Gotham and they start *improving* the paintings, throwing bright coloured paint and spraying graffiti on the masterpieces of Rembrandt, Renoir, and Degas. Impressionism is commonly regarded as an expression of beauty, luminosity, and joy, contrary to the dark and dramatic canvas that Joker decides to spare. The only place safe from destruction is *Figure with Meat* (1954) by Francis Bacon. He further gives another proof of his artistic taste when he joins Vicky Vale (Kim Basinger) at the table and starts to check her portfolio. While he considers that her fashion shots are "crap," he admits that he admires her photographs of war events and dead bodies. He declares himself as an artist and his disfigured victims as works of art.

Bacon's image of a screaming pope enclosed in a transparent cage and surrounded by sides of beef is the exact opposite of the paintings they have just destroyed. It is based on Velázquez's portrait of Pope Innocent X. Bacon admitted to being obsessed by this painting; he kept several reproductions of it in his studio, and he painted numerous figures inspired by it since the late 1940s (*Head VI*, 1949). What differentiates his rendering of the portrait of the Pope from its original is the expression of fear and pain shown by Bacon's figure; the pope is grabbing the chair and screams. His features are deformed and blurred. He is kept captive in a transparent cage, like a war criminal or a dangerous offender. In the Velázquez's painting, the pope sits confident and relaxed in his chair. He is a representation of power, while Bacon's pope is powerless.

The motif of the scream in Bacon's work is inspired by the screams of the nurse from Eisenstein's 1925 silent film *Battleship Potemkin* and from Poussin's *Massacre of the Innocents* (1626–1627). This frequent theme that represents an abstract idea of violence rather than visual horror was already present in his first paintings, such as *Abstraction from the Human Form* (1936),[5] but it became more noticeable in the 1940s and 1950s, in the series of *Heads* and popes. The lonely screaming figures from his paintings reproduce not only the sensation of sound but also of silence. The lack of sound contributes to the sensation of the uncanny, and, as

David Toop observes in his book, "all silences are uncanny, because we became estranged from absence of sound."[6] The empty desolated spaces and almost monotone dark palette of his works from the 1950s re-create the atmosphere of the night or a nightmare, which Freud linked to irrational fears of childhood.

In his famous essay, Freud describes the uncanny (*Unheimlich*) as a sensation caused by something new or unknown, something that is familiar yet distorted enough to be rendered unfamiliar, so as to produce fear in the observer. According to Freud, this perception belongs to the prehistory of the individual or of the human race. Freud follows Jentsch's definition of the uncanny and points out that "the essential condition for the emergence of the sense of the uncanny is intellectual uncertainty."[7] This kind of rational doubt can be represented as confusion between dream and reality, between animal and human, or between inanimate and human and is present in Bacon's painting. His odd sceneries and surreal figures escape rational understanding and produce an uncanny sensation in the viewer of being trapped in a nightmare.

The element of confusion between reality and dream is also present in Christopher Nolan's *Inception* (2010). The protagonist, Dom Cobb, as played by Leonardo Di Caprio, is a thief who has the ability to steal ideas and valuable information by invading the unconscious minds of his victims while they dream. A Japanese millionaire hires him for an apparently impossible task, *Inception*, which consists of implantation of an idea into a target without his consent. Cobb and his team are able to induce a multilevel "dream inside a dream" using designer drugs. The characters of the film are not always completely aware of whether they are awake or dreaming. In their dreams, they are able to manipulate the laws of physics, turn familiar places unfamiliar, creating spatial paradoxes.

In one of the first scenes, Cobb's wife Mal (Marion Cotillard) looks at a painting of Francis Bacon hung in a bedroom in a Japanese mansion. We will further know that this scene is part of a dream, as Mal is in reality dead and she only exists in Cobb's mind. He performed the act of *Inception* on her, implanting an idea that made her question the reality, until she was unable to distinguish between dream and real life. Eventually she decided to kill herself by jumping from a hotel window on the anniversary of their wedding, perceiving that this was the only way to wake up.

The painting on the wall is *Study for Head of George Dyer* (1967), a portrait of Bacon's lover. It shows his profile, and it is deliberately deformed. Dyer committed suicide in 1971 in a Paris hotel room, ingesting barbiturates and alcohol, on the day of the opening of the retrospective of Bacon's work at Grand Palais. Bacon painted numerous portraits of him, even after his death, so the memory and the image of his late lover were kept alive in his paintings. This tragic event marked Bacon's life and art, and to some extent, he felt guilty for his death. In the same way, Cobb feels responsible for his wife's suicide and he keeps her alive in his dreams.

In the film, people that appear in the dreams are described as projections of the subconscious and are based on the record the dreamer kept of them in his mind. Cobb's projection of Mal is violent and self-destructive; she attacks her husband and attempts to spoil his plans. Even if Bacon always pretended to avoid any kind of Freudian interpretation of his works, he was well aware of the importance of the subconscious in his creative process:

> I really think of myself as a maker of images. The image matters more than the beauty of paint. . . . I suppose I'm lucky in that images just drop in as they were handed down to me. . . . I always think of myself not as much as painter but as a medium for accident and chance . . .[8]

Bacon insisted that his works were a result of unconscious choices and accidents occurred in the studio. In many interviews, he described his *Painting* (1946) as an example of such successful accident, as he started painting a bird of prey, which gradually developed into an umbrella. Bacon maintained that he had no control of how the result would look like and his paintings were created almost unconsciously.

In Adrian Lyne's 1990 film *Jacob's Ladder*, the protagonist Jacob Singer (Tim Robbins) suffers a series of bizarre hallucinations and flashbacks related to his past as a soldier in the Vietnam War. He is often unable to distinguish between reality and nightmare, the familiar sceneries become *unhomely*, and people whom he trusted transform themselves into reptile-human hybrids. The mirages are allegedly caused by an experimental drug called "the ladder" given to the soldiers without their consent in order to improve their performance at war and increase their brutality. In one of the scenes of the film, the drug is described as a trigger that causes "a fast trip straight down the ladder, right to the primal fear, right to the base anger." It permits the fighters to abandon their moral restrains and return to a more primitive form of humanity. Under the effects of "the ladder," the soldiers from Singer's unit attack each other instead of the enemy; the incident results in a gruesome massacre. The scenes of the postwar hallucinations suffered by Jacob were inspired in Francis Bacon's painting. The director used a technique that consists of recording the movements of the body at low frame and then played back, resulting in an uncanny movement that deforms the features and dehumanizes the subjects that appear in Jacob's nightmares.

The first film of the *Alien* series (1979), directed by Ridley Scott, also explores the sense of uncanny characteristic to Bacon's painting. The extraterrestrial monsters are the embodiment of pure evil as they naturally lack moral boundaries, even though they appear to be intelligent forms of life. The aliens are also the perfect product of natural selection, unrepressed by norms imposed by society. Richard Dawkins argued in his *Selfish Gene* (1976) that the definitive sense of life is to transmit genetic material in the maximum possible number of copies. The aliens prey on other organisms, using them as aliment and for their own reproduction, brutally destroying them in the process. They implant an embryo into the human body, that later breaks its way through the chest. They are almost impossible to defeat and their functioning escapes human reason.

Ridley Scott's *Alien* also contains an element of confusion between dream and reality. In the first scene of the film, the crew of the mining space craft *Nostromo* wake up from hibernation, unconscious that they are going to experience a real-life nightmare. *Nostromo*, whose name is an allusion to Joseph Conrad's novel, is deliberately sent to answer a strange SOS signal emitted from a remote planet and to capture the alien organism and bring it to Earth, where it would be examined and possibly used as a weapon. The only member of the crew who is aware of the real purpose of the mission is Ash, who is later revealed to be an android. He is physically identical to a human, but he lacks feelings and any moral principles, just as the aliens. He admits that he admires the creature for its perfection.

The form of the alien in its three stadia of development was designed by the Swiss sculptor H. R. Giger. The "chestbuster," the second stadium was inspired by the *Triptych 1944: Three Figures at the Base of a Crucifixion*, described by John Russell as depiction of pure evil. The alien creature, eyeless head with a mouth full of sharp teeth, bursts from Kane's chest (John Hurt), screams and rushes away, leaving the group in shock. As David J. Skal observed in his book, one of the monsters from John Carpenter's *The Thing* (1982), represented as a creature merged from human and alien cells in the form of a human head on spider legs, could be also inspired by the same canvas.[9]

The 1944 painting is Bacon's first triptych and his first mature work. It represents three semi-human biomorphic figures, inspired by the revengeful Furies from Aeschylus's *Oresteia* and modelled on Picasso semi-abstract works from the 1930s. The three Erinyes are represented as eyeless creatures with screaming mouths full of teeth; their heads are supported on long ostrich-like necks and a shapeless torso, devoid of extremities. There is an element of intellectual uncertainty, whether it is a human or animal figure. The combination of unrecognizable biological form with human features, the scream, and the expression of pain inherent to the theme of crucifixion produce a deeply uncanny sensation in the observer. Bacon painted both human and animal screams and also often represented human faces with animal features. The abundance of atavistic elements in his works is associated with the artist's fascination with the primal side of man. Bacon was interested in Darwin's theory of evolution, zoology, and anthropoid forms of life. He used images of animals, photographs of African wildlife by Peter Beard, and torn leaves with images of apes as source material for his painting of human figures. Bacon's paintings show the essence of the human being, which is not necessarily moral or good.

Charles Darwin in the *Descent of Man* (1871) argued that morality is not naturally inherent to human nature and even the social instincts are evolved. Richard Joyce in his book observes that it is the natural selection "that made us sociable, able to enter into cooperative exchanges, capable of love, empathy and altruism—granting us the capacity to take a direct interest in the welfare of others without a thought of reciprocation and has designed us to think of our relations with one another in moral terms."[10] In the films mentioned in this chapter, the paintings of Francis Bacon were used to illustrate the idea of evil as a form of regression to the primordial instincts, sexual desires, and fears inherited from our nonhuman ancestors. It is the evolutionary process then that made Dom Cobb live with the overwhelming sensation of guilt after his wife's death, and this is why Jacob Singer is tormented by the flashbacks from his unintended killing spree. The psychopathic villains Lecter and Joker, who are emotionally closer to the aliens or the robot Ash, than to human beings, are products of a moral de-evolution to a predator. The extraterrestrial monsters inspired by Bacon's 1944 *Triptych* naturally lack moral boundaries as they did not develop them in a process of natural selection; they epitomize a perfect example of "a mindless voracity, an automatic unregulated gluttony, a ravening undifferentiated capacity for hatred."

NOTES

1. John Russell, *Francis Bacon*, Rev. ed., World of Art Series (New York: Oxford University Press, 1979), 10.

2. "Triptychs . . . are the things I like doing most, and I think this may be related to the thought I've sometimes had of making a film," quoted in David Sylvester, *Looking Back at Francis Bacon* (London: Thames & Hudson, 2000), 100.

3. Frank Maubert, *L'odeur Du Sang Humain Ne Me Quitte Pas Des Yeux: Conversations Avec Francis Bacon* (Paris: Mille et une nuits, 2009).

4. Georges Bataille, *Literature and Evil*, trans. Alastair Hamilton (New York: Marion Boyars, 1985), iv.

5. Michael Peppiatt, *Francis Bacon in the 1950s* (New Haven, CT: Yale University Press, 2006).

6. David Toop, *Sinister Resonance: The Mediumship of the Listener* (New York: Continuum, 2010).

7. Sigmund Freud, *The Uncanny,* trans. David McLintock (London: Penguin, 2003), 124–25.

8. Sylvester, *Looking Back at Francis Bacon*, 185.

9. David J. Skal, *The Monster Show: A Cultural History of Horror*, Rev. ed. (London: Macmillan, 2001), 313.

10. Richard Joyce, *The Evolution of Morality*, Life and Mind (Cambridge, MA: MIT Press, 2006), 222.

CHAPTER 15

Disney's Sorcerers, Magicians, and Wicked Witches and Why Disney's Approach to Evil Spoke to America

Martin J. Manning

What is evil and how does it relate to Disney, the epitome of wholesome living and good thoughts? Quite a bit, actually. A study of Disney the man and the characters he created in his films, both animated and live action, reveals levels of negative actions and deeds completely at odds with the image that Disney has come to represent to a global audience.

Since the early 1920s, Walt Disney's characters have been a part of our culture. From the first simple animation to the elaborate, computer-enhanced feature films of the early years of the 21st century, the Disney image continues to be magical. Generations have grown up on Donald Duck and Mickey Mouse. Today, the Disney characters are recognized as global icons, a source of enchantment and magical wonder to all ages, and now a growing impact of these Disney products in the world. Disney's major overseas businesses include distribution of the company's films and TV products as well as a billion-dollar products merchandise empire that Disney first pioneered with early films such as *Snow White and the Seven Dwarfs*. Its publications are among the most popular worldwide and the Disney logo that accompanies it is instantly recognizable everywhere. In 1984, Disney's revenues from countries outside the United States totaled $142 million, or about 8.4 percent of the company's consolidated revenues of nearly $1.7 billion. Ten years later, overseas revenue totaled approximately $2.4 billion, or 23 percent of total Disney revenues of $10.1 billion. This was a growth of 30 percent for revenues outside the United States and includes revenues from Tokyo Disneyland but not Disneyland Paris (Euro Disney). In fiscal 2011, the net income attributable to

Disney was a record $4.8 billion, an increase of 21 percent over 2010, and the revenue was a record $40.9 billion, up 7 percent from previous year.[1]

Yet the man who created the image, and the company that carried on his work after his death in 1966, was the opposite of the avuncular persona that audiences got to know through his visits to Disneyland, the theme park he created in Anaheim, California, and on Sunday night television.

"EVIL" MAN

Disney was an official FBI informant (Special Agent in Charge) in Hollywood who reported several of his colleagues and workers as possible Communist sympathizers. The Communist Party had thoroughly infiltrated Hollywood during the 1930s and 1940s. Disney participated actively in the movement to rid the film industry of such Communist influence in the 1940s.

Then half of his artists went on strike in 1941 against him, protesting his dictatorial style, the low wages and lack of credit for their work, and his refusal to bargain with the Screen Cartoonists Guild as his employees' representative. It was this strike that, in a sense, changed Disney's focus from animation to what can best be described as "spying": he became an FBI informant around 1940 in which he reportedly consented to provide the bureau with the names of writers, actors, technicians, and union leaders whom he suspected of subversion.

Disney characterized the strike as part of a Communist conspiracy to dominate the Hollywood film industry. This was really the turning point in Disney as evil. The creator of such comforting images as Disney and his other animated characters that became global icons was actually quite embittered by this strike. In fact, it can be argued that this strike ended what had been, up to 1941, Disney's Golden Age.

In 1944, Disney joined a group of fellow conservatives, including John Wayne and Gary Cooper, to form the Motion Picture Alliance for the Preservation of American Ideals (MPA); he agreed to serve as one of the organization's first vice presidents in which he helped draft the alliance's "Statement of Principles," which pledged the organization to fight the film industry's "domination by Communists, radicals, and crackpots." Disney also requested a congressional investigation of Communist influence in the film industry, which did happen in 1947.

Disney used his testimony before the House Un-American Activities Committee (HUAC) on October 27, 1947, as a "friendly" witness. He named names, particularly a few who he blamed for the strike and for other problems that befell his studio. These included the Cartoonists' Guild, and the League of Women Shoppers, a nonpolitical consumers' organization that was founded on the principles that working conditions were important considerations in the purchase of goods, which supported the Screen Cartoonists Guild during the 1941 strike and announced it would not patronize any theaters where Disney movies were being shown until his dispute with labor was settled. Disney misspoke in his testimony, referring to the League of Women Voters, to whom he apologized.[2]

In 1954, an FBI memo (dated 12/16/54 to FBI director J. Edgar Hoover) recommended Disney be promoted to full Special Agent in Charge (SAC) status because of his position as the "foremost producer of cartoon films in the motion picture industry and his prominence and wide acquaintanceship in film production matters, it is believed that he can be of valuable assistance to this office" but two years later, Disney himself suffered from the anti-Communist hysteria when an FBI memorandum [March 21, 1956, FBI memo] questioned his loyalty, citing Disney as a sponsor of rallies staged by allegedly subversive organizations in 1943 and 1944. These included a "Night of the Americas" event with Walt Disney as one of the sponsors; it honored Vicente Lombardo Toledano, president of the Confederation of Latin American Workers. The other was the Art Young Memorial with Disney once again as one of the sponsors; it was sponsored by "New Masses."[3]

When this mistake was discovered, FBI director J. Edgar Hoover tried to make amends to Disney with a letter that praised his contributions as an American but Disney remained unmoved; he later portrayed the FBI in an unflattering light in several productions (e.g., *Moon Pilot*, *That Darn Cat*) produced by his studio.

DISNEY VILLAINS

Evil also spoke in Disney characters and later in the criticism the company took for character portrayals or "misrepresentation of ideals," beginning with his early success in adapting fairy tales as animated features. Disney was just one of many authors, folklorists, playwrights, and illustrators who first discovered traditional folk and fairy tales then embraced the parts of the story they liked and discarded anything else that took away from the major point or focus that they wanted to make in retelling their theme. In fact, many of Disney's early animated features were based on the fairy tales he heard as a child and then as an adult in Aesop's Fables, Hans Christen Andersen, and the Grimm Brothers. Disney used them as the basis for feature films and even shorter cartoons. Indeed, Disney's versions of some of these stories are sometimes better known than the originals, especially in the United States. Not without truth, many Disney critics have noted how stories that Disney wanted to bring to the screen underwent a metamorphosis (Disneyfied) during the production process which usually involved cleaning up the original story with a happy ending often not present in the original tale.

In *Snow White and the Seven Dwarfs* (1937), Disney deleted much of the complicated ritual of the folk story, such as the magical birth of Snow White, the anonymity of the dwarfs, and fleshed it out by adding a love affair, providing each dwarf with a separate personality, and giving the whole a pleasing glow of charm and romanticism fairly distant from the grim detail and horrifying ending of the original tale. He diluted a psychologically charged tale to serve his own needs: a film that generated good will and optimism.[4] Other fairy tales that received the Disney treatment, all but obliterating their rather grim and often tragic originals would include *The Little Mermaid* and *Sleeping Beauty*.

Disney produced his first cartoon series, "Alice in Cartoonland" (Alice Comedies), in 1923, then, five years later, he created his most famous character, Mickey Mouse. Then, in 1937, Disney had his first great critical and financial success with *Snow White and Seven Dwarfs*. With this film, he pioneered the marketing of film merchandise, which continues today under ominous conditions: Walt Disney Company's rigid control of copyright and image. During this same period, Disney launched other successful cartoon characters, including Donald Duck and Pluto.

Classic Disney includes characters that are usually quite predictable as Disney animators followed careful formulas in creating characters and stories, which typically revolved around heroes and heroines who are strikingly beautiful/handsome, with an upper-class aristocratic background. There is always a villain, who is typically the opposite of the hero/heroine, often ugly, extremely fat or extremely thin, with exaggerated facial features. Think Cruella de Vil.[5]

Disney villains in particular are some of the most exciting and memorable characters in popular culture. The first was Peg Leg Pete, a surly strongman with a cigar and a wooden leg, who made his debut with the Alice series of shorts, 1923–1927, but the first Disney villain to achieve real stardom was the Big Bad Wolf in *Three Little Pigs* (1933). Four years later, after he achieved great advances in story and in animation, Disney introduced, in *Snow White and the Seven Dwarfs*, the wicked queen with her vengeful stalking of the innocent title character. From that film on, Disney presented a gallery of intimidating rascals, running the whole range from comic to truly evil.

The earliest characters were often used as propaganda, such as the dwarfs (*Snow White and the Seven Dwarfs*) who were commissioned by the National Film Board of Canada in *The Seven Wise Dwarfs* (1941) to invest the diamonds from their mine in war savings, and in *All Together* (1942), also for the National Film Board, in which they sold war bonds. However, the true wartime Disney star of the war effort was Donald Duck. Along with *Der Fuhrer's Face*, the cranky web-footed aquatic appeared in all manner of short films.

During World War II, three Disney short subjects served as anti-Nazi propaganda but they did not use the major Disney characters. However, evil was specifically defined during World War II when the clear-cut villains were the Nazis and later the Japanese, the enemy that Disney used incessantly, often in stereotypes that became an embarrassment after the war, a fact not uncommon to propaganda films produced by other Hollywood studios, as well, to support the war effort. Many of these still cause the viewer to cringe at the blatant stereotyping and racism!

Yet the image that Disney always wanted to project in his films was one of wholesomeness and family but these same films, both cartoons and real-life adventures, have contained characters that represent evil. Whether you love or hate Disney, it cannot be denied that his filmmakers and animators came up with great villains through their moviemaking history.

Start with Mickey Mouse. Ironically, Disney's most famous creation is actually based on a rodent, more specifically a rat, one of the most loathsome and scary of all mammals. Yet this cartoon character has become a global icon, recognized worldwide. How many believers in the Disney fantasy know that it is actually a rat, which is definitely not lovable and certainly not funny?

A list of the most repugnant of the cartoon canon would include Stromboli (*Pinocchio*, 1940), a completely heartless showman who burns his marionettes for firewood when they have grown too old to perform. This film was based on a well-known fairy tale. It was another story that Disney changed from the original tale, which dealt with fundamental issues of trust and the nature of humanity, yet he still retained some very harrowing scenes. For author and critic John Culhane, the most upsetting moment in the whole picture was when the Coachman was testing each donkey to see if any remnants of the boy remained. He asked one donkey what his name might be. The trembling voice replied, "Alexander." The gruff Coachman flung him aside, yelling, "This one can still talk! Put him back."[6]

Bambi's (1942) unseen killer, the huntsman, who is responsible for the death of Bambi's mother, initiates one of the most heart-rending scenes in a Disney film, animated or live action, in a sequence that is still debated among parents and educators as to whether such a scene is too disturbing for children in an otherwise beautiful film. Also, the image of Bambi, as a gentle, cuddlesome little deer, is completely out of sync with the real one, as any driver can testify who has had one dart in front of their automobile, particularly at night, when the driver spots one in the headlights. Real deer, under these circumstances, cause extensive damage to cars and even serious injury or death to the driver and other passengers.

Another scene that is still scary is the imprisonment of little *Dumbo*'s (1941) mother. She is eventually released but the sequence is not comforting. This signifies the mother as prisoner. This is another Disney image that makes no attempt to even portray the real thing. Elephants are not cuddly animals; they are huge and fearsome, if provoked, and nothing like the Disney cartoon.

Brer Fox and Brer Bear (*The Song of the South*) are often considered the "villains" in this combination animated—live-action film but the film was critically attacked for its interpretation of the Uncle Remus tales which were significantly distorted in the Disney version and which were highly selective in recreating only a few of the more than 100 original stories. Then there were the condescending stereotypes in which the blacks were portrayed in this film, beginning with the character of Uncle Remus who appeared more as an Uncle Tom or a racist stereotype than the dignified storyteller he was in the original Joel Chandler Harris book. The film was withdrawn from circulation in the late 1950s but it reappeared on video and excerpts are still included in Disney compilations.[7]

Then there is the animal-hating Cruella de Vil (*101 Dalmatians*, 1961), perhaps Disney's greatest villainess since the Wicked Queen in *Snow White and the Seven Dwarfs*. According to Neil Sinyard, "one of Alfred Hitchcock's golden rules for successful moviemaking was: the stronger the villain, the stronger the picture. Disney would support that, with one important modification: the stronger the villainess. Disney's greatest wrongdoers are almost all women and if 101 Dalmatians is remembered with a shiver of pleasurable affection, the reason is the character of Cruella de Vil."[8]

The manipulative Ursula (*The Little Mermaid*, 1989) was another great Disney villainess, in a story that romanticized what was actually a very dark Hans Christian Andersen fairy tale, another instance of Disney giving the fairy tales a happy ending while removing all the ugly parts of the original. Yet one could also argue that the so-called heroine Ariel is also a villain since it is her defiance of authority which leads her to Ursula in the first place. In fact, Ariel is quite unlikable, an irritant actually, who flaunts the rules and parental authority; she was definitely not a Snow White or Cinderella but then those two characters often appeared too good to be true!

The greedy Governor Ratcliffe (*Pocahontas*, 1995) who attacks the Native Americans for gold he desperately wants is usually depicted as a nasty, evil character. Here again, Ratcliffe was not the real villain in this animated film. The portrayal of women, especially the interpretation of their bodies, depicted an unreal presentation of the human female form and represented a bad image for young girls. Then there were the inaccuracy of the historical facts and, finally, another racist and stereotypical portrayal of Native Americans.

Other dastardly villains include the evil sorcerer Jafar (*Aladdin*, 1992); Shan-Ya (*Mulan*, 1998), the ruthless leader of the Huns determined to conquer China; and Scar (*The Lion King*, 1994) who kills his own brother in an attempt to become King of the Pride Lands.

Then there are the scoundrels from such classic films as *Peter and the Wolf* (1946), *Lady and the Tramp* (1955), *Robin Hood* (1973), and *Dumbo*, but film audiences really enjoy a scoundrel as opposed to a villain. It brings out the sly, wink-wink, catch-me-if-you-can mischief maker in us.

Yet Disney also created memorable villains in his post–World War II live-action films, like the gold-digging fiancée (*The Parent Trap*, both versions, 1961 and 1998), the pirates (*Swiss Family Robinson*, 1960; *Pirates of the Caribbean*, 2003), the bankers (*Mary Poppins*, 1964), and even adult authority figures (veterinarian father, *Three Lives of Thomasina*, 1963; Aunt Polly, *Pollyanna*, 1960) whose evil demeanor is more perceived by the children in the film although their actual positive qualities are seen by the end of the story. But children themselves were often the villains.

Children as villains? Disney films are populated with child actors yet they are not always nice. Two examples will suffice. The youngest son in *Swiss Family Robinson*, Kevin Corcoran as Francis Robinson, actually puts the family in danger on several occasions. He constantly wanders away from the family quarters, disobeying his parents, to play with animals that in any other situation would be in a zoo and he constantly questions situations not for his knowledge. He is rather loathsome compared to his two brothers in how he conducts himself and you actually find yourself rooting (wishing?) that either one of the animals or a particular bloodthirsty pirate will take him away. While the pirates are a looming threat that the viewer knows will eventually confront the family at the end, Francis is present throughout (and always irritating!).

Even more dangerous, and actually quite chilling for a Disney film, is the young girl, Mary McDhui in *Three Lives of Thomasina*, who declares her father dead to her after he refuses to cure her cat, Thomasina. As her depression worsens, she will have nothing more to do with her father, telling others, "My father's dead," and, "My daddy's dead. I killed him." At the same time, her young friends successfully plot to end the father's veterinary practice. Much of this film is intensely psychological, based on the Paul Gallico story, with the motherless daughter and the widowed veterinarian father who loves his daughter but has seemingly closed himself off to everyone else in his village.

Even one of Disney's best-loved films, *The Parent Trap* (1961 and its 1998 remake), has the viewer questioning a situation in which twins are separated from birth and do not know of each other's existence or that of their other parent until they happen to meet at summer camp. What subversive reason do the parents have in keeping the daughters apart? The film makes you believe that it was to keep the parents from seeing each other ever again, but to keep sisters from ever seeing each other? Thank God for summer camp!

After Walt Disney's death, his company produced a compilation of his greatest villains. It aired several times on television.

Wonderful World of Disney: Disney's Greatest Villains. Producer: Ron Miller Prepared for TV by George Petlowany, Bob King, Jim Love [and] Irwin Kostal. Airdates: May 15, 1977; June 11, 1978; October 26, 1980; May 21, 1983.

This show was an edited version of the 1955–1956 season episode entitled "Our Unsung Villains." For the later reruns, the program was edited to feature scenes from current Disney films.

The show emphasizes that every hero needs a villain for balance; without them, there would be no heroes. There are clips from numerous Disney films.

IMAGE REPRESENTATION

Disney was often accused of practicing forms of censorship in his company's adaptations of materials from other sources, such as the films he adapted from fairy tales (*Snow White, Pinocchio; Sleeping Beauty*, 1959; *Cinderella*, 1950). Later, in animated films made after Disney's death, there was something like *Pocahontas* in which Disney played freely with the historical fact, such as an important one that the heroine in the story converted from paganism to Christianity, or that the Native Americans caricatured so freely in the cartoon film were actually dignified and brave warriors who were defending their land against encroaching white "civilizers."

Yet the heaviest criticism leveled toward Disney has been the distorted version of femininity presented in Disney movies. The viewers, often young girls, are exposed to highly sexualized female characters who always seem to be in need of a brave male to rescue them or enhance their feeling of self-worth. Such examples: Snow White cleans the dwarfs' cottage to ingratiate herself with the little men who are keeping her safe; Ariel gives up her voice to win the prince in *The Little Mermaid; Mulan* almost single-handedly wins the war only to return home to be romanced; and Belle in *Beauty and the Beast* (1991) endures an abusive and violent beast in order to redeem him.

Then there are the representations of race and ethnic cultures that Disney insults to the point of stereotyping and caricature. Blacks especially are poorly treated, as appeared so blatantly in *Song of the South*, but there were others, such as the "jive" crows in *Dumbo* who appear as little more than Amos 'n' Andy caricatures, and the human-wannabe orangutans in *Jungle Book* (1967). Also, they are not a lot of them, especially in the animated features produced in Disney's lifetime.

Witness such characters as the irresponsible Chihuahuas in *Lady and the Tramp* and in *Oliver and Company* (1988); Latinos and African Americans who are depicted as street-gang thugs in *The Lion King*; Asians who are stereotyped as treacherous Siamese cats in *Lady and the Tramp*; Arabs who continually characterized as barbarians in *Aladdin*; and Native Americans who are still rendered as savages, starting with *Peter Pan* (1953) and later in *Pocahontas*.

CRITICISM AND OPPOSITION FOR CHARACTER PORTRAYALS AND PRODUCT CONTENT

Not surprising, Disney's image as a promoter of wholesome family entertainment has come under attack from religious groups who often see images or intents that really may not be there. In 1997, the Southern Baptist Convention (SBC), with over 16 million members, challenged the Disney Company over the "unchristian and immoral material" they claimed that Disney was promoting in American homes as "family entertainment." One target was ABC-TV's Ellen DeGeneres' open lesbian show; ABC is a subsidiary of the Disney Company. SBC actually had a lot of problems with their perceptions of homosexuality in Disney films and even in the theme parks, where they claimed, among other charges, that Disney sponsored "Gay Days" at the parks and that staff portraying the much-loved characters (e.g., Mickey Mouse, Minnie Mouse, Donald Duck, Snow White, Cinderella) were often gay themselves. Out of all this, SBC and other religious, tax-exempt groups such as the Assemblies of God, the Catholic League, and the American Family Association, started a boycott of Disney products and its subsidiaries "for abandoning the commitment to strong moral values" and "to return to the values that strengthen and build this nation, such as honesty, respect, integrity, decency and trust." However, there have been different claims about its effectiveness.[9]

An earlier controversy was over the Disney film, *Priest* (1994) in which a young priest, torn between his vocation and his secret life as a homosexual with a gay lover, is frowned upon by the Catholic Church. The Southern Baptists protested what they perceived as not just evil in the plot but an abominable lifestyle while the Catholic Church, including the Knights of Columbus, condemned the film in which the young priest is seen in gay bars and the older priest, the pastor, lives openly in the rectory with his housekeeper. Actually, the priesthood itself was savagely lampooned in this film and the real villain was the hypocrisy of the unseen Catholic hierarchy.[10]

After Disney's death, his empire became a global phenomenon (television, music, theater productions of its films, theme parks) but it further generated its negative image (another form of evil) of iron-clad copyright control and expensive lawsuits to any perceived violators of its intellectual property.

NOTES

1. Robert A. Iger, *Walt Disney Company Fiscal Year 2011 Annual Financial Report and Shareholder Letter* (Burbank, CA: Walt Disney Company, 2012), 1, https://docs.google.com/gview?url=http://dapsmagic.com/news/wp-content/uploads/2012/01/WDC-10kwrap-2011.pdf&chrome=true (accessed May 12, 2013).

2. Walt Disney's testimony in United States Congress House Committee on Un-American Activities, *Hearings Regarding the Communist Infiltration of the Motion Picture Industry*, vol. 2, 83 (Washington, DC: US Government Printing Office, 1947).

3. Illustrations in Marc Eliot, *Walt Disney: Hollywood's Dark Prince—a Biography* (Secaucus, NJ: Carol Publishing Group, 1993). Eliot's book, which achieved a certain notoriety, is an "expose" biography that delves into Disney's work as an FBI informant, his alleged anti-Semitism and anti-Communism, and his antilabor management style.

4. M. Thomas Inge, "Walt(Er) (Elias) Disney," in *American Writers for Children, 1900–1960*, ed. John Cech (Detroit: Gale Research, 1983), 22.

5. Janet Wasko, *Understanding Disney: The Manufacture of Fantasy* (Cambridge, UK: Polity; Malden, MA: Blackwell, 2001), 115.

6. Ollie Johnston and Frank Thomas, *The Disney Villain* (New York: Hyperion, 1993), 71. This is actually the first book that explores the villains, for many Disney fans the most interesting characters in many of the Disney films.

7. Wasko, *Understanding Disney: The Manufacture of Fantasy*, 140.

8. Neil Sinyard, *The Best of Disney* (Greenwich, CT: Twin Books; Portland House: Distributed by Crown Publishers, 1988), 94.

9. Wasko, *Understanding Disney: The Manufacture of Fantasy*, 214.

10. Debate on Disney continues. Other titles of interest on the subject of Disney as "evil" include the following: Brenda Ayres, *The Emperor's Old Groove: Decolonizing Disney's Magic Kingdom* (New York: P. Lang, 2003); Henry A. Giroux and Grace Pollock, *The Mouse That Roared: Disney and the End of Innocence*, 2nd student ed. (Lanham, MD: Rowman & Littlefield Publishers, Inc., 2010); Jamey Heit, *Vader, Voldemort and Other Villains: Essays on Evil in Popular Media* (Jefferson, NC: McFarland, 2011). A different approach is taken by Douglas Brode, *From Walt to Woodstock: How Disney Created the Counterculture* (Austin: University of Texas Press, 2004). Brode believes that no other filmmaker has had such a deep and lasting impact on American popular culture as has Disney.

CHAPTER 16

Bad Psychiatrists in *Batman*:
A Mirror into a Murderer's Mind?

Sharon Packer

Midnight. Midsummer. A movie mall. A man slips out of the shadows. His gas mask hides his face. Metal body armor covers neck and groin, limbs, and torso. The gunman points, shoots. Gas canisters roll down the aisles. Smoke spreads through the theater.

The scene recollects William Castle–style special effects, from the 1950s.[1] Few people believed it was for real. Then chaos erupts.

Twelve people die, including a child. A pregnant woman loses her baby—and permanent use of her legs. The *Batman* movie massacre was one of America's worst mass murders.[2]

The paragraph above is *not* a recap of an action-adventure movie trailer. It is *not* a screen scene from a police procedural. This was reality, albeit a sad and scary reality that occurred in Colorado, in July 2012. These events *did not* occur at Columbine, Colorado, which had been the site of a high school shoot-up that happened a mere 10 miles away. This massacre took place in Aurora, in a seemingly ordinary suburb that will never seem ordinary again. Sad to say, evil occurs in everyday life in America, and is not merely a figment of a single individual's twisted imagination. Evil impacts everyone.

What was inside the mind of the murderer? What motivates a man to shoot women, children, family men, a teenage boyfriend, a mother's son? We may never know the whole truth, even after the trials are over. We do know that this horrific event happened at a late-night screening of a *Batman* movie, and therein may lay some clues.

The suspect allegedly identified himself as the Joker, Batman's historic archenemy.[3] The Joker wears signature green and violet, and sports a slimy, over-sized, unchanging grin. Half a year later, at the trial about the shooter's sanity, we learned that he filled his rented room with *Batman* memorabilia and that he literally was a "die-hard" *Batman* fan.[4]

In the previous *Batman* blockbuster, the one that starred the now-deceased Heath Ledger, the Joker ditched his customary costume and dressed in drag, in a nurse's uniform. The scene was striking: Joker was visiting D.A. Harvey Dent, who was resting in the hospital, recuperating from the death-defying explosion that scarred his soul as much as his face. Dent turned into the villainous Two-Face after that event, and then devoted himself to seeking revenge on Batman.

In this hospital scene, the Joker strolls through the halls, pushing his way through packed wards. He exits the hospital complex calmly, still wearing a white nurse's uniform. A starched nurse's cap perches atop his head. Once outside, the Joker presses a remote that he holds in his hand and ignites explosives that he hid inside the building. He glances back as he walks away, shrugs his shoulders, and moves on. The building blows up in the background.

Curiously, the mother of the Colorado shooting suspect is also a nurse. Even more curiously, she showed no surprise when authorities arrived and suggested that her son might be a murderer. Is this correspondence a coincidence, or a chance correlation, or does some meaning lie beneath the surface? At this point, no one knows. Yet we do know of many, many correspondences between *Batman*'s bad characters and a few facts concerning the Colorado movie massacre.

We know that the troubled young neuroscience student planned and plotted months ahead, ordering weapons, ammunition, and combat apparatus, well in advance of that dreadful day. Those who know more about the expansive *Batman* universe—which exists in comics, film, TV shows, cartoons, graphic novels, video games, children's toys, Halloween costumes, school lunch boxes, pencil cases, and much more—may also know that many sinister psychiatrists and deranged neuroscientists populate *Batman* stories. It is easy to understand how an unstable mind might gravitate to stories about powerful but pernicious mental health specialists, especially when that unstable person is studying the neuroscience of schizophrenia himself.

In psychiatric practice, we sometimes encounter unstable persons who develop a "psychotic identification" with fictional characters. Their ego boundaries blur. Distinguishing a hazy sense of self from well-defined fantasy actors becomes an impossible chore. Most people can draw a line between themselves and fictional roles seen on-screen—but not everyone can. Spectators typically identify with specific actors as the movie plays, "suspending disbelief" and temporarily accepting fiction as fact. Once the credits roll, and lights turn on, most audience members return to reality and separate themselves from the screen.

A person whose mind is disintegrating into psychosis may not be able to make this shift, and might adopt those easily identifiable identities from the drama. One might go so far as to announce that he is "the Joker," as happened in Aurora, Colorado. If that particular troubled person is an aspiring neuroscientist, and one who wants to research serious psychiatric disorders (as is the case with the murder suspect), he can find a host of villainous psychiatrists and neuroscientists in the *Batman* universe. In fact, I cannot think of any series of stories, novels, or comics that includes more sinister psychiatrists than *Batman.* New sinister psychiatrists pop up on a regular basis, with Dr. Meredith from February 2013 being the latest.

In the hours that followed the summer shootings, much was made of the fact that suspect James Holmes identified himself to the police as the Joker. Press reports (and photos) emphasized the suspect's orange hair, taking that as confirmation that he did indeed identify with the Joker— even though the Joker has green hair. For the moment, we can excuse the press's errors about comic book iconography, and examine the many other reasons why this Joker identity could be an important link to evil in American pop culture.

Although the Joker is neither a psychiatrist nor a neuroscientist, the Joker has multiple links to both psychiatry and psychosis. Joker had extensive contact with mental health professionals and spent much time in psychiatric facilities, so that we wonder if the Joker's secondary career as a mental patient meant as much to the suspect as Joker's primary criminal career. Joker's criminal capers drive many plots, and often act as the "MacGuffin" of some *Batman* stories, but the Joker's psychiatric escapades introduce spicy subplots that pepper *Batman* comics, graphic novels, and, most recently, video games.

Specifically, after the Joker is arrested for his crimes, he is confined to Arkham Asylum for the Criminally Insane. He is sprung by an attractive young psychiatrist who is assigned to treat him in his prison cell. The fictional Dr. Harlene Quinzel falls in love with her grinning patient, even though he chokes her and mistreats her, and even though professional ethics forbid romantic encounters between doctor and patient. At the time of this writing, there is a reasonable chance that Holmes himself will enter a forensic facility for the so-called criminally insane, just like his mentor, the Joker. Still, the fate that awaits Holmes is still far away, especially since his January 2013 hearing found him capable of standing trial.

It is interesting to speculate about Holmes's reaction to the love-smitten psychiatrist who abandons her post as an Arkham medical staff member and joins the Joker. Dr. Quinzel disposed of her white coat, turning into a harlequin, and adopting the name "Harley Quinn." This one-time high school gymnast becomes Joker's helpmate and his acrobatic partner in crime. In later stories, Harley Quinn befriends another *Batman* villainess, Poison Ivy. Ivy is an equally evil but stunningly beautiful botanist, and a redheaded one at that. Poison Ivy's face and physical form are modeled after Bette Paige, the immodest pinup model from the 1950s. Poison Ivy's red hair reminds us of the redheaded prostitutes that the suspect preferentially patronized.[5]

As time goes on, Quinn attempts to abandon her evil ways, and joins a team of high-minded, high-powered female superheroes. At this moment, we are left wondering what the disturbed young man was thinking when he sought treatment from a female psychiatrist at his university's Student Health Service. Did he harbor secret fantasies that his doctor would join him after he sent her a package about his plans? Alternatively, was he chagrined that his disturbed mental status was not taken seriously enough by his doctor? Alternatively, perhaps his mind was working well enough for him to hope that she could stop him. Unfortunately, the university mail system failed, and his package of deadly plans was not delivered until the event was over.

Right now, we can only speculate about what lurked within the dark recesses of James Holmes's mind, and assumptions made without solid facts rarely do anyone any good, not even curious readers. So let us return to the imaginary *Batman* universe, where we can turn the comic book pages, to see the scheming but plain-looking young medical student who steps up to the plate after Harley Quinn departs. That student is Alyse Sinner. Her name is sometimes spelled Alice Synner. Either way, she is aptly named. Appearance-wise, Alice-Alyse is no *femme fatale*, but mentally, her mind is as dark as the darkest shadows from 1940s-era *film noir*.

While working at Arkham Asylum for the Criminally Insane, Alyce befriends Dr. Jeremiah Arkham. He becomes her mentor. She conducts a romance with this older psychiatrist, and encourages his evil activities, both overt and covert. Her paramour secretly calls himself the Black Mask. As the Black Mask, he organizes other evil scientists into a collective. When he is treating, or mistreating, his patients at Arkham Asylum, Black Mask is none other than Dr. Jeremiah Arkham, a direct descendent of the deranged clan that started the Arkham Asylum.

As the Black Mask, Dr. Jeremiah Arkham collects a cadre of evil scientists: The Reaper, Dr. Hugo Strange, Dr. Death, and Fright (Dr. Linda Frittawa), an albino. The hard-hearted, redheaded botanist, Poison Ivy, is noticeably absent from this collective. This "Ministry of Science" should not be confused with Fritz Lang's *noir* classic, *Ministry of Fear* (1944)— even though *Batman*'s creators were strongly influenced by *film noir*'s aesthetic and by Lang's *Metropolis* (1926) in particular. Bob Kane specifically based Gotham City on the *Metropolis*'s towering Art Deco buildings, and the dark shadows that they cast over the deep caverns that lay between.

In *Batman*, Ministry of Science members merge their minds and collaborate on evil deeds. Their goals form a sharp contrast with the goals of the DC comics' Justice League or Justice Society. In those organizations, superheroes join forces to help humankind and improve society.

Some Ministry scientists are starkly mad, while others, such as the Reaper, were deceived by other evil-minded Ministry members. The Reaper is a rageful Holocaust survivor who does not set out to commit evil acts. Yet he is so ensnared in the web of his rage that he becomes easy prey for villains who lure him into their fold. Most of the other Ministry of Science members are stereotypical science fiction "mad scientist" villains. They recollect the fact that mad scientists were the most common type of science fiction villain until the mid-to-late 20th century.

Those stereotyped mad scientists fell out of favor as the 20th century progressed, and as scientific advances became less frightening and more understandable to more people. Education increased among Americans, thanks in no small part to the GI bill that sent veterans to college, where science classes were readily accessible. In the 1950s, there was Sputnik and the Race to Space, and Dr. Jonas Salk's miraculous vaccine to prevent polio. TV broadcasts of the Cape Canaveral space shuttle launch, plus TV's popular "Mr. Science" children's show, turned scientists into kindly creatures to be admired, even emulated, rather than feared. Most importantly, the successes of Alfred Hitchcock's *Psycho* (1961) and John Carpenter's *Halloween* (1978) proved that murderous mental patients were scarier than the mad scientists that populated the screen earlier in the century.[6] *Batman* stories added a bit of both.

As the asylums emptied in the late 1950s, thanks to the introduction of Thorazine (chlorpromazine), mental patients suddenly headed for home. Thorazine stopped the disturbing and sometimes dangerous voices and visions of schizophrenia. Until Thorazine's invention, the seriously mentally ill seemed destined to spend their lives locked inside state hospitals. Then Thorazine opened the floodgates and largely negated the need for long-term institutionalization.

The push for "deinstitutionalization" gained momentum. The goal was to send patients home—but not everyone had homes, and not everyone had neighbors that welcomed them back. So more ex-mental patients headed for the street or the shelters. Many meandered into public parks, after being rejected by family or returning to uncaring or fractured families. Deinstitutionalization was eventually deemed a naive move, but its impact remained, both in public mental health policy and in movie themes.

Fears of being attacked by a maniac—or an escaped mental patient who left the wards before being completely cured—became a more realistic fear than ever before. The ever-inventive *Batman* writers tapped into these fears, and created ever more intense villains. They turned science fiction's time-honored mad scientists into escaped psychiatric patients that had been locked in Arkham Asylum for the Criminally Insane, until they wrangled their way out of the locked wards, to menace society again. A prime example was the Joker, who seduced his psychiatrist and convinced her to free him from Arkham.

Batman story arcs reflect these fears and parallel other shifts in psychiatric theory and practice. Two decades earlier, in the late 1930s, electroconvulsive therapy (ECT) arrived in America and introduced an era of machine-mediated neuropsychiatric care. (Hydrotherapy, such as that depicted in a 1909 Georges Méliès movie,[7] cannot correctly be classified as mechanical or technical, even though its props resemble primitive Jacuzzis.) Shock therapy uses dramatic and potentially dangerous apparatus. The invention of the electroencephalogram (EEG) that traces brain waves made ECT possible. ECT machinery proved well suited for gadget geeks like Bruce Wayne, Batman, and Alfred the Butler, as well as the villains who oppose them and mechanically minded comics fans that follow their escapades.

Brain machines proliferate in *Batman*, and understandably so. In a 1990s cartoon, Dr. Hugo Strange uses brain machines to extract memories and steal identities. World War II–era "Japanazi" Dr. Daka drains brains and makes zombies via a brain machine that anticipates the apparatus of contemporary transcutaneous magnetic stimulation (TCMS). Characters such as Skulldugger, Riddler, Mad Hatter, and even aliens have access to brain machines. When aliens extract Bruce Wayne's memories, they reexperience the impact of his losing his parents, but cannot tolerate the pain and begin to self-mutilate, like real-life persons with borderline personality disorders who also endured severe personal trauma. It is striking to see 70-year-old *Batman* serials and their eerily premonitions about modern-day neuroscience.

Mad scientists—or simply mean scientists—are abundant in 20th-century films (and in 19th-century literature). Since these characters are so common, it is unreasonable to suggest that such characters automatically unravel minds. However, if a mind is already starting to unravel, that mind could overreact, and these hostile characters could tip the balance, as shown by numerous studies. If a neuroscience student senses that he is going mad himself, he might be attracted to bad role models in his chosen profession. Such a person could be unduly influenced by *Batman*, and go so far as to develop a special interest that borders on obsession. He might even dye his hair orange, identify himself as the Joker, and maybe even open fire on *Batman* fans that flock to opening night of the latest *Batman* movie.

Arkham Asylum psychiatric staff and members of Black Mask's Ministry of Science are a treasure trove of bad examples of psychiatrists, neuroscientists, and other scientists that might "speak" to someone of this ilk. Still, I emphasize that these over-the-top figures appeal to the public at large. Their appeal is not at all limited to the fringes of society. It is the general public that still buys *Batman* comics, stands in line to see *Batman* films, dresses their children in *Batman* costumes on Halloween, and packs school lunches in *Batman* lunch boxes. Let us not forget that Batman remains the most popular superhero of all time. He has stayed "alive" since the start of the superhero genre, and is one of only three superheroes that survived nonstop.

More than any other superhero, Batman persisted when interest in superheroes waned in the mid-1950s and when anticomics crusades almost annihilated superheroes. *Batman* owes his longevity to his ability to function as a detective as much as a superhero. Because he is completely human, and owes his physical agility, martial arts training, and mental maneuvering to exercise and perseverance—rather than extraterrestrial origin or life-threatening radiation exposure—his special powers seem to be within the reach. That makes it easier to identify with Batman. In addition, Bruce Wayne's handsome face, generous heart, and extreme wealth make him appealing in other ways, to both men and women.

Batman comics revolve around Bruce Wayne, who inherited his family's wealth after he was orphaned as a boy. Bruce perfected skills to fight crime, and used his money for crime-fighting gadgets, such as the Batmobile. The orphan theme holds special appeal for children, even though children are no longer *Batman*'s prime audience. Orphan stories address children's fears of abandonment, as they wonder if their missing parents will return. Orphan themes reconcile the conflicts between children's wishes to outdo their parents, so they will no longer need them, and will be free to become independent. Orphans invoke fears that outdoing one's parents metaphorically kills off one's parents and cuts the ties that bind them to their families.

Oedipal overtones permeate almost all orphan stories. They reference Freudian theories about boys who wish their fathers dead, so that they can possess their mothers. In Bruce's case, this "unresolved oedipal complex" leaves Bruce unable to leave the nest, and impairs his ability to establish adult relationships with women. Bruce is doomed to live his life in prepubescent fashion, essentially entombed in a family mansion with Alfred the Butler, and later reliant upon an eternally boyish companion named Robin, who himself was orphaned when his parents were murdered while performing as circus acrobats. Whether or not Freudian theories are accurate is unimportant, what is important is that this motif reflects the cultural currency and mirrors the broader social concerns of the era in which it was created—the World War II–era.

Batman stories are known for their colorful villains. These villains are foils for the agile—and altruistic—hero who is sometimes misunderstood and occasionally mistaken for a villain himself. Villains add texture to the stories, making them more dramatic and multidimensional. The age-old appeal of "good versus evil" persists in *Batman* and in superhero stories in general.

The Joker is not the only villain to pass through the pages of *Batman* comics, but he is the best known and one of the earliest. Historically, *Batman* villains attracted Hollywood's most talented actors. The first Joker was a buffoon, played by a jovial Cesar Romero in the TV series. Then a petulant Jack Nicholson made his mark in Tim Burton's movie versions of *Batman.* Most recently, the drug-addled Heath Ledger portrayed the most diabolical Joker ever. Unfortunately, Ledger's life ended with a drug overdose before he could collect the Oscar he posthumously won for Best Supporting Actor in Christopher Nolan's dark interpretation of *The Dark Night.*

There is a trend among *Batman* villains that deserves more mention here. True, most of these villains are motivated by deep psychological wounds and unresolved personal traumas, as would be expected of villains that were invented soon after Freud died in 1938, when psychoanalytically informed story structures gained greater cache.[8] Some characters (Two-Face, in particular) show influences from Jungian psychology, which talks about masks and public faces (personas) and how those false personalities compare to private identities. In contrast, villains from the Dick Tracy comic strip, which premiered in 1931, are physically disfigured (and hence easily identifiable), but are not necessarily psychologically maimed.

In *Batman*, psychiatrist-villains and neuroscientist-villains are particularly prominent, and stand out among the standard-brand "mad scientists" from science fiction stories. If we recall that superhero stories are a subgenre of science fiction, and that early superhero authors were strongly influenced by the emerging genre of SF promoted by Gernsback's magazine, we become less surprised to see so many bad doctors and sick scientists in *Batman* story arcs.[9]

Geneticists are also common, and received extra attention because *Batman* began when the Nazis controlled Germany. For the Nazis justified their genocide and "racial purity" policies through their spurious eugenics theories. In fact, *Batman* began just after World War II erupted in Europe. Nazi Germany had already annexed Austria, and invaded parts of Czechoslovakia and Poland. *Batman* appeared in the same year—1940—that the Reich launched "Operation T-4." Killing centers opened. They soon became training grounds for SS who ran death camps.[10]

For the most part, German psychiatrists were the henchmen for theoretically minded German geneticists. Therefore, it makes sense that a

1940s-era *Batman* geneticist morphed into a practicing psychiatrist once the time was ripe. Psychiatrists personally chose which chronic mental patients and inveterate alcoholics led "lives not worth living." They decided who went to the gas chambers that were built for mental patients (before chambers were reappropriated for the annihilation of Jews and gypsies). Significantly, the first commandant of Treblinka was a psychiatrist and was the only physician to command a Nazi death camp. He gained his "expertise" through his experience as superintendent of Brandenburg Psychiatry Hospital.

Unlike the mass murders of the Jews and gypsies that were skillfully concealed for some years, Nazi plans for wholesale destruction of mentally and physically handicapped persons became public knowledge. These plans inspired so much protest from clergy and others that the process was halted—but not until 200,000 lives were lost. Curiously, Batman is the only World War II–era superhero who does not fight Nazis directly—yet *Batman*'s Nazi-like scientists and diabolical "Japanazi" mind doctors such as Dr. Daka (from 1943 serials) make strong statements in their own way. Such statements may not be strong enough to speak to contemporary audiences that do not know as much about the Reich's eugenics policies as 1940s readers knew.

As for neuroscientists, several of them exist in the *Batman* universe. One of the most memorable is the orange-haired Mad Hatter, who is adapted from the famed *Alice in Wonderland* story. Mad Hatter's flame-colored tresses recollect James Holmes's orange hair, which drew immediate comparisons with the Joker (who has green hair rather than orange!). Mad Hatter uses dream machines to steal dreams or insert dreams. He hypnotizes victims with his pop-out eyes and sometimes controls victims by implanting brain chips.

Some latter-day psychiatrist-villains began their comics' careers as neuroscientists, and transformed into psychiatrists much later, when *Batman* writers wreaked revenge on psychiatrists in attempt to retaliate against one particular psychiatrist, Fredric Wertham, MD.[11] In contrast to the professional confusion that occurs in many films and earlier comics, and even in clinical situations to this day, *Batman* writers knew that Dr. Wertham was trained as an MD. Therefore, they made a point of vilifying psychiatrists specifically, rather than denouncing all mental health professionals. In fact, clinical psychologists who treat patients—rather than just administer tests—had not been invented when Dr. Wertham began his anticomics crusade in the 1950s.

Dr. Wertham labored to bring down the comics industry by testifying before Congress, hosting anticomics academic conferences, and writing a best-selling book about the evils of superheroes. *Seduction of the Innocent* (1954) played off the New Testament theme of the "massacre of the innocents," when King Herod ordered the murder of newborn baby boys.

Wertham vilified gruesome horror comics from the 1950s, and lampooned many superheroes, but he singled out the *Batman* more than others, pointing out the Batman-Robin "man-boy love" relationship and thereby casting Bruce Wayne as a pedophile. Wertham was born in Europe in 1895. When an extra dose of Eisenhower-era conservatism and McCarthy-era paranoia from the 1950s compounded his stolid Victorian-style values, he reached conclusions that sound quaint today, if not outright offensive or patently illegal. In recent decades, Wertham's crusade against Batman and Robin inspired comedy spoofs on Saturday Night Live (SNL) and cartoons. Inexplicably, Wertham was far more progressive than his peers were when it came to race relations.

Still, some very bad doctors appear in early *Batman* comics, well before Wertham hit the scene. An important one arrived shortly after the Joker's 1940 debut: Dr. Hugo Strange. Dr. Hugo Strange should *not* be confused with Marvel's 1960s-era psychedelic superhero, Dr. Stephen Vincent Strange, the disabled neurosurgeon who denounces his past bad behavior and moves to Tibet, where he studies magical medicine and performs good works upon return.

DC Comics' Dr. Hugo Strange begins as a geneticist. He is not as a psychiatrist per se, although he trolls psychiatric institutions in search of subjects for his strange studies. Dr. Strange frees asylum inmates, and experiments on them, turning them into monsters. By the 1960s, Dr. Strange has morphed into a full-fledged psychiatrist. He is qualified to conduct psychological stress tests of Wayne Enterprise employees. Hoping to confirm his suspicions about Bruce Wayne's secret life as Batman, Dr. Strange exposes Bruce Wayne to hallucinogens prior to conducting a psychiatric interview with the iconoclastic philanthropist.

We later learn that Hugo Strange was abandoned as a child and reared in state-run homes, where he was mistreated. Hugo's childhood poses an obvious contrast to Bruce Wayne's. Bruce, too, lost his parents at a young age, but he was accidentally orphaned (rather than intentionally abandoned). Bruce also had strong social support from his butler. Importantly, Bruce found a mission in life and so he became hero, rather than a villain, like Hugo Strange.

Another early psychiatrist is Dr. Crane, who goes by the name "Scarecrow." Invented in 1941, Dr. Crane began his career as a psychology professor who studies phobias and the psychology of fear. After he fires a gun inside a crowded classroom and wounds a student—somewhat like the neuroscience graduate student who opened fire in a crowded movie theater—Professor Crane loses his job. To avenge his job loss, Crane murders those professors who recommended his termination. He goes on to lead a life of crime. In a film version, this retired professor (Cillian Murphy) becomes head of a forensic hospital, where he mistreats mobsters.

Comics stories can be confusing and contradictory, and *Batman* comics are no exception. There are several versions of Dr. Crane's encounters with young Tommy Elliot, the one-time neighbor of the Wayne family who starts out as a child murderer and then becomes a surgeon. According to one version, Dr. Crane is asked to evaluate Tommy when he is still a young boy, albeit one who just attempted to murder his parents. Dr. Crane is intrigued by the developmental process of evil children, and is completely unconcerned with the moral conduct of others or with his personal professional responsibilities.

To see what happens to this evil child when he matures, Dr. Crane, a forensic psychiatrist, gives Tommy a clean bill of health that allows his release from the mental hospital.

This evil boy goes on to become an equally evil surgeon, thanks to Dr. Crane's evil-inspired intervention. Dr. Elliot goes by the name of "Hush." Hush has a life-long "sibling rivalry" with his neighbor Bruce, who is also an only child without other sibs. Hush has a plastic surgery that permits him to impersonate Bruce and assume his identity. Dr. Elliot also develops an obsession with Batman, and struggles to uncover Batman's secret civilian identity. The Hush-Scarecrow duo evolves into psychodynamically informed adventure (and misadventure) stories.

The Arkham clan of psychiatrists is arguably even more evil than any of their predecessors, if that is imaginable. The Arkhams are later inventions, and were mentioned only in passing in comics' stories. Arkham Asylum is not fully fleshed out until a graphic novel came about. The video game about *Arkham Asylum* (2009) expanded our knowledge of Arkham, its origins, and its twisted hospital staff. The elder Dr. Arkham opened the Arkham Asylum for the Criminally Insane after he euthanized his psychotic mother, who suffers from some nondescript neurodegenerative disorder. His mother already transmitted her "degenerative" genes to her progeny, who staff the asylum and torture patients with shock therapy. Some Arkham psychiatrists drug patients and turn them into zombies that follow their doctors' evil instructions.

The stories about sinister psychiatrists and nasty neuroscientists in *Batman* are always evolving and show no signs of fading away. As late as February 2013, yet another sinister and psychotic psychiatrist appeared in *Batman* comics. Dr. Meredith commands his patients to kill, in much the same way that Dr. Caligari did, in the German Expressionist classic from 1919.[12] Dr. Meredith recognizes the horrors inherent in the insanity defense. He dreads hospitals for the criminally insane, and is devastated when an even meaner court psychiatrist declares him psychotic and sentences him to Arkham, rather than Blackgate, the more benign prison facility.

Does this story arc anticipate events that will occur in the James Holmes story, as it evolves? That is anyone's guess—but there is no need to guess. All we need is patience, for now, we can be certain that telling details will reveal themselves in the months and years to come. At present, we can say with certainty that evil exists in American pop culture, and that pop culture both forms and reflects the evil that is sadly inherent in some human souls, ever since our species was cast out of Eden, and long, long, long before America was established.

NOTES

1. For details about kitschy gimmicks (floating paper skeletons, miniature coffins on theater seats) displayed during screenings of William Castle's 1950s-era horror films, see Sharon Packer, *Movies and the Modern Psyche* (Westport, CT: Praeger, 2007); Sharon Packer, *Cinema's Sinister Psychiatrists: From Caligari to Hannibal* (Jefferson, NC: McFarland, 2012). When home TV sets became increasingly common, Castle found ways to compete against television and bring viewers back to movie theaters.

2. By fall of 2012, other bizarre massacres occurred, most notably at an elementary school in Sandy Hook, Connecticut.

3. Richard Esposito et al., "Aurora 'Dark Knight' Suspect James Holmes Said He 'Was the Joker': Cops," Video, http://abcnews.go.com/Blotter/aurora-dark-knight-suspect-joker-cops/story?id=16822251 (accessed February 2013).

4. Sam Quinones, Kim Murphy, and Joe Mozingo, "Aurora Suspect's Profile Grows Murkier," *Los Angeles Times*, July 23, 2012, http://articles.latimes.com/2012/jul/23/nation/la-na-colorado-shooting-sider-20120723 (accessed February 17, 2013).

5. Kate Sheey, "Redheaded Hooker Says Theater 'Gunman' James Holmes Copied Her with Hair Dye," *New York Post*, July 30, 2012, http://www.nypost.com/p/news/national/joker_hooker_hairdo_AzlVI3vR1wETqaiQG9AojN (accessed February 17, 2013).

6. Andrew Tudor, *Monsters and Mad Scientists: A Cultural History of the Horror Movie* (Cambridge, MA: Basil Blackwell, 1989). Tudor chronicles the shifts in protagonists in American horror films.

7. See Georges Méliès' *Hydrothérapie Fantastique* (Méliès, 1909).

8. Wieder D. Sievers, *Freud on Broadway; a History of Psychoanalysis and the American Drama* (New York: Cooper Square Publishers, 1970).

9. For additional bibliographic references, see Sharon Packer, *Superheroes and Superegos: Analyzing the Minds behind the Masks* (Santa Barbara, CA: Praeger/ABC-CLIO, 2010).

10. Rael D. Strous, "Nazi Euthanasia of the Mentally Ill at Hadamar," *The American Journal of Psychiatry* 163, no. 1 (2006): 27.

11. This hypothetical connection between Wertham and bad *Batman* psychiatrists as well as neuroscientists is not universally shared. Some *Batman* writers, such as Dennis O'Neil, state that they were not "conscious" of such an association when they wrote about characters such as Harley Quinn. Other comics' editors, such as Danny Fingeroth, claim that they see the Viennese-born villain, Dr. Faustus, as a closer spinoff of Dr. Wertham. Panel Discussion, "Surely You're Joking, Dr. Wertham," Gallery for Digital Art, Soho, NYC, NY, March 20, 2013.

12. See Packer, *Cinema's Sinister Psychiatrists: From Caligari to Hannibal.*

CHAPTER 17

The Care and Feeding of Serial Killers: Covert Cultural Values Feed the Market for Murderabilia

Katherine Ramsland

The Criminology Museum (*Il Museo Criminologico*) in Italy displays wax replicas of offenders such as Ted Bundy and Andrei Chikatilo, providing their stories through headphones. Among other ghoulish things, visitors can see a re-creation of the living room where John Wayne Gacy had handcuffed each of his 33 victims before raping and strangling them with his infamous "rope trick." A reviewer, disgusted by the displays, still called the museum "the most entertaining venue" in Florence. His ambivalence expresses the edgy allure of certain extreme crimes. We can be attracted to things that repel us because we move toward energy, and sometimes this energy has a horrific frame. Murder and mayhem radiate it. In a way, the murderabilia market is similar to the allure of battlefields, extreme sports, and scary movies. Intensity makes our hearts beat faster. Throw in fame and the "contagion effect" and we can see not only why people want to possess ghastly items but also why some items command high prices.

Crime scenes and murder trials have attracted gawkers since the 1800s, and the Internet's reach has enhanced visibility and access. One can find a sizeable community of sellers and buyers for items featuring or made by—or just touched by—serial killers. It could be dirt from a victim's grave, crime scene souvenirs, or an X-ray of a killer's brain. Some items are more enticing than others. Depraved child killer and cannibal Albert Fish's autograph bears a price tag of $30,000, for example, while a licked envelope from the lesser-known David Gore goes for just $8.

Andrew Kahan, director of the Mayor's Crime Victims Office in Houston, coined the term, "murderabilia" in his enduring fight to make this commerce illegal.[1] Since then, it has become a pervasive meme. At its surface, the market for murderabilia seems reserved for fringe elements, but during some eras it grows quite popular and even members of the social elite have been collectors. In 1895, for example, San Francisco's upper class threw "Durrant parties" when Theodore Durrant, the "monster of the Belfry," was tried for killing two women. They also got reserved seats in the courtroom.

Seeking items related to mass or serial killers derives from our embrace of celebrity, coupled with a desire to get close to perceived vitality. At an inarticulate level, we sense power in acts like torture and murder. It feels active and alive. The popularity of murderabilia is a manifestation of a latent collective attraction that offers the opportunity to consider cultural values that form our collective identity. This market is not just about fringe elements; it expresses our pervasive attraction to violent crime. More correctly, it expresses our drive to get close to intense emotion, even (sometimes especially) when this can be dangerous. We should try to understand why we can preserve in one form the very thing we condemn in another, and yet fail to see the contradiction.

IT STARTED WITH EDUCATION

During the late 19th century, philosophies that emphasized empirical data inspired the first "crime museums," which were used for education.[2] Objects were exhibited from crime scenes, and even from deceased perpetrators (usually their skulls). When Austrian criminologist Hans Gross noticed that knowledge about crime and criminology quickly grew obsolete, his observations inspired museum developers to create displays of actual objects to establish a visual history and provide a fuller education. They included a variety of items, such as the preserved brains of offenders, as well as the instruments of crime investigation, such as the weapons used, blood samples, photographs, microscopes, and samples of handwriting. In Rome, they even included a cauldron in which a female killer had boiled her victims to remove the flesh.

Such museums popped up in several major cities under the supervision of prominent criminologists, such as Hans Gross and Cesare Lombroso. Initially meant for professionals, they soon opened to the public. In Rome, for example, the Prison Administration acknowledged that "the public is enormously interested in the vicissitudes and the phenomena of criminal life" when it set up the Museo Criminologico.[3] These officials realized that statistical gazettes were "dead letters," so they decided to offer a more immediate experience by putting crime items on open display. They created tableaus of torture narratives, executions, and criminal acts to demonstrate how science was useful in criminal investigations.

These exhibits also introduced visitors to the experience of being close to violent acts, which proved to be titillating. This, in turn, inspired intense curiosity. Observant vendors looking to tap this resource sold morbid products. For example, after the press covered the sensational case of H.H. Holmes and his murder castle in Chicago during the 1890s, an enterprising police officer acquired the lease and sold entrance fees (15 cents). Before he got his new business off the ground, however, the building went up in flames.[4] In 1908, when Belle Gunness's pig farm turned up numerous bodies and body parts, some 15,000 curious people arrived to see the sights. People were even allowed to tramp through the pig shed to see the decedents laid out. On this site, crime entrepreneurs sold grizzly pictures, and tourists picked up charred bricks from the fire-decimated house or dirt from the makeshift cemetery.[5]

Over the past 30 years in America, the frenzy to purchase and own things that killers have touched, created, or grown has hyped them into a celebrity status akin to sports or rock stars. English professor David Schmid traces today's dramatic rise of interest in murderabilia to the 1980s. Serial killers, he states, have become "iconic figures." He thinks this arises from America's socially approved narrative, which makes killers into the bad guys and law enforcement into the good guys. However, beneath the surfaces is also a disavowed narrative that killers are fascinating. The more exposure a given figure achieves via an audience-grabbing story, the greater the celebrity allure.[6] Schmid views the combination of celebrity and death as the force behind morbid commerce, but his explanation falls short. What, we must ask, makes this combination so compelling. It must be more than just the entwinement of fandom and fear.

CLOSER THAN THEY APPEAR

Serial killers show up in numerous entertainment venues, from opera to film to bestselling novels. John Malkovich toured internationally in a stage play about an international serial murderer and successful writer, Jack Unterweger. The various crime series, such as *C.S.I.* and *Law and Order*, are natural venues for plots about murder investigations. *Criminal Minds* is devoted almost entirely to how profilers track down serial offenders. The long-running Showtime series, *Dexter*, features a lovable serial killer who kills other killers, and similar projects are currently in the works. *Dark Minds* actually uses an unnamed serial killer to help solve cold cases.

Some people carry on numerous correspondences with incarcerated killers, design trading cards or board games, or purchase items that killers have made. Internet auction sites like eBay have carried such items as an FBI document with Gein's fingerprints, a hatchet from his farm, wood from his ramshackle house, and a painting of him done by killer John Wayne Gacy. At the time of Gein's sensational arrest in 1957 for the murders of two women in Wisconsin (not to mention his stash of preserved body parts), entrepreneurs confiscated his Ford sedan and charged gawkers money to look at "the car that hauled the dead from their graves."[7]

Today, there are quite a few online auction sites, such as Serial Killer Central, Supernaught, and Ghouls Like Us. Items found for sale over the years have included:

- A bible that John Wayne Gacy had supposedly used, as well as the rosary that supplied the stick for his fatal "rope trick"
- Notes and envelopes from Ted Bundy, Dennis Rader, Angelo Buono, Tommy Lynn Sells, and any number of other killers
- Choker necklaces from Albert deSalvo
- Origami items from Charles Ng
- Bricks from the apartment building where Jeffrey Dahmer had lived before it was torn down
- Empty prescription bottles, driver's licenses, sunglasses, hair clips, used soap, dirty socks, and anything else that could be demonstrated to have been owned or touched by a serial killer
- Toenails supposedly clipped by Glen Rogers and locks of hair from Nightstalker Richard Ramirez
- Some items were real prizes, such as the freezer in which Dahmer stored his victims' heads

In addition to these authentic items, one can find plenty of serial killer kitsch. There are black velvet images of Dorothy Puente and David Berkowitz; coffee mugs featuring Charles Manson, Ed Gein, and Jeffrey Dahmer barbeque aprons; Night Stalker snow globes; and action figures for Jack the Ripper, Ted Bundy, and Lizzie Borden. The Jeffrey Dahmer "Slay Set" featured a doll in a zippered suit that held plastic parts of a dismembered victim.

Lustmord: The Writings and Artifacts of Murderers, published by Bloat Books, includes killer artifacts such as journal entries, letters, drawings, and poetry. In this category we also find graphic novels, serial killer board games, and coloring books.

A handful of artists set up exhibits or online marketplaces for items made by Richard Ramirez, Ted Bundy, and Jeffrey Dahmer. A few have settled for selling their own unique depictions of these offenders. Among the most notorious is an artist named Joe Coleman, who creates "outsider art," or depictions of social misfits. His paintings are elaborate and usually feature murder weapons, victims, and other reminders of the killer's particular violent expression. Coleman also admitted on camera to stealing the original copy of the letter that Albert Fish had written to Grace Budd's mother about cannibalizing the little girl after he had killed her.[8]

Julian P. Hobbes filmed *Collectors* (2000), to feature people obsessed with serial killer culture, and there are other such documentaries in the works. John Borowski, the producer of documentaries about Albert Fish, Carl Panzram, and H. H. Holmes, is currently collecting stories about serial killer culture for his next film.

Hobbes focused much of his documentary on Louisiana mortician Rick Staton and his business partner, Tobias Allen. Staton had asked several incarcerated serial killers to do some artwork for his "Death Row Art Shows." He started with John Wayne Gacy and then acquired pieces from Richard Speck, Elmer Wayne Henley, Ottis Toole, and Henry Lee Lucas.

Only a special type of collector seeks the most intimate objects. They want something a killer has touched, worn, used, made, or grown. This opens the market to the offenders themselves. Eight states ban killers from profiting from their crimes, but these laws are difficult to enforce.

ART OF DARKNESS

Imprisoned murderers have time on their hands, and some have turned to art to explore creative outlets as well as make money via outside agents. Elmer Wayne Henley was the infamous assistant to "Candyman" Dean Corll, who had tortured, raped, and murdered at least 29 boys in Houston, Texas, during the late 1960s. In prison, Henley took up painting and showed real skill. Art calms him, he says, and his preference is for sunsets, flowers, and seascapes. Still, he sometimes indulges in depicting the very thing that got him into prison—nude young boys. Staton includes them in his displays.

Death row inmate Derrick Todd Lee, the "Baton Rouge Killer," found a way to sell his art online.[9] He made a pencil drawing of a panda eating bamboo, which was offered for $75. Another featured a pair of swans. These paintings went to a website that sells serial killer handiwork, along with a letter that Lee had written. The swan painting sold on the day it was posted, and an investigation turned up a payment made to Lee. The website is run by a couple who once had worked in real estate and graphic design. They decided to correspond with inmates to procure items to sell and found a lucrative occupation.

In 2005, the State of Massachusetts took on the issue of killers profiting from their art when sexual predator Alfred Gaynor's art showed up in an online auction. His sketch, "A Righteous man's Reward," which featured Jesus Christ, provoked a hot public debate over whether he had the right to sell art and make money. On Gaynor's side was the Fortune Society, a prisoners' advocacy group, which insisted on his right of free speech.

The most violent offenders can easily find buyers, because they are considered the elite. Gacy reportedly earned over $100,000 from his paintings, which featured anything from his rendition of Disney's seven dwarves to depictions of other serial killers. Gacy's self-portraits in his clown suit commanded high prices. As often occurs after the deaths of artists of genuine cultural merit, Gacy's death (by execution) enhanced the value of many of his paintings, although some collectors claimed they had brought bad luck.

While alive, Richard Ramirez, the Night Stalker, maintain his reputation as a "minion of Satan" by drawing demons. Gerard Schaefer, who was convicted of two murders but suspected in more, illustrated and published a collection of short stories. He said they were fiction, but law enforcement believed they were actual murders he had committed. Lawrence Bittaker creates greeting cards, and murder cult leader Charles Manson once sold puppets he had knit himself from yarn he had pulled from his socks.[10]

The question remains, why do people even want them? True crime writer Harold Schechter states that collecting items that killers have touched or owned has a "talisman effect." From dipping handkerchiefs into the bullet wounds of gangster John Dillinger to purchasing Ted Bundy's Volkswagen Beetle, there will always be people who want to possess items closely associated with violent death.[11]

Relatives of victims are horrified that some people consider it fun to own a Dahmer doll, Ripper trading cards, or the calculator that had once belonged to Virginia Tech shooter Seung-Hui Cho. Many call the exhibition or sale of such items tasteless, sensationalistic, obscene, and exploitive. Some protesters have even had public bonfires. They say it poisons the memory of the victims and that it signals a culture in spiritual decline.

The aforementioned Andy Kahan mounted a fierce crusade against eBay for its blatant hosting of the sale of "murderabilia," and his efforts got results. Members of victims' rights groups signed a petition to the effect that if no limits were imposed on certain practices, the Internet's function as a network for millions of people could have a detrimental effect on society. The glorification of killers, the argument went, and the frenzy to purchase and own things that they touched, glamorizes serial murder and rewards the offenders. It might also encourage others toward violent ambitions.

In fact, more than one young killer has said that the desire for fame had inspired him. In April 2010, a teenage boy followed the lead of a serial killer character in a British soap opera to kill a neighbor. He bludgeoned her to death with a hammer before setting her house on fire. Several shocking murders have been linked to *Dexter.* In Edmonton, Canada, Mark Twitchell lured men to his "movie studio" to participate in his feature about a sword-wielding serial killer. One was murdered and the other managed to escape. Twitchell had adopted the persona "Dexter Morgan" on his Facebook page and had made a brief movie that had scenes that were similar to how Dexter operates on the TV show. In a different incident, Andrew Conley admitted that *Dexter* had inspired him to strangle his 10-year-old brother. After killing his brother, Conley put a plastic bag over the boy's head, mimicking Dexter's post-murder ritual, and calmly went to his girlfriend's house to watch a movie. Then, in the United Kingdom, James Hamill was tried and convicted for the murder of a man he believed was a drug dealer. Hamill cited *Dexter* as his inspiration.

Although Kahan's protest inspired eBay to ban the sale of certain types of murderabilia, other sites continue to offer it. Murderabilia remains a thriving business. Some merchants acknowledge that victims' families might be hurt by something like the sale of soil where the bodies were buried, but they stand by their right to free trade.

THE CONTAGION EFFECT

Researchers at the Yale School of Management published a study in the *Journal of Consumer Research* that examined why people purchased objects once owned by celebrities. They included items associated with infamous criminals. In some cases, they found, consumers made such purchases as investments or because the objects evoked positive associations. However, of most interest for this article were those who said they hoped to gain some special access to, or degree of intimacy with, a celebrity who had handled the object. Actual celebrity contact counted for a *lot.* Purchasers were willing to pay more for a celebrity's sweaty shirt than the same shirt laundered, or for a sweater that a celebrity liked and wore rather than a sweater that he or she had merely owned. Thus, among the study's findings was a "contagion effect," which operates on superstitious or magical thinking. The logic of magical thinking holds that once two things come in contact, their essence remains in contact even after they part.

The purchasers in the study seemed to have sought the celebrity's essence as much as, or more than, the item itself.[12]

Given the general population represented in this study, there were probably few genuine murderabilia collectors. However, we can surmise that the contagion effect still applies, because many of these collectors view items touched by killers to be enhanced through contact, and even to be protective (or, alternately, they had become scary and therefore intriguing). An edgy aura enhances such items, so ownership is desirable apart from any potential market value. In other words, collectors of items that killers touched might believe that part of the killer's soul adheres to certain items: the pen that eight-time rapist and killer Michael Ross used to write his legal briefs would still "feel" like he is holding it. A brick from Lizzie Borden's house (despite her acquittal) would "feel" permeated with the energy and presence of the perpetrator of a double homicide there. Celebrity associations are part of the calculation, as there is more market value in a famous killer's items than in those owned by someone who had garnered little media attention.

We might enhance these findings with studies on the motivations of the ultimate murderabilia collectors: serial killer groupies. Such women want to embrace the aura so much they actually marry these offenders. Mental health experts have compared this type of infatuation to the most extreme forms of fanaticism. Such women are usually dismissed as insecure females who cannot find love any other way, or as "love-avoidant" females who seek relationships that cannot be consummated. Yet while this might be true in some cases, several devotees have been strikingly beautiful and educated. Many have even been married. A few have been lawyers or judges. Women who are attracted to killers are usually in their 30s or 40s. Their motives for getting so passionately involved vary, but they share a fierce sense of protection over the relationship.

Some theorists hypothesize that certain women view aggression as a feature of the definitive male. Comparing them to humans, Richard Wrangham and Dale Peterson examined Orangutans.[13] They found that female primates preferred the larger, louder, more aggressive males that were ready to scrap with other males. After a victory, females approached them for sexual relations. Generalizing this finding to humans, the researchers suggested that women who seek out dangerous men might be confusing brutality with masculinity. It is also possible that they anticipate an intense sexual encounter. Essentially, the logic goes like this: The aggressive alpha-male is perceived as larger-than-life, so he will deliver *more* than an ordinary man. Such relationships will be superior to what other women have.

If we translate this into the realm of serial killer groupies (at least, the female version), we might say that women who love serial killers want to possess the killer's alpha qualities because it feels both special and protective, perhaps even transcendent. In a way, these women model a larger cultural value, an ironic fascination with power that could actually harm or destroy us.

COVERT INFLUENCE

Psychologist Michael Apter considered the attraction to danger and suggested that something that is viewed as "dangerous" can exert a magical allure. The closer we get to it, the more alive we feel.[14] However, since it also raises anxiety, we tend to develop what Apter labels "protective frames." These frames are narratives about an evildoer that builds a buffer of safety around us. It gives us a weapon or shield against the monster. Thus, we can indulge in the *frisson* of excitement while dampening the anxiety.

It is easy to see how this concept applies to the enticement of murderabilia, especially considering the perceived transfer of a killer's essence. The meaning with which a collector imbues the object creates the frame: the thing feels dangerous, which makes the heart beat faster. Getting close to the intensity of murder and the reality of torture and death assists those who own these objects to obtain a sense of raw contact with that electricity. Yet because they are not actually in the presence of an ongoing murder, they feel safe.

Although this murderabilia marketplace might seem like just a morbid margin of society, it arises from the energy sparked by conflicted social values that operate below our awareness. Even as we express disgust over people who love violence, we collectively embrace psychopathic mindsets poised for predation. People who purchase murderabilia might actually be more attuned to a divided cultural mentality that embraces the energy of violence while pretending to condemn it.

As a culture, we might verbally disavow it, but our behavior says otherwise. We ensure high ratings for violent TV shows, films, and fiction, but this is just a surface expression. Covertly, we honor social institutions that protect criminal acts at higher levels. Such people become our leaders. They control our lives. We are the groupies to the alpha-humans who gain positions of power so they can strip the environment, cut corners on safety, endanger our economy, and harbor prejudices that dehumanize whole groups. In bad faith, we say serial murder is evil, but then support corporations and politicians that harm and plunder us on a larger scale. Take whatever you need, is our unspoken philosophy; use us however you will. Protect yourself and survive, no matter what it takes. When we let those in power do whatever they will, with little or no accountability, we support—even honor—the same narcissistic philosophy that feeds the acts of serial killers.

So, we denounce murderabilia collectors while we make murder and mayhem a staple in our entertainment venues, and predation a viable leadership style. We protect, and even institutionalize, the very thing that we claim to decry. As long as we sanction a psychopathic approach to business, politics, and banking, but simultaneously *pretend* that we do not, we fuel the behavior of those who act out the negative side of our collective contradictions. We empower merchants of death and darkness in any form.

It's all about vigor. We seek the spark of life, so we move toward that which is most intense, and this can draw us straight toward evil. We eroticize the killer's egoism and fetishize his acts. We go through the motions to destroy him, but then we want another to replace him. We want the game to continue. Fascination with murder is about an attraction to energy that defies restrictive and suffocating boundaries. Attunement to the serial killer tale, whether through crime TV or murderabilia collections, keeps our fingers on a lusty, if disturbing, pulse. It also diverts our attention from a more devouring evil in our midst that we subconsciously accept.

SUMMARY

Our contemporary value system has built-in philosophical slippage that allows us to use whatever moral context we need to suit our purposes. Thus, we can turn a blind eye to how we enjoy evil so that we can claim to be a moral society that has the right to denounce murderabilia collectors. We wish to avoid this truth, but the existence of an active murderabilia market nevertheless expresses it. Rather than condemn it, we might benefit from understanding that suppressed part of ourselves that gives it life.

NOTES

1. Thomas Vinciguerra, "The 'Murderabilia' Market," *New York Times*, June 5, 2011.

2. Susanne Regener, "Criminological Museums and the Visualization of Evil," *Crime, History & Societies* 7, no. 1 (2003): 43–56.

3. Assunta Borzacchiello, ed. *Museo Criminologico* (Rome, Italy: Department of Prison Administration, 2003), 10.

4. John Borowski, *H.H. Holmes: America's First Serial Killer* (Waterfront Productions, 2004).

5. Sylvia Shepherd, *The Mistress of Murder Hill: The Serial Killings of Belle Gunness* (Bloomington, IN: 1st Book Library, 2001), 85–86.

6. David Schmid, *Natural Born Celebrities: Serial Killers in American Culture* (Chicago: University of Chicago Press, 2005), 6–8.

7. Sign on exhibit, photo in Harold Schechter, *The Serial Killer Files: The Who, What, Where, How, and Why of the World's Most Terrifying Murderers* (New York: Ballantine, 2004), 396.

8. Joshua Lipton, "Abnormal Rockwell: Joe Coleman," *Spin*, July 23, 2003.

9. Koran Addo, "Serial Killer Art Sold Online," *The Advocate*, January 30, 2012.

10. Katherine M. Ramsland, *The Human Predator: A Historical Chronicle of Serial Murder and Forensic Investigation* (New York: Berkley Books, 2005), 242–43.

11. Schechter, *The Serial Killer Files: The Who, What, Where, How, and Why of the World's Most Terrifying Murderers*, 394–97.

12. George E. Newman, Gil Diesendruck, and Paul Bloom, "Celebrity Contagion and the Value of Objects," *Journal of Consumer Research* 38, no. 2 (2011): 215–28.

13. Richard W. Wrangham and Dale Peterson, *Demonic Males: Apes and the Origins of Human Violence* (Boston: Houghton Mifflin, 1996).

14. Michael J. Apter, *The Dangerous Edge: The Psychology of Excitement* (New York: Free Press, 1992), 11–30.

PART III

Newscasts, Courtroom Cases, and Political Polemics

CHAPTER 18

A Touch of Evil: Rewriting True Crime in Pop Culture

Michael Butterfield and Michael D. Kelleher

Evil is unspectacular and always human
And shares our bed and eats at our own table . . .
—*W.H. Auden*, Herman Melville

Human beings who walked the earth centuries ago had no psychologists or criminal profilers to explain the many mysteries regarding human evil. Our ancestors never uttered the phrases "antisocial personality disorder," "psychopath," or "serial killer." Instead, the preferred explanations often blamed evil spirits, demons, or satanic forces which had somehow corrupted and controlled the helpless humans who committed inexplicable acts of violence. Some theories suggest that the serial killers of yesterday inspired the popular myths and legends of vampires and werewolves. When confronted with the discovery of a savaged corpse next to a set of retreating human footprints, people were sometimes reluctant to accept that another person could be responsible for such brutality. Therefore, they chose to believe that a human being had somehow been transformed into an animal and then driven to kill. This explanation conveniently excused the very human origins of evil while blaming external forces in a more acceptable scenario. According to this rationale, a murderer was an inhuman monster.

The desire to rewrite the truth about the dark side of humanity is evident in the celebrated depictions of fantasy violence throughout history. Sensational stories of mayhem and murder satisfy the appetite for the gruesome and grotesque, and each new tale of terror provides an opportunity to revise and improve upon the eternal effort to ignore the ugly truths about humankind. Evil is portrayed as an external enemy rather than an internal impulse. Human beings are transformed into killers by the bite of a werewolf, demonic possession, or even divine direction. Pop culture also absorbs real-life crimes and horrors in a repackaged and more palatable form. When confronted by its reflection, society seeks to sanitize its sins and recast its villains.

One of the most celebrated cases of evil began in 1888, in a part of Victorian London known as Whitechapel. The upper class enjoyed the safety and security of wealth, privilege, and entitlement in the West End while a far lower class lived in the poverty and disease-ridden slums of the crowded East End. Whitechapel was plagued by crime and violence, and police were overwhelmed by the drunks, petty criminals, thieves, and sexual predators. Prostitution was rampant throughout Whitechapel as desperate and destitute women sold their bodies in order to buy a meal or a flea-infested bed. Customers prowled the streets in search of anonymous sex, and many men were abusive and violent. Those who were not forced to live in such conditions often knew little about London's dark underbelly and few had much sympathy for its inhabitants. As a result, the horrors of the East End were largely ignored until someone began murdering the women of Whitechapel.

The body of Mary Ann Nichols was discovered in the hours before dawn on August 31, 1888. Nichols had worked as a prostitute, and a client had mutilated her body with several strokes of a sharp blade. The story hit the newspapers and the public became fascinated by the unfolding mystery. The search for a villain quickly settled upon the theory that the brutal murder was the work of an outsider, most likely of Jewish origins. This theory was not supported by the evidence but was rooted in the already-established anti-Semitism of the time. Rumors and sensational speculation in the newspapers identified a Jewish butcher known as "Leather Apron," and he soon became the target of angry citizens seeking justice. A second murder further terrified the public and a group of vigilantes took to the streets under the name "Mile End Vigilance Committee." The Central News Agency then received a letter from someone who claimed to be the killer. The message read in part:

> That joke about Leather Apron gave me real fits. I am down on whores and I shant quit ripping them till I do get buckled. . . . The next job I do I shall clip the ladys ears off and send to the police officers just for jolly wouldn't you.

The letter was signed, "Yours truly Jack the Ripper," and added, "Dont mind me giving the trade name." The author also laughed at the popular theory regarding his identity, writing, "They say I'm a doctor now. ha ha."

At the request of police, the letter was not printed for public consumption. Doubts about the authenticity of the letter were balanced with the possibility that the author's warning about the next crime was sincere. Less than three days after the "Ripper" letter warned of an impending attack, the bodies of two women were discovered in the East End. The evidence indicated that the unseen assailant had killed the first woman but may have been interrupted and then fled to select the second victim. According to the police surgeon who examined the victim at the scene of the crime, "The lobe and auricle of the right ear were cut obliquely through." Many observers believed that this detail proved that the killer had written the Ripper letter while other skeptics believed that the killer would have removed the ears if he wanted to do so.

In an effort to help identify the individual responsible for the Ripper letter, police informed the public and pleaded for assistance from anyone with information about the message or the murders. Days later, a second letter arrived at the CNA, once again signed with the name "Jack the Ripper." The author explained that he did not have time to remove the ears of the victim, reinforcing the theory that the writer was, in fact, responsible for the killings. Police requested that the media suppress this letter due to concerns about false confessors and hoaxes. Soon, the leader of the Mile End Vigilance Committee received a letter sent "From hell" which was accompanied by a human kidney. According to the police surgeon, the left kidney of the fourth victim had been removed. This fact fueled speculation that the killer had sent the letters and the kidney, but some investigators and others began to suspect that the Ripper messages were the work of a prankster or even a clever reporter. In his book *Days of My Years* (1914), Assistant Commissioner Sir Melville Macnaghten wrote, "In this ghastly production I have always thought I could discern the stained forefinger of the journalist. . . . But whoever did pen the gruesome stuff, it is certain to my mind that it was not the mad miscreant who had committed the murders." Detective Chief Inspector George Littlechild described the "Ripper" persona as "a smart piece of journalistic work."

The media frenzy surrounding the murders satisfied the public appetite for horror, but the coverage also shed light on the appalling conditions in London's East End. On Monday, September 24, 1888, *The Star* newspaper published a letter by the famous Irish playwright George Bernard Shaw. According to *The Star* editor, Shaw's letter concerned "the hideous and squalid tragedies which, occurring in the East, have stirred up the West End to unusual and unaccustomed interest in the fate of the poor and the disinherited of the nation." Under the title "Blood Money to Whitechapel," Shaw wrote that he and "conventional social Democrats" tried to draw attention to the horrors facing the working class, but the "proprietary class" and newspapers of London remained indifferent to the "scum who dared to complain that they were starving." Shaw then sarcastically referred to the Ripper as an "independent genius" who had "taken the matter in hand" and put the issue in the spotlight "by simply murdering and disemboweling four women."

The Ripper saga became a worldwide sensation, but the story seemed to end just as society had become addicted to the nightmare. After the discovery of a fourth victim, the killer appeared to vanish into the fog-filled streets of Whitechapel. Police were unable to identify the Ripper and the case became the greatest mystery in crime history, spawning hundreds of books, documentaries, films, and websites throughout the following century.

The murders of prostitutes were common in communities damaged by poverty, inequality, drugs, and crime, and such conditions often produced Ripper-like monsters. The public fascination with the timeless mystery turned to more entertaining explanations which conveniently ignored the source of the evil. Popular theories portrayed the Ripper as a doctor or even a member of the Royal family. Other theories blamed the secret society of Freemasons or an official conspiracy. FBI profilers and other experts later examined the crimes and concluded that the killer was most likely a mentally disturbed loner who managed to avoid detection in the congestion and chaos of the East End. Many of the so-called Ripperologists who studied the mystery believed that the killer did not write the many letters attributed to the Ripper. Reluctant to accept the monster as a product of his environment, society desired a more attractive Jack the Ripper, a brilliant madman who penned taunting letters and delighted in his evil deeds while wearing a mask of sanity in his daily life. The living conditions of London's East End had produced a real nightmare, but future exploitation of the tragedy rarely mentioned the true horrors as anything more than a backdrop for the fiction of modern entertainment.

In the 1950s America, a middle-aged man named Ed Gein began to display very unusual behavior after the death of his mother. Left alone in the family farmhouse, Ed disappeared into his fantasy life and became convinced that he could resurrect the ghost of his dead mother in the body of another woman. Ed crept onto the grounds of the local cemetery, where he often spent hours digging up the corpses of recently deceased women. He took the bodies home to perform some ritual which he believed would recapture his mother's spirit. Ed then began killing women and carving their flesh in order to create a suit of skin which he wore during bizarre moonlight dances. He also collected vaginas, noses, and other body parts for his fantasy world. At the time of his arrest, Ed Gein had the headless body of his latest victim hanging in his summer kitchen, sliced open just as a hunter would prepare a dead animal.

Citizens of Gein's rural Wisconsin community were outraged by his shocking crimes, although some ambitious entrepreneur reportedly considered turning the Gein farmhouse of horrors into a freak show attraction for curious tourists. The property was then destroyed by a mysterious fire. Court-appointed psychiatrists examined Gein and concluded that he suffered from schizophrenia. A court ruled that Gein was mentally incompetent and therefore could not contribute to his defense as required by law. He was institutionalized until 1968 when doctors declared him sufficiently sane to stand trial.[1] By the time Gein's trial began, the world had already absorbed his nightmare through pop culture and the classic horror film *Psycho* (1960). The movie was based on the book by author Robert Bloch and its Gein-like character Norman Bates. Bloch also transformed the Gein house into what became known as the "Psycho house," where Bates lived with the preserved corpse of his dead mother. The house overlooked the roadside Bates Motel, where Bates donned his mother's dress and her persona while murdering unlucky guests. Bloch's Norman Bates was unlikable, unattractive, even pathetic. For the 1960 film version of the story, director Alfred Hitchcock cast actor Anthony Perkins as a likable, attractive, and sympathetic Norman. Perkins delivered one of the most unforgettable performances in movie history, but the pop-culture version of the Ed Gein story bore little resemblance to the truth. Unlike the original inspiration for the character, Norman wore his mother's clothes and assumed her identity in what the film explained as a case of a split personality. Gein's bizarre suit of female flesh was forgotten in favor of the now-iconic image of a knife-wielding Perkins wearing a tattered dress and wig.

Ed Gein's strange use of body parts inspired the murderous family of cannibals in the cult horror film *The Texas Chainsaw Massacre* (Tobe Hooper, 1974). A member of the clan known as "Leatherface" wears the faces of his victims as a death mask and, like Gein, inhabits a remote farm house filled with fixtures made from human bones and other assorted frights. The film inspired several sequels and remakes, putting Leatherface on the list of American horror movie icons, alongside Michael Myers of *Halloween* (John Carpenter, 1978) and Jason Vorhees of the *Friday the 13th* series of films. These killers wore masks which rendered them faceless, anonymous, and inhuman monsters. Society had developed an appetite for violence and the vicarious thrill of so-called slasher films, yet most of these fictional killers were simplistic representations which avoided troubling questions about the human origins of true evil and celebrated a fantasy version of real horror.

Decades after his crimes shocked the world, Ed Gein inspired yet another fictional character in the book *The Silence of the Lambs* (1988) by author Thomas Harris. In this story, a serial killer nick-named "Buffalo Bill" skinned his victims and constructed a suit of female flesh to wear while he danced in front of a video camera. The novel and film adaptation also included another character which became one of the most famous and influential villains in the history of cinema, psychiatrist and serial killer Hannibal "The Cannibal" Lecter. The devilish doctor had originally appeared in a previous novel by Harris titled *Red Dragon* (1981). The lesser-known film *Manhunter* (Michael Mann, 1986) featured veteran actor Bryan Cox as a deeply disturbed and scheming Lecter. In contrast, famed actor Anthony Hopkins offered a different interpretation in the film *The Silence of the Lambs* (Jonathan Demme, 1991) and the sequel *Hannibal* (Ridley Scott, 2001). This Lecter was witty, charming, and refined, a polite yet diabolical character who appealed to audiences and provided a more attractive face of evil. The Oscar-winning performance inspired countless imitations and further depicted human evil in cartoon-like caricature.

America's most notorious and elusive serial killer walked in the shadow of his predecessor Jack the Ripper. In the summer of 1969, a series of murders captured public interest when newspapers in the San Francisco Bay Area received letters from someone who claimed to be responsible for the attacks.[2] The author identified himself as "The Zodiac" and threatened to kill a dozen people if his letters were not published. Unlike most killers, the Zodiac wore a bizarre, hooded costume which featured his chosen symbol, a crossed-circle. The Zodiac also called police to report his crimes and even sent coded messages which he claimed would reveal his identity. After his last known murder, the Zodiac sent another letter in an envelope which contained a blood-stained scrap of the victim's shirt. The killer further terrorized the Bay Area with subsequent letters and threats to assassinate school children, but the Zodiac apparently vanished in 1974. According to one theory, the Zodiac spree was an elaborate terror campaign orchestrated by a secret sect of Satanists which included Charles Manson, the leader of the notorious "Family" responsible for several horrific slayings at the time. Other theories suggested that the Zodiac was a Harvard lecturer, a wealthy businessman, a noted doctor, and even the infamous "Unabomber" Ted Kaczynski, who mailed explosive devices to universities and airlines to protest the evils of modern industrial civilization. Books, movies, and websites cast the Zodiac as a super-villain rarely seen in reality but often found in popular fiction.

Shortly after the Zodiac disappeared, a similar monster appeared on the other side of the country in New York. The so-called Son of Sam killed without apparent motive and bragged about his crimes in taunting letters. Police arrested David Berkowitz, a loner who worked for the post office and harassed his neighbors with bizarre letters. Handwriting experts concluded that Berkowitz had also written the "Son of Sam" letters. Berkowitz confessed several times to doctors, investigators, and others, claiming that a demonic dog had ordered him to kill (a story he later recanted). Alternate theories of the crime blamed alleged accomplices and offered more entertaining explanations. The most popular theory cast Berkowitz as a helpless pawn in a massive conspiracy created by an elite network of devil-worshipers who engaged in satanic rituals, sacrificed human beings, sexually abused young children for pornography, and produced "snuff films" of actual murders. The image of Berkowitz as a calculating killer who had acted alone was lost in the rush to blame evil outsiders who were also responsible for every other imaginable horror.

Haunted by unspeakable crimes, society struggled to explain evil aberrations like the Zodiac and "Jack the Ripper." In the 1800s, the accepted term for an expert on the subject of mental illness was an "alienist," derived from the French word aliéniste and aliéné (insane). The word "alienist" clearly defined the mentally ill as aliens, beings apart from the rest of society. The same logic was used to define the evil acts committed by the morally ill, those who killed for pleasure, greed, revenge, or other motives. Child molesters, serial killers, rapists, and other criminals were often described as "monsters" or "inhuman." Evil had been consistently defined as an outside force, an external enemy, and those who committed evil acts were therefore defined as outsiders rather than threats from within. For some, this logic manifested in the belief that evildoers were compelled by outside forces. Despite centuries documenting a consistent pattern of human depravity, society blamed other causes, such as drugs, traumatic childhoods, absent parents, peer pressure, liberal excesses, right-wing extremism, sex and violence in the media, or even the devil himself.

In 1974, gun lover Ronald "Butch" DeFeo shot and killed his mother, father, two brothers, and two sisters inside the family home in the village of Amityville, in Long Island, New York. DeFeo staged the discovery of the bodies and then suggested that a reputed mobster may have been responsible for the brutal attack. DeFeo changed his story many times until he finally confessed, although his true motives remained a mystery. DeFeo had a volatile relationship with his father due to his ongoing use of heroin, LSD, and other drugs, and some evidence suggested that DeFeo had hoped to profit from the death of his family.[3] During his trial, defense attorneys tried to convince jurors that DeFeo was insane at the time of the murders. Ronald DeFeo also testified that he heard voices which had somehow compelled him to kill his entire family, but many observers dismissed his claims as a transparent attempt to deny responsibility for his horrific crimes.[4] DeFeo was convicted and sent to prison, but the story of the Amityville nightmare had just begun and soon became a modern American legend.

The DeFeo murders had shocked the country, and, like the Gein farmhouse, the scene of the crime became an infamous house of horrors. The Lutz family moved into the former DeFeo home and then claimed that they had been tormented by demonic forces. The story was the subject of the highly fictionalized, best-selling book by Jay Anson titled *The Amityville Horror* (1971). The subsequent film version was further fictionalized, as was the follow-up prequel which depicted Ronald DeFeo as a reluctant killer possessed by an unseen evil. When the film series was relaunched in 2005, the story blamed the haunted happenings on the spirits of a sinister Satanist and the victims he had tortured and killed inside the Amityville house decades earlier. Once again, Ronald DeFeo was portrayed as the victim of demonic possession rather than a ruthless killer. The public and the media celebrated the so-called Amityville curse, and the story continued to change and expand to more sensational heights with countless films, documentaries, books, and websites.

The Amityville murders occurred shortly after the theatrical release of the blockbuster film *The Exorcist* (William Friedkin, 1973), which told the story of a young girl possessed by a demon. The controversial film caused a worldwide sensation and some audience members even collapsed in the theater from fear and shock. The financial success of the movie inspired a failed sequel and a fury of imitations, including *The Omen* (Richard Donner, 1976) and its story of the anti-Christ as a young boy. Some critics and skeptics believed that the public fascination with demonic forces had inspired the Lutz family to concoct the story of the Amityville haunting which became one of the most lucrative and enduring commercial enterprises in history. Years later, supernatural fantasies were a fixture of cable television with shows such as *Haunting Evidence* and *Ghost Hunters*, and Ronald DeFeo appeared with self-proclaimed psychic Jackie Barrett in the A&E program *Amityville: The Final Testament* (2010). DeFeo embraced the popular explanation for the seemingly inexplicable murder of his entire family and claimed that he had been haunted by an inescapable evil entity during his years in prison. He once again changed his story and blamed the eldest DeFeo sister as a co-conspirator in the murders. Barrett traveled to the Amityville house with a camera crew, described her visions of the DeFeo slayings, and predictably blamed a sinister spirit inside the cursed home. The successful marketing of the Amityville media machine indicated that society preferred to believe that supernatural villains were responsible for human horror.

In the 1970s, society found a new name for modern monsters, the "serial killer", a phrase which was reportedly created to describe a charming law student named Ted Bundy. A volunteer at a suicide-prevention hotline, Bundy murdered dozens of young women during his long and prolific career as an insatiable sexual predator. As one of the first serial killers in the age of modern media, Bundy challenged the public perceptions, assumptions, and expectations of a human monster. Attractive, articulate, and intelligent, Bundy did not resemble the popular portrait of a murderer and many observers believed his claims of innocence. Defended by his many supporters and glamorized by a media obsessed with the new and emerging phenomenon of such killers, Bundy found instant fame as a classic antihero figure and a deadly object of desire.

Ted Bundy was also a prolific shoplifter, a thief, and a liar who relied upon his charm to deceive and victimize others. Bundy was arrested for the kidnapping of a young woman in Colorado and linked to the murders of many missing women in several Northwestern states. Despite evidence of his guilt, including an eyewitness identification, Bundy was able to convince his many followers that he was wrongly accused, the victim of a horrible injustice rather than a remorseless killer. Friends, family, and others raised money for Bundy's defense, and his subsequent conviction did not deter his defenders.

Most of the world was introduced to Ted Bundy during sensational, televised images from trials for crimes he committed during his brief escape to Florida where he claimed more victims in a sorority house. Two women were killed and two others were severely wounded when Bundy set upon the sleeping victims with a large, wooden club. During the attack, Bundy forced an aerosol hair spray can into the rectum of one woman and he bit the second victim on the buttocks, leaving evidence later used to convict him. Bundy was also linked to the murder of a 12-year-old girl, but media accounts identified him as the killer of young coeds rather than a depraved child killer. The good-looking murder suspect who defended himself in court also defied the accepted definition of evil. Despite the overwhelming evidence of his guilt, including an eyewitness identification, Bundy was still able to charm his many followers. Women vied for his attention and sought a romantic relationship with Bundy, and he eventually married and fathered a child with one of his supporters.[5]

Other serial killers such as David Berkowitz (the "Son of Sam") and John Wayne Gacy were depicted as deranged loners, but Ted Bundy was described as attractive and engaging. When Bundy's story became a TV-movie of the week, audiences experienced the case and the crimes through the performance of actor Mark Harmon, then dubbed People Magazine's "Sexiest Man Alive." In subsequent tellings of the same story, Bundy was portrayed by other actors noted for their "sex appeal," including Cary Elwes and Billy Campbell. Popular portraits of Bundy often sanitized and sexualized the killer, further cementing the image of a likable and intelligent Dr. Jekyll instead of the more accurate face of a grotesque Mr. Hyde.

The standard description of Ted Bundy usually stated that he charmed and lured women to their deaths. His use of a fake arm-cast to elicit sympathy was often cited as an example of his clever criminal mind. However, Bundy's later confessions revealed that he was impulsive, often incompetent and usually drunk during his crimes. Impatient and desperate to experience even greater thrills of sexual violence, Bundy could barely maintain the superficial small talk necessary to deceive and distract his victims before he launched a surprise attack with a preplaced tire-iron. Bundy was often described as a cunning killer who abducted, raped, and then murdered his victims, yet his confessions revealed that he sometimes murdered and then raped his victims, even interacting with his dead victims after decomposition began.[6] In at least one instance, Bundy admitted that he had taken the severed head of a victim to his home, where he used a brush and makeup to create a glamorous masturbation tool. When the decapitated head had decayed beyond its use, Bundy burned the gruesome evidence in the fireplace at his girlfriend's home. Bundy's other victims were often found with their heads removed and placed apart from the rest of the body, an indication that he had repeated his masturbation fantasy with the heads of other victims. The man who used a severed head as a sex toy was also an American sex symbol.

Bundy's attempts to delay his impending execution by finally confessing to his crimes proved unsuccessful. In his last days, Bundy was interviewed by James Dobson of the religious organization known as the Family Research Council. Dobson's interview was included in a subsequent antipornography video. In keeping with Dobson's agenda and in a further attempt to escape his own guilt, Bundy blamed his horrific crimes on the evil influence of hardcore pornography. Dobson's documentary did not mention that Bundy's confessions contradicted this convenient attempt to deflect responsibility for his actions. According to Bundy, he was sexually aroused by the images of terrified, glamorous women and imposing, anonymous male figures which appeared on the covers of popular true crime magazines of the 1960s and 1970s. These publications often featured gruesome crime scene photographs and graphic descriptions of grisly murders. In the staged interview with James Dobson, Ted Bundy blamed the porn industry. In private confessions, Bundy implicated the mainstream media and pop culture.[7]

While Dobson and others named pornographers as the true villains, society sought the usual suspects in an attempt to reconcile the two faces of Ted Bundy, the handsome young Republican versus the murderous pervert. Bundy was initially raised by his grandparents and lived with his older sister. Later, he was finally informed that his grandfather was not his real father and that his sister was actually his mother. Bundy was reportedly devastated by the truth that he was an "illegitimate bastard," a child born outside of marriage, and media reports seized on his alleged confusion regarding his identity as a possible explanation for his violent acts. Other theories suggested that Bundy was driven to kill after being rejected by his socialite girlfriend. News reports frequently stated that Bundy's girlfriend had long hair which was parted in the middle and then noted the similarity to the appearance of the murder victims as proof to support the rejection theory. In fact, Bundy's motives remained largely unknown and his life of fantasy and violence began long before he met the woman who later rejected him. Many investigators, psychologists, and experts dismissed the theory that Bundy's identity crisis caused him to kill, noting that many people had suffered more severe trauma and abuse yet did not grow up to murder other human beings for personal pleasure. In his confessions, Ted Bundy spoke of his own failed efforts to understand his dark side and revealed that he could not identify any single spark which had ignited his murderous appetite.

Bundy's victims and pursuers were offended by the attempts to excuse his actions, as dramatized in the television mini-series about Bundy and his crimes titled *The Deliberate Stranger* (Marvin J. Chomsky, 1986). In one scene, a reporter sympathizes with Bundy's childhood confusion, provoking the sarcastic reply from detective Bob Keppel, "My heart bleeds. Lots of people grow up gettin' mixed messages, but they don't always go around crackin' girls' heads open." The line reminds viewers that easy answers often elude those who seek to explain the origins of human evil.

William Shakespeare wrote that the fault lies not in the stars but in ourselves. As the nature of evil evolves, so does pop culture and its ability to adapt and absorb even the most hideous of human faces. In the process of repackaging evil for public consumption, pop culture blames demons and other sinister forces, but the footprints found at the scene of the crime are always those of a human being.

NOTES

1. Robert D. Hare, *Without Conscience: The Disturbing World of the Psychopaths among Us* (New York: Guilford Press, 1999), 22–23.

2. The "Zodiac" letters and envelopes addressed to *The San Francisco Chronicle, The San Francisco Examiner,* and *The Vallejo Times-Herald* newspapers (California, 1969).

3. Gerard Sullivan and Harvey Aronson, *High Hopes: The Amityville Murders* (New York: Dell, 1982), 161.

4. Hans Holzer, *Murder in Amityville* (New York: Aspera Ad Astra, Inc., 2007), 33, 101.

5. Polly Nelson, *Defending the Devil: My Story as Ted Bundy's Last Lawyer* (New York: W. Morrow, 1994), 215.

6. Robert D. Keppel, PhD, as quoted in Patrick Bellamy, "Robert D. Keppel Ph.D. An Interview," Crime Library, http://www.trutv.com/library/crime/criminal_mind/profiling/keppel/3.html (accessed May 24, 2013).

7. Robert D. Keppel, *The Riverman: Ted Bundy and I Hunt for the Green River Killer* (New York: Pocket, 1995), 455.

CHAPTER 19

Ted Bundy: Celebrity Slayer

George R. "Bob" Dekle

As I was leaving Florida State Prison after attending the execution of Ted Bundy, a reporter asked me if I thought I would ever have another case like Bundy. I dodged the question by saying "No comment." If I had answered the question, I would have had to say "As a matter of fact we are preparing to indict a nomadic serial killer whose case is very similar to the Bundy case." As it turned out, this second serial killer idolized Bundy and felt honored to be tried by the same prosecutors who had sent Bundy to death row. During the course of the prosecution, I noticed many more striking similarities between the two crimes and the two criminals. To borrow a phrase from Yogi Berra, trying the man was like "*déjà vu* all over again" except that the news media almost completely ignored the case. In the final analysis, Ted Bundy was a remarkably unremarkable killer. I have been involved with cases which were far more complex and prosecuted men who were far more dangerous. Ironically, the thing which makes Bundy most like other serial killers is one of the things which people point to as making him unique—his personality.

There is almost universal agreement that Bundy was a classic example of the psychiatric condition known as sociopathy or antisocial personality disorder.[1] I have been involved in the prosecution of many men who fit the FBI's definition of a serial killer, and all of them have been sociopaths. Oddly enough, almost all these men had qualities which I would have found admirable if they had been employed for good rather than evil. In my first serial murder investigation as a prosecutor, I was sorely tempted to admire the courage and audacity displayed by the killer, but the sadism, brutality, and deviance of his crimes prevented me from thinking of him as anything but despicable. This is the paradox of sociopathic serial killers. Although many of them exhibit superficial charm, or even charisma, they also display a variety of unlovely and even repulsive behaviors. Dr. Hervey M. Cleckley, who pioneered this area of forensic psychiatry, described the sociopath as unreliable, untruthful, insincere, shameless, unremorseful, egocentric, lacking judgment, lacking insight, unable or unwilling to learn from experience, incapable of love, and likely to engage in poorly motivated antisocial behavior. Once, when my work carried me to the mental institution at Chattahoochee, Florida, a psychiatrist summed up the sociopathic personality for me. He said the sociopath was a "bum, hobo, [and] criminal." Most sociopaths engage in garden-variety criminal behavior, but some carry criminality to unsettling levels of evil. Dr. Robert Hare seeks to distinguish these "supercharged" sociopaths by calling them psychopaths. Hare's psychopath has all the characteristics of a sociopath, but in addition to antisocial behavior, Hare's psychopath engages in socially deviant behavior. Dr. Michael H. Stone eschews the term "sociopath" for antisocial personality, but he seems to agree that the psychopath is a sort of supercharged sociopath. He sees male serial sexual killers as being psychopaths who also have schizoid and sadistic personalities. Stone describes 22 levels of evil and places psychopathic killers at the pinnacle of his hierarchy of evil. We can thus see three levels of evil in Ted Bundy. He was not just a sociopath; Hare specifically categorized him as a psychopath, and Stone placed him in the inner circle of the most evil psychopathic killers.[2]

Many serial killers gain a modicum of notoriety during their criminal careers and subsequent prosecutions, but they achieve only regional and transitory fame. Bundy achieved notoriety which is not only worldwide; it is enduring. A mere week before Bundy's second trial in Florida, for the murder of Kimberly Diane Leach, Bantam published the first Bundy book. Bantam released it on January 1, 1980, with a run of 150,000 copies, and by January 4, was preparing a second run of similar size. Two other books came close on the heels of Bundy's second conviction, and over the following decades numerous others have seen print. The year 2011 alone has seen four volumes published, and at this writing another book nears publication.[3]

Richard Hauptmann, who kidnapped the Lindbergh baby, is the only other modern American killer who has generated as many books. There is a stark difference between the two bodies of literature, however—one focuses on whether, the other on why. The authors of the Hauptmann corpus engage in a lively debate of Hauptmann's guilt or innocence while the Bundy authors try to understand how a seemingly normal person could commit such unspeakable crimes. Although the case against Hauptmann was far stronger than the case against Bundy, many authors vociferously contend for Hauptmann's innocence, some even going so far as to accuse the prosecution of criminal conspiracy. Had Bundy emulated Hauptmann and refused to confess, he might be the subject of a similar body of revisionist literature. But he confessed in the forlorn hope that he could stave off his execution by giving the details of his crimes, and the world had to confront the awful truth that attractive, seemingly normal human beings can commit unspeakable crimes.

Despite the fact that he displayed all the unlovely characteristics of the sociopathic personality, and despite the perversity of his crimes, Bundy has become the "Rudolph Valentino of the serial killer world."[4] Bundy's career as a folk celebrity began almost as soon as he became a suspect in an unsolved string of murders occurring in the Far West. He first came to public notice as a beleaguered innocent hounded by relentless officers bent on arresting somebody, anybody, for the crimes. Although this perception waned, it lingered in some quarters up until Bundy unleashed a torrent of confessions on the eve of his execution. Before his execution, people would often challenge me, contending Bundy was innocent and questioning how I could have been involved in the prosecution of such a nice young man. Even after his execution, I receive occasional queries from those who doubt his guilt. The latest of these queries came on the heels of the recent announcement that Bundy's DNA had been profiled using the blood sample we collected from him over three decades ago. My questioner wanted to know why we did not settle the issue of Bundy's guilt once and for all by comparing Bundy's DNA profile against the foreign body fluids on our victim's clothing. I replied that, firstly, in light of Bundy's confession it would be a waste of time, and secondly, that all the tangible evidence in our case had been destroyed years ago on the heels of Bundy's execution. It was only by accident that the vials of blood were overlooked when everything else was destroyed.

As the public came less and less to regard him as Bundy the Beleaguered, he took on the persona of Teflon Ted, a wily bad boy who could confound and confute the police at every turn, a "Golden Boy" who was "beloved by the media." His two escapes from the Colorado jail where he awaited trial for the murder of Caryn Campbell merely added to his luster as an antiestablishment mastermind. Before he came to Florida, the persona of Teflon Ted assumed mythic proportions, as the public actually celebrated him. Entrepreneurs began selling Bundy cocktails and T-shirts bearing the inscription "Ted Bundy is a One-Night-Stand." At least one enterprising capitalist even began selling the Bundy burger, which had no meat in honor of the fact that many of his victims were skeletonized when their bodies were found.[5]

In the wake of his Florida convictions, Teflon Ted became Bundy the Bedeviled, a brilliant young man whose great potential was destroyed by the demons of mental illness. Possibly the greatest contributing factor in the shift from Teflon Ted to Bundy the Bedeviled was a remark made by Circuit Judge Edward Cowart when he sentenced Bundy to death for the Chi Omega Murders. Just before Bundy was led from the courtroom, Cowart said: "It's a tragedy for this court to see such a total waste of humanity that I've experienced in this courtroom. You're a bright young man. You'd have made a good lawyer, and I'd have loved to have you practice in front of me—but you went another way, partner. Take care of yourself. I don't have any animosity to you. I want you to know that."[6]

Bundy the Bedeviled became the central character in one of the early books on his career. When originally published in 1983, Stephen G. Michaud and Hugh Aynesworth's book, *The Only Living Witness*, bore the subtitle *A True Account of Homicidal Insanity*. Michaud and Aynesworth took up an offhand remark I made shortly after Bundy's conviction and featured it prominently in their book. A reporter had remarked to me that she could hardly believe such an articulate, well-groomed, nice-looking young man could be capable of such horrible crimes. I replied, "People think a criminal is a hunchbacked, cross-eyed little monster with warts all over his face slithering through the dark leaving a trail of slime. But they're not; they're human beings." Michaud and Aynesworth seized upon the hunchback metaphor and made it a theme of their book, mentioning Bundy's hunchback persona no fewer than 11 times. Bundy the Bedeviled began to lose steam with the Federal habeas corpus hearing held before Judge Kendall Sharp in December 1987. Bundy's lawyers had convinced the Eleventh Circuit Court of Appeals that there was reason to believe he was mentally incompetent, and that an evidentiary hearing should be held on the issue. Sharp held a multiday hearing in which an array of witnesses testified on the issue of Bundy's competence. Finally, Sharp released a lengthy opinion carefully assessing the defense claims and the testimony of the witnesses. He summed up his analysis by finding Bundy competent. Michaud and Aynesworth's book never mentioned the hunchback in their second book on Bundy, and when they rereleased *The Only Living Witness* in 1999, they changed the subtitle from *A True Account of Homicidal Insanity* to *The True Story of Serial Sex Killer Ted Bundy*. Bundy, in his final public incarnation, was (and is) the embodiment of evil. Bundy once told a team of police interrogators that he had a vampire component to his personality.[7] Vampire Ted, like the vampires of modern fiction, continues to engender both fascination and revulsion in the American public.

Just as Dracula had female admirers, Bundy had female admirers. During the proceedings against him, we noticed several young women who would come to the court proceedings and sit in the audience admiring him from afar. We gave one of his admirers the nickname "The Lady in Black" because she always wore black to court. She would sit in the courtroom and divide her time between casting longing looks at Bundy and staring daggers at the young lady who eventually became Mrs. Ted Bundy.

Bundy's future wife steadfastly advocated his innocence from the time of his arrest throughout the trial proceedings. The two were married in a bizarre "ceremony" which Bundy conducted while he examined her as a witness during the penalty phase of his trial in Orlando, and she stood by him right up until the time that he began to confess his crimes on the eve of his execution. I completely lost track of her after the execution, but I was told by prison personnel that Bundy's confessions devastated her.

Bundy is not unique in having inspired such a devoted following. During his trials and tribulations following the disappearance of Natalee Holloway, Joran van der Sloot acquired at least one such advocate. Van der Sloot's admirer held a responsible position as a radiologist at a Veterans Affairs Hospital when she took up his cause in 2010. Since that time she has appeared on the *Today Show* and in *Newsweek* proclaiming his innocence. She was recently quoted as saying "The more I know Joran, the more I know there's a beautiful person in there," and declaring that although she has no romantic interest in him, "I love him unconditionally."[8] Van der Sloot's recent plea of guilty to the murder of Stephanie Flores might prove a severe test for that love.

Decades after his crimes and execution, Bundy continues to fascinate. There is at least one very active comment thread on the Internet which engages in a lively continuing discussion of all aspects of Bundy's personality and the cases against him. People still ask me about him, and the question they most commonly ask is "Tell me, what was he really like?" Ann Rule reports similar experiences and gives as an example a conversation she had at a hospital. As she lay on the table in the operating room and the anesthesiologist prepared to sedate her, one of the nurses leaned toward her and asked "Tell me, what was Ted Bundy really like?" How can this be? How can Americans continue, over two decades after Bundy's execution, to be so fascinated by him? Many writers have weighed in on the subject, and each of their observations serves as a piece which we can fit into the puzzle as we seek to understand the phenomenon of Bundy's celebrity. Robert Ressler thinks it was because Bundy was so "photogenic and articulate." David Schmid opines that Bundy represented an "especially roguish example" of the stereotypical heterosexual ladies' man. Hare confesses that he is mystified by such a phenomenon but offers the suggestion that "notoriety is confused with fame." Ann Rule believes that Bundy's popularity comes from the public's selective memory. They remember Teflon Ted while they gloss over his horrific crimes. But even those who fully appreciate his criminality can still compartmentalize their thinking so as to find him fascinating.[9]

Whatever it is in the human psyche that causes us to be attracted to evil, it is not new. One of the oldest stories in Western literature tells how Adam and Eve ate the forbidden fruit because "it was pleasant to the eyes;" and Aristotle, in his *Poetics*, makes the point that we quickly become bored with a protagonist who displays only good qualities. Our heroes must be good, but not too good. Thus we find Jacob, the wily trickster and con man, more appealing than his father Isaac, the homebody; and David, the adulterer and murderer, is more attractive than his descendant Josiah, the religious reformer. We find a rather remarkable example of this in Milton's portrayal of Satan in *Paradise Lost*. Satan is, of course, the villain; but he displays such courage, audacity, determination, and resourcefulness that we come to like him. Satan's heavenly counterpart, Michael, suffers in comparison. Michael's personality is simply too bland to inspire admiration. Milton has been accused of being a closet atheist for his sympathetic portrayal of Satan, and the criticism reached such a level that in his *Preface to Paradise Lost*, C.S. Lewis felt compelled to write a chapter defending Milton and explaining why Satan appears to be such a hero in the epic. Lewis attempts to rescue Milton by admitting that his Satan is a magnificent character, but distinguishing two senses of the term "magnificent character." He argues that Milton wrote a magnificent portrayal of Satan, but that Milton never intended his Satan to be someone we ought to admire.[10]

Lewis contends that it is the "Satan in us" which causes us to admire Milton's Satan, but merely blaming the attraction on Original Sin is too simplistic an explanation. We admire Milton's Satan for the same three reasons that we admire villains like Bundy: First, we do not fully appreciate the depths of the harm resulting from the evil done by such people—we are disconnected from the suffering caused by the evil. It is one thing to acknowledge intellectually that someone has committed an evil act; it is something else entirely to appreciate fully the suffering caused by that act. It's the difference between knowing that hitting our thumb with a hammer will hurt and feeling the pain when we actually hit it with a hammer. We often look upon minor, victimless rule breaking as if it were a practical joke. We find it humorous because the appearance of danger from the joke is not real. Practical jokers and minor rule breakers, so long as they hurt no one, amuse us. If we can insulate ourselves from the pathos of villainous crimes, we can treat them as practical jokes. Thus, instead of being horrified by Ted Bundy's murders, we can buy Bundy burgers and wear T-shirts saying "Ted Bundy is a One-Night-Stand."

Second, we forget that "good" does not always equal "moral," "ethical," or "saintly." There are many morally neutral qualities that are "good" to possess, and when people possess these qualities, we see them as "good" in the moral or ethical sense. Consider courage. We all agree that it is good to have courage, and we admire the courageous. But evil people can display courage as readily as good people. Other attributes such as competence, skill, strength, intelligence, and affability are morally neutral. It is "good" to have them, and we sometimes forget that having them does not make us morally good. Bundy's affability, resourcefulness, intelligence, and physical beauty were all "good" but they were neither ethical, moral, nor saintly. I once heard a defense attorney argue that his client was unworthy of the death penalty because he was a highly skilled mechanic. In another case, such a skill might be a mitigating circumstance, but in this case the defendant had used that mechanical skill to build the homemade gun with which he killed his wife. "Good" qualities are not good if they are used in the service of evil.

Third, we confuse suffering with martyrdom. When a villainous killer is finally prosecuted for his misdeeds, he suffers. When a martyr is prosecuted for standing on her principles, she suffers. There is a universe of difference, however, between the suffering of Sir Thomas More and the suffering of Timothy McVeigh. If we do not appreciate the reason for the suffering, we can confer undeserved sainthood on the sufferer. When these three factors converge, Bundy and those like him can evoke our sympathy and collect a cadre of supporters. This happens almost every day in prosecutions throughout the land, although few people like Bundy reach the lofty heights of nationwide celebrity because we disconnect from the suffering caused by their crimes, mistake their "good" qualities for ethical and moral qualities, and consider them saintly merely because they suffer the consequences of their evil deeds.

As I see things, a pedestrian murder case becomes a *cause célèbre* when the circumstances of the killing add three additional factors to the equation—beauty, celebrity (or its counterfeit, notoriety), and innocence. These three additional factors can reside exclusively in the victims, as in the Tate-LaBianca murders, or they can be shared among killer and victim, as in the O.J. Simpson case. The Simpson case provides an example of perceived innocence on both sides. On the one hand, neither Ron Goldman nor Nicole Simpson deserved the fate they suffered, and on the other Simpson's lawyers successfully portrayed him as the victim of police misconduct. In our culture, we equate being unjustly prosecuted with being innocent. This is why many perceive Richard Hauptmann as innocent of the Lindbergh kidnapping. Looking at the trial, we see the prosecution doing all sorts of things which at the time were legal, but which have come to be condemned as violations of constitutional rights. We retroject our more stringent requirements for a fair trial into a situation where they did not apply, and we conclude that Hauptmann was the victim of an unjust prosecution and therefore innocent.

Bundy's case provided a perfect storm of faulty reasons and *cause célèbre* factors—counterfeit celebrity (Teflon Ted), beauty ("The Rudolph Valentino of serial killers"), perceived innocence (Bundy the Beleaguered), disconnecting the harm done from the evil ("Ted Bundy is a One-Night

Stand"), equating "good" with "moral" ("You're a bright young man"), and mistaking the protagonist's suffering for sainthood (Bundy the Bedeviled). The public found itself confronted with a young man accused of committing a string of unspeakable crimes against a series of beautiful young women, a young man who turned out to be handsome and well-spoken, and to have a flair for outrageous courtroom conduct. He presented us with the paradox of beauty and unspeakable evil dwelling in the same body. The paradox was so marked that many believed him to be an innocent victim of police misconduct—right up until he began confessing his crimes.

Probably the most important of the six factors is the disconnect between evil and harm. Ted Bundy and people like him would not become celebrities if we would simply refuse to disconnect from the suffering they have caused. When I was chose to be witness to the execution, I feared that seeing him collect the wages of his sin would be traumatic. In order to disconnect from Bundy's suffering, I prepared myself on the eve of the execution by reconnecting the suffering he caused. I went into the archives of the State Attorney's Office and reviewed the crime scene photographs. At least one of the official witnesses was profoundly shaken by the execution. He probably had failed to prepare himself by fully reconnecting with the evil done by Bundy.

Most Floridians stayed connected to the evil. They celebrated each death warrant and bemoaned each stay of execution. When Governor Martinez signed the final death warrant and it looked as though he really would be executed, a North Florida disc jockey known only as "the Greaseman" began playing the sound of frying bacon in honor of the event. Two central Florida disc jockeys cut a record to the tune of *American Pie* in which they crooned "Bye bye Ted Bundy, bye bye." Caravans were organized to convoy celebrants to Florida State Prison for the execution. Upon leaving the death chamber and returning to the prison parking lot to drive home, I looked across the road into the normally empty field in front of Florida State Prison and saw a crowd of hundreds of people. With most executions, only death penalty foes gathered outside the prison, but death penalty advocates heavily outnumbered them this particular morning.

Another factor that we might consider is distance in time. We can admire historical figures like Vlad the Impaler (1431–1476) because their crimes are so far in the past that we are insulated from the evil. For some, however, the passage of time can never obscure the evil. To this day you will find few admirers of Bundy in Lake City, Florida, his last victim's home town. Over three decades later, he is universally despised by those who lived through the ordeal of Kim Leach's disappearance and discovery, and the spectacle of his prosecution. Lake City never disconnected from the evil and consequently never lost sight of where the true beauty and innocence lay—in a pretty little 12-year-old girl who was robbed of her bright future by unspeakable villainy.

NOTES

1. Robert D. Keppel, *The Riverman: Ted Bundy and I Hunt for the Green River Killer* (New York: Pocket, 1995), 417; Richard W. Larsen, *Bundy: The Deliberate Stranger* (Englewood Cliffs, NJ: Prentice-Hall, 1980), 299, 300; Stephen G. Michaud and Hugh Aynesworth, *The Only Living Witness*, Updated ed., Signet Non Fiction (Irving, TX: Authorlink Press, 1999), 13; Ann Rule, *The Stranger Beside Me* (New York: Pocket Books Reprint, 2009), 81, 480. "Psychopathy" is an older term for the condition. See Hervey M. Cleckley, *The Mask of Sanity: An Attempt to Clarify Some Issues about the So-Called Psychopathic Personality*, 5th ed. (Augusta, GA: Emily Cleckley, 1988).

2. Most of these men were diagnosed as sociopaths by mental health professionals. All exhibited the behavioral characteristics associated with sociopathy. Cleckley, *The Mask of Sanity: An Attempt to Clarify Some Issues about the So-Called Psychopathic Personality*, 337–64; Robert D. Hare, *Without Conscience: The Disturbing World of the Psychopaths among Us* (New York: Guilford Press, 1999), 23–25; Michael H. Stone, *The Anatomy of Evil* (Amherst: Prometheus Books, 2009), 33, 315–18.

3. Steve Winn and David Merrill, *Ted Bundy: The Killer Next Door* (New York Bantam, 1980); John S. Gholdston, "Sales of Bundy Book Reflect Trail of Convicted Murderer's Past," *Orlando Sentinel-Star*, January 4, 1980.{Larsen, 1980 #202}; Rule, *The Stranger Beside Me*. See, for example Michaud and Aynesworth, *The Only Living Witness*; Stephen G. Michaud, Hugh Aynesworth, and Ted Bundy, *Ted Bundy: Conversations with a Killer* (Irving, TX: Authorlink Press, 2000); Kevin M. Sullivan, *The Bundy Murders: A Comprehensive History* (Jefferson, NC: McFarland, 2009); Rebecca Morris, *Ted and Ann: The Mystery of a Missing Child and Her Neighbor Ted Bundy* (Indianapolis: Dog Ear, 2011); George R. Dekle, *The Last Murder: The Investigation, Prosecution, and Execution of Ted Bundy* (Santa Barbara, CA: Praeger, 2011); L. H. Victoria, *Conquering the Haunting Memories of Ted Bundy* (Frederick, MD: PublishAmerica, 2011); Stephen G. Michaud and Robert D. Keppel, *Terrible Secrets: Ted Bundy on Serial Murder* (Irving, TX: Authorlink Press 2011); "Advertisement for Richard A. Duffus," *Ted Bundy: The Felon's Hook* (Darksider Press, 2012), http://www.darksiderpress.com/ (accessed December 17, 2011).

4. Robert K. Ressler and Tom Shachtman, *Whoever Fights Monsters* (New York: St. Martin's Press, 1992), 72.

5. Rule, *The Stranger Beside Me*, 350. Jay Cowan, "Aspen Scandals: Part I," *Aspen Sojourner*, Summer 2009.

6. Rule, *The Stranger Beside Me*, 335.

7. Michaud and Aynesworth, *The Only Living Witness*, 13–15, 19, 20–22, 24, 78, 120, 242; *Bundy v. Dugger*, 816 F.2d 564 (11th Cir., 1987); *Bundy v. Dugger*, 675 Fed.Supp. 622 (M.D. Fla., 1987); Michaud, Aynesworth, and Bundy, *Ted*

Bundy: Conversations with a Killer; Dekle, *The Last Murder: The Investigation, Prosecution, and Execution of Ted Bundy*, 50.

8. Anne Geggis, "Woman Wants to Be Van der Sloot's Guardian Angel," *Gainesville Sun*, January 13, 2012.

9. "1989: Ted Bundy, Psycho Killer," *Executed Today*, January 24, 2009 http://www.executedtoday.com/2009/01/24/1989-ted-bundy-psycho-killer/; David Schmid, *Natural Born Celebrities: Serial Killers in American Culture* (Chicago: University of Chicago Press, 2005), 215; Hare, *Without Conscience: The Disturbing World of the Psychopaths among Us*, 150; Rule, *The Stranger Beside Me*. "pointu mais passionnant"; Ann Rule, *The Stranger Beside Me* (New York: Pocket Books Reprint, 2009), 618; Robert K. Ressler and Tom Shachtman, *Whoever Fights Monsters* (New York: St. Martin's Press, 1992) 72.

10. Genesis 3:6 (KJV). Aristotle and Jonathan Barnes, *The Complete Works of Aristotle: The Revised Oxford Translation*, 2 vols., vol. 2, Bollingen Series (Princeton: Princeton University Press, 1984), 2327–29; C. S. Lewis, *A Preface to Paradise Lost* (London: Oxford University Press, 1961), 94, 101.

CHAPTER 20

Evil Empire and Axis of Evil: The Evocation of Evil in Political Rhetoric

Glen M. E. Duerr

INTRODUCTION

In the recent history of the United States, two presidents are remembered specifically for their invocations of the concept of evil. Both statements were used as a means of implementing a more combative form of foreign policy aimed at changing what they perceived to be threats to liberty in the international arena. President Ronald Reagan described the Soviet Union as the "evil empire" and President George W. Bush described the countries of Iraq, Iran, and North Korea as part of an "axis of evil." Describing international issues in moral terms is not new in American politics. Other presidents such as Bill Clinton used the concept "rogue states," Franklin Roosevelt identified "four freedoms," and Woodrow Wilson wanted to make the world "safe for democracy."[1] The statements by Ronald Reagan and George W. Bush, however, by invoking the notion of evil as applied to an enemy, marked a change from statements made by other presidents. A clear line was drawn between "evil" enemies and the "good and benevolent" United States. These statements became defining moments of their respective presidencies.

President Reagan delivered his remarks on the evil empire to the National Association of Evangelicals in Orlando, Florida, on March 8, 1983. President Bush delivered his famous axis of evil line during his State of the Union address in Washington, D.C., on January 29, 2002.[2] Both sets of remarks highlight the importance and use of the term "evil" in American political rhetoric. By invoking the term "evil," both presidents were tapping into a contested part of the national narrative that the United

States is exceptional, and a force for good in the world. The term "evil" implies that both good and evil exist in the world and that countries can— at a given point in history—be classified as one or the other. This is not to say that countries in the world fall into a simple dichotomy of good or evil; rather, the world is full of grey and abstract issues, but some things— like the actions and policies of some authoritarian leaders—can be measured at the extremes of good and evil.

The act of judging something or someone as evil can be categorized into three broad categories. The first category argues that nothing can be described as evil, that the world is too complex for an absolute judgment. The second category argues that some events and some decisions are undoubtedly evil. Many people, for example, would describe the holocaust as an evil atrocity carried out on millions of innocent people, or would consider the Rwandan genocide as an evil act. The final group argues that evil exists and should be labeled wherever and whenever it is judged so. Ronald Reagan and George W. Bush both fit into the final category of people. They were both willing to label a country (or a group of countries) as evil and align foreign policy strategies with ridding the world of that evil.

This chapter will investigate the use of evil in American political rhetoric. I start the chapter by discussing the foreign policy context in which both presidents delivered their famous lines invoking the concept of evil. I then move on to discuss what was said specifically and how different people distinctly view Presidents Ronald Reagan and George W. Bush in light of their comments on evil. Finally, I discuss their respective legacies and how their comments on evil have been viewed over time.

FOREIGN POLICY DECISIONS IN CONTEXT

Ronald Reagan was president during the Cold War, an era stretching from the end of World War II to 1991, wherein the United States and the Soviet Union were two global superpowers fighting for influence across the rest of the world. The United States supported the ideology of capitalism (and on paper, democracy; but much less so in practice), whereas the Soviet Union supported the ideology of communism. By the time George W. Bush became president of the United States in January 2001, the world was very different. The Cold War was over and the United States was left as the sole superpower in the world, but an old tactic of warfare, terrorism, emerged in a new and more deadly way. While terrorism had been used as a tactic of warfare for decades in diverse parts of the world, 9/11 spectacularly changed the scope of terrorist attacks, given the high-level targets, the sheer number of casualties, and the toll on the world economy. The decisions and statements made by Presidents Ronald Reagan and George W. Bush took place in specific contexts wherein as commander-in-chief, the president had to enact a foreign policy vision in line with what they thought was the best approach to retaining and promoting American interests in light of the major global power dynamics at play. Both presidents were in their first terms and would seek reelection.

EVIL IN AMERICAN POLITICAL RHETORIC

All human beings believe in some form of morality. Each individual and society has norms as to what constitutes moral behavior. In the United States, moral discussions are debated more regularly than in Western Europe, but are less prevalent than in the Middle East and South Asia. A discussion of morality in American politics is nothing new, though. As noted earlier, presidents from Wilson to Roosevelt to Clinton all invoked moral messages in their foreign policy speeches. Ronald Reagan and George W. Bush were, however, different from these other examples. Both carefully specified what they thought was clearly right and wrong, marking two distinct categories. The historian and journalist David Halberstam notes, ". . . many of the Reagan people had cared not just about national security but rather which side was right and which side was wrong. Not by chance had Reagan himself called the Soviet empire 'evil.'"[3] What is interesting about this is that Reagan imposed a moral absolute on the Soviet Union, and George W. Bush did the same with Iran, Iraq, and North Korea. The underlying principle at work for these presidents is that the United States is exceptional and has an obligation to stand up against evils in the world.

However, both Reagan's "evil empire" and George W. Bush's "axis of evil" were also meant to appeal to voters who held religiously based distinctions between good and evil. Specifically, George W. Bush was often linked with Evangelical Christians and he gained significant support from this group, mainly because he publicly identified as an evangelical. Ronald Reagan, however, did not publicly identify himself as an evangelical (unlike his opponent in 1980, Jimmy Carter). Reagan was generally viewed as a Christian, though, and publicly professed Christian faith. Christian distinctions of good and evil are invoked by religious and political leaders to provide clear moral instruction in an otherwise abstract and ambiguous world. There are major debates in Christian circles as to the extent of how and when Christians should confront aggression. Some argue that Christians should simply love their enemies, others say that aggression should be confronted within the tenets of *Just War* theory, and still others note that it is a moral imperative to stand up for the weak and those that have been exploited wherever they may be. Ronald Reagan and George W. Bush fall into the latter category, as leaders that should take moral stands and oppose those they perceive to be carrying out evil acts and who are deemed to be exploiting other people and/or countries.

RONALD REAGAN'S EVIL EMPIRE

As a result of their decisions, the statements invoking evil deserve closer individual scrutiny. Reagan frequently castigated Soviet leaders noting, pointing to such things as their immorality, aggression, and oppression. Reagan openly confronted the Soviet Union in a manner that was much more confrontational than his predecessors. He saw the Soviet empire spreading communism and stifling liberty and freedom, especially in Eastern Europe and Southeast Asia, and also in parts of Latin America and Africa.

Reagan's statement, in many respects, overturned U.S. policy toward the Soviet Union. Instead of following the traditional path of George Kennan's "containment," Reagan chose to increase the pressure on the Soviet Union.[4] In many respects, Reagan was quite successful. His legacy of introducing the strategy of "rollback" instead of Kennan's strategy of "containment," which had been the central U.S. strategy since the start of the Cold War, was on paper very successful. Containment was successful on paper because the United States avoided a nuclear and/or military war with the Soviet Union, but it also meant that communism remained credible in much of the world. Reagan's decision to put more and greater pressure on the Soviet Union is often cited by Republican and Democratic presidential hopefuls. For example, former speaker of the House of Representatives and former 2012 Republican hopeful, Newt Gingrich, has spent much time trying to position himself as a Reaganite leader.

Typically, most Americans argue that Reagan should be applauded for his efforts to defeat the Soviet Union. Several prominent commentators make this case below.[5] Former Secretary of State, Condoleezza Rice, argues that Reagan "issued the final challenge to the Soviet Union at the dawn of the 1980s, calling it an evil empire and pushing through huge defense budgets that spent it into the Ice Age." Journalist Tom Brokaw notes that "(Reagan) so skillfully kept the pressure on the Soviet Union that its end was inevitable." Former Vice President, Dan Quayle, argues that Reagan was right in challenging the Soviet Union economically and on the issue of "Star Wars." Quayle argues that "while the rest of the world was growing richer, the Soviet empire was getting more miserable and poor." Quayle's implication is that through increased pressure on the Soviet Union, Reagan's policies directly correlated with its downfall.

Moreover, Quayle argues that in implementing the Star Wars program, the Soviet Union was forced to spend more money to keep up with the United States in terms of technology, which also added strain to the Soviet economy and the Soviets' ability to function as a legitimate superpower. Finally, author Dinesh D'Souza explains that Reagan made some very bold remarks about confronting the Soviet Union even when experts in the field foresaw a strong and vibrant Soviet Union, which, they claimed, would continue to exist.

There is, of course, debate on this subject. Other commentators argue that Reagan should not be given credit for the fall of the Soviet Union.[6] Scholar Frances Fitzgerald, for example, argues that the collapse of the Soviet Union had little to do with Reagan or with his Strategic Defense Initiative ("Star Wars"). Likewise, Gwynne Dyer argues that the Soviet command economy stalled in the 1960s while defense spending still matched the Americans'. In effect, Reagan's defense budget increase in 1982, Dyer argues, only served to "flog an already dead horse." Nonetheless, despite some critiques, the pressure from Reagan ultimately helped to speed up the downfall of the Soviet Union, but as with any major change, it should be seen as a cumulative effect of several presidencies, not just Reagan's. All presidents, from Truman through Carter, also deserve some of the praise for winning the Cold War.

President Ronald Reagan's declaration that the Soviet Union was the "evil empire" served to confront the Soviet Union sternly. It is also noteworthy, however, that Reagan's tone and demeanor changed in his second term with the arrival of Mikhail Gorbachev as secretary general of the Communist Party and president of the Soviet Union. Reagan and Gorbachev had a much more cordial relationship and they began to discuss a range of different ways of cooperating including the issue of reductions in nuclear armaments.

GEORGE W. BUSH'S AXIS OF EVIL

President Bush delivered the "axis of evil" line at the 2002 State of the Union address to a joint session of Congress in Washington, D.C. The axis of evil includes three countries: Iran, Iraq, and North Korea and speechwriter David Frum took credit for inserting the phrase into the speech. In his autobiography, *Decision Points*, President Bush discusses the axis of evil statement. He argues that media took the statement to mean that Iran, Iraq, and North Korea were in an alliance, which he says missed the point. Rather, President Bush argues, the axis "referred to . . . the link between the governments that pursued weapons of mass destruction (WMD) and the terrorists who could use the weapons."[7]

The "axis of evil" statement was defended by Henry Kissinger who argued that the Bush administration had uncovered some important facts in the international arena. Kissinger argues that Bush "raised a central issue to international security: the nexus between large, well-organized and deadly terrorist organizations (such as al-Qaeda), states that have used and supported terrorism (such as Iran and North Korea), and states that have developed (and, in the case of Iraq, used) WMD."[8]

At the time of the speech (and also since then), President Bush received significant criticism domestically and globally. The "axis of evil" speech should, however, be seen as part of the larger Bush Doctrine, which is composed of several components. Two major components include: American primacy and preemptive war (and strikes). Some other components of the Bush Doctrine include: challenging and stopping states that harbor terrorists, and democratic regime change through advancing liberty.[9]

Bush's proclamation of an "axis of evil" spoke to many people in the American polity, but resonated most clearly with foreign policy hawks and religious voters. Amongst foreign policy hawks, the argument is that the United States is an exceptional country and has the responsibility to make sure that threats to liberty and freedom are confronted wherever they exist in the world. Given this starting point, an exceptional and benevolent United States must take the fight for liberty and justice to authoritarian despots wherever and whenever it is deemed necessary.

The other intended audience of the statement, Evangelical Christians, formed a significant voting bloc for Bush in 2000 and 2004 and the invocation of evil was a frame of reference most in tune with this group. The separation of good and evil into distinct categories is an important way to view the world for Evangelical Christians, and this includes foreign policy. Although many commentators and analysts characterize evangelicals as simplistic for categorizing people or actions as evil, most evangelicals would argue that the world has its complexities, but that simple distinctions between good and evil do sometimes exist and need to be categorized as biblical or unbiblical.

In 2004, 79 percent of white evangelicals voted for Bush, while 21 percent voted for Kerry. (Most African American evangelicals, on the other hand, voted overwhelmingly for Kerry in 2004.) Since 2004, however, the number of young (18–29 years) white evangelicals approving of President Bush dropped dramatically from a high of 87 percent in 2002 to just 45 percent in 2007.[10] This shows, in part, that while the term "axis of evil" was used to target evangelicals, many evangelicals, especially young ones, began to disapprove of Bush's job as president, which was tied to his foreign policy and handling of the Iraq War. Bush was reelected in 2004 with the support of millions of evangelicals, but that support did not remain through the end of his presidency.

The main policy outcome of the "axis of evil" speech was the invasion of Iraq in 2003 in order to rid the country of WMD and install a democratic system of government. Despite an initial military victory, there were failures of policy such as not finding the WMD, ethnic and sectarian violence amongst Kurds, Sunni, and Shia, and the problems of forming a government in a timely matter. Democracy takes time, but there were numerous problems. And, these problems have remained to the detriment of the Bush legacy. It is still possible that Iraq will turn into a functioning, open, and contested democracy, but that has not happened yet.

In their book *An End to Evil: How to Win the War on Terror*, David Frum and Richard Perle defend the use of evil in political rhetoric. Frum and Perle argue that "terrorism is the greatest evil of our time" and that "Iran and North Korea are working frantically to develop nuclear weapons."[11] These authors invoke evil as a means of declaring some countries to be enemies, which need to be confronted either directly through force or indirectly through sanctions and other tactics. Frum is important to the discussion on the "axis of evil" because he was the speechwriter who inserted the line into Bush's speech. The line was then cleared by several high-level experts in the administration including Condoleezza Rice and then the president himself.

The Bush administration used moral language in discussing foreign policy on more than one occasion. During George W. Bush's second term, his Secretary of State, Condoleezza Rice, pinpointed six "outposts of tyranny," including Cuba, Belarus, Zimbabwe, Burma, Iran, and North Korea. The announcement was similar to the "axis of evil" speech, but was much less well publicized. However, in identifying six outposts of tyranny, Rice linked six states, which are dictatorial and abuse human rights. This list of six states is selective because others could fit here, but it still increased pressure on all of these regimes. Applying pressure to restrictive regimes was something that the Bush administration was very good at. This was seen as part of the larger strategy of the freedom agenda (discussed later) wherein economic, political, and religious freedoms should be encouraged throughout the world.

A SHARED THEME OF EVIL

A common theme in both the "evil empire" and "axis of evil" speeches was an overarching point—advocated by both Reagan and Bush—that good states need to keep evil leaders in check. In a 2009 book chapter, I argued that Bush is not a neoconservative, but rather an evangelical realist. Where evil leaders exist, the evangelical realist will seek—where possible—to spread human liberties.[12] Reagan's rhetoric, in many respects, was designed to have a similar impact. These statements appeal to a more religious audience for whom moral absolutes exist. Often, the president expresses some level of sympathy for the people under a given authoritarian regime, but military and economic pressures are also mounted against said enemy.

With Reagan and Bush, both leaders—for right or for wrong—took a moral stand against their enemies. The implication here is that leaders like Reagan and Bush are more likely to draw moral lines in the sand and stand against people and/or regimes they consider to be evil. This type of stance can be overtly confrontational and can cause needless deaths. These confrontations can, however, also change the trajectory of history for a given set of people. Examples of this include Russia in the 1990s after the dissolution of the Soviet Union and Burma at the present, which, as of the time of writing (June 2012) has undergone numerous important democratic reforms.

A useful source for the foreign policy stances of both Ronald Reagan and George W. Bush is the work of Reinhold Niebuhr. Niebuhr was a theologian and foreign policy advocate in much of the middle part of the 20th century who argued that Protestants should stand against tyranny and that they had a moral calling to confront injustice in the world. Niebuhr was writing against the backdrop of World War II and the legacy of many of his contemporaries having argued that the United States should not get involved in the conflict against Germany. Niebuhr argued that biblically there was no evidence that one should cower or avoid confrontation; rather, he argued that the Christian had the responsibility to stand up and confront evil wherever it exists.[13] Aspects of this lesson have been applied by both Reagan and Bush, although Niebuhr might well disagree with some of the applications.

LEGACY

The use of moral and/or religiously inspired political language has the potential for both policy success and failure. Reagan's "evil empire" speech emboldened U.S. policy toward the Soviet Union and ended up being successful with the dissolution of the USSR and the end of the Cold War. It also ushered in an era when America became the world's sole superpower, which has led to U.S. primacy globally. In many respects, the legacy of Ronald Reagan is still seen as very strong given the frequency of citation amongst Democrats and Republicans alike. Reagan's legacy has also stood the test of some time; although, as with any legacy, more time will help to clarify whether he made the correct policy decisions. The downside of Reagan confronting the Soviet Union so boldly is that he did not balance the national budget and the national debt increased during his presidency, something that is a contemporary issue and could still undermine his legacy.

Since the dissolution of the Soviet Union in 1991, the world has been more peaceful than at any other era in human history by some measures. This cannot be credited directly to Reagan by any means, but the end of the Cold War created the conditions for greater peace. With the United States as the sole superpower in the world—and a largely benevolent one at that—great power rivalries were no longer the most immediate threat. The United Nations has functioned better and both interstate and intrastate wars received more international attention—and by proxy, more incentives were given to stop these wars. Reagan cannot be credited with this, but he did contribute to speeding up the end of the Cold War and in so doing allowed for a greater window to decrease global conflict.

The Soviet Union no longer poses a threat to the United States and the Cold War has been won. However, Russia did not become a legitimate and functioning democracy as hoped by Reagan and Gorbachev. Vladimir Putin came to power in 2000 and has remained in office by manipulating the constitution and bending the electoral rules to give himself more legitimacy. It is not likely that Russia will pose a major threat to the world, but Russia has bullied its neighbors and still exerts significant power in the former-Soviet sphere. Reagan's legacy is solid, but there are some related issues that are contested.

The legacy of George W. Bush is not clear yet. The Iraq War was costly, selective, and undermanned, but democracy is (so far) holding in the country. The Arab Spring of 2010–2012 (and still going at the time of writing) also relates to the axis of evil line and Condoleezza Rice's "outposts of tyranny" speech, which were both effective in that they targeted various dictators around the world. George W. Bush confronted what he saw as evil in the world and based a major foreign policy decision on this moral notion, which may have emboldened others to do the same thing.

Critics, however, argue that there are numerous problems with the Bush legacy: the image of the United States seriously declined throughout the Muslim world (in particular), Saddam was contained and not an immediate threat, and future issues with WMD (such as Iran and North Korea) were set back because of the speed at which Bush decided to go into Iraq without proof of WMD stockpiles. Relatedly, critics argue that Iran is now the strongest power in the Middle East and the United States paid to get rid of Iran's biggest rival. Finally, some critics argue that Bush ignored the wider issue of power in the world. He weakened the United States by massively funding the wars in Iraq and Afghanistan while great power rivals like China and Russia became relatively stronger during the same period. Geostrategically, these critics argue, Bush made a major mistake, which has cost the United States in military and economic power relative to the nearest rivals.

Bush's legacy has some bright spots, though. Iraq is free from a violent dictator. Democracy has stood up to several tests. Iraq is not, despite numerous predictions, in the midst of a civil war (although some analysts argue that it was in 2006–2007). The freedom agenda is on the march and revolutions have (as of the time of writing in June 2012) taken down dictators in Tunisia, Egypt, Libya, and Yemen while major constitutional reforms have been promised in Morocco, Jordan, Oman, and Kuwait. It is difficult to explicitly link the success of the Arab Spring with the Iraq invasion, but it is not outside the realm of possibilities that this link will be strengthened in the history books given the commonality of both Bush and the Arab Spring protesters to take a moral stand against perceived evil in the Middle East. The manner of change in Iraq will be the major point of the debate here, though.

Bush coupled the idea of confronting evil with providing political, economic, and religious freedom. Whether or not freedom and democracy can be accomplished through violence is a matter of debate. The cases of Germany and Japan post–World War II were both noteworthy and successful. However, there have been a range of other cases that have not been successful, and the concept of regime change is contested.

The other countries listed in the axis of evil, Iran and North Korea, also remain problematic. North Korea developed and then tested two nuclear weapons in 2006 and 2009 (a third test is scheduled in 2012). The country remains highly authoritarian and steadfastly so even after the death of Kim Jong-il. Iran has not yet developed and tested a nuclear weapon, but they are getting much closer. The Green Movement—a major protest movement to gain more accountability and openness in the Iranian government—has thus far been quashed. Moreover, tensions periodically flare between Iran and Israel and the United States. The Bush legacy remains, overall, intertwined heavily with the Iraq War. Despite the focus of the Bush administration in Iraq, the other two countries named in the axis of evil, North Korea and Iran, are still major concerns in the international community. Both countries are in similar situations as they were in the Clinton era and remain potentially problematic for future American leaders. President Obama is still dealing with similar problems in North Korea and Iran; neither case has changed dramatically despite being described as "evil" and this inaction—whether to confront these countries or to normalize relations with them—is still tied to the Bush legacy.

The invocation of evil in speeches made by Presidents Ronald Reagan and George W. Bush were both extremely controversial at the time. Reagan's invocation of evil has largely been upheld in a mostly—but not universally—positive light and the legacy of his remarks and policies have so far done well across time. President George W. Bush was roundly criticized at the time of his speech and the Iraq War did not go as planned. However, democracy is still holding in Iraq—albeit barely. The Arab Spring may in time help his legacy with regard to the axis of evil statement, but it is still unknown as to how George W. Bush will be viewed across time. His legacy is not strong at this point, but he must be judged through the lens of history, and his story is thus far incomplete.

NOTES

1. Steven W. Hook, "Beyond the Bush Doctrine," in *Perspectives on the Legacy of George W. Bush*, ed. Michael Grossman and Ronald Eric Matthews (Newcastle upon Tyne: Cambridge Scholars Publishing, 2009), 164.

2. Bob Woodward, *Bush at War* (New York: Simon & Schuster, 2002), 329.

3. David Halberstam, *War in a Time of Peace: Bush, Clinton, and the Generals* (New York: Scribner, 2001), 58–59.

4. X (George Kennan), "The Sources of Soviet Conduct," *Foreign Affairs* 25, no. 4 (1947): 566–82.

5. Condoleezza Rice, *No Higher Honor: A Memoir of My Years in Washington* (New York: Crown, 2011), 24; Tom Brokaw, *The Time of Our Lives* (New York: Random House, 2011), 13; Dan Quayle, *Standing Firm: A Vice-Presidential Memoir* (New York: HarperCollins, 1994), 166; Dinesh D'Souza, *Ronald Reagan: How an Ordinary Man Became an Extraordinary Leader* (New York: Free Press, 1997).

6. Frances FitzGerald, *Way Out There in the Blue: Reagan, Star Wars, and the End of the Cold War* (New York: Simon & Schuster, 2000); Gwynne Dyer, *Future: Tense: The Coming World Order* (Toronto: M&S, 2004), 117.

7. George W. Bush, *Decision Points* (New York: Crown, 2010), 233.

8. Henry Kissinger, *Does America Need a Foreign Policy?: Toward a Diplomacy for the 21st Century* (New York: Simon & Schuster, 2002), 294.

9. Bush, *Decision Points*.

10. Dan Cox, *Young White Evangelicals: Less Republican, Still Conservative*, (Washington, DC: 2007), http://pewforum.org/Politics-and-Elections/Young-White-Evangelicals-Less-Republican-Still-Conservative.aspx (accessed November 30, 2011).

11. David Frum and Richard N. Perle, *An End to Evil: How to Win the War on Terror* (New York: Random House, 2003), 4–9.

12. Glen Duerr, "Faith in Foreign Policy: Evangelical Realism, Not Neoconservatism in the Presidency of George W. Bush," in *Perspectives on the Legacy of George W. Bush*, ed. Michael Grossman and Ronald Eric Matthews (Newcastle upon Tyne: Cambridge Scholars Publishing, 2009), 131.

13. Reinhold Niebuhr, *Christian Realism and Political Problems* (New York: Scribner, 1953).

CHAPTER 21

Child Sexualization, Abuse, and Evil in Pop Culture

Gregory K. Moffatt

Among the most significant issues facing any culture are the nurture and protection of children, who rely on adults for their well-being. Without a doubt, caring for children should be a matter of paramount concern for individuals, families, and the society as a whole. Unfortunately, some children, both in poor and affluent neighborhoods, are neglected and abused, sometimes without evil intent. At the same time, some people ignore the needs of children or take advantage of them intentionally. Despite accounts of highly publicized cases of seemingly random violence against children, however, a family member, neighbor, a teacher, religious leader, or a coach is more likely to be the perpetrator than some stranger who lurks behind bushes and in dark alleyways, snatching children without warning. Confusion about other matters related to the abuse of children abounds. American pop culture—including the news, movies, music, and television—has presented sexual and physical abuse of children in nearly every possible way. Children have been presented as innocent victims as well as instigators of physical and sexual abuse. In some cases, sexualization of children is even encouraged, either intentionally or unintentionally, through advertising, music, and marketing practices.

This chapter addresses the problem of sexualization of children in the media, the presentation of physical and sexual abuse of children in movies, television, and advertising and its effect on culture and how we view child abuse. This chapter also examines the much-discussed concept of the "pedophile priest," the inaccurate portrayal of church leaders in the media, and child abuse and the law.

PHYSICAL ABUSE IN THE MEDIA

Accounts of physical abuse of children in the news most often are either sensational cases where a child has been randomly attacked by a stranger or outrageous cases of extreme abuse by parents or caregivers. Both types of stories present a skewed view of the typical abuser. There is no question that extreme cases exist. For example, Jaycee Dugard was kidnapped at age 11 and held captive in a California house for 18 years. During that time she was not allowed to leave the house, was zapped with a stun gun, threatened with vicious dogs, and sexually molested. She bore two children by her captor and was so terrorized that she did not even try to escape. Likewise, Elisabeth Fritzl was held captive by her father in the secret basement of an Austrian home for 24 years. Like Dugard, she was tortured and sexually abused. But this level of evil is not that of the average abuser. Instead, the more likely abuser is a parent, stepparent, boyfriend, teacher, coach, or youth leader who uses the opportunity of the relationship to either deliberately take advantage of a child or who engages in poor parenting practices that qualify as abuse by law. While extreme cases exist, most abuse is subtle enough to go undetected for years. Psychological maltreatment, terroristic threats, neglect, consensual incestuous sex between an adult and a minor, and other forms of abuse that are hard to identify unless witnessed directly make up the majority of the abuse cases. This does not mean that these forms of abuse do not have an effect on victims. It merely points out that the news media give the impression that abusers are characteristically "evil" strangers who stalk and attack children and harbor them in dungeon-like basements or behind false walls.

Physical abuse themes have found their way into films many times. In the 1984 film *Places in the Heart,* actress Sally Field finds herself confronted with raising her son alone after the murder of her husband. When her son requires punishment, she discusses with him what "daddy would have done." Her son honestly says that his father would have given him a number of lashes with his belt. Field, attempting to be a good mother, retrieves her deceased husband's belt from behind a door and lashes her son several times with it. Following the spanking, as a voice-over in the film she concludes she would never do that again. Her character intuitively knew that such behavior was abusive, even though the standard of the day said it was not. Numerous other films have dealt with the issue of abuse, as well as its effects on children, including *The Great Santini* (1979), *Mommie Dearest* (1981), *Antwone Fisher* (2002), and *Radio Flyer* (1992). These films correctly portray abusers as often parents, stepparents, or others known to the child. While some films have examined the issue of abuse of children by other children, this is still an issue, other than bullying, that remains a topic relegated to thrillers (i.e., *The Good Son* [1993]) and films involving the supernatural (i.e., *Damien: The Omen II* [1978]). Pop culture has largely ignored the role of stepsiblings in both sexual and physical abuse.

SEXUALIZATION OF CHILDREN IN MEDIA

Television, movies, and music rate among the most powerful "conveyors of these societal ideals" (Choate and Curry, 2009). These media are laden with sexual themes that directly affect children, and these images are powerful. These concerns are not new to the digital age. "Purity activist Elizabeth Blackwell, for example, cautioned parents on the dangers of sexuality in children in her 1884 *Counsel to Parents on the Moral Education of their Children in Relations to Sex*" (Egan and Hawkes, 2008, p. 310). The transition in how sex has been portrayed on television and in the movies, however, is noticeable. In the 1960s, popular television couples like Rob and Laura Petrie of the *Dick Van Dyke Show* were not permitted by the Federal Communications Commission (FCC) to sit on the same bed on-screen. During the 1950s, even Lucille Ball and Desi Arnaz, married in real life, had been held to the same standard on the *I Love Lucy* show. Today, nearly anything can be seen in prime time television, with the exception of full frontal nudity, and sexualized content has transitioned to include child characters. Television reality shows, including a 2011 season premiere of *Toddlers in Tiaras*, accentuate sexualized young girls through beauty pageants. Child beauty pageants were not part of the mainstream media interest until the 1996 murder of six-year-old JonBenét Ramsey. After the sensational murder and repeated showings of the Colorado toddler dressed in glamorous clothing and makeup, numerous stories questioned the judgment of parents who would subject their daughter to the adult-like world of beauty pageants. Fifteen years later, this behavior is mainstream and in some ways what the Ramseys did seems antiquated. Today's parents do not stop with makeup and toddler-sized evening gowns. Some mothers have admitted dressing their toddlers in fake breasts and augmented rear ends. Others have invested thousands of dollars in surgical breast augmentations and other surgical adjustments for children as young as six or seven. The fact that there is even an audience for something like this says something about our culture. This does not mean that children should be presented in some asexual manner. All cultures acknowledge sex. The issue is whether or not children should be displayed in sexual ways (eroticized) as if they were adults.

On that note, some researchers have argued that a distinction should be made between "proper" and "improper" sexualization of children.[1] This argument supposes that children are inherently sexual (as opposed to erotic), and that proper sexualization includes, for example, dresses for girls and blue jeans for boys. Improper sexualization might be thought of as eroticization of the child and this, no doubt, is displayed in programs such as *Toddlers in Tiaras*. Compare the arguably proper portrayal of childhood femininity in the popular *American Girl* dolls with the seemingly improper sexualization of young girls in *Barbie* or *Bratz* dolls. *American Girl* dolls accentuate feminine clothing and hairstyles, but avoid sexual clothing, poses, or body shape. The sex of the *American Girl* dolls is portrayed by traditional fabrics, colors, and patterns. There is nothing physically sexual about them, but they are clearly female. On the other hand, *Barbie's* overly exaggerated breast size, hip-to-waist-to-breast ratio, and long legs give her a hypersexual appearance. *Bratz* dolls are even worse, often "wearing sexualized clothing such as miniskirts, fishnet stockings, and feather boas."[2]

Magazines marketed to young girls also highly sexualize young girls. In the United States, magazines like *Teen* and *Seventeen* are culprits, but this practice can be found around the world. Australia's highly popular magazine *Dolly* portrays girls in makeup and in sensual poses, and they stare at the camera with alluring looks. "*Dolly* presents many images of young, slim, attractive females, with perfect smiles and flawless complexions."[3] These images accentuate the *sexuality* of the models, rather than the sex of the models.

Likewise, advertisers rely heavily on sexuality to sell their products and, in recent years, children have become prominent in sex-laden advertisements. In some Ralph Lauren advertisements, children that appear to be younger than 10 years of age are dressed in skimpy clothing and posed in adult-like situations. As recently as fall of 2011, the French clothing line Jours Après Lunes launched a series of underwear for babies and children that some say borders on Victoria's Secret. But it is not just fashion designers and marginal outlets that promote sexuality in children. Mainstream chains such as JC Penny and Target have marketed padded bras and thong panties for children.[4] Sexualization is not limited to girls. Best known may be Calvin Klein ads that have been highly criticized for sexualizing both boys and girls. However, an executive task force of the American Psychological Association (APA) report noted that 85 percent of sexualized children are female.[5]

Sexual clothing is marketed to young children, mostly girls. Young teens commonly wear thongs, a type of lingerie that was once reserved for prostitutes or sexual experimentation between married couples. The argument by young girls for wearing thongs is that it avoids visible panty lines, which raises the question of why a young teen should even been concerned with panty lines at all. One researcher summarized the absurdity of sexualizing children through such products as "thong underwear sized for young girls printed with slogans such as 'wink wink'" and "Playboy Bunny merchandise marketed to preteens."[6]

THE PROBLEM OF CHILD SEXUALIZATION

The sexualization of children in the media presents our culture with several problems. First, any behavior that is encouraged or glamorized will be repeated. When children see commercials of other children playing with a certain toy or consuming a certain food, they want it. Either through advertising or direct messages, children are exposed to what culture accepts. For example, when a pop singer like Katy Perry tells her listeners to put their hands on her in her skintight jeans and "we'll go all the way tonight," it should not surprise us when teenage girls dress seductively and engage in these very behaviors. In one small survey of 24 subjects aged 14–18, subjects reported that "sex in the media desensitized them to risks of, and increased their perceived pressure for participating in sexual activity."[7] Second, Western culture has deleted adolescence, launching girls from childhood directly into sexual adulthood when we know that their social, cognitive, and emotional development still lags far behind. This encourages the idea that Egan and Hawkes call an "ultimately irresolvable category—girl-woman or 'miniature adult,'" which leads to victimization.[8] Finally, this sexualization creates the image that young girls are objects to be consumed. For the "tweenie" herself, this creates the image that she is *primarily* a sexual object. Media portrayals of sexualized children socialize young girls "to believe that their power and worth are primarily based upon their sexual appeal."[9] Research is clear that one problem in treating sexual offenders is that they see their victims as objects and, therefore, they do not see any problem abusing them.

Interestingly, this effect is not seen in boys. While boys do succumb to the sexualization of girls in the media, popular culture is not very effective in portraying boys as sexual objects and the negative effects of that process eludes boys. "It also should be noted that while boys are also affected by sexualization, it does not seem to pervade their overall sense of self the way that it does for girls."[10]

There is no doubt that media presentation of sex has an effect on viewers. But TV does not "cause" sexualized children nor does it cause adults to abuse them. Sexualization of children is reciprocally determined. It is evident that culture responds measurably and directly as a result of media presentations. Consider the then-relatively new field of product placement in movies back in 1982. The candy Reese's Pieces was featured in the film *E.T.: The Extra Terrestrial* for just a few minutes, but sales exploded more than 65 percent. Embedded marketing is now commonplace in most major films. But culture affects what media portrays, as well. Consider again, for example, the pop musician Katy Perry. Sexually explicit lyrics in her song "Last Friday Night" describes waking with someone in her bed, getting drunk, dancing naked, and most explicitly, a ménage à trois. This type of music, targeted toward teens, in turn creates a normalization of sexual behavior. Normalization increases the likelihood that it will be displayed. That, in turn, makes it more likely other media will present such images to consumers. How naive it must seem historically to think that in the late 1950s Elvis Presley created a firestorm because he thrust his hips when he danced and in the early 1960s the Beatles created controversy because their hair touched their ears. It is equally naive to suppose that the correlation is a simple one.

There may be differential effects of sex in the media in regard to race. It has been established, for example, that African American children, who watch more television than children of any other race—nearly an hour and a half more viewing per day than the average U.S. teen—may also be at greater risk because of their viewing habits, which may contribute to a stunning list of issues for African American teens including "the highest prevalence of sexual behaviors as well as Sexually Transmitted Infections (STIs) and nonmarital pregnancies" and "an established association between exposure of sexual content on television and attitudes and behaviors of adolescents." Moreover, researchers have demonstrated that African American adolescents' sexual behavior can be "delayed with exposure to sexual risk and sexual responsibility messages."[11] Consequently, African American children might be more prone to the detrimental effects of television viewing, including sexualization of self.

The effects of the sexualization of children in the media are two sided. On the one hand, children are sexualized and introduced to sexual themes that change the way they behave. On the other hand, sexually themed programming feeds the perpetrator's lusts and advancing technologies make trolling and acquiring victims easier than ever. Perpetrators have access to Facebook, MySpace, texting, the World Wide Web, and a host of other digital devices/software that allow them to contact, seduce, and eventually meet victims, and it is access to victims that is most challenging in preventing abuse. Priests who have abused children have taken advantage of their easy access to children as they perpetrated their crimes against them.

THE CATHOLIC CHURCH AND PEDOPHILE PRIESTS

More than a decade after the beginning of the revelations in the world press of sexual abuse in the Catholic Church, evidence is clear that the church failed to protect its members. Numerous documented accounts exist of priests who molested children only to be moved on to other churches by church leaders where they repeated their crimes against children. Even in cases where the church attempted to treat the offending priests, church officials still relocated them to new parishes without warning church members and seemingly without supervision to ensure they were not continuing to perpetrate their crimes against minors. For example, one Boston priest named John J. Geoghan "serially molested young boys for years while his superiors responded by periodically shipping him off for therapy, then recycling him into new parishes without warning parents there."[12] In at least a few of these cases, the cycle went on for more than 25 years.

The problem is not a new one. There is a long history of sexual issues within the Catholic Church. As early as AD177, "adulterers and pederasts were dealt with in the most severe manner possible" and Church leaders were given specific "advice for dealing with clerics who molest boys and girls."[13] So, for at least two millennia, a priest's conduct in regard to sexual behavior with children has been a concern. Speculation has circulated that priesthood in the Catholic Church attracts pedophiles, or that there is something about the priesthood that causes pedophilia. These are ridiculous accusations. Child molesters go where the children are. Molesters exist in various religious organizations, scouting, coaching, teaching, or anywhere else where they can access children. There is no evidence that being celibate causes pedophilia. Likewise, it is a myth to assume that priests are more likely to molest than any other form of clergy. About "4% of Catholic clergy in the United States sexually victimized minors between 1950 and 2002. No credible research evidence has been published at this time that can claim that this 4% figure is significantly higher than clergy from other faith traditions or from the general population of men."[14]

It is reasonable to suppose that some men who struggle with abnormal sexual urges may seek the protective cloak of religion to battle their sinful selves by pursuing the priesthood, hoping that a focus on a religious life might help them overcome their drives, only to be thrust into what they experience as a sexual smorgasbord with little or no accountability when they are assigned a parish. In these cases, the Devil within overwhelms them and leads to their abusing the very people they are sent by the church to protect. Others may enter the priesthood specifically to have access to children. It would seem counterintuitive to the reasons why one might assume men would enter the priesthood, but that intuition is flawed. People enter any profession—the priesthood included—for a variety of reasons. For example, some sociopaths ("antisocial personality disorder" according to the *DSM IV-TR*) have pursued careers as doctors, nurses, or paramedics, specifically to control and/or kill their patients, not save them. For example, Dr. Michael Swango eventually went to prison for killing, or attempting to kill, numerous patients over many years as a paramedic and later as a physician.

Researchers have offered number of ideas as to why priests molest children in their parishes. Dale and Alpert group the theories of why priests molest the children in their care into five "themes" that include societal influence (i.e., the media), abuse of power (sociopathology, pedophilia), forgiveness (being sent for treatment), the pressures of moral perfection, and effects of celibacy in the priesthood.[15] Perhaps it is more likely a bit of all of them. But most of these ideas can be boiled down to two primary reasons why priests molest children. Molesters who are priests are either (1) already struggling with their own sexuality and/or pedophilia and the lack of supervision and accountability in the church allows them to pursue their lusts or (2) they are deliberately seeking to access children and the priesthood provides the freedom and lack of oversight a predator lives for.

CHILD SEXUAL PERPETRATION AND THE LAW

The history in the United States has a less-than-stellar history of legally protecting children. The first documented case of the courts protecting children from abuse in the United States was in 1874. A social worker in New York City investigated a report that a child was being beaten daily and abused by her mother in other ways, but there were no state or federal laws on the books to protect her. There were, however, laws that protected farm animals from abuse by their owners. So the social worker argued in court that the child was a part of the animal kingdom, won her case, and the mother was sent to prison. Children are no longer considered animals and sexually or physically abusing a child has been illegal in all states for a long time. However, as recently as the 1960s, even though child abuse was against the law, many jurisdictions were hesitant to meddle with parenting choices so a parent could often physically abuse a child under the guise of discipline and get away with it. Incest and intrafamilial molestation was often ignored altogether.

In what may be argued has been an overreaction, today sexual offenders receive among the harshest punishments short of execution. In some states, a person could murder another human being, be arrested and convicted, and eventually be released from prison. When his/her probation is finished, the sentence has been served and the convict's rights are restored. This is not true for sexual perpetrators. In many states, they must register as sexual offenders even after completing their sentences and often their names can never be removed from the sexual offender rolls. This might sound reasonable, but states have not been very good at determining exactly what constitutes a sexual offender. Rapists and child molesters qualify, of course, but in some states, something as simple as public urination can qualify as a sexual offense if the event is witnessed by a minor. Even though a state statute may say it is not considered abuse if it is "by accidental means," such cases are not unheard of. I have personally worked with several cases where perpetrators were convicted based on this issue alone.

Other problems in distinguishing predators from perpetrators of other crimes also exist. Until recently, a 17-year-old male who had consensual sex with his 15-year-old prom date could be convicted as a sexual offender. Both public urination and consensual sex with a date, in the eyes of the court, would look the same on paper as a stranger who snatched a child from the sidewalk, dragged her into the bushes, and molested her. Only recently have state legislators begun to propose laws that differentiate between types of sexual perpetration.

The effects of such prosecution are long term. Upon release from prison, sexual offenders must, like all parolees and probationers, contact their probation officers in the county where they will reside. They must also notify the county sheriff's department in the county where they will reside. Both the sheriff's department and the probation office have the right to tell the convict that he cannot reside where he is living or work where he has found employment. Sexual offenders in some counties are required to report to a detention facility on Halloween where they stay locked up for the evening. They also must notify their probation office if they plan on moving. If they move or if they get a new parole officer, they have to start the process again.

This one-size-fits-all approach to sexual crimes makes it difficult for convicted felons to reintegrate into society. For example, Colorado's department of public safety website includes a list of "facts about sexual offenders," but should more appropriately note facts about *some* sexual offenders. All sexual offenders are not the same. Some are evil and fit a traditional sexual offender stereotype while others are men who had bad lawyers. For those offenders who want to rehabilitate, the road is not an easy one. A powerful film starring Kevin Bacon entitled *The Woodsman* portrays the difficulties of a recently released child molester. Bacon's character desperately wants to get his life together, but he is confronted with brick walls at every turn. He is shunned by his coworkers when they discover his history, the police harass him without cause, and eventually he finds himself losing no matter what he does. The person charged with being a sexual offender for urinating in public faces this same stigma. He is a registered sexual offender—period.

MIXED MESSAGES AND DOUBLE STANDARDS

Mixed messages, especially in regard to sexual behavior, create a cultural dilemma. Consider the 1999 hit movie *American Beauty*. The main character in the film, played by Kevin Spacey, struggles with his infatuation with a teenage girl. She was only a teenage girl in her character (interestingly, the actress was 20 years old in real life), but she was overtly sexual and was presented very much as a woman in dress and behavior. If the character played by Kevin Spacey had indeed had a sexual relationship with her, the viewer would have been repulsed that a 45-year-old man would sleep with a teenager. Yet in the 2004 film *Birth*, starring Nicole Kidman, she believes her husband has been reborn in the body of a 10-year-old boy (11 years old in real life), and in one seductive scene they are in a bathtub together. Imagine the public outcry if Kevin Spacey had been shown in the bathtub with a 17-year-old girl, much less a 10-year-old girl. In all likelihood, a scene between any adult male and a 10-year-old girl in a bathtub would never have made it past censorship. But the Kidman scene went forward without resistance.

Interestingly, just as there has been a double standard in film regarding the sex of a perpetrator, the same double standard has existed in the prosecution of pedophiles. Consider teachers that have had sexual relationships with their students. For several decades, any male teacher who had a sexual relationship with a student, even a consensual sexual relationship with a high school student, faced decades in prison for sex crimes and was labeled a pedophile. But it was not until the turn of the 21st century that female teachers began facing similar prosecution. Prior to 2000, many cases of female perpetrators never even made the news. Those cases that went to court often ended with the woman sentenced to probation, community service, or minimal 90-day sentences. The "evil" pedophile was the male. Females had merely engaged in poor judgment. Similarly, it is not difficult to find stories of priests who have engaged in sex with children in their parishes, yet mainstream stories of nuns who had sex with a child are hard to imagine. While such stories do exist, they rarely make headlines. Again, priests are "evil," but nuns who abuse children appear to be considered culturally irrelevant.

CONCLUSION

The sexualization of children in our global culture has global consequences. Child sex trafficking is a growing global market. Eastern and
Western Europe, Asia, Latin America, and Africa, along with the United
States, have seen an increase in child prostitution and sex trafficking. For
example, "the International Labor Organization estimates that 15 percent of India's 2.3 million commercial sex workers are children under 14,
and most of them are girls."[16] But the problem is not just in India. It is a
global problem. Over one million children are trafficked every year and
almost all of them are girls.[17] I'm not suggesting that this is due exclusively to sex in the media, but how could one argue that sexualizing of
children is not a factor? No one would argue that regular doses of com-
mercializing of a product had no effect on sales and no political candidate
would say that his/her advertising dollars meant nothing toward his or
her getting elected.

As technology advances faster than the culture knows what to do with
it, risk of perpetration increases. Prior to the Internet, perpetrators had
to physically leave their homes to hunt for victims and those victims had
to be available to perpetrators outside of the supervision of adults. With
ever-advancing technology, perpetrators can feed their lusts from hand-
held devices, movies, and even commercials. They can troll for victims
from the comfort of their living rooms and victims can unwittingly make
themselves available from the privacy of their own bedrooms. As Choate
and Curry note, "As potential perpetrators may have access to these girls
through online interactions, the risk of exposure to offenders, exploitation, and victimization is increased."[18]

NOTES

1. R. Danielle Egan and Gail L. Hawkes, "Endangered Girls and Incendiary Objects: Unpacking the Discourse on Sexualization," *Sexuality & Culture* 12,
no. 4 (2008): 291–311.

2. Laura Choate and Jennifer R. Curry, "Addressing the Sexualization of
Girls through Comprehensive Programs, Advocacy, and Systemic Change: Implications for Professional School Counselors," *Professional School Counseling* 12,
no. 3 (2009): 213–22.

3. Fiona Brookes and Peter Kelly, "*Dolly* Girls: Tweenies as Artefacts of
Consumption," *Journal of Youth Studies* 12, no. 6 (2009): 606.

4. Diane E. Levin and Jean Kilbourne, *So Sexy So Soon: The New Sexualized
Childhood, and What Parents Can Do to Protect Their Kids* (New York: Ballantine,
2008), 42.

5. Task Force on the Sexualization of Girls American Psychological Association, *Report of the APA Task Force on the Sexualization of Girls* (Washington, DC: 2010), http://www.apa.org/pi/women/programs/girls/report-full.pdf (accessed April 20, 2012).

6. Choate and Curry, "Addressing the Sexualization of Girls through Comprehensive Programs, Advocacy, and Systemic Change: Implications for Professional School Counselors," 213–22.

7. Georgia N.L. Johnston Polacek et al., "Media and Sex: Perspectives from Hispanic Teens," *American Journal of Sexuality Education* 1, no. 4 (2006): 51.

8. Egan and Hawkes, "Endangered Girls and Incendiary Objects: Unpacking the Discourse on Sexualization," 305.

9. Choate and Curry, "Addressing the Sexualization of Girls through Comprehensive Programs, Advocacy, and Systemic Change: Implications for Professional School Counselors," 213–22.

10. Choate and Curry, "Addressing the Sexualization of Girls through Comprehensive Programs, Advocacy, and Systemic Change: Implications for Professional School Counselors," 213–22.

11. Brian C. Gordon, Mike A Perko, and Michael Taylor, "A Review of Sexual Content in Black-Themed Television Programming," *American Journal of Health Studies* 22, no. 4 (2007): 217–23.

12. Carol M. Cannon, "The Priest Scandal," *American Journalism Review* 24, no. 4 (2002): 20.

13. Kathryn A. Dale and Judith L. Alpert, "Hiding Behind the Cloth: Child Sexual Abuse and the Catholic Church," *Journal of Child Sexual Abuse* 16, no. 3 (2007): 61.

14. Thomas G. Plante, "Why Are So Many So Misinformed Nine Years after the Clergy Abuse Crisis in America?," *Human Development* 32, no. 2 (2011): 28.

15. Dale and Alpert, "Hiding behind the Cloth: Child Sexual Abuse and the Catholic Church," 64.

16. Meenakshi Gigi Durham, *The Lolita Effect: The Media Sexualization of Young Girls and What We Can Do about It* (Woodstock, NY: Overlook Press, 2008), 58.

17. Durham, *The Lolita Effect: The Media Sexualization of Young Girls and What We Can Do about It*, 57.

18. Choate and Curry, "Addressing the Sexualization of Girls through Comprehensive Programs, Advocacy, and Systemic Change: Implications for Professional School Counselors," 213–22.

CHAPTER 22

From Theodore Roosevelt's "Dark and Evil Spirits of Malice and Greed" to George W. Bush's "Axis of Evil": Evil in American Political Rhetoric

Hans C. Schmidt

Ours is a world that is no stranger to atrocity. The mention of actions such as genocide and slavery, places such as Auschwitz and Goree Island, or people such as Adolf Hitler, serve as grim reminders that the list of atrocities visited upon humankind, by humankind, could fill volumes. But when does that which is atrocious, immoral, or inhumane transcend to the level of evil? Understanding this differentiation is a challenge, in part because a singular definition of evil is difficult to establish. Within the Judeo-Christian tradition, the Book of Genesis establishes evil as the opposite of good, in its reference to the "tree of the knowledge of good and evil." Similarly, Western philosophers have considered the issue. In antiquity, Plotinus defined evil as being simply the "absence of good." In the 19th century, Friedrich Wilhelm Joseph von Schelling contended that evil is manifested in the grandiose exaltation of self-will, and Friedrich Nietzsche considered it a violent manifestation of resentment. More recently, Emmanuel Levinas suggested that evil involves a total break from ethical normativity through excess nihilism.

Such definitions are helpful, yet leave plenty of room for individuals to decide for themselves what constitutes evil. Because of this, the philosophical debate that has spanned centuries continues. But in the modern political world, evil has come to be a term of political expediency; it means whatever politicians want it to mean.

According to William Casebeer, "evil" in political rhetoric can be used to accomplish four purposes: motivation, counterforce, division, and evaluation.[1] Motivation involves simply motivating groups to act; counterforce involves responding to others' use of the rhetoric of evil; division involves using the rhetoric of evil to make groups feel different from or superior to other groups; evaluation involves making a normative judgment of the morality of a situation.

Clearly the rhetoric of evil can be a powerful thing, and using it to achieve any of these four objectives is nothing new. It is especially telling, though, to consider the rhetoric of evil in political discourse. In recent decades, this rhetoric of evil has become especially identifiable because of oft-quoted phrases like Ronald Reagan's "evil empire" and George W. Bush's "axis of evil." But Reagan and Bush were hardly the first to employ "evil" rhetoric in presidential speech. To the contrary, the rhetoric of evil has been a mainstay in presidential communication throughout the past century. Yet, what has changed over time is the way in which "evil" has been used by America's leaders. By understanding how the rhetoric of evil has been used over time, we learn not only about the changing nature of political discourse, but also about the contemporary conceptualization of evil today. Accordingly, it is beneficial to consider how the rhetoric of evil has evolved from the dawn of the 20th century up to present times.

FROM THEODORE ROOSEVELT TO CALVIN COOLIDGE

Theodore Roosevelt did not shy away from "evil"; his first State of the Union address in 1901 included seven references to evil. Roosevelt suggested that anarchists possess "dark and evil spirits of malice and greed, envy and sullen hatred" and that Native Americans living on reservations faced a host of social evils. Roosevelt saved much of his "evil" language to describe certain industrial practices, suggesting in 1901 that trusts can possess some "real and grave evils."[2] A year later, Roosevelt stated that congressional regulation was needed to prevent "monopolies, unjust discriminations, which prevent or cripple competition, fraudulent over-capitalization, and other evils in trust organizations and practices which injuriously affect interstate trade."[3] Roosevelt's tone is representative of the way in which "evil" was used by presidents throughout most of the 20th century. Roosevelt refrained from using "evil" as a label; he never suggested that specific corporations or politicians were evil. Rather, he used "evil" in a broad and evaluative sense, suggesting that certain, unspecified practices of these groups were evil in nature.

William Howard Taft similarly saw economic evil. When accepting the Republican presidential nomination in 1908, Taft stated, "For more than ten years this country passed through an epoch of material development far beyond any that ever occurred in the world before. In its course, certain evils crept in. Some prominent and influential members of the community, spurred by financial success and in their hurry for greater wealth, became unmindful of the common rules of business honesty and fidelity and of the limitations imposed by law upon their action."[4] Additionally, in his speeches, Taft mentioned the need for regulation to curb "manifest evils in corporate management,"[5] referred to the need to support China's efforts to eradicate the "opium evil"[6] and suggested the importance of ending the evil of "white slavery."[7]

Woodrow Wilson used "evil" when describing economic and governmental policy. In his first Inaugural address, Wilson suggested that in America's industrialization "evil has come with the good. . . . We have squandered a great part of what we might have used, and have not stopped to conserve the exceeding bounty of nature. . . ." Later, in the same speech Wilson urged against government corruption, suggesting that evil could exist within American government itself. Stated Wilson, "Justice, and only justice, shall always be our motto. . . . The Nation has been deeply stirred, stirred by a solemn passion, stirred by the knowledge of wrong, of ideals lost, of government too often debauched and made an instrument of evil."[8]

Upon America's entry into World War I, Wilson used "evil" as a motivational device, yet refrained from turning the might of "evil" rhetoric directly on America's enemies. Wilson referred vaguely to the war as a battle against evil, stating that the allied powers desire "peace by the overcoming of evil, by the defeat once and for all of the sinister forces that interrupt peace and render it impossible. . . ." However, Wilson stopped short of actually calling Germany evil, instead referring to Germany as having practiced an "intolerable thing," as possessing an "ugly face," and being "without conscience or honor."[9]

After World War I drew to a close, Wilson's 1919 State of the Union address made reference to the "evil consequences" which America had witnessed. But, Wilson quickly refocused the "evil" rhetoric back on American domestic social issues which required attention, suggesting that "high rates of income and profit taxes," "extravagant expenditures," and "unemployment" were "attendant evils" that America would need to address in peacetime.[10] Similarly, in his final State of the Union address in 1920, Wilson urged America to champion democracy and democratic practices both abroad and domestically, and to "remedy any injustices or evils that may have shown themselves in our own national life."[11]

Warren G. Harding continued the trend of identifying evils within American governmental and economic policies. In his speech to accept the 1920 Republican presidential nomination, Harding suggested that it was important to "strike at government borrowing which enlarges the evil" of the depreciation of the dollar and inflation.[12] In his 1921 Inaugural address, he spoke of the need to prevent the "evil consequences" of "modern industrialism,"[13] and in his second State of the Union address, Harding referred to the evil of child labor.[14]

Calvin Coolidge mentioned unspecified domestic evils in his third and fourth State of the Union addresses. Later, in 1929, Herbert Hoover referred to deteriorating conditions at federal prisons as an evil which needed to be relieved,[15] and referenced the "evils of the liquor traffic" in his speech accepting the 1932 Republican presidential nomination.[16]

FROM FRANKLIN D. ROOSEVELT
TO JIMMY CARTER

Franklin D. Roosevelt mentioned "evil" many times during his four terms in office. He started early, in his 1933 Inaugural address. Here, Roosevelt spoke of "evils of the old order" in reference to the economic practices that led to the stock market crash of 1929 and the ensuing depression.[17] Roosevelt continued to use the rhetoric in later speeches. In his second Inaugural address, Roosevelt suggested that people no longer tolerate "evil things formerly accepted."[18] In the 1937 State of the Union address, Roosevelt stated that "Overproduction, underproduction and speculation are three evil sisters who distill the troubles of unsound inflation and disastrous deflation."[19] In the third Inaugural address, Roosevelt suggested that Americans have "put away many evil things."[20]

Yet, like Wilson before him, Roosevelt was very cautious about unleashing "evil" on America's enemies even after entering World War II. In the 1942 State of the Union address, Roosevelt stated, "We are fighting to cleanse the world of ancient evils, ancient ills."[21] Yet, Roosevelt did not specifically identify a particular nation as evil; rather the rhetoric of evil was used motivationally to position the war within a historical context. Similarly, the following year, Roosevelt stated that "Hitlerism, like any other form of crime or disease, can grow from the evil seeds of economic as well as military feudalism."[22] Again, the carefully phrased statement did not call Nazis evil; instead it suggested that the Nazi movement had grown out of evil circumstances.

For Roosevelt, "evil" was a term primarily used to describe domestic economic troubles. By 1943—as the war reached a turning point—Roosevelt had already begun to return to his rhetorical suggestion that economic insecurity was the main evil of the day. In his 1943 State of the Union address, Roosevelt stated, "When you talk with our young men and women, you will find that with the opportunity for employment they want assurance against the evils of all major economic hazards—assurance that will extend from the cradle to the grave. And this great Government can and must provide this assurance."[23]

Like Roosevelt, Harry Truman primarily applied "evil" rhetoric to domestic economic issues. Truman's 1948 State of the Union address stated that "economic distress is a disease whose evil effects spread far beyond the boundaries of the afflicted nation."[24] The next year, he also criticized economic practices that lead to "the evils of boom and bust" and warned against the "dangers of recession and against the evils of inflation."[25]

When discussing foreign policy, Truman was careful with the use of "evil" language. In 1946, Truman referred to Nazi and Japanese war criminals as "evildoers," but refrained from using "evil" divisively or expanding the label beyond the scope of certain individuals.[26] Instead, when criticizing hostile nations, Truman used much less inflammatory language and linked communism and totalitarianism with "want and misery," "poverty and strife," and "terror and oppression."[27] In 1951, Truman referred to Soviet aggression in Korea as an "evil war by proxy."[28] But it was the war which Truman labeled as evil, not the enemy. Again, Truman refrained from turning the power of "evil" language on outside nations; instead "evil" was used as an evaluative term for conditions in which people suffered, especially when that suffering was related to economic disadvantage.

Dwight D. Eisenhower continued in the same tradition. A firm critic of the USSR, Eisenhower referred to evil in his speeches, but always stopped just short of actually calling the Soviet Union evil. Eisenhower's 1953 Inaugural address suggested that America is aligned with faith and goodness, stating that "forces of good and evil are massed and armed and opposed as rarely before in history" and suggested that the "power to achieve good or to inflict evil surpasses the brightest hopes and the sharpest fears of all ages."[29] Later, in 1957, Eisenhower restated that new nations across the Earth have the power to bring "great good or great evil to the free world's future."[30] Yet, in such instances, Eisenhower associated "evil" with something to be avoided, but not as that which is embodied by any particular enemy.

John F. Kennedy similarly did not call the nation's enemies evil. Instead, when Kennedy referred to evil, it was to suggest the challenges faced by all nuclear powers. In his 1963 speech on the Nuclear Test Ban Treaty, Kennedy stated, "That is why the continuation of atmospheric testing causes so many countries to regard all nuclear powers as equally evil; and we can hope that its prevention will enable all those countries to see the world more clearly, while enabling all the world to breathe more easily."[31]

Lyndon B. Johnson referred to Kennedy's assassination as an "evil moment" and called upon Americans, saying, "So let us put an end to the teaching and the preaching of hate and evil and violence. Let us turn away from the fanatics of the far left and the far right, from the apostles of bitterness and bigotry, from those defiant of law, and those who pour venom into our Nation's bloodstream."[32] Otherwise, however, Johnson only rarely used the word "evil," even as the nation proceeded through the Cold War years. One instance came during the 1967 State of the Union address, when Johnson justified the war in Vietnam by quoting Thomas Jefferson, who said, "It is the melancholy law of human societies to be compelled sometimes to choose a great evil in order to ward off a greater evil."[33] Yet, again, Johnson's "evil" was not specified and not linked to a particular enemy.

Richard Nixon employed even more conciliatory language. In a televised speech to the Russian people in 1974, Nixon stated, "I reflected on the fact that our efforts now must be directed not against any one nation or group of nations, but against the evil of war itself."[34] Otherwise, when Nixon spoke of "evil," it was in reference to domestic issues. Stated Nixon in the 1973 State of the Union address, "We must do a better job in community development—in creating more livable communities, in which all of our children can grow up with fuller access to opportunity and greater immunity to the social evils and blights which now plague so many of our towns and cities."[35]

Gerald Ford went even further, acknowledging the way in which some individuals felt that America itself was evil. In his 1976 State of the Union address, Ford stated, "The American people have heard too much about how terrible our mistakes, how evil our deeds, and how misguided our purposes. The American people know better. The truth is we are the world's greatest democracy."[36] Similarly, Jimmy Carter's rhetoric reflected his less provocative stance toward international relations and the Cold War; Carter avoided the use of "evil" in his Inaugural address and all State of the Union addresses while in office. This tone changed quite dramatically with the Reagan presidency.

RONALD REAGAN AND THE "EVIL EMPIRE"

Ronald Reagan's first use of "evil" as president in reference to totalitarianism occurred in a 1982 speech in the British House of Commons. Reagan positioned America against the communist bloc, stating, "Must freedom wither in a quiet, deadening accommodation with totalitarian evil?" Later in the speech, Reagan asserted his position, stating that "the forces of good ultimately rally and triumph over evil."[37] Reagan initially used "evil" in the traditionally broad and motivational sense, referencing unspecified evils associated with totalitarianism. While establishing a rhetorical agenda similar to that of wartime presidents like Wilson and Roosevelt, and positioning America's "crusade for freedom" within a salvation narrative, Reagan initially refrained from using "evil" as a label attached to any particular country.

Yet, Reagan took a rhetorical leap the following year, and began using "evil" as a tool of division. Speaking on August 8, 1983, at the Annual Convention of the National Association of Evangelicals, Reagan built on the ongoing theo-political narrative and created the contrast: good versus evil; America versus the Soviet Union; American Christianity versus the USSR's "godless communism." Reagan stated, "While they preach the supremacy of the State, declare its omnipotence over individual man, and predict its eventual domination of all peoples on the earth, they are the focus of evil in the modern world." Then, Reagan famously elaborated, saying, "So, in your discussions of the nuclear freeze proposals, I urge you to beware the temptation of pride—the temptation of blithely declaring yourselves above it all and label both sides equally at fault, to ignore the facts of history and the aggressive impulses of an evil empire, to simply call the arms race a giant misunderstanding and thereby remove yourself from the struggle between right and wrong and good and evil."[38]

For Reagan to move from describing the practices of an enemy power as "evil" to labeling the nation itself as an "evil empire" was a significant rhetorical leap. Yet, despite the fact that "evil empire" went on to enter the cultural vernacular, Reagan himself soon abandoned this rhetorical escalation. The theological rhetoric continued, and Reagan continued to create a contrast between American virtue and perceived Soviet ills. Yet, the divisive "evil empire" rhetoric disappeared. By 1986, Reagan wished the Soviet people goodwill and peace in his televised New Year's greeting, going so far as to state that, "Yes, there are enormous differences between our two systems, but there is also something the American and the Soviet people share—something as universal and eternal as what a mother feels when she hears the cry of her newborn child. . . ."[39] And, speaking to reporters in Moscow in 1988, Reagan suggested that the "evil empire" of the Soviet Union was "another time, another era."[40] This is not to say that Reagan became a "see no evil" president; to the contrary, Reagan saw evil everywhere in the world and used the term "evil" in a total of 87 presidential speeches during his two terms as president. But the nature of Reagan's "evil" changed, and he came to use the word in an evaluative sense in reference to a wide variety of criminal, social, and political topics including terrorism, war, corruption, communism, drugs, crime, and deficit spending.

"EVIL" RHETORIC AFTER THE REAGAN YEARS

Such evils persisted in the world after Reagan left office; the term "evil" has been used in over 1,100 presidential speeches since 1989. This was the case despite the fall of the Soviet Union. The point was clear; "evil" was powerful language; "evil" was effective language; "evil" could be applied to whatever enemy or obstacle surfaced next.

While more rhetorically cautious than his predecessor, George H. W. Bush indirectly associated evil with Iraq under the regime of Saddam Hussein. In his 1991 State of the Union address, Bush suggested that America can confront evils abroad and at home, stating, "We are resolute and resourceful. If we can selflessly confront the evil for the sake of good in a land so far away, then surely we can make this land all that it should be."[41]

William Clinton also referred to evil in his speeches. At times, "evil" was used in a vaguely motivational and unspecific sense, as was the case in the 1994 State of the Union address in which he urged America to "once more stand strong against the forces of despair and evil because everybody has a chance to walk into a better tomorrow."[42]

At other times, "evil" was used to evaluate specific actions and condemn terrorism. Speaking just days after the 1995 bombing of the Alfred P. Murrah Federal Building in Oklahoma City, Clinton stated, "We pledge to do all we can to help you heal the injured, to rebuild this city, and to bring to justice those who did this evil." Later, in the same speech, he referred to evil within a religious context. Stated Clinton, "St. Paul admonished us, let us 'not be overcome by evil, but overcome evil with good.'"[43] Clinton's use of "evil" was in the tradition of most presidential rhetoric; "evil" was used to motivate or evaluate actions and events, but not label groups or create division.

"EVIL" RETURNS AFTER SEPTEMBER 11, 2001

No presidential administration since that of Ronald Reagan has embraced the rhetoric of evil as much as that of George W. Bush, who spoke of evil from the very start. When accepting the Republican presidential nomination on August 3, 2000, Bush referenced evil stating, "My father was the last president of a great generation. A generation of Americans who stormed beaches, liberated concentration camps and delivered us from evil."[44] Initially, Bush used "evil" in the traditionally vague sense, mentioning an unspecified evil that was not linked to any particular individual or nation.

This general motivational tone continued in speeches that immediately followed the terrorist attacks of September 11, 2001. In a televised speech on the evening of September 11, Bush referred to an unspecified evil while placing the nation's struggles within a Judeo-Christian moral perspective. Quoting a verse from Psalm 23, Bush stated, "Even though I walk through the valley of the shadow of death, I fear no evil, for You are with me." Then, he went on to state, "Thousands of lives were suddenly ended by evil." In contrast, America was given the rhetorical high ground. Bush stated, "America was targeted for attack because we're the brightest beacon for freedom and opportunity in the world. . . . And no one will keep that light from shining."[45]

Theopolitical in its tone, this speech fit comfortably into the long tradition of presidential speeches that employed the rhetoric of evil in an evaluative and motivational manor. Yet, within a few months the rhetoric escalated dramatically, and Bush came to use "evil" as a proper noun used to label specific ideologies and nations.

This happened with the emergence of the phrase "axis of evil," in the State of the Union address on January 29, 2002. In one of five references to "evil" in the speech, Bush stated that Iraq, Iran, North Korea, "and their terrorist allies constitute an axis of evil, arming to threaten the peace of the world." This was contrasted with the "power, wonder-working power, in the goodness and idealism and faith of the American people."[46]

Within the span of several months, "evil" turned from being an evaluative device into a label of specific nations and a tool of division. Of course, grouping America's enemies together rhetorically was not new. In 1990, George H. W. Bush grouped together enemies as "states that have contempt for civilized norms,"[47] and in 1998 Clinton identified "outlaw states."[48] Bush's rhetoric, however, was dramatically more powerful. Labeling certain enemy states as "evil" ramped up the rhetorical intensity to an extent not seen since Reagan's "evil empire."

The phrase became the political buzz of the moment, and was often repeated in American news media and defended by administration officials. Within a few months, future U.S. Ambassador to the United Nations John Bolton even went to far as to suggest that the axis should be expanded "beyond the axis of evil"[49] to also include Libya, Syria, and Cuba.

But the phrase also quickly became controversial, meaning vastly different things to different people. To some, the phrase reflected an accurate assessment of international relations. As then Secretary of State Condoleezza Rice stated, "It was a pretty good analysis, wasn't it? It really was."[50] To others, like former Secretary of State Madeline Albright, "it was a big mistake to lump those three countries together."[51]

More than anything else, however, the trouble with the phrase was that it could create no meaningful policy directions; fighting terrorism was possible, but ridding the world of "evil" is an impossible foreign policy.

Eventually, Bush backed away from such heated rhetoric in the same way as Reagan had done nearly two decades prior. By the end of the second Bush administration, the "axis of evil" rhetoric had long since faded from use.

Barack Obama distanced himself from the hyperbolic language of previous administrations, but his worldview also identified the existence of evil, and he acknowledged its presence in his Nobel Peace Prize acceptance speech. Obama stated, "For make no mistake: evil does exist in the world."[52] Obama struck a different tone than his predecessor; while he suggested the existence of unspecified evil abroad, he refrained from connecting the term to any specific nations. Otherwise, Obama refrained from using the word "evil" in his Inaugural and State of the Union speeches.

EVIL AND THE AMERICAN WORLDVIEW

The use of the word "evil" as a rhetorical tool is nothing new. It has been a mainstay of presidential speech throughout the past century, as the "good versus evil" narrative is used to galvanize the nation against whatever issue looms largest in the national consciousness. In American political rhetoric, evil is anything that ails or assails America, ranging from joblessness, to corporate corruption, hunger, poverty, anarchism, Nazism, communism, or terrorism.

But the problem is not just that "evil" is used frequently. Admittedly, it is used so often and defined so broadly that its power could become diluted. Yet, the real problem is not one of linguistics. Instead, the way in which the rhetoric of evil has come to be used suggests that we, as a culture, have developed a delusional view of ourselves, and our own supposed virtue.

Over time, Greek mythology came to present its gods as less omnipotent, and as more troubled, with more human foibles and weaknesses. It has been said that as the Greek gods became more human, the humans came to view themselves as more godlike. The same process is happening with our understanding of evil. It might be said that the more evil we make other people, the more good we believe ourselves to be. Indeed, in earlier political rhetoric, "evil" was often used to describe the problems that everyone faces; it was a human universal against which everyone struggles. Now, "evil" has come to be used as a divisive label to describe others who are different.

In the past, economic and social evils could exist within America. Political rhetoric constructed an American narrative in which the country fought against its evils, and triumphed with good. Evil was linked to domestic problems and international conflicts alike. Yet, with the exception of references to the terrorist attacks in 1995 and 2001, no president since Nixon has hinted at the existence of any form of evil within the nation's borders during any State of the Union or Inaugural addresses. Instead, "evil" has come to be used exclusively to describe or label problems abroad. Such political rhetoric suggests that we are inherently good, and triumph over the evils which exist exclusively among others. "Evil" has become confused with "otherness;" "good" has become confused with "similarity." Confusing "evil" with otherness promotes xenophobia; confusing "good" with similarity promotes sanctimony.

Thus, American political speeches of recent years have demonstrated an increasingly xenophobic, sanctimonious view of the world. But "evil" in political discourse need not be used to promote such negative cultural attributes. After all, real evil does exist in the world. There is much which is absent of any goodness and which stretches the bounds of inhumanity. Using the rhetoric of evil in an evaluative manor to describe true atrocities serves a practical purpose. But using language to promote division is harmful, and ultimately serves to create a distorted view of oneself and the world. The key is to use language carefully, and in so doing protect society's view of the world so that evil can be seen wherever it really abides.

NOTES

1. William D. Casebeer, "Knowing Evil When You See It: Uses for the Rhetoric of Evil in International Relations," *International Relations* 18, no. 4 (2004): 441–45.

2. Theodore Roosevelt, "First Annual Message," Speech, December 3, 1901. The American Presidency Project, http://www.presidency.ucsb.edu/ws/index.php?pid=29542#axzz1dtpNZ2bj (accessed November 16, 2011).

3. Theodore Roosevelt, "Second Annual Message," Speech, December 2, 1902. The American Presidency Project, http://www.presidency.ucsb.edu/ws/index.php?pid=29543&st=evil&st1=#ixzz1qL1iGBOh (accessed November 16, 2011).

4. William H. Taft, "Address Accepting the Republican Presidential Nomination," Speech, July 28, 1908. The American Presidency Project, http://www.presidency.ucsb.edu/ws/?pid=76222 (accessed November 17, 2011).

5. William H. Taft, "First Annual Message," Speech, December 7, 1909. The American Presidency Project, http://www.presidency.ucsb.edu/ws/?pid=29550 (accessed November 17, 2011).

6. William H. Taft, "Third Annual Message," Speech, December 5, 1911. The American Presidency Project, http://www.presidency.ucsb.edu/ws/?pid=29552 (accessed November 17, 2011).

7. William H. Taft, "Fourth Annual Message," Speech, December 3, 1912. The American Presidency Project, http://www.presidency.ucsb.edu/ws/?pid= 29553 (accessed November 17, 2011).

8. Woodrow Wilson, "Inaugural Address," Speech, March 4, 1913. The American Presidency Project, http://www.presidency.ucsb.edu/ws/?pid=25831 (accessed November 17, 2011).

9. Woodrow Wilson, "Fifth Annual Message," Speech, December 4, 1917. The American Presidency Project, http://www.presidency.ucsb.edu/ws/?pid= 29558 (accessed November 17, 2011).

10. Woodrow Wilson, "Seventh Annual Message," Speech, December 2, 1919. The American Presidency Project, http://www.presidency.ucsb.edu/ ws/?pid=29560 (accessed November 20, 2011).

11. Woodrow Wilson, "Eighth Annual Message," Speech, December 7, 1920. The American Presidency Project, http://www.presidency.ucsb.edu/ ws/?pid=29561 (accessed November 20, 2011).

12. Warren G. Harding, "Address Accepting the Republican Presidential Nomination," Speech, June 12, 1920. The American Presidency Project, http://www.presidency.ucsb.edu/ws/?pid=76198 (accessed November 20, 2011).

13. Warren G. Harding, "Inaugural Address," Speech, March 4, 1921. The American Presidency Project, http://www.presidency.ucsb.edu/ws/?pid=25833 (accessed November 20, 2011).

14. Warren G. Harding, "Second Annual Message," Speech, December 8, 1922. The American Presidency Project, http://www.presidency.ucsb.edu/ ws/?pid=29563 (accessed November 25, 2011).

15. Herbert Hoover, "Annual Message to Congress on the State of the Union," Speech, December 3, 1929. The American Presidency Project, http:// www.presidency.ucsb.edu/ws/?pid=22021 (accessed November 22, 2011).

16. Herbert Hoover, "Address Accepting the Republican Presidential Nomination," Speech, August 11, 1932. The American Presidency Project, http:// www.presidency.ucsb.edu/ws/?pid=23198 (accessed November 16, 2011).

17. Franklin D. Roosevelt, "First Inaugural Address," Speech, March 4, 1933. The American Presidency Project, http://www.presidency.ucsb.edu/ ws/?pid=14473 (accessed November 16, 2011).

18. Franklin D. Roosevelt, "Second Inaugural Address," Speech, January 20, 1937. The American Presidency Project, http://www.presidency.ucsb.edu/ws/? pid=15349 (accessed November 16, 2011).

19. Franklin D. Roosevelt, "Annual Message to Congress," Speech, January 6, 1937. The American Presidency Project, http://www.presidency.ucsb.edu/ ws/?pid=15336 (accessed November 16, 2011).

20. Franklin D. Roosevelt, "Third Inaugural Address," Speech, January 20, 1941. The American Presidency Project, http://www.presidency.ucsb.edu/ws/? pid=16022 (accessed November 16, 2011).

21. Franklin D. Roosevelt, "State of the Union," Speech, January 6, 1942. The American Presidency Project, http://www.presidency.ucsb.edu/ws/?pid= 16253 (accessed November 25, 2011).

22. Franklin D. Roosevelt, "State of the Union," Speech, January 7, 1943. The American Presidency Project, http://www.presidency.ucsb.edu/ws/?pid= 16386 (accessed November 25, 2011).

23. Roosevelt, "State of the Union," January 7, 1943.

24. Harry S. Truman, "Annual Message to the Congress on the State of the Union," Speech, January 7, 1948. The American Presidency Project, http://www .presidency.ucsb.edu/ws/?pid=13005 (accessed November 25, 2011).

25. Harry S. Truman, "Annual Message to the Congress on the State of the Union," Speech, January 5, 1949. The American Presidency Project, http://www .presidency.ucsb.edu/ws/?pid=13293 (accessed November 25, 2011).

26. Harry S. Truman, "Message to the Congress on the State of the Union and on the Budget for 1947," Speech, January 21, 1946. The American Presidency Project, http://www.presidency.ucsb.edu/ws/?pid=12467 (accessed December 1, 2011).

27. Harry S. Truman, "Special Message to the Congress on Greece and Turkey: The Truman Doctrine," Speech, March 12, 1947. The American Presidency Project, http://www.presidency.ucsb.edu/ws/?pid=12846 (accessed November 1, 2011).

28. Harry S. Truman, "Annual Message to the Congress on the State of the Union," Speech, January 8, 1951. The American Presidency Project, http://www .presidency.ucsb.edu/ws/?pid=14017 (accessed November 25, 2011).

29. Dwight D. Eisenhower, "Inaugural Address," Speech, January 20, 1953. The American Presidency Project, http://www.presidency.ucsb.edu/ws/?pid=9600 (accessed November 25, 2011).

30. Dwight D. Eisenhower, "Second Inaugural Address," Speech, January 21, 1957. The American Presidency Project, http://www.presidency.ucsb.edu/ws/? pid=10856 (accessed November 25, 2011).

31. John F. Kennedy, "Radio and Television Address to the American People on the Nuclear Test Ban Treaty," Speech, July 26, 1963. The American Presidency Project, http://www.presidency.ucsb.edu/ws/?pid=9360 (accessed November 29, 2011).

32. Lyndon B. Johnson, "Address before a Joint Session of the Congress," Speech, November 27, 1963. The American Presidency Project, http://www .presidency.ucsb.edu/ws/?pid=25988 (accessed November 25, 2011).

33. Lyndon B. Johnson, "Annual Message to the Congress on the State of the Union," Speech, January 10, 1967. The American Presidency Project, http:// www.presidency.ucsb.edu/ws/?pid=28338 (accessed November 28, 2011).

34. Richard M. Nixon, "Radio and Television Address to the People of the Soviet Union," Speech, July 2, 1974. The American Presidency Project, http:// www.presidency.ucsb.edu/ws/?pid=4282 (accessed November 28, 2011).

35. Richard M. Nixon, "State of the Union Message to the Congress: Overview and Goals," Speech, February 2, 1973. The American Presidency Project, http://www.presidency.ucsb.edu/ws/?pid=3996 (accessed November 28, 2011).

36. Gerald R. Ford, "Address before a Joint Session of the Congress Reporting on the State of the Union," Speech, January 19, 1976. The American

Presidency Project, http://www.presidency.ucsb.edu/ws/?pid=5677 (accessed November 28, 2011).

37. Ronald Reagan, "Address to Members of the British Parliament," Speech, June 8, 1982. The American Presidency Project, http://www.presidency.ucsb.edu/ws/?pid=42614 (accessed November 1, 2011).

38. Ronald Reagan, "Remarks at the Annual Convention of the National Association of Evangelicals in Orlando, Florida," Speech, March 8, 1983. The American Presidency Project, http://www.presidency.ucsb.edu/ws/?pid=41023 (accessed November 21, 2011).

39. Ronald Reagan, "New Year's Radio Address to the People of the Soviet Union," Speech, December 31, 1986. The American Presidency Project, http://www.presidency.ucsb.edu/ws/?pid=36848 (accessed November 16, 2011).

40. James Mann, "Reagan at the Berlin Wall," *The Los Angeles Times*, November 6, 2009, http://articles.latimes.com/2009/nov/06/opinion/oe-mann6 (accessed December 5, 2011).

41. George H. W. Bush, "Address before a Joint Session of the Congress on the State of the Union," Speech, January 29, 1991. The American Presidency Project, http://www.presidency.ucsb.edu/ws/?pid=19253 (accessed November 28, 2011).

42. William J. Clinton, "Address before a Joint Session of the Congress on the State of the Union," Speech, January 25, 1994. The American Presidency Project, http://www.presidency.ucsb.edu/ws/?pid=50409 (accessed November 28, 2011).

43. William J. Clinton, "Remarks on the Bombing of the Alfred P. Murrah Federal Building in Oklahoma City, Oklahoma," Speech, April 19, 1995. The American Presidency Project, http://www.presidency.ucsb.edu/ws/?pid=51239 (accessed November 15, 2011).

44. George W. Bush, "Address Accepting the Presidential Nomination at the Republican National Convention in Philadelphia," Speech, August 3, 2000. The American Presidency Project, http://www.presidency.ucsb.edu/ws/?pid=25954 (accessed November 16, 2011).

45. George W. Bush, "Address to the Nation on the Terrorist Attacks," Speech, September 11, 2001. The American Presidency Project, http://www.presidency.ucsb.edu/ws/?pid=58057 (accessed November 14, 2011).

46. George W. Bush, "Address before a Joint Session of the Congress on the State of the Union," Speech, January 29, 2002. The American Presidency Project, http://www.presidency.ucsb.edu/ws/?pid=29644 (accessed November 28, 2011).

47. George H. W. Bush, "Remarks and a Question-and-Answer Session at a Luncheon Hosted by the Commonwealth Club in San Francisco, California," Speech, February 7, 1990. The American Presidency Project, http://www.presidency.ucsb.edu/ws/?pid=18128 (accessed November 18, 2011).

48. William J. Clinton, "Address before a Joint Session of the Congress on the State of the Union," Speech, January 27, 1998. The American Presidency Project, http://www.presidency.ucsb.edu/ws/?pid=56280 (accessed November 16, 2011).

49. John Bolton, "Beyond the Axis of Evil: Additional Threats from Weapons of Mass Destruction," May 6, 2002, http://www.heritage.org/research/lecture/beyond-the-axis-of-evil (accessed November 25, 2011).

50. Associated Press, "Rice: Bush 'Axis of Evil' Reference Was Accurate," *MSNBC*, October 24, 2006, http://www.nbcnews.com/id/15406560/ns/politics/t/rice-bush-axis-evil-reference-was-accurate/ (accessed March 21, 2012).

51. "Transcript: Rice on Fox News Sunday," *Fox News Sunday*, February 3, 2002, http://www.foxnews.com/story/0,2933,44645,00.html (accessed March 21, 2012).

52. Barack Obama, "Remarks by the President at the Acceptance of the Nobel Peace Prize," Speech, December 10, 2009. The White House, http://www.whitehouse.gov/the-press-office/remarks-president-acceptance-nobel-peace-prize (accessed December 5, 2011).

CHAPTER 23

Pornography as Resilient Popular Evil

Joseph W. Slade

For Americans conflicted about bodies and their sexualities, pornography has long functioned as a sign of iniquity, not quite a source of dread, but resiliently sinister all the same. Over time, medical advances, economic necessity, First Amendment guarantees, changing lifestyles, conceptions of privacy, gender disputes, and the relentless spread of mass communication have eroded both the credibility and the salience of many of pornography's alleged evils. Artists have discovered beauty in subjects considered taboo for centuries, and the fashion industry now routinely discovers inspiration in marginal tastes. Commerce itself has sanitized, even domesticated, speech and pictures that shocked Americans a few decades ago. Evolutionary biologists, revising understanding of the mechanics of sexual attraction, have bestowed legitimacy on images previously condemned as "unnatural." As some objections to sexual expression have lost traction, however, opponents have at various stages found new reasons to demonize it. Attacks today tend to be religious, moral, esthetic, or cultural, but for most of its history, America dealt with pornography's perceived evils through legal sanctions.

Pornography has been linked to the rise of both modernity and industrialization, a circumstance that has contributed to resistance. According to Walter Kendrick, *pornography* is less a thing than an argument,[1] but it usually refers to words or images whose capacity to arouse exceeds that of mere *erotica*, a term with more respectable connotations. The word "pornography" entered the English language only in 1850. Prior to that, the regulation of sexual expression was subsumed by conceptions of obscenity themselves shaped by religion and politics. Historians root prohibitions against obscenity in early Christian characterizations of human bodies as impure vessels easily corrupted by animalistic sexuality. Western ecclesiastics chastised stimulating words and pictures as sacrilegious, blasphemous, or "unnatural"; certainly American religious leaders have done so. In 1744, for example, Jonathan Edwards condemned popular sex manuals in Northampton, Massachusetts. His fear, widely shared, was that reading such texts led to masturbation, the mythical evils (blindness, lesions, madness) of which still resonate today.

In the political run-up to democracy, dissenters in Europe used obscenity as a weapon against "divine right," denouncing kings and queens as decadent symbols of "the body politic." Antimonarchists launched obscene attacks against the English crown during the 17th century, just as Jacobins later flooded Paris with obscene pamphlets lampooning debauched aristocrats to ignite the French Revolution. "By the end of the eighteenth century," says one historian, "pornography had significantly undercut the credibility of aristocratic privilege and played a vital role in modernity's emergence."[2] That role came at a cost: the cruel sexual invective of revolutionaries such as the Marquis de Sade established an enduring—if often mistaken—link between pornography and violence and—more convincingly—between pornography and social upheaval. But most pornographers merely titillated. European and English erotic classics followed colonists to the New World (to be shelved in the libraries of Benjamin Franklin and William Byrd); in 1821 Massachusetts convicted two men of distributing John Cleland's *Fanny Hill* (1748). Low literacy and the expense of printing limited traffic, though. Visiting in 1831–1832, Tocqueville observed that the United States had few laws against "licentious books" because lack of demand meant that no Americans wanted to write them.[3]

Industrialization, however, eroticized the urban landscapes it created. The opening of the Erie Canal (1825) transformed northeastern cities into centers of manufacturing and distribution. Booming economies commercialized leisure for thousands of young men who labored in factories and businesses by day and caroused by night. Saloons, whorehouses, gambling dens, racetracks, and prizefights catered to them, but so did purveyors of private amusements. During the Jacksonian era, masculine pursuits spawned a "sporting press," scandal sheets such as *The Whip, The Weekly Rake,* and *The Libertine.* Sometimes as partisan crusaders, sometimes as blackmailers, editors of these pornographic papers charged political opponents with immorality and hypocrisy for patronizing prostitutes and bawdy establishments. Book publishers in New York churned out seamy volumes, followed by similar entrepreneurs in New Orleans and Cincinnati, as the appeal of transgression boosted the number of writers specializing in salacious topics. When these vulgar enterprises concentrated themselves in municipal underbellies, pornography seemed a form of urban blight.

Industrialization also created a new middle class that set itself apart from lower classes not only by status and affluence but also by standards of decorum and respectability. For those citizens, pornographic amusements undermined puritanical and capitalist work ethics. Licentious entertainment offended the (mostly) male arbiters of this class, who were even more disturbed by the changes wrought by immigration, education, science, and incipient feminism, all of which they thought dangerous. For conservatives, moral innocence was in retreat, overwhelmed by evil; for progressives, pseudoinnocence simply masked hypocrisy, an evil in itself. Sexual wars pitted traditionalists against advocates of free love, sexual health, and birth control. Feminist "dress reformers" pushed bloomers and pantaloons; communitarian movements practiced both celibacy and sexual experimentation; faddists promoted sexual diets and regimens; markets for sexual appliances soared; women bought romance novels and medical texts by the armload. Dr. Frederick Hollick's *Marriage Guide* (1851), for example, was shocking because it discussed masturbation, went through 500 editions. Worse, publishers began dabbling in homosexual genres, a development regarded as even more pernicious, as reaction to Walt Whitman's *Leaves of Grass* (1855) would soon demonstrate. For traditionalists, mediated perversions encroached on the natural order of things; they struggled to control "easily swayed" women, immigrants, and urban masses, hoping that censorship could prevent erosion of class and gender boundaries.

The Civil War swelled the market for sexual materials, with publishers on both sides selling explicit pictures, books, and novelties to troops in trenches. After the War, proliferating transportation systems and high-speed presses distributed sexual materials on a frightening scale. In 1873, Anthony Comstock, a former grocery clerk with strong convictions and influential allies, launched the New York Society for the Suppression of Vice to prosecute evils such as blasphemy, gambling, violent sporting events, birth control advocacy, indecent theatrical performance, and lewd writing and pictures. Similar vice-societies sprang up in Boston, St. Louis, Chicago, Louisville, Cincinnati, and San Francisco. Comstock lobbied Congress to add sections 1461, 1462, and 1463 (collectively called the Comstock Act of 1873) to Title 18 of the U.S. Code. These prohibited the publication, manufacture, importation, interstate transportation, and advertising of materials for "indecent or immoral use," a category that included sexual expression and erotic devices as well as contraceptive information and medical advice on reproduction. Comstock was also appointed Special Agent for the Post Office to interdict obscenity in the mails. In his federal and state capacities, Comstock prosecuted marginal publishers, producers of risqué and avant-garde theatrical performances, and artists, photographers, and distributors of "indecent" drawings, paintings, photographs, and appliances.

Later reviled for failing to distinguish between artistic or scientific and trashy expression, Comstock at first drew support not simply from conservatives but also from progressives concerned about urban crime and social ills, especially rampant prostitution and venereal disease. Not for the last time, many Americans assumed that sexual discourse spurred both violence and promiscuity. Members of the perennially insecure middle class redoubled efforts to distance themselves from the imagined rapacious sexual appetites and loose morals of lower classes by policing obscenity that might undermine social hierarchies. Legal justification for suppression, however, was still linked to blasphemy and libel. American courts, following English common law, prosecuted transgressive works using as precedent *Regina v. Hicklin* (1868), which was originally designed to suppress political dissent, not ordinary sexual expression. *Hicklin* allowed condemnation of a book if any passages were deemed likely to "deprave and corrupt" those "whose minds are open to such immoral influences," in other words, children, women, lower classes, and foreigners.

Well into the 20th century, most American cases of obscenity were decided at local levels, often in small magistrates' courts, where sexual texts and pictures were regarded as clear evidence of guilt. Breakthroughs in obscenity case law required celebrated examples of high culture or defenses too expensive for all but the well heeled. Judicial doubts appeared during prosecution of Daniel Carson Goodman's novel *Hagar Revelly;* while upholding *Hicklin* in *U.S. v. Kennerly* (1913), federal judge Learned Hand questioned the wisdom of prohibiting books because they were unsuitable for children. Comstock having died in 1915, the New York Society for the Suppression of Vice reacted to the loosened post–World War I cultural climate by joining a Clean Books Campaign that peaked in the early 1920s. Because it attempted to retard both emerging mainstream literary realism and modern art, the alliance eroded the standing of the Society, which went into decline. Not surprisingly, nationwide campaigns to suppress prostitution stimulated interest in sexual representations and performances. As the new medium of motion pictures siphoned audiences from theaters, entrepreneurs countered by staging dramas on prostitution and homosexuality, designing revues around scantily dressed showgirls, and introducing striptease artists whose celebrity captivated fans. Paintings and photographs reproduced human figures more boldly, while scandal newspapers and romance magazines foregrounded sexuality—all flirtations with the forbidden probably accentuated by the public's weariness with the restrictions of prohibition (1919–1933).

Genuine pornography went underground, into surreptitious markets for crude comic books, indecent photographs, and pornographic movies, while official culture waffled over mainstream expression. In *Mutual Film Corporation v. Industrial Commission of Ohio* (1915), the Supreme Court denied motion pictures the protection of the First Amendment on the grounds that moving images were a species of spectacle, not speech. When Congress declined to pass federal film censorship, state and municipal boards proliferated so quickly that the Motion Picture Producers and Distributors of America began to self-regulate movies to counter piecemeal local censorship. In the contentious year 1930, the MPPDA established a strict Production Code; a Catholic bishop founded the National Organization for Decent Literature; and Massachusetts banned Dreiser's *An American Tragedy* and D.H. Lawrence's *Lady Chatterley's Lover.* On the other hand, that year federal judge Augustus Hand (cousin of Learned) reversed the conviction of an educational pamphlet, *The Sex Side of Life*, by Mary Ware Dennett, and Congress reduced the roles of the Post Office and the Customs Department by vesting the power to determine obscenity solely with courts. Two important decisions widened space for expression. In *Near v. Minnesota* (1931), the Supreme Court ruled that government may not engage in "prior restraint" of scandalous material, and in *U.S. v. One Book Called "Ulysses"* (1933), Judge John M. Woolsey eviscerated *Hicklin*, ruling that James Joyce's masterpiece was not obscene. Appellate justices Augustus and Learned Hand upheld Woolsey's argument that a work must be considered as a whole. At the same time, in the 1934 Communications Act, Congress dealt with yet another new technology by forbidding "indecency" (requiring a much lower threshold of proof than obscenity) in broadcast media.

The contrived cultural blandness that followed World War II was shattered by the Kinsey Reports (1948 and 1953), which reported on the sexual habits of Americans. Magazines skirted restrictions by submerging sex in increasingly violent contexts until *Playboy* (founded in 1953) linked female nudity with affluent lifestyles, and argued for the recreational aspects of sex, a concept anathema to conservatives convinced that intercourse's primary purpose was procreation. In another blow to conservatives, the FDA in 1960 approved the oral contraceptive pill Enovid. As television cut into audiences for motion pictures, the Supreme Court reversed itself by extending First Amendment protection to cinema in *Joseph Burstyn, Inc. v. Wilson, Commissioner of Education of New York* (1952), a decision that permitted movies to compete by depicting scenes not permitted on the airwaves. It was similarly apparent to mainstream publishers that censorship had to go if their industry were to flourish. High-profile cases cleared D.H. Lawrence's *Lady Chatterley's Lover* (1960), Henry Miller's *Tropic of Cancer* (1964), and John Cleland's *Fanny Hill* (1966). In 1964,

Britain's Home Secretary filed a protest against the more than 1 million lurid American paperbacks swamping his nation.[4]

Pornography nonetheless retained its power to complicate definitions of protected speech. Between 1957 and 1967, the 9 Supreme Court justices filed 55 *different* concurring or dissenting opinions in 13 major obscenity cases. In *Roth v. U.S.* (1957), Justice Brennan said that "all ideas having even the slightest redeeming social importance—unorthodox ideas, controversial ideas, even ideas hateful to the prevailing climate of opinion—have the full protection of [the First Amendment]." According to *Roth*, "[The test for obscenity is] whether to the average person, applying contemporary community standards, the dominant theme of the material taken as a whole appeals to prurient interest." In subsequent cases, the Court calibrated "contemporary standards" on a "national" scale, said that the "appeals to prurient interests" must be "patently offensive," and reduced the threshold of "slightest" to "no redeeming social importance."

Along the way, the Court, headed by Earl Warren, dealt with nudity ("nudity in itself and without lewdness or dirtiness is not obscenity in law or in common sense . . .," *Excelsior Pictures v. Regents of the University of the State of New York* [1957]); "ideological obscenity" ("an idea," and therefore protected, *Kingsley Int'l Pictures v. Regents of the University of the State of New York* [1959]); homosexual magazines ("cannot be deemed so offensive on their faces to affront current community standards of decency," *Manual Enterprises v. Day, Postmaster General* [1962]); and "pandering" intent (which *was* prosecutable, *Ginzburg v. U.S.* [1965]). After *Redrup v. New York* (1966), censorship of questionable books virtually ceased because the Court limited prosecution to *distribution* that pandered or targeted children or unwilling audiences. Moreover, in *Stanley v. Georgia* (1969) the Court held that a citizen's right to privacy meant that it was not illegal to possess obscene materials for personal use.

Taking advantage of pornography's still-ambiguous status, mob-connected entrepreneurs such as Reuben Sturman, operator of Parliament News, began trafficking in hard-core magazines and in 8-mm loops, the successors to the hard-core stag films that had titillated men in American Legion halls for decades. The latter quickly mutated into 35-mm feature films exhibited in public cinemas. The most notorious of these, *Deep Throat* (1972), financed by organized crime, became so popular that it made pornography chic for middle-class audiences. To clarify matters, President Lyndon Johnson established a Commission on Obscenity and Pornography. In 1970, the Commission's report, buttressed by massive research, concluded that pornography had few antisocial effects, and recommended that its production and distribution be decriminalized for consenting adults. Ignoring the recommendation, a more conservative

Supreme Court under Warren Burger in *Miller v. California* (1973) reformulated the prurient interest test as "whether the work depicts or describes, in a patently offensive way, sexual conduct specifically defined by state law," a stipulation that allowed states to prohibit acts and representations. Burger weakened the "utterly without redeeming social value" test so that it read "whether the work, taken as a whole, lacks serious literary, artistic, political or scientific value." Significantly, also, the Court revised "contemporary standards" to mean those of a local, not a national, community. Moreover, in a companion case, *Paris Adult Theatre v. Slaton* (1973), the Court revived provisions of *Hicklin*, asserting that government may "protect the weak, the uninformed, the unsuspecting, and the gullible" by prohibiting certain expression, in this instance by closing an adult theater. The notion of innocence as a defense against evil seemed resurgent. When the state of Georgia promptly convicted as obscene the mainstream film *Carnal Knowledge*, an embarrassed Supreme Court in *Jenkins v. Georgia* (1974) reversed the conviction, a signal that local censors did not have "unbridled discretion."

Although *Miller* remained the law, in practice juried convictions were so rare that local communities adopted a variety of strategies short of outright censorship. One revived the idea that pornography could corrupt public places, an obvious evil; zoning restricted the location of adult businesses so that they would not blight a neighborhood. In *Young, Mayor of Detroit v. American Mini-Theatres* (1976), the Supreme Court said that Detroit could prevent sex businesses from clustering together and thus lowering property values. Five years later, however, in *Schad v. Borough of Mt. Ephraim* (1981), the Court reminded municipalities that they could not use zoning to eliminate such businesses altogether. The Court also at last ended Comstock's ban on advertising contraceptive devices through the mails in *Bolger v. Young Drug Products* (1983). While many Americans responded gratefully to the decriminalization of birth control advice, others continued to insist that such information was pornographic and immoral.

Zoning gradually became moot as new technologies enabled Americans to consume explicit materials in their homes. Pornography in fact drove the market for videocassette recorder-players; more than 50 percent of all videocassettes marketed during the 1970s were pornographic.[5] Proliferating satellite and cable systems quickly secured audiences eager to watch content that the Federal Communications Commission (FCC) did not regulate because such services required subscriptions. Economically threatened, but still forced by their public licenses to avoid "indecency," broadcast radio and television cautiously flirted with mild sexual themes, constrained by the FCC's 1978 prohibition of "seven dirty words" (*FCC v. Pacifica Foundation*).

Opponents of explicit expression next tried to characterize entrepreneurs as public nuisances because of their shabby premises, crowd-attracting entertainment, and excessive noise; the Supreme Court briefly upheld such restrictions, allowing municipalities to use nuisance-abatement ordinances to close adult businesses (e.g., *Arcara v. Cloud Books* [1986]). Such interdictions failed. Explicit books, magazines, artifacts, movies, and videotapes circulated so widely that they provoked a backlash from antipornography feminists, who asserted that pornography caused rape and sexual violence. Finding a scapegoat in a scabrous movie in which an actress was allegedly killed during intercourse on screen, antiporn feminists mounted massive demonstrations against exhibition of *Snuff* (1976). Revelation that the film was a fraud (footage had been recut by a producer who spread the rumor that the star had actually been murdered) did not end wild tales that still circulate (no authentic "snuff" film has ever been discovered), a reminder that some evils are at base folklore.[6] In a more serious challenge to sexual expression, Catharine MacKinnon, a legal scholar responsible for legislation against sexual harassment in work places, and Andrea Dworkin, an activist who claimed that men routinely victimized women, redefined pornography as discriminatory words and images designed to oppress women. In 1984, the Minneapolis City Council adopted an ordinance by MacKinnon and Dworkin making it possible for women to sue producers and distributors of pornography provided that they could prove the materials harmful. Undeterred by the mayor's veto of the ordinance, MacKinnon and Dworkin wrote a similar one for Indianapolis. American Booksellers, the trade organization of book publishers and dealers, contested its adoption, and won in 1985 (*American Booksellers v. Hudnut*). Ironically, defining pornography in ideologically gendered terms actually elevated it to the much more protected category of political speech.

Antiporn feminists next allied themselves with President Reagan's conservative Attorney General Edwin Meese, whose 1986 Commission on Pornography aimed to roll back the recommendations of the 1970 Commission on Obscenity and Pornography. By now, however, psychologists and sociologists had conducted dozens of studies of pornography. Leading scholars agreed that pornographic films (the most explicit genre) appeared to have negative effects *only* when violence was joined to sexual content. Unable convincingly to demonstrate antisocial consequences, and undercut by dissent from its members, the Commission's insistence that pornography was harmful persuaded few. Though admonished by courts for overzealousness, Meese's National Obscenity Enforcement Unit continued to harass pornographers, using tactics such as forum-shopping (i.e., finding a community conservative enough to convict) and RICO (Racketeer Influenced and Corrupt Organization Act) legislation.

The antiporn feminist position unraveled when a MacKinnon-endorsed study claiming that the majority of images on the Internet were pornographic[7] proved to be bogus (the actual figure was less than 1%), and when successive annual Department of Justice reports indicated that sexual assaults against women fell during the period when pornographic industries surged. More important was a counterreaction from other feminists, who began to find in pornography positive implications for female sexual freedom. Gays and lesbians declared that pornography had historically functioned to create a sense of community among gender outcasts, and women and minorities began to produce pornography to advance their own agendas. Patti Reagan Davis, daughter of President Reagan, posed nude for *Playboy* (1994).

The Meese Commission had declined to target literary eroticism on the grounds that pornography meant audiovisual expression, not books. Licentious expression magnified and delivered by electronics became the new evil, to be combatted by protecting children, by now the only legal strategy for curtailing sexual expression that could compel wide assent. In 1985, prodded by the Parents Music Resource Center, founded by wives of Washington politicians, the Senate held hearings on explicit and violent lyrics in music recordings; the industry responded by agreeing to affix warning labels to record and CD jackets. In 1989, the Supreme Court invalidated Congressional attempts to curtail the transmission of pornographic messages (dial-a-porn) via telephones (*Sable Communications v. FCC*). On the other hand, courts let stand Section 2257 of Title 18, added in 1995, a requirement that producers of visual sexual materials prove that all performers, no matter how elderly, were 18 or older; ironically, the legislation stabilized a previously disordered industry by forcing it to keep records.

In passing the Telecommunications Act of 1996, Congress mandated that television sets manufactured after 1998 be equipped with an electronic V-chip that can read ratings of televised sexual and violent content to be provided by broadcasters and cable casters; the provision made parents rather than distributors responsible for what children watched. Dealing with the Internet was more problematic. The Internet mooted one evil by reducing the role of organized crime, which could no longer control distribution of sexual materials, and it not only destroyed the market for pornographic magazines by transmitting explicit images to any computer connected to the World Wide Web, but also made those images available to children. The Communication Decency Act (1996) sought to criminalize the knowing sending of indecent or obscene messages via the net to minors, but the Supreme Court (*Reno v. ACLU* [1997]) struck down its overly broad provisions. Second and third attempts, the Child Pornography Prevention Act (1996) and the Child Online Protection Act

(1998) met similar fates (*Ashcroft v. Free Speech Coalition* [2002] and *Ashcroft v. ACLU* [2004]) though the Court let stand the Children's Internet Protection Act (2000), which called for filters to be installed on computers in schools and libraries.

Broadly speaking, while obscenity is still illegal in America, pornography featuring adult performers intended for adults is not. Here again, legislative efforts to protect children from being exploited as subjects have led to unforeseen consequences. Prodded by the United States over the last decade to adopt child pornography laws as strict as its own, Western countries by anathematizing child pornography have also legitimized pornography for adults, and thus increased production of the latter. Great Britain, for example, which clung to censorship of sexual representations even for mature consumers into the 1990s, now prosecutes materials involving minors instead of regulating content for those old enough to vote. Largely unstated economic motives may have driven legal agreements to combat child pornography because they helped regularize international trade in sexual materials; cash-hungry Eastern European nations like Hungary in particular have as a result benefitted from pornography exported by home-grown industries. However laudable, international cooperation in catching child pornographers can do little to restrict access by minors to Internet-delivered pornography intended for adults.

Calculating market size is difficult because few Americans agree on whether such genres as women's romances, nude performances, R-rated movies, cable programs, and television soap operas should be designated pornographic. Exaggeration further clouds arguments. Reports that the adult video industry is larger than the mainstream film industry are inaccurate; Hollywood's billions in annual revenue are more than five times those of pornographers. But they are still impressive figures, a source of pride to porn entrepreneurs, and of dismay to those who view such growth with alarm. The United States is now the world's largest exporter of pornographic materials, an embarrassment to those who think such trade blemishes the nation's reputation. Estimates of the size of the total *global* market, usually expressed in tens of billions of dollars, vary widely; suffice it to say that Osama bin Laden easily acquired a large personal library of explicit DVDs.

In America, pornography has emerged from shadows long enough to permit recycling of the louche glamor of the 1970s, the so-called Golden Age of Porn. Hollywood producers are readying not one but two biographical motion pictures on the late Linda Lovelace, star of the iconic *Deep Throat*, herself once depicted as a victim of pornography. Old battles constantly resurface. Conservatives still view sexuality and its expression as moral issues bounded by norms both real and imaginary. Vaguely defined "family values" serve as moral flash points even as numbers of Americans abandon ideal conceptions of marriage. Pornography continues to be a third rail for politicians, though one Republican presidential candidate called for new restrictions on sexual materials in 2012.

The unease of progressives is just as vague. The *New York Times* defines that unease as "the awareness of everything perilous about the modern world: the degradation of the environment, nuclear energy, religious fundamentalism, threats to privacy and the family, drugs, pornography, violence, terrorism."[8] Thousands of Americans of all genders circulate pictures and video clips of themselves nude or in intercourse on the Internet, and millions more download them. Seemingly obsessive consumption has led to worries that pornography is addictive, though psychiatrists dispute the appropriateness of the term (as well as "sexual addiction"). Threats to health still garner attention. Los Angeles, home to the adult video industry because the city does not equate making pornography with engaging in prostitution, recently passed an ordinance requiring actors to wear condoms, partly to protect the actors against sexually transmitted diseases, and partly because adult movie stars might serve as role models for viewers.[9]

Just as worrisome is pornography's alleged tendency to redirect sexual expectations in partners toward behavior so kinky that it obscures mutually fulfilling experience. The new edition of the *Diagnostic and Statistical Manual of Mental Disorders* (*DSM-5*) will probably downgrade many previously recognized sexual fetishes to the status of inclinations rather than disorders, in keeping with a broader cultural tendency to think of traditional moral dicta as matters of taste.[10] Practices in pornography once deemed manifestly evil now seem normal, at least to those who enjoy them. Many Americans nonetheless think of interest in pornography as a sign of sexual dysfunction. Nested within free-floating anxieties is the fear that pornography, because it promotes solitary masturbation, displaces actual sex with synthetic versions bereft of emotion. Theorists such as Jean Baudrillard claim that humans now live within media-synthesized simulacra. Still others, like Georges Bataille, argue that technology itself sexualizes the human condition, making artifice more exciting than reproductive intercourse.[11]

A spectrum of engineering advances has darkened those visions, forcing Americans to confront the disturbing implications of digital technologies capable of enormous verisimilitude. *Expression*, the term traditionally applied to pornographic discourse, inadequately registers the impact of electronic *representation*. When digitized audiovisual assemblages supplant words, when intimate performance of authentic sex erases mere simulation, such representations become much more mimetic than symbolic expression. On the one hand, pornography in digitized modes dematerializes sex, removing from it the sweaty physicality of intercourse and the bio-logical imperatives of reproduction. On the other, digital renderings of naked bodies in intercourse lack the distance that ordinarily separates the sounds and images of television and motion pictures from actual experience; their no-longer closeted presence is intrusive, a violation of the public nature and detached consideration of art. Mediation becomes embodiment, a form of representation whose fidelity aspires to virtualization.

Taking note of sales in sexual appliances (from mechanical aids to sex dolls), by reports that young people are more enraptured by cyberspace than by automobiles, by advances in artificial intelligence and machine learning, and by the construction of humanoid robots by manufacturers such as Honda, digital experts such as David Levy believe that humans will soon mate with androids within 50 years. Not surprisingly, antiporn activists agree, prophesying that sexual technologies will lead to an apocalyptic "acceleration of perversions."[12] The ancient charge that pornography is somehow unnatural seems to have come full circle, though the focus is where it logically should be, on mediation as opposed to sex itself. Deciding whether virtual sex representations will come to pass is not as important as observing that pornography will remain an issue of contention, striking some as liberating if humanly challenging, and others as unremittingly demeaning and offensive. For the present, at least, pornography continues to trigger apprehension, to hint more than ever at an evil that is primal.

NOTES

1. Walter M. Kendrick, *The Secret Museum: Pornography in Modern Culture* (New York: Viking, 1987), 31.

2. Melissa M. Mowry, *The Bawdy Politic in Stuart England, 1660–1714: Political Pornography and Prostitution* (Aldershot: Ashgate, 2004), 2.

3. Alexis de Tocqueville, *Democracy in America*, trans. Henry Reeve, 2 vols., vol. 1 (New York: Knopf, 1966), 265.

4. "U.S. Pornography Irks British," *New York Times*, April 13, 1964, 58.

5. Jonathan Coopersmith, "The Role of the Pornographic Industry in the Development of Videotape and the Internet," in *Women and Technology: Historical, Societal, and Professional Perspectives: Proceedings: 29–31 July 1999, New Brunswick, New Jersey*, ed. IEEE Society on Social Implications of Technology (New York: IEEE, 1999), 173–87.

6. Eithne Johnson and Eric Schaefer, "Soft-Core Hard-Core and How a Low-Budget Exploitation Feature Turned Porn on Its Ear—*Snuff* as a Crisis in Meaning," *Journal of Film and Video* 45, no. 2–3 (1993): 40–59.

7. Marty Rimm, "Marketing Pornography on the Information Superhighway: A Survey of 917,410 Images, Descriptions, Short Stories, and Animations Downloaded 8.5 Million Times by Consumers in over 2000 Cities in Forty

Countries, Provinces, and Territories," *Georgetown Law Journal* 83, no. June (1995): 1849–934.

8. Daniel Smith, "It's Still the 'Age of Anxiety.' or Is It?," *New York Times*, January 15, 2012, 14.

9. Ian Lovett, "Law on Condoms Threatens Tie between Sex Films and Their Home," *New York Times*, March 8, 2012.

10. John Cloud, "What Counts as Crazy? This Is the Book Doctors Use to Define Mental Illness—and It's All About to Change," *Time*, March 19, 2012.

11. Jean Baudrillard, *Simulacra and Simulation*, The Body, in Theory (Ann Arbor: University of Michigan Press, 1994); Georges Bataille, *Death and Sensuality: A Study of Eroticism and the Taboo* (New York: Walker, 1962).

12. David N. L. Levy, *Love + Sex with Robots: The Evolution of Human-Robot Relations* (New York: HarperCollins, 2007); Rich Deen, "Why Sex with Robots Is Always Wrong: The Impending Demise of the Human Species," www.godandscience.org/doctrine/sex_with_robots.html.

PART IV

Myth and Religion

CHAPTER 24

The Future Unwritten: How We Learned to Love the End of the World

Ryan P. Doom

Few people really want the world to end. Only a small minority pray for society to crumble, for the final cataclysmic event that erases civilization as we know it. Sure, some might sarcastically beg for ruin during moments of despair, heartache, or anger, but outside stock James Bond villains, few actually plan for the destruction of earth. Hopefully. While Americans live, earn paychecks, consume, spend, and pay taxes and bills, we take our surroundings for granted—except when tragedy strikes. Then we notice the trivial things, the important things. Only when things vanish do we miss them. It is a reason for crises to exist, to remind us that in a flash everything and everyone could evaporate. That is why throughout history, we have awaited the "big one," the apocalypse, a seemingly definitive threat to humanity told through religious prophesies, ancient calendars, and misinterpretation. It is only human to fear the end of our species. Dread of the apocalypse gives all Americans a shared sense of mortality, which in turn creates unified paranoid fear. When evil looms, it is the American way to panic over possible and inevitable apocalyptic events. Regardless of race, religion, or creed, Americans have been bred into paranoia. We seemingly understand an expiration date for civilization waits in the near future caused by a flipped switch for nuclear destruction, a vengeful Mother Nature, infectious disease, or just bad luck. Luckily, the apocalypse has not arrived (at the time of this publication) though that has not kept popular fiction (film, novels, poems, TV, video games) from prophesying about life post-Armageddon.

Though collectively fearing the apocalypse, mass audiences find entertainment in representations of what remains after the dust settles, especially since the nuclear bomb. Yes, films like *War of the Worlds* (Byron Haskin, 1953) exist that show the moment of destruction, but sometimes they lack the depths of social commentary found within the post-apocalypse. Much like effectively produced futuristic science fiction (space movies), the distant, surreal nature of a scathed post-apocalyptic environment and a fallen civilization creates an elevated literary quality. Here, we can observe the societal devastation and deterioration as the genre acts like an experiment, combining psychological and sociological elements, which allows for drama at the rawest level—the aftermath as humans unravel, cope, and survive. The observation of the post-apocalypse has made a recreation, a voyeuristic study of the erosion of moral, social, and ethical codes, a place to witness those who can withstand punishment and those who cannot.

This initially explains our consistent attraction to the popular culture of the post-apocalypse. As American society has seemingly drifted further away from its initial fundamental religious roots that founded the country, our basic understanding of why we are drawn to this material has also diminished. Jerome F. Shapiro notes that the term *apocalyptic* has been continually misinterpreted that it "has also come to be misused as a term denoting a kind of mass psychopathology, as well as disaster and destruction. Thus, the word has lost its currency."[1] When the post-apocalyptic genre is viewed without religious ramifications, Shapiro is correct. Post-apocalyptic films are concerned with how survivors alter mental and social conduct in transition with events. Viewers without a religious background might grasp historical religious implications, but not necessarily the reasons behind the end or why society remains eternally paranoid about it. That is why post-apocalyptic fiction has expanded beyond the Book of Revelation. To contain our fears to only religious concepts would only result in heightened paranoia and more misinterpretation. Fictional works help relive those concerns as director J.J. Abrams notes, "Stories in which the destruction of society occurs are explorations of social fear . . . it's a way to process these fears that are mostly bottled up."[2] Post-apocalyptic fiction plays out this angst in a safe manner, focusing on life after devastation, whereas apocalyptic fiction focuses on life during said devastation. But questions remain. What joy do we receive in witnessing the aftermath of the wrath of the apocalypse? How do remnants of everything we hold dear equate with satisfying entertainment? Lastly, do we comprehend why we are drawn to such material?

The post-apocalypse has proved a profitable thematic classification, growing in popularity each year with varied speculation of the end's arrival. Themes range from greed, to overconsumption, to paranoia, to fear. Some years, nuclear devastation is in vogue. Other times, technology has overtaken its creators. Alternatively, perhaps aliens have invaded or

Mother Nature has reclaimed the planet. Filmmakers take what appears to be an affliction of society and give it a fictitious treatment for easy mass consumption. Lately, the zombie apocalypse has staggered back into popular culture and expanded beyond the cinema. Americans are currently obsessed with undead franchises of films, books, video games, and TV with projects like the *Resident Evil* series, Max Brooks's *World War Z*, the *Left for Dead* games, and various comic book series. TV has seen AMC's *The Walking Dead* (2010–) with its depiction of an America ruled by villainous zombies. In this post-apocalyptic subgenre, zombies make for surface level evil (enjoying human flesh = bad), but a well-made zombie tale means perceived evil derives from humanity's actions while in survival mode. In general, post-apocalyptic material—zombie or not—means traditional morals and values vanish along with standard heroics while instability, paranoia, and violence rise. Characters usually fall into two categories. For example, some, such as Rick Grimes (Andrew Lincoln) in *The Walking Dead*, retain their faith while trying to adhere to previous ethical and moral codes of right and wrong in order to maintain order, family, and humanity. Others in the series, like Shane Walsh (Jon Bernthal) or the Governor (David Morrissey), lose their faith and understand that old ways no longer prove practical—they get people dead. Once ethical values vanish, the line between good and evil becomes less defined in the post-apocalyptic world, as it becomes a matter of point of view.

No matter the threat or decade, the post-apocalypse audience continually returns to witness humanity's reaction to complete destruction. Marina Warner claimed, "Brilliant techniques of illusion propel fantasies into reality."[3] Movies like *The Day the Earth Stood Still* (Robert Wise, 1951), *Night of the Living Dead* (George A. Romero, 1968), *Planet of the Apes* (Franklin J. Schaffner, 1968), *Zardoz* (John Boorman, 1974), *Logan's Run* (Michael Anderson, 1976), *Mad Max 2: The Road Warrior* (George Miller, 1981), *Resident Evil* (Paul W. S. Anderson, 2002), *The Road* (John Hillcoat, 2009), *The Book of Eli* (Albert and Allen Hughes, 2010), and many more demonstrate possible scenarios by mimicking current anxieties. For each generation's perception of evil, Hollywood conveniently manufactures a nightmare narrative for capital gain, which not only helps to maintain apocalyptic thought, but also creates entertainment where we explore the dread.

Before the nuclear bomb, Hollywood often defined evil through supernatural or unnatural villains, but with the bomb came a new genre movement. At first, Hollywood responded with mostly B movies like *Captive Women* (Stuart Gilmore, 1952) and *Five* (Arch Oboler, 1951), along with mutated monsters like *Them!* (Gordon Douglas, 1954) and *Godzilla* (Ishirô Honda, 1954) or aliens in *The Thing from Another World* (Christian Nyby, 1951) and *Earth vs. the Flying Saucers* (Fred F. Sears, 1956). As

America transitioned into the Cold War, Hollywood paralleled the nuclear holocaust threat, producing an evil far greater than the lurking vampire or brooding wolf man. The threat appeared tangible in *The Last Man on Earth* (Ubaldo Ragona, 1964), *Dr. Strangelove: Or How I Learned to Stop Worrying and Love the Bomb* (Stanley Kubrick, 1964), and *The Omega Man* (Boris Sagel, 1971). Notably, *A Boy and His Dog* (L. Q. Jones, 1975) demonstrated man's return to animal instinct when free from standard moral values. As the Cold War progressed and neared an end, new economic worries developed during the oil crises of 1973 and 1979, reflected effectively in Australian George Miller's *Mad Max* trilogy. Here, within a ruined world, humanity no longer quarreled over food or shelter; they died for oil. *The Road Warrior* was a part of the genre's arguably most effective era (the late 1970s through the late 1980s) with *Escape from New York* (John Carpenter, 1981), *The Terminator* (James Cameron, 1984), *Night of the Comet* (Thom E. Eberhardt, 1984), *Day of the Dead* (George A. Romero, 1985), and *The Quiet Earth* (Geoff Murphy, 1985) among others. When the 1990s ushered in the Internet boom, for once, apocalyptic mindset seemed dampened, at least cinematically, as only a handful of notable entries of a more abstract evil via environmental destruction in *Twelve Monkeys* (Terry Gilliam, 1995), *Waterworld* (Kevin Reynolds, 1995), and *The Postman* (Kevin Costner, 1997). *The Matrix* (Andy and Lana Wachowski, 1999)—and to a lesser extent films like *Johnny Mnemonic* (Robert Longo, 1995)—effectively explored the threat of new technology.

However, the magnitude of September 11 reawakened post-apocalyptic interest with at least 35 major releases since 2002 such as *28 Days Later* (Danny Boyle, 2002), *Dawn of the Dead* (Zack Snyder, 2004), *Children of Men* (Alfonso Cuaron, 2006), *I Am Legend* (Francis Lawrence, 2007), *City of Ember* (Gil Kenan, 2008), *Zombieland* (Ruben Fleischer, 2009), *The Road*, and *The Book of Eli* among others. These films helped reinstall America's fear and provided evils that could destroy the American way of life not seen since the Cold War. Though the genre had not disappeared before 9/11, that event added a fresh layer of realism to fiction. Despite its release date, one could view *The Terminator* as an important 9/11 film with its prediction that the unknown terrorist's strike would replace the traditionally known enemy as terrorists blended among us, desiring our complete eradication. Hero Kyle Reese (Michael Biehn) explains to his savior's mother, Sara Connor (Linda Hamilton), that the enemy operates without the ability to reason or negotiate. Obviously, Reese defines Schwarzenegger's villain, but more so, he defines America's, if not the world's, current paranoid state over an embedded evil.

While Hollywood perpetually reminds audiences of civilization's potential fate, it is important to note the term "apocalyptic" remains bigger than the American entertainment industry. Post-apocalyptic narratives rarely focus on the prophesized Biblical events and often discount historic religious and cultural impact, creating a new perspective on apocalyptic prophesies. However, for audiences (religiously aware or unaware) to unravel the popular culture of post-apocalypse, we must decipher our initial belief in the apocalypse's eventual existence and why we fear and fantasize over it.

The apocalypse's origin story, believed to have begun around 586 BCE with Babylon's conquering of Jerusalem, shows that century after century, the "good" always encounter a new "evil" reinvented to fit modern problems as each new enemy is willing to trigger annihilation. When Jerusalem fell, it destroyed Israel's freedom as the Jewish people were exiled from their homeland. This action helped establish roots for a Jewish and Christian apocalyptic mindset in which an evil always waits (the devil/anti-Christ). Over time, Jerusalem and Babylon symbolically stood for good and evil, respectively. Babylon equaled an oppressive state, one of exile, while Jerusalem became a place of refuge, producing a conflict that remains at the heart of apocalyptic belief. Each perceived evil the Jewish people encountered prevented a return to Jerusalem, which created a lasting impact on not only desire, but also on maintaining faith.

The most well-known apocalyptic text remains the Book of Revelation, which Christians place as the Bible's final book, bringing the Holy Text full circle with tales of creation and destruction, a reminder of God's mighty power. Revelation could be the most adapted text ever as even during the 4th century, St. Augustine "railed against the 'ridiculous tales' that even some Christians had elaborated from the text."[4] From Revelation derives the Christian belief in the ultimate clash between good and evil, serving as the basis for nearly all future post-apocalyptic work where all people have two choices: be a believer or an unbeliever. Have belief in God, follow His Word, and have no worry. The unbelievers, who abandon God, will discover eternal damnation. Marian Warner states that Revelation is a "riddling story" that "remained ambiguous as well as controversial from the start."[5] With Revelation's "ambiguous" story, the exact moment or catalyst for the end leaves only the most devoted feeling secure. Everyone else is left guessing. It is no wonder a paranoid civilization developed, and after decades of zombies, aliens, bombs, mutants, disease, ecoterror, and technology, the genre has spawned new apocalyptic thought. As Abrams suggests that we need stories to explore "social fear," Shapiro believes the post-apocalypse's long survival comes from it being "proven adaptable to many social situations. This is because, in part, a fundamental characteristic of the apocalyptic tradition is the assimilation of other literary traditions by authors trying to reach a broader audience."[6] To ensure a widely spread message, authors "address experiences such as persecution, culture shock, political powerlessness, social change, 'the dismal fate of humanity,' and death."[7] If Revelation purposely confused and remains a "riddling story," then interpretation from artists, writers, poets, and filmmakers remains an unwritten future, giving them free rein to create moral and ethical narratives to reflect modern discontent.

Obviously, the Book of Revelation was written before America's founding, yet denying its impact on American culture clouds our ingrained apocalyptic beliefs and our mentality toward civilized ethics and values. America has been religiously cultivated to burden ourselves with the future. For example, when the Puritans escaped the Church of England, they established roots in America with a firm apocalyptic mindset as they continually battled perceived "evil" with witch trials. They lived perplexing lives as some followers believed they were destined for eternal damnation regardless if they maintained a pure existence. Despite hardships and setbacks, Americans endured and established a Christian ideology foundation for future generations. Even as those generations drift in and out of religion, America remains embedded in cataclysmic thought with every era fearing that the next will lead to eventual erosion. It is only natural for us to expect the worst: We have been bred to fear the end, making Americans innately paranoid. One might assume that as a society matures, the old ways of thought might diminish. The modern world, however, has increased the convenience of these thoughts since today we seemingly cannot disconnect ourselves from endless information about eventual cultural extinction via cable, computers, smartphones, and tablets, providing consumers with unlimited and instant depictions of doom. For every event, there's a proclamation utilized on a multitude of platforms to reach many. No wonder people continually return to apocalyptic religious conventions. Every year a new unstoppable evil looms. The more technology expands, the more some might consider civilization on the brink of destruction (events like December 21, 2012, and Y2K illustrate how endless media outlets and discussion can fester paranoia). Each new nemesis is potentially the annihilation catalyst. Just as one threat rises, finds resolution, or simply passes, another nemesis emerges to repeat the process.

If paranoia can dictate American behavior, then unsurprisingly we consistently speculate about a yearly increase in violence that brings the apocalypse closer. It seems as a generation ages, every era views the next as increasingly dangerous. It is an idea discussed in Cormac McCarthy's (and the Coen Brothers' 2007 adaptation) *No Country for Old Men*—an older generation remains at odds with the young, disapproving and failing to understand its actions. Sheriff Ed Tom Bell repeatedly complains of a new form of violence, one he cannot comprehend. He has lost belief in his ability as a lawman. Near the conclusion of the film, Bell is reminded that violence, that evil has always been a part of America. "What you got ain't nothing new. This country is hard on people. You can't stop what's coming." The movie, while not part of the post-apocalyptic genre, has little faith that good can conquer evil. The old no longer prove effective, playing into the notion of a generational and societal decline.

The belief in increased violence seems a moot point considering America's rich tradition of bloodshed against perceived evil. Another part of the annihilation allure comes from America's inherent affinity for outlaw behavior and its inevitable bloodshed because it is a country rich in outlaw tales of those outside established society. In particular, the majority of post-apocalyptic works evoke the lore of the American Wild West in films like *A Boy and His Dog*, the *Mad Max* films, the *Resident Evil* films, and *The Book of Eli* among others. They incorporate an exaggerated, fantastical mixture of unparalleled freedom and absolute chaos as humanity seemingly brushed off moral standards in turbulent times. The violent lawlessness in an uncivilized country has always maintained appeal, something the post-apocalyptic genre often emulates by creating a neo-Western world. The Western folklore has merged with truth just as post-apocalyptic fiction possibly has as "brilliant techniques of illusion propel fantasies into reality." America remains a unique society that worships violence and peace simultaneously. Public outcries for horrific real tragedies remain frequent (like the shootings at Columbine, Aurora, and Newtown), yet we continue to flock to theaters and focus on TV programs that remain overridden with violence. It is easy to see why post-apocalyptic work grows in popularity as it not only shows "explorations of social fear," but reconnects audiences with outlaw allure.

Perhaps movies depicting an enduring humanity in a devastated society, regardless of the cause, comfort us, letting Americans know we can survive and continue as long as we maintain standard values. If we don't, we have narratives to foreshadow the future. But maybe it is more than that. Perhaps the idea of building a new culture or hitting the reset button to clean civilization's plate remains a natural appeal to the post-apocalyptic culture. According to the genre, when the apocalypse occurs, everything we depend on will vanish, allowing a reboot of society. This is best illustrated at the end of *Escape from L.A.* (John Carpenter, 1996) when main character Snake Plissken (Kurt Russell) has a choice of either maintaining a decayed civilization or destroying all electrical equipment, sending earth back into the Stone Age. He chooses the latter, allowing his desecrated world to start anew. It could be argued that post-apocalyptic concern with societal leftovers is oxymoronic because the end is never absolute. It is simply an exercise in crisis management. Though life continues, the reaction and decisions of the survivors depicts the quality of their existence, an element audiences enjoy.

Thematically, post-apocalyptic films can be categorized in the previously mentioned religious apocalyptic divisions: the believers and the unbelievers. Faith films do not necessarily mean religious belief, but faith that something or someone exists that will set the proper path for humanity. To prevent the end from being the end. Characters with belief who demonstrate that devotion remain and endure while the unbelievers are left without hope or purpose. It is easy to comprehend why characters in a post-apocalyptic world end up nihilistic, apathetic, corrupt, paranoid, and give into violent, animalistic instincts. *The Walking Dead*'s TV serial format (and the ongoing comic series) allows for a lengthy discussion of the believers and the unbelievers for contemporary audience comprehension. After all, if trust is placed in something unsuccessful, how can someone still maintain devotion? Can people believe in religion, government, relationships, employment, or society when each continually underperforms? Time and time again, the things people believe in fail. Yet, clichés state that good always triumphs over evil and that the cowboy with the white hat will always triumph over the cowboy with the black hat. In reality, societal evil remains an abstract concept that only finds definition in the eye of the beholder. In fictitious works, the line between the two always finds explanation based on the character's perspective. Only heroes, individuals embracing faith in something, can transcend and show the downtrodden the proper path. In the case of *The Walking Dead*, the main characters remind society that moral and ethical codes existed for a reason.

Without social boundaries, chaos will rule shown through the bleak perspective of faithless films, best illustrated by *The Road Warrior*. The only hope exists in living to survive, and without the belief in something more, a world without hope only breeds undirected anarchy. Faithlessness lacks the belief, the blind trust that someone possesses the power to save. When traditional society decays and shared human ethics fall, the line between good and evil evaporates as well. It becomes a world where survival of the fittest returns to the animalistic definition, and becomes the only thing that matters. In *The Road Warrior*, groups form in order to increase the chances of survival as two warring factions battle over the control of oil. The "good" controls the oil while the "evil" desires more. Both act violently, yet both show love still exists within their groups. The ethical line reappears within traditional moral codes. The outsiders act as savages, raping, torturing, and invading though we are never given their true motive. The "good" are given the benefit that they want humanity to resume based on point of view and screen time. They hope to find remnants somewhere and rebuild. If the evil were allowed to give their perspective, maybe they understand only the strong survive; civilization is gone. The film becomes faithless because the main character, Mad Max (Mel Gibson), is an unbeliever. He understands the old world is dead, which stands in contrast to the "civilized" people he encounters who still have belief that "normal" society remains somewhere. For Max, he is not out to preserve the old ways and helps others reluctantly when it benefits his survival.

Out of the 35 releases since 2002, two films in particular demonstrate the genre's division of believers or unbelievers: *The Book of Eli* and *The Road*. *The Book of Eli* is a perfect example of holding faith with religious conviction, as is *Children of Men*. Both depict the standard gloomy future where main characters are determined to save something and preserve, protect that something while evil, violent forces surround them. By both film's conclusions, they maintain faith because no matter the dire circumstances of the future, society can be saved as both movies apply Biblical overtones, adding a subtle (and sometimes not so subtle) layer without turning off mass audiences. In *The Book of Eli*, it is the Book, and in *Children of Men*, it is the immaculate child.

Nevertheless, *The Book of Eli* demonstrates faith most effectively in Denzel Washington's character Eli. While paranoia surrounds him, he believes he can bring change to a suffering, world of unbelievers (where religion has vanished) and will lead the lost to salvation through a copy of the Bible. Eli understands the need for religion in a desolate world, and though he is not a savior in a Christ-like role along the same lines of a John Connor or Mr. Anderson/Neo, he delivers the message the people need. "People had more than they needed. We had no idea what was precious and what was not. We threw away things people kill each other for now." He trusts—he believes in—the power of the Word. Eli will prevail in spite of obstacles and hardships based upon his conviction that he is on a holy mission.

With the exception of Eli, most characters within *The Book of Eli* are portrayed as savages. Only a handful of survivors have preserved intellectual thought, led by Gary Oldman's ruthlessly civilized villain, Carnegie, who will not stop until he captures Eli's "book" (a brail Bible) and can present the messages within it through his vision and "evil" perspective. When Eli and Carnegie face off, a clichéd battle of good and evil emerges for the Book's control in order to decide how others should interpret it. From Eli's perspective, the violent, paranoid savages under Carnegie's control will learn manipulated faith through his twisted word and selfish rule. Eli has met his anti-Christ. Carnegie clearly represents the evil character even though he has created a new civilization, a functioning Western town where people can resume some sort of daily routine with a sense of order and control the lawlessness. Nevertheless, he comprehends the power of the Book and its ability to control. He knows that a faithless people remain a danger. Carnegie acquires the evil label due to his blatant desire to manipulate the message. Society deems this action as evil, however, how many times has the Bible or other religious text been translated and reformed to fit a "modern" people? And when this occurred, how was the messenger received? Since *The Book of Eli* remains Eli's perspective, we can only trust that Eli and his Book speak the truth.

The Road proves difficult to classify as it contains blatant religious overtones yet remains faithless in the end, creating an interesting case study. The novel was a best-seller, landing on Oprah's powerful book club list and making Cormac McCarthy a household name. Still, the film failed to live up to the hefty expectations (a box office and awards disappointment) even if the message remained the same. Audiences were not prepared for a faithless film that lacked a standard tough guy antihero. Instead, audiences received a father and son seeking a safe haven, a New Jerusalem, continuing faith only to find failure. The man (the father) preserves the convictions of fatherhood, on the existence of good people despite the surrounding horror, and that the human soul is worth saving. The father repeatedly reminds his son to keep a light within him while encountering various "prophets" along the way. The father hopes for the continuation of humanity despite nothing remaining.

This may seem like faith, but in the end, the characters have nothing to believe in. Paranoia and violence overwhelmed them, as everything around them remains faithless and no saviors appear to give humanity a reason to live in the face of turmoil as in *The Book of Eli*. "In *The Road* also, what is saved, redeemed, and hoped for does not echo a narrative completion or end. It is, rather, in the persistence and memory of that which refuses to be forgotten."[8] This notion of the lingering memory effectively summarizes the father's mission. He is passing the life he once had onto his son, knowing it will never be anything but past tense. The difference between *The Road* and *Book of Eli* comes from "the absence of referents for forging new values, new rules, and new duties."[9] *The Road*'s world is empty without an ability to refuel. To present a reason to live, the man presents small victories that account for nothing other than false hope. They move further down the road only to remain alive even as the man knows the world is bankrupt. Nothing waits for them. *The Road* clenches onto dead memories. Without God, without something to believe in for the future, the characters become faithless. No clear antagonist exists in *The Road* minus the road itself, showing a dead America. *The Road* still represents absolute freedom, but now it means something else as roaming cannibals present an obvious threat, though they do not linger on-screen long enough. They have no agenda minus survival at any cost. Only the elements prove to be a true foe for the man and boy. Hope for the future arrives at the end when the boy finds a surrogate family after the man dies, but will they have a better chance? Even if they do, the faithlessness of their environment, the lack of a savior, and the lack of a future will overtake them.

Perhaps Kubrick's *Dr. Strangelove* summarizes our love for the post-apocalypse best. It shows that it is not something other worldly or planetary will cause the apocalypse, but man's own incompetence. Our paranoid fear of evil and the potential chaos it could create triggered our own destruction. *Dr. Strangelove* shows that misplaced trust (the film depicts the government's incompetence in protecting and maintaining peace) is worthless. Only faith, as seen in *The Book of Eli*, can restore humanity. However, if the bomb drops, machines revolt, Mother Nature evicts us, or the dead walk, we might as well stop worrying and learn to love a post-apocalyptic world. And with the current zombie fetish, perhaps we already have. *The Walking Dead* has brought post-apocalyptic work to the mainstream like no work since perhaps Revelation itself. Characters who lack hope "find only time to dash from one crisis to the next; like the coward who dies a thousand deaths, they suffer a thousand ends of the world."[10] If we use apocalyptism responsibly, we will trust in something and continue living, knowing the end is near.

The world is resilient. It will repair itself. In nearly all post-apocalyptic films, characters with devotion maintain their faith in the face of paranoid and violent world. They understood the wrath would come. Some hold the belief that someone will come to save them, while others become scavengers, fending for survival. It is all part of the plan, depending on the perspective.

NOTES

1. Jerome F. Shapiro, *Atomic Bomb Cinema: The Apocalyptic Imagination on Film* (New York: Routledge, 2002), 26.

2. Lev Grossman, "Apocalypse New," *Time*, January 17, 2008, http://www.time.com/time/magazine/article/0,9171,1704694,00.html (accessed December 18, 2010).

3. Marina Warner, "Angels & Engines: The Culture of Apocalypse," *Raritan* 25, no. 2 (2005): 15.

4. David E. Nantais and Michael Simone, "Apocalypse When?," *America: The National Catholic Review*, August 18, 2003, http://americamagazine.org/node/146591 (accessed January 10, 2012).

5. Warner, "Angels & Engines: The Culture of Apocalypse," 13.

6. Shapiro, *Atomic Bomb Cinema*, 26.

7. Shapiro, *Atomic Bomb Cinema*, 28.

8. Stefan Skrimshire, "'There Is No God and We Are His Prophets': Deconstructing Redemption in Cormac Mccarthy's the Road," *Journal for Cultural Research* 15, no. 1 (2011): 12.

9. Skrimshire, "'There Is No God and We Are His Prophets': Deconstructing Redemption in Cormac McCarthy's the Road," 5.

10. Rodney Clapp, "Overdosing on the Apocalypse," *Christianity Today*, October 28, 1991, 29.

CHAPTER 25

Canonical Evil: The Demonic, the Satanic, and the Persistence of Catholic Paradigms in American Supernatural Horror

Brenda Gardenour Walter

THE PARANORMAL: GATEWAY TO EVIL

America is haunted. From the signs and wonders of Cotton Mather's *Magnalia Christi Americana* (1702) and the sinister woods of Nathaniel Hawthorne's *Young Goodman Brown* (1835) to Edgar Allan Poe's ghostly *Lenore* (1843), the cultural landscape of America is laced with dark shadows that suggest things are not as they seem.[1] More recently, the American fascination with the unseen world has manifested in paranormal television programs, many of which purport to be "reality shows." Popular programs such as *Scariest Places on Earth* (ABC Family, 2001–2006), *A Haunting* (Discovery, 2005–2007), *Ghost Hunters* (SyFy, 2004–), *Ghost Adventures* (Travel Channel, 2008–), and *Paranormal State* (A&E, 2006–) thrill audiences as they explore the hidden and horrible histories of primarily American localities and families. To different degrees, each of these shows looks to prove scientifically the existence of a shadowy realm that lurks just below our visible and often mundane world. Drawing from traditional horror fare, gothic structures such as old asylums and prisons make up some of the haunted locales investigated on these programs. Here, ghosts perform for their interlocutors by causing drafts and chills, rapping on walls, stomping along empty corridors, and sometimes calling out in menacing voices. For the most part, however, the haunted locations on these shows are far more quotidian in nature: ranch homes from the 1950s, new and renovated houses, trailer homes, and even apartments. These homes, each a manifestation of the American Dream from different socioeconomic perspectives, should inspire not fear but instead a feeling of security: "Safe as houses," as the saying goes. Yet, these places, according to paranormal experts, might house the most horrific of secrets and the most dangerous of entities, far worse than those lurking in old prisons and graveyards.

The local cinema is also a locus of haunting. Films such as *The Sixth Sense* (1999), *The Others* (2001), and *The Devil's Backbone* (2001) attempt to humanize the denizens of the supernatural, thereby making them objects of sympathy and compassion. Far more common, however, are movies like *The Changeling* (1980), *House on Haunted Hill* (1959, 1999), *Thirteen Ghosts* (1960, 2001), and *Poltergeist* (1982, 1986, 1988) that depict spirits as hateful and dangerous to the living. These two themes are interwoven in the *onryou*, or sorrowful and avenging spirit of Japanese folklore, which now haunts the quiet subdivisions of the American mind through films such *The Ring* (2002, 2005, 2012) and *The Grudge* (2004, 2006, 2009, 2012).[2] Perhaps the most pervasive message about the supernatural realm in American culture comes from movies like *White Noise* (2005, 2007) and *Paranormal Activity* (2007, 2010, 2011, 2012) that warn us against our own curiosity of unseen entities and the shadowy world between life and death. According to these films, even the most seemingly benign of spirits, be they the invisible friends of children or cold vapors in the hallway, might not be ghosts at all but completely *inhuman entities* that are toying with our naive and gullible human sympathies.

The supernatural realm as an alluring gateway with the potential for evil is a foundational tenet across almost all representations of the paranormal in America. The viewer is repeatedly warned that venturing into the invisible world is so precarious that it requires the guidance of experts in the form of scientists and investigators who have the wisdom to prevent unexpected horrors from occurring. The consequences of amateur dabbling in the paranormal might be a more intense haunting of one's home or the opening of a portal to the dead that cannot be closed without expert assistance. The stakes are far higher, however, in cases of inhuman or demonic entities, for the presence of true evil—which in American popular culture is nearly always satanic evil—requires the summoning of very particular experts with very old and powerful knowledge. In the world of the paranormal, those experts might include Catholic demonologists such as Ed Warren and his psychic wife, Lorraine, famous for their participation in the Amityville Horror case. Since Ed's death in 2006, Lorraine has continued as a consultant in the most difficult of hauntings, and is often brought in when demonic activity is suspected by investigators.[3] Ultimately, however, almost all cases of demonic infestation and possession require the intervention of the Catholic Church, which conducts an inquest into the haunting and discerns the nature of the offending spirits. Should the Church's investigation yield evidence of the demonic, it gives permission to send in an exorcist, a Roman Catholic priest, who understands the ways of God's enemy, Satan, and how to banish him from the houses and bodies of the faithful and, strangely enough, even the faithless.

SATAN AND HIS SERVANTS AMONG US

In American popular culture, Satan, Satanism, and demonic evil are inseparable from the institutional authority and secret knowledge of the Catholic Church, like two sides of the same coin ever-spinning through a dark well. On the dark side of the coin, demonic evil has remarkably salient and persistent characteristics, the cultural markers of which are writ large in the genre of supernatural horror.[4] At the center is Satan, the ringleader of evil, whose goal is to seduce souls away from the goodness and light of God and into his own dark kingdom. When he is shown at all, the host of hell is often depicted in his historically accepted form as a satyr with a goat's head, horns, and glowing eyes; the Goat of Mendes from *The Devil Rides Out* (1968), the goat-faced Satan of *The Devil's Rain* (1975), and the fantastically horned red-skinned devil of *Legend* (1985) all play upon this theme. The Father of Lies, however, takes many shapes, including a well-dressed man (*The Devil's Advocate*, 1997), an androgynous but somehow strangely seductive woman (*The Passion of the Christ*, 2004), an amorphous goo (*The Prince of Darkness*, 1987), and a dark mist (*End of Days*, 1999). The second-most-powerful character in the realm of demonic evil is the Anti-Christ, the only-begotten son of Satan, who is forever struggling to be born into our world. Because American popular culture demands that the Anti-Christ be the *actual* son of Satan and not merely an agent of evil as proposed in the Book of Revelation, Satan must find a bride (*Lost Souls*, 2000) or, at the very least, a concubine to bear his spawn (*Rosemary's Baby*, 1967; *To the Devil a Daughter*, 1976). In movies such as *The Omen* (1976), adoption of the Anti-Christ allows us to skip the drama of satanic courtship, impregnation, and unnatural birth so that we might move more swiftly into the effects of the evil child on the helpless adults around him.

In their work, Satan and the Anti-Christ are assisted by minions, the most powerful of which are demons, unnatural beings, dark and horrid, who can fly, change shape, see the future in a limited capacity, possess people and places, steal unwary souls for their master, and even provide lurid sexual pleasure to sleeping humans. In films such as *Night of the Demon* (1957), the demon looks much like his master, with a strangely animalistic snout, large fangs, goat's ears, and pointed horns. This particular demon, added to the film against director Jacques Tourneur's will, is also of Godzilla-like proportions and enrobed in ethereal flames. In a different vein, *The Unholy* (1988) features a demon who walks the streets of New Orleans as a sexy vixen and attempts the seduction of a devout priest. Demons, however, are not always so bold; *The Mothman Prophecies* (2002), for example, suggests that the tall, shadowy, winged beings that plague a small town are actually demonic in nature. Paranormal television programs almost always depict demons as "shadow figures" that leave three-clawed scratch marks on walls (*Paranormal State*, "I am Six") and flesh (*A Haunting*, "Where Demons Dwell"; *Paranormal State*, "The Devil in Syracuse"). Not content with inhabiting our homes, demons often seek to possess our bodies as their own; so pervasive is the idea of demon possession that it has become its own horror subgenre. The 1973 release and subsequent success of Friedkin's *The Exorcist*, based on William Peter Blatty's novel of the same name, spawned myriad possession films, the most recent of which include *The Exorcism of Emily Rose* (2005), *Exorcismus* (2010), *The Last Exorcism* (2010) and its sequel, *The Last Exorcism 2*, which was released in 2012.

With so much dastardly work to be done, the Devil does not rely on supernatural minions alone; according to the paradigm of satanic evil in America, he also has legions of human followers willing to fulfill his commands. In some ways more disturbing than their supernatural counterparts, these human manifestations of evil look benign and more often than not like good American citizens, our neighbors, and friends. From Old New England (*Horror Hotel*, 1960) to the Wild, Wild West (*The Devil's Rain*, 1975) to New York in the last millennium (*Rosemary's Baby*, 1968; *The Sentinel*, 1977) and the new (*Bless the Child*, 2000), our communities are infested with individuals who have not only given their own souls over to the Devil, but have also sought the company of others like them in the form of satanic cults. Just out of our range of vision, these cults poison the minds of others, seeking their conversion to Satanism; they also search for victims, preferably nubile young virgins, children, or infants, to be sacrificed in the dreaded Black Mass. This dark ritual is at once evil, ancient, and somehow completely familiar; it is a world turned upside down and inside out, where its symbols and rituals, such as inverted crosses, black candles and vestments, reversed Latin, acts of promiscuity, and infant sacrifice, are merely the symbols and rituals of Catholicism, the most medieval and ritualistic form of Christianity, in reverse (*To the Devil a Daughter*, 1976; *The Devil Rides Out*, 1968; *The Exorcist III*, 1990). Because of this, combatting Satanism, Satan, and other forms of demonic evil in American popular culture requires the use of crucifixes, holy water, Biblical verses, the seven sacraments, sacred vestments, Latin invocations—in short, the wisdom of pre-Vatican II priests who remember their Latin, believe in the Devil, and know what to do about him.

The deep-rooted belief in the power of the Catholic Church over the demonic and its resonance in both Protestant and secular culture is best evidenced in the original case that inspired Blatty's *The Exorcist*. Although the following events are purportedly true, the details of the case, much like *The Exorcist* itself, have become the stuff of legend. In 1949, in a small Maryland town, a 13-year-old Lutheran boy named Robby and his spiritualist aunt visiting from Saint Louis frequently played with a Ouija Board in an attempt to communicate with the spirit world. After his aunt's return home and subsequent death, a disconsolate Robby once again turned to the Ouija Board, in hopes that he might contact her. His foray into the paranormal had, it would seem, opened the dreaded gateway to demonic evil; invisible claws scratched at the walls of the house, his shaking mattress, and ultimately his flesh. After initial consultations with mental health professionals, his family brought him to their Lutheran minister, the Reverend Schulze, who assumed that Robby was merely undergoing some sort of psychic trauma or perhaps manipulating his parents into believing he had strange powers. To dispel this myth, Schulze invited Robby to stay with him overnight, and what he saw disturbed him: the movement of chairs while the boy was asleep, the shaking of the mattress, and the dragging of the boy under the bed by some unseen force. The following day, the Lutheran Reverend Schultz advised the family to find a Catholic priest because "the Catholics know about things like this." Once in the hands of the Jesuits at Saint Louis University, Robby underwent a Catholic conversion and myriad exorcisms that culminated in a vision, seen by both the boy and Jesuits at a local church, of the Archangel Michael defeating Satan's minion in battle. Robby was free, his parents converted to Catholicism, and they lived, so we are told, happily ever after.[5]

"CATHOLICS KNOW ABOUT THINGS LIKE THIS."

Where do these images of demonic evil (including possession, Satanism, the Black Mass, and ritual sacrifice) and its equally matched opponent, the Catholic Church, come from? Why is it that the Catholic Church "knows about things like this" and is the main line of defense against the demonic? The answer lies in the Middle Ages, not as some would have it in the absolute authority of the Church or in the irrational superstitions of folklore, but in the rational world of the medieval university, where theologians used the philosophy of Aristotle to organize already held beliefs into a coherent system of paradigmatic good and evil.

Throughout the 13th century, Aristotle's philosophy became the primary lens through which scholars understood the natural world. Aristotle's *On Logic* provided a binary system of argumentation in which everything that exists must have an inverted opposite, producing inverted symmetrical worlds. *On Physics* offered a detailed hierarchical structure for the cosmos, with a world of ethereal perfection beyond the moon and a world of corruption and change due to the shifting of the four elements (earth, water, air, fire) and the clashing of binary qualities (hot, dry, cold, wet) below the moon.[6] According to Aristotle, the sublunary material world was composed of individual things with binary qualities that might then be organized into larger categories, again with binary qualities, and for each of these things and categories there existed a symmetrically inverted opposite. For example, the male body was warm and dry, muscular and hairy; the female body, on the other hand, was cold and moist, spongy and hairless. In Aristotle's schema, that which was warm or male was closer to perfection and more alive, while that which was cold or female was seen as corrupt and closer to death.[7]

Aristotle's system of binaries and categorical inversion provided scholastic scholars such as Thomas Aquinas and Pseudo-Albertus with a detailed, systematic, and concrete framework for organizing the folkloric and learned, visible and invisible worlds of canonical good and its inversion, canonical evil. Canonical good might be envisioned as a triangle with its base on the surface of the earth and its apex in the highest heavens. At the very peak of this triangle sat God the Father, followed by his son, Jesus Christ, the angels and the saints. This heavenly hierarchy continued into the earthly realm where canonical goodness was embodied in holy and chaste individuals such as monks, nuns, and mystical virgins, as well as in the organized Church, the Mass, and the seven sacraments. Goodness permeated the devout Christian through the cleansing water of baptism and the consumption of the transubstantiated Eucharist, bread and wine that were truly flesh and blood. According to the Aristotelian paradigm of categorical inversion, as theologians elaborated the detailed structures of the Church and canonical goodness, it simultaneously formulated the invisible structures of canonical evil, the Anti-Good Anti-Church.

Unlike the Christian triangle that extended beyond the moon into the heavens, the Anti-Christian and therefore evil triangle had its base in the earthly realm and its apex below the earth's crust in the icy pits of the deepest hell. At the very bottom of this triangle was Satan, the evil force in opposition to God the Father. Because God warmed the Christian heart with ardent prayer and Aristotle argued that warmth was a sign of perfection, the Devil was believed to be cold in nature—thus Dante places Satan in an icy pit. Aristotle had further argued that the most corrupt matter was the heaviest and sunk to the very center of the cosmos, the center of the earth. Satan, therefore, was the dross of creation, an embodiment of chaos and an affront to the natural order. Up until the 13th and 14th centuries, Satan was commonly depicted as either a human with horns or as a small black imp. By the 14th century, however, he had been transformed into a figure of monstrosity, an inversion of nature with a fanged mouth, leathery wings, "horns on knees, calves, or ankles and with faces on chest, belly, and buttocks."[8] As God elevated and nurtured souls and promised ultimately to resurrect purified human bodies, the Devil tormented souls and both tortured and consumed corrupt human flesh. And while God had established a holy kingdom in heaven through the communion of souls and on earth through the Church, so Satan sought to build his own empire of converts both on earth and below its surface in fiery hell. This basic vision of Satan elaborated in the late medieval university is still with us in films such as *Häxan: Witchcraft through the Ages* (1922), *The Devil Rides Out* (1968), and *Legend* (1985), each of which features a truly monstrous Devil with horns and hooves in search of an evil congregation.

Satan's unholy congregation was populated by a full complement of evil minions, the first of which was his only son, the Anti-Christ. Some medieval theologians argued that the Anti-Christ would come as a phantom to terrorize the earth, while others held that he would be merely a wicked man controlled by the Devil.[9] A third and increasingly popular view was that the Anti-Christ would be the physical son of Satan, preferably conceived through a violent sexual act committed upon a whore, thus inverting the impregnation of the Virgin Mary. If Christ was the product of the ethereal divine word and virgin earthly flesh, the Anti-Christ was to be born of carnality and physically polluted female flesh. The convoluted attempt at procreating Astaroth in *To the Devil a Daughter* (1975), the rape of Rosemary in *Rosemary's Baby* (1968), and the strange insemination in *The Prince of Darkness* (1987) are the legacy of such beliefs. In another twist on this theme, black-haired Damien of *The Omen* (1976), himself an inversion of the blond-haired Jesus of mainline American Protestantism, was born of Satan and a jackal, making him a son of a bitch as well as the son of the Devil.

Satan was further assisted in his evil plot by earth-bound demons with leathery wings and cold, slimy bodies, the inversion of the pure and ethereal angels of heaven. Following Aristotle's schema, demons performed angelic functions in reverse by attacking the faithful, tempting them to sin, possessing human flesh, and seducing souls into Satan's service through inquisition-like torture. The Devil's ranks were filled out by his devout worshipers, warlocks, and nefarious witches, who brought others into his coven. Unlike the virgin saints and mystic visionaries of Christianity with their pure bodies and porcelain skin pink with the blush of ardent prayer, witches were corrupt and old with green-grey skin, mottled with witches' teats and the claw marks of the Devil. These poisonous women lured others into the worship of Satan, inviting them to the witches' Sabbath held in the darkness of the forest. Here, converts would sign satanic pacts written in their own blood, receive baptism in blood, trample upon the cross and other sacred Christian objects, consume unbaptized infants in a mockery of the Eucharist, kiss the Devil's posterior as an inversion of the kiss of peace, participate in orgies with demons and fellow worshippers, and ultimately fly home through the use of magical ointment. The elements of the witches' Sabbath would be elaborated in the Black Mass, essentially the Catholic Mass in reverse, all of the trappings of which might be found in movies from *Häxan* (1922) and *The Devil's Rain* (1975) to the spate of exorcism movies released since *The Exorcist* in 1973.

The real-world legacy of the medieval construction of canonical good and evil is terrifying and long lived. At its foundation, Aristotelian philosophy in the service of theologians provided a rational framework for invisible fears and irrational beliefs which divided the world into a strict binary system of good and evil since there existed no intermediary categories between Christian good and non-Christian evil, those who did not fit into the rigidly constructed Christian paradigm—heretics, folk healers, midwives, Jews, and Muslims—were assumed to be in league with the Devil. Worst of all, this demonization of the "other" was defended using the authority of Aristotelian philosophy and learned medicine, making "otherness" seem objectively true and therefore provable. It was this system that was elaborated upon in the *Malleus Maleficarum*, an inquisitor's manual written by Jakob Sprenger and Heinrich Kramer in the 15th century, which was designed to help identify witches and define witchcraft so that both might be rooted out and destroyed. The text is filled with salacious details about the deviant activities of witches, their lust for Satan and his demons, their unholy orgies, as well as their desire to poison good Christians and seduce them into the service of the Devil. Its explicit content matter and its confirmation of long-held beliefs about Satan and the proliferation of witches and their craft made the *Malleus* an early modern best seller, one that escalated fears of satanic witchcraft festering in the shadows of Europe and set the witch-hunts of the 16th and 17th centuries ablaze. At the same time that the *Malleus* rationalized evil, it offered an authoritative solution to the problem; Satan, demons, and witchcraft might be combatted with their opposites, the weapons of Catholic ritual. That is why Catholics know about these things—because Catholic theologians constructed satanic evil in the later Middle Ages and professed Catholic ritual as its only remedy.

FROM THE CINEMA TO THE COURTHOUSE: SATAN AND SOCIETY IN 1980S AMERICA

The elements of canonical evil constructed in the medieval university and disseminated in the *Malleus Maleficarum* have proliferated in the Western imagination, haunting and shaping the Romantic and Gothic movements,[10] Fin-du-Siècle Spiritualism,[11] the works of Montague Summers, and modern supernatural horror fiction and film. In the first half of the 20th century, satanic imagery, especially that of the Black Mass, remained a staple of horror comics, short stories, and movies such as *The Black Cat* (1934) and *The City of the Dead* (1960), but the Devil himself was rarely taken seriously as a force of evil; in comparison to world war, fascism, economic depression, and the threat of nuclear annihilation, perhaps Satan simply did not seem so scary. It was not until the 1960s and the flowering of the Charismatic Christian movement that a very real Satan once again became the focus of human fears as the source of earthly suffering.[12] Charismatic preachers embraced the Pentecostal idea that demons could manifest as human sins and might be cast out through the descent of the Holy Spirit or Pentecostal Fire into the body of the afflicted. The Counter-Cultural Revolution with its rampant questioning of authority, free love, drug culture, and rock and roll, all of which seemed to come together in the "occult" Manson killings in 1969, offered Charismatics proof that America was under attack by satanic forces. It was in the wake of Christian revival and widespread violence that William Friedkin released *The Exorcist* (1973) to near-hysterical audiences who fainted, vomited, and waited hours in line to experience it again and again. Perhaps, *The Exorcist* was a confirmation that America's youth were possessed by evil forces, or that feminism and the women's liberation movement had put the nation's youth at risk, that audiences found so compelling. Or perhaps it was the strange familiarity of Regan's (Linda Blair) possession embedded with elements that signified true demonic evil, such as Regan-Demon's sexual abuse of the Crucifix, aversion to holy water, knowledge of Latin, and fear of the Mass Priest whose knowledge of sacred rituals made him the only one who might banish the demon to hell. What is clear is that in 1973, a world of escalating violence, economic despair, and social chaos, *The Exorcist* made America a desperate promise—that satanic evil existed and was the true source of modern suffering, and that God's faithful had the weapons to combat it.

Throughout the 1970s, America accepted the existence of satanic evil and blamed Satan and Satanists for all that was deemed threatening or inexplicable, including the decadence of disco, the corruption of youth, the stabbing and slashing of serial killers, and the purportedly mysterious mutilation of cattle. The fear that demons and Satanists, lurking just out of sight, were wreaking havoc on predominantly white middle-class Americans escalated into a "satanic panic" in the 1980s and 1990s, a time when fictions created in the medieval academy and kept alive in popular culture stepped from the horror film and the pulpit into the therapist's office, the courtroom, and the news.[13] The decade began with Lindsey and Carlson's *The 1980's: Countdown to Armageddon,* a purportedly nonfiction follow-up to their earlier works, *Late Great Planet Earth* (1970) and *Satan Is Alive and Well on Planet Earth* (1972).[14] Satan and his followers were busy, they argued, building their secret networks and preparing for the Apocalypse, and many Americans, including a multitude of mental health professionals, soon agreed with them. For example, Lawrence Pazder, a Canadian therapist and Charismatic Catholic, interpreted and shaped the dreams of his patient and future lover, Michelle Smith, through a satanic lens. Using techniques of coercive inquiry that guided the patient to a predetermined set of answers, Pazder and Michelle "reconstructed" a repressed past filled with satanic rituals and sexual abuse performed by members of an extensive and hidden satanic network. Following Pazder's lead, a spate of psychotherapists in Canada and the United States applied his techniques and unsurprisingly yielded the same results: repressed memories of satanic abuse, or satanic Ritual Abuse (SRA), as it would be labeled by some professionals. In books such as *Michelle Remembers* (1980) and *Satan's Underground* (1988), authors claimed that they had survived ritual abuse at the hands of their parents and other satanic cult members.[15] Young children, usually female, were brought in darkness by black-robed men to a hidden altar with all of the trimmings of the Black Mass; there, they were sexually assaulted with ritual objects and sometimes raped by the priests of the cult. Many women claimed that they were forced to bear infants used in ritual sacrifice and cannibalism; almost all blamed their parents, their spouses, and Satan for the sorry state of the present lives. Many readers accepted their stories because they confirmed what they already believed was true, that Satanists were everywhere, even in the nicest of families, and that children were especially vulnerable because they were necessary ingredients in satanic ritual.

The authoritative language of modern psychotherapy, which had validated and codified Satanism as worthy of scientific investigation, was reinforced by the Federal Bureau of Investigation (FBI) and local police departments that formed "occult units" responsible for working satanic cases, and news agencies that attributed crimes large and small to the work of satanic cults. When Judy Johnson claimed in 1983 that her toddler son had suffered satanic abuse at the hands of Ray Buckey, an attendant at the McMartin Preschool in Manhattan Beach, California, America was ready to listen and believe her twisted tale. Following Johnson's claims that her son had been routinely sodomized and forced to drink a sacrificed infant's blood in an old church, Children's Institute International (CII) was charged with taking testimony from other children at the day care. Using coercive techniques and offering rewards for "right answers," CII created an increasingly bizarre image of SRA conducted in "dark tunnels" below McMartin, one imbued with the tropes and schemes of satanic horror fiction. The McMartin trial, which would become the longest and most expensive in U.S. history, spawned satanic accusations in day cares from Stuart, Florida and Edenton, North Carolina to Fells Acres, Massachusetts and Spring Valley, California. In not one of these cases was any physical evidence of satanic activity produced—but then again, none was needed. The existence of Satan and the child-endangering works of his followers had been defined and proven a priori, from the *Malleus Maleficarum* to *The Exorcist*.

LINGERING SULPHUR

Twenty-first-century America remains haunted, "a cursed land where the Devil and his children still walk with earthly feet."[16] We are a nation obsessed with the paranormal, the world beyond death, with the dark shadows lurking in the corner. Sometimes those shadows contain evidence of the demonic, vestiges of canonical evil defined in the medieval university that have haunted the Christian imagination for centuries. What began as a theological construct supported by learned authority in the later Middle Ages became codified in the *Malleus Maleficarum*, a text that shaped learned and popular ideas about evil and fueled the witchcraft trials of the 16th and 17th centuries. The invisible had been "proven," had moved from fiction to fact, from church to trial, and innocent lives were lost to the flames. This same process was repeated in the satanic panic of the 20th century, during which satanic fictions moved from the horror film and the pulpit to the police station and the courtroom where they would ruin countless lives. Somewhere between fiction and fact, paranormal television continues this quest to prove the unseen and the existence of pure evil; predictably, Catholic paradigms pervade the proof and defeat of the demonic. The paradigm of canonical evil likewise remains in the news. In 2008, Fr. Moligano of St. Martin de Porres Catholic Church in Florida attributed a recent theft to the work of "satanic cults in the local area" who "need consecrated hosts" for the "black mass to be properly conducted ritually." The thefts were followed by the appearance of snakes, one of which was found on the accused's bicycle. "I'm not saying that this individual was satanic or possessed or anything of that sort, but again, *evil exists.*"[17] Like the lingering smell of sulphur, the Devil remains with us, haunting the American imagination, safe from exorcism.

NOTES

1. For a good introduction to these themes, see H. P. Lovecraft, *Supernatural Horror in Literature* (New York: Dover, 1973).

2. For more on J-Horror and East Asian Horror more generally construed, see Vivian P. Y. Lee, *East Asian Cinemas: Regional Flows and Global Transformations* (Basingstoke: Palgrave Macmillan, 2011).

3. See Gerald Brittle, *The Demonologist: The Extraordinary Career of Ed and Lorraine Warren* (Bloomington, IN: iUniverse, 2002).

4. For an excellent overview of Satanism in film, see Carrol L. Fry, *Cinema of the Occult: New Age, Satanism, Wicca, and Spiritualism in Film* (Bethlehem: Lehigh University Press, 2008).

5. For more on the original case, see William Peter Blatty, *William Peter Blatty on The Exorcist: from Novel to Film* (London: Bantam, 1974); Steve Erdmann, "The Truth Behind *the Exorcist*," *Fate: The World's Mysteries Explored,* January 1975; and the Discovery Channel's reconstruction *In The Grip of Evil* (Charles Vanderpool, 1997). See also *Possession,* a Showtime production released in 2000. For the role of exorcism in American culture more generally, see Michael W. Cuneo, *American Exorcism: Expelling Demons in the Land of Plenty* (New York: Doubleday, 2001).

6. Also see Book I of Aristotle, "On Generation and Corruption, Book 1," in *The Works of Aristotle,* ed. W. D. Ross (Franklin Center, PA: Franklin Library, 1978).

7. On moisture and warmth as the foundation of life, see Aristotle's *On Longevity*; on the dichotomy between male and female bodies in Aristotle, see Lesley Dean-Jones, *Women's Bodies in Classical Greek Science* (Oxford: Clarendon Press, 1994).

8. Jeffrey B. Russell, *Lucifer, the Devil in the Middle Ages* (Ithaca, NY: Cornell University Press, 1984), 210.

9. Adso Montier-en-Der, *Letter on the Origin and Time of the Antichrist,* ca. 950.

10. See David Punter and Glennis Byron, *The Gothic* (Malden, MA: Blackwell, 2004).

11. Antonio Melechi, *Servants of the Supernatural: The Night Side of the Victorian Mind* (London: William Heinemann, 2008).

12. W. Scott Poole, *Satan in America: The Devil We Know* (Lanham, MD: Rowman & Littlefield, 2009), 112–13.

13. On the Satanic Panic, see Bill Ellis, *Raising the Devil: Satanism, New Religions, and the Media* (Lexington: University Press of Kentucky, 2000), and Bill Ellis, *Lucifer Ascending: The Occult in Folklore and Popular Culture* (Lexington: University Press of Kentucky, 2004). See also David Frankfurter, *Evil Incarnate: Rumors of Demonic Conspiracy and Ritual Abuse in History* (Princeton, NJ: Princeton University Press, 2006).

14. Hal Lindsey and Carole C. Carlson, *The Late Great Planet Earth* (Grand Rapids, MI: Zondervan, 1970); and Hal Lindsey, *Satan Is Alive and Well on Planet Earth* (Grand Rapids, MI: Zondervan, 1972).

15. Michelle Smith and Lawrence Pazder, *Michelle Remembers* (New York: Congdon & Lattes, 1980); and Lauren Stratford, *Satan's Underground* (Eugene, OR: Harvest House, 1988).

16. Bram Stoker, *Dracula* (New York: Limited Editions Club, 1965), 62.

17. "Priest Believes Satanic Cult behind Bizarre Church Incidents," *WPBF Channel*, 2008, http://www.wpbf.com/Priest-Believes-Satanic-Cult-Behind-Bizarre-Church-Incidents/-/8789538/5108722/-/ed2jel/-/index.html (accessed May 27, 2013).

CHAPTER 26

Sinister Beasts: Animal Symbolism and the Evolutionary Roots of Evil

Micah Issitt

In the pantheon of evil, few characters rank higher in the American collective consciousness than Satan, or "The Devil," the archenemy of Jesus who has come to be known by hundreds of other names. Satan is not purely a Christian creation and his genesis owes elements to many cultures, from Asia to prehistoric Europe. The earliest known illustration of Satan in a Christian text appears in the Rabbula Gospels of 586 CE, where Satan is depicted as a faceless, shadowy figure, somewhat ghost-like in appearance. Since that time, he has undergone a host of stylistic makeovers, and somewhere along the way, he became animalistic in character. The image most popular today—a red-skinned, half-animal monster—is derived largely from literary interpretations like Dante's *Inferno* and Milton's *Paradise Lost*.[1]

Milton compared the Devil with a toad, raven, cormorant, and wolf, and Satan often appeared with the hooves and horns of a goat in 14th-century renderings. The creatures used to represent Satan, or his evil manifested on earth, reveal the underlying symbolism that fuels Western ecological imagination. These preferences and prejudices are still a dominant force in determining how animals are portrayed in films, literature, and other manifestations of popular culture.[2] The wolf, raven, cat, spider, snake, pig, and goat are only a few of the creatures that have been maligned because of their imagined associations with evil, while swans, sheep, doves, and lions are among those creatures chosen to represent the side of righteousness and justice because they are seen to have qualities representative of purity and morality.[3]

Christian mythology is a dominant influence in Western animal symbolism, but there are other motivations at play in determining how we ascribe moral value throughout the environment. The demonization or deification of a species may be motivated by historical, political, social, economic, aesthetic, and evolutionary motivations and there are often multiple influences collectively active in determining the symbolism attached to a particular species. In this chapter, we will examine species from the A-list of the Devil's bestiary and will see how various factors converge to create the mythology of animal morality that pervades Western art and popular culture.

THE WOLF AND THE RAVEN

The grey wolf (*Canis lupus*) and the common raven (*Corvus corax*) are described together because of the important ties between these two species and their relationship with humans. Nearly 300,000 years ago, during the Pleistocene, early humans, ravens, and wolves shared the boreal forests of Europe and North America. Ravens, ever the efficient scavengers, learned to follow both wolves and humans to their kills in the hopes of snatching scraps of meat. Wolves followed ravens to locate carrion and to find prey animals. Humans, in turn, learned to attend to the behaviors of both wolves and ravens in an effort to mimic these species' survival skills.[4]

The relationships between these three species became so close that some evolutionary biologists classify it as an instance of "coevolution," where all three species were shaped, through natural selection, to be attentive to the behaviors of the other two. Over thousands of years, wolves and humans became so intermeshed that wolves engaged in a kind of "self-domestication," integrating themselves into the human tribe. Humans eagerly accepted the attentions of wolves, using them to find prey, to guard their settlements, and increasingly over the millennia, as companions.

Given the prehistoric nature of human relationships with both species, the mythology concerning wolves and ravens stretches to the very beginnings of human culture. The relationship between wolves and humans is particularly complex, spanning the spectrum from despised rival to familial love. The wolf was one of humanity's most ancient enemies, but from a rivalry and shared behavioral repertoire grew one of our species' most enduring interspecies friendships.

The association between wolves and evil has three motivations. The first and most primary would be fear, as wolves are potentially dangerous to humans and at times certainly hunted and killed our ancestors. The second is competition, as wolves have been competing with humans for prey since prehistory and have been known to steal food from humans directly, either in the form of scraps pilfered from a kill or livestock stolen from a herdsman. Third, wolves scavenge carrion and are not above eating dead humans, which places them within the liminal, metaphysical world of creatures that represent the connection between life and death.[5]

As humans transitioned from hunter-gatherers to a herding, agricultural lifestyle, hatred of wolves increased. Wolves are capable of killing and stealing livestock and while this occurs less than one would think given the vehemence with which ranchers have poisoned, hunted, and killed wolves, it was a driving force in the designation of the wolf as evil.[6] Once the wolf was separated from the domestic dog (by generations of selective breeding), the wolf became the enemy of civilization while the dog became a symbol of loyalty, fealty, and servitude.

Associations between wolves and evil are so common that they have become cliché in pop culture. The Big Bad Wolf, of both Aesop's Fables and Grimm's Fairy Tales, is one of the most famous of all literary villains. He is portrayed as a slave to his insatiable hunger and through his behaviors, lessons regarding the dangers of greed and violence are demonstrated with trite moral rectitude. Wolves are perhaps the creatures most associated with feral nature and the dangers of the untamed wild. Even in cultures where wolves are admired and deified, they are still often invoked to symbolize the dangers of nature. In American lore, the wolf is perhaps the most fitting example of Alfred Lord Tennyson's description of nature as "red in tooth and claw," a realm in which survival is earned by shedding blood.

The lycanthrope, or werewolf, a blend of human and wolf that has become a favorite of gothic horror and fiction, has symbolic meaning with ancient roots. Among prehistoric tribes, the idea of blending human and animal characteristics featured prominently in mythology. This was perhaps a representation of the desire to be endowed with the abilities of the beasts, thereby becoming better at avoiding danger, finding food, and surviving environmental perils. Werewolves emerged from these prehistoric chimeras, representing the human reversion to its savage heritage. In films and literature, werewolves are often invoked to address the duality of culture vs. instinct and humanity vs. animality. This allows for an exploration of what divides humans from animals and how much of this connection still remains after the transition from the more ecologically dependent society of early humans to the modern, industrial human condition.[7]

Ravens, like wolves, scavenge from dead bodies and this places them within the category of animals most closely associated with death. For this reason, ravens have been romanticized and villainized as harbingers of war, pestilence, and mortality. In Native American and Norse mythology, the raven was a teacher and messenger, and elements of this mythological role influence the animal's modern pop cultural mystique. In the West, the raven is typically portrayed as somewhat shadowy, often possessing foreknowledge of death and perhaps in league with dark forces.

Hatred of the raven (and its smaller cousin, the crow) deepened with the development of agriculture. This was because ravens are pests to a farmer, eating crops and posing threat to the farmer's livelihood. Crows found it far easier than ravens to adjust to life within larger human communities and for that reason, much of the animosity and suspicion once given to the raven has been refocused on the crow.[8]

There is also an aesthetic component to the demonification of ravens and crows, because they typically appear in black and, in the West, black is one of the colors most closely associated with evil and death (though it is also the color of sensuality and intrigue). American pop culture has inherited aesthetic values from colonial European culture, which was in turn derived from the classical traditions of the Greeks and Romans. The color black has not always been associated with evil in the Western tradition. In the Old Testament, for instance, red and white were symbolic of evil. It was in the Middle Ages that the association of blackness with evil was firmly committed, though some historians have noted that black was also associated with evil in ancient Greece.[9]

Ravens are rarely portrayed as the arch villains in fiction and are more likely to fill the fantasy role as portents of doom. Shakespeare wrote of ravens in both *Othello* and *Macbeth*, using them as symbols for approaching death and war. In his poem "The Raven," Edgar Allan Poe used the inky bird to symbolize his protagonist's descent into misery and madness over the loss of his love. Poe's raven speaks only a single word, "nevermore," thus infuriating the hero with its reticence as it simultaneously drives him further into depression. Throughout, Poe makes references connecting the raven to the occult, images derived from centuries-old symbolic associations.[10]

While both the raven and the wolf have been linked to evil, they are among the most variable totems in the Western symbolic fauna. Both creatures also serve as symbols of natural wisdom and power. They are perhaps the best representations of the malleability of animal symbolism; despised for some aspects of their character and admired for others. We see in the symbolism of ravens and wolves both our fear of the untamed, uncontrollable aspects of nature and our enduring fascination and attraction to these same qualities.

THE GOAT AND THE PIG

Unlike wolves and ravens, whose evil association stems from their associations with danger and death, pigs (*Sus*) and goats (*Capra aegagrus hircus*) have both been associated with evil because they are seen to represent human vices and sins. As domestic creatures, the symbolism surrounding them differs substantially from that ascribed to feral animals, relying more on the way that these species were used in the foundations of human society.

The relationship between humans and pigs was born in antiquity, and archaeological evidence from the Middle East indicates that pig breeding was popular 8,500 years ago, though it likely began thousands of years prior to that.[11] In some cultures, the pig is revered for its capability for survival, extremely acute senses, and intelligence. In Papua, New Guinea, where there is a variety of feral and domesticated pig species, the animal is among the most sacred creatures in tribal mythos.

One reason why pigs have been among the most hated and loved of cultivated creatures is their similarity to humans. Their skin has a similar pigment, they eat similar foods, and it has long been recognized that their flesh is the most human-like of all animals except primates. Some Polynesians who practiced cannibalism even went so far as to refer to human meat as "long pig."[12] These similarities have played an important role in determining how humanity has chosen to represent symbolically the pig and its association with morality.

Associations between pigs and human vices like gluttony and greed can be found in writings derived from ancient Egypt, and these prejudices have perpetuated into the modern era. Followers of Old Testament dietary guidelines (Jews and Moslems) abstain from pork and it is commonly believed that this is because pigs are "unclean" animals. In common English parlance, the word "pig" has become an insult signifying gluttony and a lack of manners or hygiene. The myth of the "filthy" pig is based largely on medieval pig husbandry, when pigs were often forced to live in cramped pens littered with their own waste. If given the choice, pigs are fairly hygienic, though they do wallow in mud in an effort to shield their sensitive skin from the sun.[13]

Undercooked pork was scientifically linked to the illness trichinosis in 1859, which seemed to provide scientific justification for the Old Testament pork prejudice. However, this connection was unknown to the Old Testament authors and was probably not an important motivating factor given the worldwide popularity of pork at the time and the fact that undercooked beef can be just as hazardous.[14] The passage banning pigs literally says that humans may consume any animal that "chews the cud," which is where pigs differ from cows and sheep in that pigs lack the digestive capacity to consume grass.

It may be that the Old Testament authors were simply attempting to promote husbandry of the most useful creatures, as cows, sheep, and goats were the most economically viable cultivated species because they provided milk in addition to meat. Pigs are omnivores, like humans, and therefore represent competition for food that could be used to feed humans, while ruminants live on grass, a resource that is basically wasted on humans as we also lack the necessary digestive mechanisms to consume it.

While Christians raised and ate pigs, blissfully free from the pork prohibition, they also demonized the species, often using them as metaphors for sinful and immoral behaviors. Throughout European history, pigs have been labeled as unintelligent, unhygienic, and gluttonous, and these prejudices became part of Christian tradition as it developed. Pigs are conspicuously absent from Jesus's manger, though they were every bit as popular in Christian agriculture as the ass, camel, sheep, and ox who generally appear at the scene. Most notably, three times in the Gospels, Christ casts the sin out of humans and into pigs. This is perhaps the most revealing of the Christian denigrations toward the pig: the transformation of the animal into a vessel for human sin.[15]

Goats, like pigs, also have the designation of having been used in religious rituals, and this is one of the keys to understanding their association with the occult. In Leviticus, God orders the Hebrews to fetch two identical goats, one sacrificed to God and the other released into the wild for the demonic spirit, Azazel. This is the origin of the term "scapegoat," though it has come to mean one who suffers for the wrongdoings of another. In Hebrew mythology, the scapegoat was used because, as an animal, it was considered to be "without sin" and, as a cultivated beast, it was made to serve human interests.[16] The association between goats and evil may have been partially inspired by their popularity as a sacrifice to evil spirits.

One of the most famous connections between goats and evil can be seen in medieval portrayals of Satan. Since the 14th century, artistic depictions have conferred on Satan a variety of goat-like features, including horns, hooves, and the "goatee" descending from his chin. These associations might result partially from Christian disdain for the pagan gods of the cultures they replaced across Europe. The Celtic "Horned God of the West," Cernunnos, was the god of hunting, fertility, and the underworld, while the Hellenistic Greek god Pan symbolized the pastoral occupation, hunting, and the animalistic side of sexuality.[17] Both Pan and Cernunnos were horned and partially furred, resembling in many respects human-goat hybrids. From a combination of fear and politically motivated prejudice, Christians chose the bodies of pagan gods for their demons, none more so than Pan, who has often been used to represent the lascivious side of human sexuality.[18]

Interestingly, Europeans typically raise goats for milk rather than their meat, and this makes them a secondary agricultural crop. In Africa and the Middle East, where goat meat is a staple, the animal is less often cast as an accomplice to evil. In Western mythology, the sheep and cow are the livestock most often associated with benign and even divine symbolism, which may speak to the importance of these creatures in agricultural life. For instance, Jesus is often compared to a lamb, the ultimate sacrificial animal because of its perceived purity and docility, qualities that are even mirrored in its color. The goat was also a common sacrificial animal, but was more often used to appease evil than to honor the divine. Therefore, the goat, in its resemblance to pagan gods and its traditional role as a sacrifice to sin, became the perfect symbol for the ultimate totem of evil: the body of Satan himself.

THE SNAKE AND THE SPIDER

Some animals pose a threat to humans because they possess defensive weapons, including natural poisons that make them every bit as deadly as any of humanity's potential predators.[19] Snakes and spiders occupy a special place in human fears, representing the hidden, unseen dangers of the natural world. To many observers, these "creepy crawlies" are more frightening than the large predators because their small size and nearly silent movement allows them to infiltrate our homes, placing them within the borders we erect to provide safety from the outside world.

Statistically speaking, more humans manifest a fear of spiders and/ or snakes than electricity or automobiles, despite the fact that the latter pose a much greater threat to human life. Evolutionary psychologists believe that the potential to develop these fears has been programmed into the human brain through natural selection. In the distant past, humans who learned to recognize and avoid potentially poisonous animals were less likely to die from envenomation and therefore left more offspring. The fear of these creatures is therefore hardwired into the human psyche, though these fears are not nearly as relevant in the modern era.[20]

In the case of spiders, for instance, there are only two species in the United States capable of delivering a fatal bite and the chances of dying by spider bite are similar to the chance of dying in a plane crash, approximately 1 in 11 million. By contrast, approximately one in every 5,000 humans will die in an automobile accident.[21] Given these statistics, a million years from now it is likely that natural selection will result in a much larger portion of the population with the potential for "motorphobia."

Even if they pose an unlikely threat, their potential danger places spiders and snakes on the short list of creatures most likely to consort with evil. Fantasy fiction pioneer J.R.R. Tolkien, for instance, used a monstrous, massive spider named "Shelob" to terrorize his noble hobbits in the *Lord of the Rings* trilogy. Tolkien describes Shelob as an evil derived from an ancient era before the sentient villains of the world were the primary threat. He reveals that she is not a naturally occurring beast at all, but in fact an evil spirit, known as an "ugoliant," that manifests in the world in spider form.[22]

More realistic depictions of spiders are found throughout literature and films, especially gothic fiction and horror. At times, spiders are used to represent the dangers of untamed nature, such as the tarantulas that often crop up in films and novels set in dense jungles or deserts. In other cases, spiders represent the dangers of the dark, appearing in basements and subterranean catacombs where they add to the sense of doom inherent in these dimly lit settings. In some cases, spiders are used to symbolize the dangers of the immediate environment, such as in the film *Arachnophobia* (1990), where an outbreak of particularly poisonous spiders terrorizes a suburban community. In each case, spiders are invoked to prey upon a fear so deeply embedded in human consciousness that even the shape of a spider is enough to cause many to recoil in fear.

The association of snakes with evil is very familiar to most Americans from the story of the serpent who tempted Eve in the Garden of Eden. Over the millennia, the snake has been unable to slough this sinister image. In the *Harry Potter* series of books and films, the chief villain Voldemort is said to have descended from a line of wizards that had the ability to communicate with snakes. This snake-evil connection is furthered in one of Voldemort's chief soldiers, a larger-than-life serpent named Nagini, who is responsible for the death of several of the story's heroes.

In Rudyard Kipling's short story "Riki-Tiki-Tavi," from *the Jungle Book*, the titular mongoose battles with snakes to keep his adopted human family safe. While Kipling casts snakes as the villains of his story, in revealing their motivations it is also shown that the snakes mean only to protect themselves and their children by removing the humans who might try to kill them. We therefore see, in Kipling, elements of the traditional Western symbolism regarding serpents combined with a more informed ecological consciousness. Kipling hints at the understanding that animals are not subject to the same sense of good and evil as humans, but behave in ways designed only to aid in their survival.

In other cultures, snakes and spiders are sometimes cast as folk heroes for their various abilities. Key among these notable features is the fact that snakes and spiders shed the outer layers of their bodies as they grow. This biomechanical mechanism has linked the snake and spider to the spiritual concepts of metamorphosis and transformation. In many stories, they are cast as creators of life and as creatures that can change their shape and appear in alternate forms. In African mythology, the spider's ability to weave webs has made her a storyteller and the "weaver" of various facets of the universe. The positive aspects of snake and spider biology have not been integrated into Western mythology significantly to alter the symbolism associated with them. Despite their function as hunters of vermin and killers of flies, snakes and spiders remain among the most popular symbols of natural terror.

THE CAT AND THE WOMAN

There is perhaps no other creature in the history of Western culture that has enjoyed and suffered such a mix of love and hate as the cat (*Felis domesticus*). Cats are the adored pets of millions around the world who dote on their feline companions with as much love and affection as is allotted to human children, but they have also been the subjects of intense hatred and persecution. In the 16th century, cats were gathered and openly burned in much of Europe, despised for their apparent connection to Satanism and witchcraft. This pattern emerged again during the anti-black-magic craze of American fame, culminating in the Salem Witch Trials.[23]

The image of the evil feline has numerous sources of inspiration. For one thing, prehistoric man's arch nemesis was the predatory cat, which was and still is the predator most likely to hunt humans. In *The Jungle Book*, Kipling casts the tiger Shere Khan as his villain, which is not surprising since the tiger is among the most feared of all large predators.[24] In the Suderbans region of India, the number of humans killed by tigers annually sometimes exceeds the number of tigers killed by humans, a record that no other predator can match.[25]

While the domestic cat is unlikely to hunt and kill humans, this ancient evolutionary association lingers in the subconscious, inspiring associations between the feline form and the potential for danger. The ambush tactics and overall stealthy, slinking nature of the cat has inspired associations with assassins and secretive, deadly intentions. Add to this the fact that cats come in black varieties, the color most often associated with death, danger, and the occult in Western aesthetics, and we have part of the answer for why the black cat became the epitome of symbolic wickedness.

The association between cats and witchcraft is ancient, and originated before Christian dominance of Europe. In the 10th century, there are written records indicating the belief that witches kept cats as familiars and could use them to do their bidding. Equally ancient is the association between cats and women. In the ancient Egyptian religions, cats were associated with the goddesses Bast, Hecate, and Isis. As a result, cats were held in high esteem and almost worshipped in ancient Egypt, a bit of trivia that delights many a cat owner looking to justify their devotion to their pet.[26] The association between feline and feminine also appeared in pagan Greece, where cats were associated with the goddess Diana and in

Scandinavian mythology, where cats accompanied Freya, the goddess of love and beauty.[27]

In the modern Western world, cats and women are still often equated together, from the sex appeal of "Cat Woman" to the stereotypical image of the "crazy cat lady." The perception is to some extent based on reality, as statistics seem to indicate that women are more likely to own cats. More than 53 percent of women who adopt a pet choose a cat, compared to only 35 percent of men, who tend to prefer dogs.[28]

It may be correct to assume, as many feminist scholars have, that the persecution of cats was partially due to Christian fear and opposition to the matriarchic and female-dominated cults of the pre-Christian pagan religions. Certainly, the symbols of worship and admiration in pagan religions, as with the goat, have become symbols of evil in Christian mythology and it is likely that political and cultural motivations likewise played a role in the denigration of the cat.

It is also appropriate to note that no animal posed more of a threat to the male-dominated culture of the West than the human female. Specifically, the power allotted to women as priestesses and religious leaders in pagan cults would likely have been viewed as a significant threat in a culture built on male-dominated social, political, and religious institutions, such as those that emerged in Christian, Moslem, and Jewish Europe and the Middle East. The goddess and her faithful feline companion may therefore have become the witch and her familiar, casting one stone to cripple both threats and leaving Western culture with an enduring image of the maligned feline as the servant of an evil female mistress.

In their association with women, cats provide a unique example of the sinister beast, hated as much for their symbolic role in socio-sexual relations as for their color, behaviors, or evolutionary significance. However, even after hundreds of years of open persecution, cats emerge as winners because human affection and their usefulness in hunting vermin have outweighed the malicious image bestowed on them. The cat therefore serves as a prime example of the transformation of evil in the West. What was once a symbol of wickedness and the occult has been transformed into an Internet meme of kittens failing to speak English. Man has moved away from nature, away from history, and into an age where nature is largely ours to reimagine. The cat, honored pet, hunter of mice, and female totem, has made the journey with us.

THE NATURE OF EVIL

The descriptions of animals presented in this chapter largely represent "traditional" manifestations of evil within the animal kingdom. In modern pop culture, writers, artists, and filmmakers sometimes fall back on these associations, but are just as likely to utilize animals in contrary symbolic gestures. The Big Bad Wolf of yesteryear may thereby become the hero in a postmodern fairy tale.

This shift has occurred for a number of reasons. Firstly, art and culture evolve partially by reimagining traditional concepts. Evoking the opposing relationship has become one way to gain fresh impact from timeworn symbolism. Secondly, Americans today enjoy access to information about wildlife and folk traditions from around the world. Today's artists may therefore use symbolism derived from cultures or ecosystems that were unknown to the Westerners who established many of the early ideas about good and evil in nature. Whereas traditional animal symbolism in the West is largely derived from Christianity, artists today might use Native American, Buddhist, or African mythology as the basis for literature, arts, and films.

Most importantly, nature plays a changing pop cultural role as America has moved further into an era of expanded (or at least *altered*) ecological consciousness. The green movement, the animal rights movement, and the conservation movement that have been building since the 19th century have played an important role in shaping American attitudes about animals. In the modern era, therefore, traditionally sinister beasts have become virtuous victims of humanity's continued domination.

It is interesting to note that while many fears of animals have their roots in prehistory, prehistoric humans probably hated far fewer creatures than in modern society. When we lived as hunter-gatherers, intimately linked to our ecosystems, each beast was a potential danger but also a teacher in a sense, demonstrating behaviors that could be used to enhance survival and to understand the natural world. As humans became farmers, herders, and later industrial workers, animals were more often simply competitors and enemies. Their value as teachers was lost, as we had less need to attend to their behaviors for guidance.

The interest in animal life and the natural environment that our ancestors needed to keep them alive has become a hobby in modern society, expressed in the ownership of pets, ecotourism, nature documentaries, and thousands of animal characters in literature and film. Dangerous animals like tigers, snakes, and wolves are among the most popular creatures with animal enthusiasts and this reflects the close association between danger and intrigue. Once the danger these species pose has been eliminated, all that remains is humanity's innate attraction to the abilities of animals, the same traits that have fueled human imagination and nightmares since the Paleolithic.

Humans have gradually abandoned the depiction of animals as villains, not because we have reintegrated with nature, but because we are now separated sufficiently that we observe the natural world from a dispassionate, intellectual point of view. Some may view this as detrimental, precipitating the era of ecological collapse that will likely result from human expansion. However, in viewing nature removed from human culture, we can see animals for what they are, neither villains nor heroes but simply survivors in a world where human morality does not apply. Further, we can see that our depictions of good and evil among animals were little more than mirrors for viewing our own nature. It is perhaps illustrative to note that while Satan is often depicted with various animal characteristics, he is always part human as well. Just as evil only exists in the human imagination, we may find that there is only one truly sinister beast, the dominator of nature and archenemy of all animals, *Homo sapiens*.

NOTES

1. Luther Link, *The Devil: A Mask without a Face* (London: Reaktion Books, 1995), 72–74.

2. William F. Hansen, *Classical Mythology: A Guide to the Mythical World of the Greeks and Romans* (New York: Oxford University Press, 2005), 278–81.

3. Arkadiusz Marciniak, *Placing Animals in the Neolithic: Social Zooarchaeology of Prehistoric Farming Communities* (London: UCL; Portland, OR: Cavendish), 51–55.

4. Steven H. Fritts et al., "Wolves and Humans," in *Wolves: Behavior, Ecology, and Conservation*, ed. L. David Mech and Luigi Boitani (Chicago: University of Chicago Press, 2003), 288–91.

5. John M. Marzluff and Colleen Marzluff, *Dog Days, Raven Nights* (New Haven, CT: Yale University Press, 2011), 146–260.

6. Barry H. Lopez, *Of Wolves and Men* (New York: Scribner, 1978), 145–47.

7. Brian M. Stableford, *Space, Time, and Infinity: Essays on Fantastic Literature* (San Bernardino, CA: Borgo Press, 1998), 171–76.

8. John M. Marzluff and Tony Angell, *In the Company of Crows and Ravens* (New Haven, CT: Yale University Press, 2005), 1–22.

9. Robert E. Hood, *Begrimed and Black: Christian Traditions on Blacks and Blackness* (Minneapolis: Fortress Press, 1994), 72–82.

10. Boria Sax, *Crow* (London: Reaktion, 2003), 122–23.

11. W.L.R. Oliver et al., "Origins of Domestication and the Pig Culture," in *Pigs, Peccaries, and Hippos: Status Survey and Conservation Action Plan*, ed. William L.R. Oliver (Gland, Switzerland: IUCN, 1993), 171–75.

12. Gananath Obeyesekere, *Cannibal Talk: The Man-Eating Myth and Human Sacrifice in the South Seas* (Berkeley: University of California Press, 2005), 24–26.

13. Per Jensen, "The Behavior of Pigs," in *The Ethology of Domestic Animals: An Introductory Text*, ed. Per Jensen (Wallingford: CABI Pub., 2002), 161–62.

14. Marvin Harris, "The Abominable Pig," in *Good to Eat: Riddles of Food and Culture* (New York: Simon & Schuster, 1985), 106–10.

15. Elizabeth A. Lawrence, "The Sacred Bee, the Filthy Pig, and the Bat Out of Hell: Animal Symbolism as Cognitive Biophilia," in *The Biophilia Hypothesis*, ed. Stephen R. Kellert and Edward O. Wilson (Washington, DC: Island Press, 1993), 310–15.

16. Jesse Goldhammer, *The Headless Republic: Sacrificial Violence in Modern French Thought* (Ithaca, NY: Cornell University Press, 2005), 20–21.

17. Jeffrey B. Russell, *Lucifer, the Devil in the Middle Ages* (Ithaca, NY: Cornell University Press, 1984), 64–65.

18. Joseph F. Kelly, *The Problem of Evil in the Western Tradition: From the Book of Job to Modern Genetics* (Collegeville, MN: Liturgical Press, 2002), 49.

19. H. Clark Barrett, "Adaptations to Predators and Prey," in *The Handbook of Evolutionary Psychology*, ed. David M. Buss (Hoboken, NJ: John Wiley & Sons, 2005), 200–10.

20. Rush W. Dozier, *Fear Itself: The Origin and Nature of the Powerful Emotion That Shapes Our Lives and Our World* (New York: St. Martin's Press, 1998).

21. Stefan G. Hofmann, *An Introduction to Modern CBT: Psychological Solutions to Mental Health Problems* (Chichester, UK: Wiley-Blackwell, 2012), 52.

22. Leslie A. Donovan, "The Valkyrie Reflex in J.R.R. Tolkien's *The Lord of the Rings*: Galadriel, Shelob, Éowyn, and Arwen," in *Tolkien the Medievalist*, ed. Jane Chance (London: Routledge, 2003), 120–23.

23. Anne Marks, *The Cat in History, Legend, and Art* (London: Elliot Stock, 1909), 35–38.

24. Rudyard Kipling, *The Jungle Book* (London: Macmillan, 1894).

25. Claudio Sillero-Zubiri and M. Karen Laurenson, "Interactions between Carnivores and Local Communities: Conflict or Co-Existence?," in *Carnivore Conservation*, ed. John L. Gittleman (Cambridge: Cambridge University Press, 2001), 284–85.

26. M. Oldfield Howey, *The Cat in Magic and Myth* (Mineola, NY: Dover Publications; Newton Abbot: David & Charles, 2004), 86–87.

27. Marks, *The Cat in History, Legend, and Art*, 26–27.

28. Philip H. Kass, "Cat Overpopulation in the United States," *Animal Welfare* 3 (2007): 137–38.

CHAPTER 27

The Trial of the West Memphis Three: Rival Visions of Evil

Joseph Laycock

The story of the so-called West Memphis Three reveals two radically different worldviews regarding the problem of evil. Following the murder of three children in rural Arkansas, some saw the face of evil in three teenagers accused of holding human sacrifices. Others saw evil in a town that would not only believe such a story, but also sentence an innocent person to death because of it. These perspectives reflect larger cultural and socioeconomic differences. The idea that a group's perceptions could be so strongly influenced by its particular understanding of evil holds disturbing implications for our justice system and the concept of a fair trial.

On May 6, 1993, the bodies of three eight-year-old boys were recovered from a creek near West Memphis, Arkansas. The boys were found naked and hog-tied with their own shoelaces. The cause of death appeared to be blunt trauma to the head. Most disturbingly, the genitals of one child had been mutilated, suggesting a sexual or ritualistic motive to the murders. With no suspects, the investigation focused on 18-year-old Damien Echols, a teenage iconoclast. On June 3, police questioned Jessie Misskelley Jr., a 17-year-old with mild mental disabilities. After a 12-hour interrogation, Misskelley not only confessed to the murders but implicated Echols and his close friend, 16-year-old Jason Baldwin. Despite the lack of any physical evidence, a jury found all three guilty of murder. Misskelley and Baldwin were given life sentences. Echols received the death penalty.

This would have been the end of the story, had it not been for documentarians Joe Berlinger and Bruce Sinofksy, who traveled to West Memphis to film the trial. This footage was turned into an HBO feature entitled

Paradise Lost: The Child Murders at Robin Hood Hills that aired in 1996. *Paradise Lost* inspired a wave of support for "The West Memphis Three." An advocacy group launched a campaign to raise awareness of the case and money for an appeal. Much of this support came from individuals who identified with Echols and felt marginalized by mainstream society. Several Pagan groups saw this as a case of religious intolerance and lent their support. Numerous musicians representing diverse genres contributed their money and their talent to the cause.

Berlinger and Sinofsky produced two sequels to *Paradise Lost, Paradise Lost 2: Revelations* (2000), and *Paradise Lost 3: Purgatory* (2011). The documentaries presented gross errors by West Memphis police in handling the crime scene and questioning suspects. They also offered evidence of questionable expert witnesses, ineffective assistance of counsel by the defendant's lawyers, and jury misconduct. In 2011, the case was reopened in light of DNA evidence found on the bodies. On August 19, 2011, the Three were retried and offered a so-called Alford Plea. This is a legal mechanism by which a defendant asserts his or her innocence while also recognizing that there is sufficient evidence for a conviction. A judge found them guilty but sentenced them to time served. This outcome not only freed the West Memphis Three, but also exonerated the legal system of wrongly imprisoning three young men for over 18 years.

Americans have long been preoccupied with fighting evil. This mentality goes back to the Puritans, who felt that Satan was actively trying to stop them from establishing their community as a "City on a Hill." Native Americans and "witches" were both seen as agents of demonic evil sent to stop them in their mission. Since the Puritans, America's preoccupation with evil has been closely allied with ideas of American exceptionalism. American political rhetoric typically frames America as a country that will ultimately triumph over evil.

However, Americans are sharply divided in their understanding of the nature of evil. Like the Puritans, many Americans perceive evil in supernatural terms. Social problems are seen as worldly manifestations of the demonic, and by fighting against them, we align ourselves with God. This view is referred to here as a "transcendent" vision of evil because it posits evil as a force that comes "from beyond." In its association with supernatural forces, evil holds an ontological status beyond our ordinary, quotidian reality. In this worldview, supernatural otherness is frequently equated with social and cultural otherness. Outsiders and the socially marginalized are often seen as the vanguards of evil's encroachment.

Other Americans have an "immanent" vision of evil, seeing it as something that lurks within rather than without. In this view, evil is not singular, but multifaceted and complex. Those with an immanent view of evil tend to be more humble both in identifying evil and in taking action against it. Rather than focusing suspicion on outsiders, the immanent vision of evil looks to more familiar places such as social prejudices and power structures that contribute to human suffering.

The story of the West Memphis Three poignantly demonstrates these rival understandings of evil. While all Americans can identify evil in the murder of three innocent children, this is where the consensus ends. Damien Echols was suspected and ultimately found guilty largely because of his otherness: his black clothing, his interest in the occult, and the fact that he enjoyed horror novels and heavy metal music. Religion scholars argue that the West Memphis Three trial was a manifestation of "satanic panic," a widespread belief that satanic cults exist throughout America and perform human sacrifices. Within this worldview, no physical evidence was needed to obtain a conviction: Echols was clearly a Satanist and murdering children is the business of those who serve Satan. While satanic panic peaked in America during the 1980s, it is the cultural legacy of Puritan belief in witchcraft and the witch-hunts of early modern Europe.

Those who defended the Three also saw the face of evil in the trial. But where the prosecution saw three teenagers as a manifestation of rampant criminal Satanism, advocates of the Three saw the Arkansas justice system as emblematic of a much larger problem of intolerance and social injustice. Many of these advocates were culturally deviant themselves, producing art and music with esoteric or dark overtones. The persecution of these teenagers resonated with their own experiences of persecution and alienation.

Trial by jury is based on an Enlightenment ideal that we share a common view of reality and are each capable of seeing evidence objectively. What is so unsettling about the case of the West Memphis Three is the possibility that evidence is seen only through larger moral and cosmological frameworks that are not objective but socially constructed. In this sense, the resolution of the case through an Alford Plea is the most disturbing detail of all. By paradoxically freeing the West Memphis Three while insisting they are guilty, it seems that these rival versions of reality will never truly be reconciled.

THE STORY OF THE WEST MEMPHIS THREE

Eight-year-olds Stevie Branch, Michael Moore, and Christopher Myers were last seen playing together the evening of May 5, 1993. When they failed to come home, a search was organized. On May 6, an officer found their submerged bodies when he inadvertently stepped on one while wading through a creek. The bodies had what appeared to be bite marks and the genitals of Christopher Myers were mutilated; the testicles and head of the penis had been removed. In the absence of any suspect or motive, the murders became a kind of Rorschach test onto which the community could project its darkest fears. Details of the apparent sexual mutilation were leaked to the press. On May 10, *USA Today* ran the headline, "'Monstrous Evil' Haunts Town." By May 12, the Associated Press described rumors of "everything from gangs to cults."

According to FBI statistics, parents and stepparents are the most likely perpetrators in homicide cases with victims aged 6–11.[1] However, the police seemed to assume that the murderer must have come from outside their community. In the first week of the investigation, police rounded up and questioned transients. Like the homeless, teenagers were marginalized members of the community and strongly suspected. Years before the murders, juvenile officers Steve Jones and Jerry B. Driver were already investigating possible teenage occultism in the county. Early in the investigation, Driver produced a list of eight teenagers believed to be involved with Satanism, including Damien Echols and Jason Baldwin. He declared that when the investigation was over, one or more of the teenagers on the list would be charged with the murders.

On May 7, police interviewed Echols because of his suspected involvement in "cult activity." In an interview with Mara Leveritt of the *Arkansas Times*, Echols said that he was first teased about being a witch in the seventh grade. He claimed he changed his name from "Michael" to "Damien" after the 19th-century Catholic saint. However, locals assumed the name referred to the horror film *The Omen* (Richard Donner, 1976). Echols was not a Satanist, but allowed others to believe that he was. Cultivating this image likely served as both a deterrent to bullying and as a way of punishing his community for their prejudice and ignorance.[2]

Jessie Misskelley was implicated through a single mother named Vicki Hutchinson, who was initially interviewed by police after her employer accused her of stealing. This charge was dropped; however, she volunteered to help police by "seducing" Echols to learn more about his cult activities. This scheme involved using Misskelley, who sometimes babysat for Hutchinson, to get to Echols. Misskelley did succeed in getting Echols to visit Hutchinson's home where the police had provided her with books on the occult and set up hidden microphones. However, Echols never made any incriminating statements during this visit. Hutchinson then told police that she had visited a Wiccan "Esbat" with Echols and Misskelley.[3] There were numerous holes in this story. For instance, Hutchinson later claimed that she was drunk and may have dreamed the entire event. She may have believed that cooperating with police would protect her from criminal charges for theft.

Hutchinson's story led police to question Misskelley. Despite the fact that Misskelley was a minor and had an IQ of 72, he was interrogated for 12 hours without the presence of a parent or attorney. Police also tricked him into believing he had failed a lie detector test. Eventually Misskelley confessed that he, Echols, and Baldwin had committed the murders. There were numerous inconsistencies in Misskelley's confession, which he later recanted. He was charged with murder and pled not guilty. The defense brought in social psychologist Richard Ofshe as an expert witness, who testified that Misskelley had given a coerced confession. Despite this testimony, a jury found Misskelley guilty of three counts of murder.[4]

Echols and Baldwin were tried separately from Misskelley. With no physical evidence, the trial focused entirely on Echols's suspected involvement in Satanism, which by association was extended to his friend, Baldwin. The prosecution brought in retired police officer Dale W. Griffis, a self-described expert in occult crime. The defense argued that Griffis was not qualified to be an expert witness because his doctoral degree came from Columbia Pacific University, an unaccredited, distance-learning school that was eventually shut down by the state of California. Griffis claimed the murder seemed satanic in nature. He also testified that criminal Satanists often wear black T-shirts and repeated searches of Echols's home had found no less than 15 black T-shirts.[5]

Because Echols and Baldwin had not confessed and Misskelley refused to testify against them, Misskelley's confession was inadmissible as evidence under an interpretation of the Sixth Amendment known as "the Bruton rule." However, a transcript of Misskelly's confession was leaked to the *Memphis Commercial Appeal*. On June 7, the paper printed parts of the confession with the headline, "Teen Describes Cult Torture of Boys: Defendant Misskelley Tells Police of Sex Mutilation." In 2010, advocates for the Three obtained an affidavit signed by attorney Lloyd Warford that alleged jury misconduct by Kent Arnold, the jury foreman. Arnold had hired Warford for help in an unrelated criminal case and had frequently discussed jury duty with him. According to the affidavit, Arnold had used deception to get onto the jury and informed his fellow jurors of the confession. Arnold had already decided on Echols's guilt before the trial began, commenting that if you looked into Echols's eyes, "you knew he was evil."[6] Echols and Baldwin were also found guilty of three counts of murder. Baldwin received a life sentence and Echols was sentenced to death.

Joe Berlinger and Bruce Sinofsky went to West Memphis intending to make a documentary about the horrors of disaffected youth. But when they arrived, they concluded that the Three were not murderers but teenagers being railroaded by a prejudiced justice system. Many who saw their documentary felt a deep sympathy for the Three, including prominent actors and musicians. *Paradise Lost* and its sequels are the only films in which the band Metallica allowed their music to be used. Punk rocker Henry Rollins sought out other artists to produce the album "Rise Above," all proceeds of which went to a legal support fund. The Dixie Chicks, Disturbed, and Pearl Jam's Eddie Vedder all came out in support of the Three. In 2010, actor Johnny Depp advocated the Three's innocence on a CBS special entitled "Cry for Justice." Comedian Margaret Cho became pen pals with Echols and called him, without irony, "the heavy metal Nelson Mandela."[7]

In 2007, attorneys for the Three filed a motion in federal court to overturn the convictions in light of DNA evidence. Further investigation found unknown DNA on the victims, but no DNA from any of the Three. The motion also brought up such concerns as the questionable testimony of Dale Griffis and the affidavit alleging jury misconduct. Furthermore, seven forensic scientists agreed that the sexual mutilation of Christopher Myers—the detail that seemed to prove the murders were "ritualistic"—was actually the result of animal predation after the bodies had been exposed to the elements. The Arkansas Supreme Court ordered Circuit Judge David Laser to consider this new evidence. Laser reached a deal with prosecutors in which a new trial would be held, provided the defendants offer Alford Pleas. In 2011, the Three were freed.

TRANSCENDENT AND IMMANENT EVIL

Both sides of the legal battle over the Three saw themselves engaged in a struggle against evil. Rival views of black-clad teenagers were indicative of a much larger divide over the nature of evil. Sociologists Christopher Bader, F. Carson Mencken, and Joseph Baker note that rival visions of evil were starkly evident in the 2008 presidential campaign. At an event in Saddleback Church, one of the largest megachurches in the country, Pastor Rick Warren asked senators Barack Obama and John McCain the question, "Does evil exist? And if it does, do we ignore it? Do we negotiate with it? Do we contain it? Do we defeat it?"

Senator McCain responded:
Defeat it. A couple of points. One, if I'm president of the United States, my friends, if I have to follow him to the gates of hell, I will get bin Laden and bring him to justice. I will do that. And I know how to do that. I will get that done. No one, no one should be allowed to take thousands of American— innocent American lives. Of course, evil must be defeated.
  Senator Obama responded:
  Evil does exist. I mean I think we see evil all the time. We see evil in Darfur. We see evil, sadly, on the streets of our cities. We see evil in parents

who viciously abuse their children. I think it has to be confronted. It has to be confronted squarely, and one of the things that I strongly believe is that, now, we are not going to, as individuals, be able to erase evil from the world. . . . Now, the one thing that I think is very important is for us [to] have some humility in how we approach the issue of confronting evil, because of evil's been perpetrated based on the claim that we were trying to confront evil.

Bader et al. conclude that the two senators' comments (and the close election between them) indicate two radically different understandings of evil. McCain responded to Warren's question with a vision of transcendent evil, while Obama responded with a vision of immanent evil. McCain described evil as a force that invades from outside—Islamic terrorism. He also invoked the supernatural through a reference to "the gates of hell." Obama described evil in our own cities and even in our own families. McCain emphasized avenging the innocent, while Obama emphasized discernment in confronting the causes of human suffering.

Survey data demonstrates that these different conceptions of evil correlate with socioeconomic, religious, and cultural differences. Bader et al. conclude, "The person most likely to view the Earth as a spiritual battleground between good and evil is a conservatively/traditionally religious person who is not faring well in the socioeconomic status system by conventional standards."[8] This profile fits the community of West Memphis perfectly. In fact, the controversy surrounding the Three was a clash of cultures more than a debate over evidence. Many of the West Memphis Three's most influential supporters came from New York and California. Berlinger and Sinofsky recounted how they were described by the locals as "New York Jew Boys" and received several death threats.[9] Locals not only saw advocates of the Three as wealthy and secular interlopers who did not share their values, but as incapable of seeing the evidence correctly. The truth about the murders was, in this sense, a local one. Advocate Burk Sauls recalls, "We were told by police that we simply didn't know that the truth; that the truth was invisible to us because we were from California, and that Damien, Jason, and Jessie's guilt was obvious to the people who had 'been there' when it all happened."[10] This quote demonstrates a profound epistemological problem arising from rival cultural worldviews.

TRANSCENDENT EVIL AND SATANIC PANIC

Survey data indicates that many Americans believe in the reality of supernatural evil. Gallup polls show that belief in the devil has risen from 55 percent in 1990 to 70 percent in 2004.[11] In the 2007 Baylor Religion

Survey, nearly 75 percent of respondents indicated that Satan "absolutely" or "probably" existed. Nearly 70 percent indicated that demons absolutely or probably exist.[12] The 2008 Pew Forum survey indicated that nearly 70 percent of Americans believe that (angels and) demons are active in the world.[13] Belief in spiritual evil may be even more widespread in Southern states such as Arkansas. The 1998 Southern Focus Poll indicated that nearly 59 percent of respondents believe "people are sometimes possessed by the Devil."[14] Furthermore, researchers have found that belief in Satan and spiritual evil are strong predictors of political participation in rallies, petitions, picketing, and social movements such as the Moral Majority.[15]

This belief in supernatural evil in the form of Satan and demons is closely linked with satanic panic, which also includes the fear that satanic cults operate in secret, performing human sacrifices. Rumors of satanic cults turned into a national phobia in the 1960s due to the rise of an anticult movement and the creation of Anton LaVey's Church of Satan in 1966. The murders carried about by Charles Manson and his "family" in 1969 convinced many that the teenage counterculture was engaged in criminal Satanism on a large scale. After Manson's arrest, the *Los Angeles Herald Examiner* ran a front-page article titled "Hippie Commune Witchcraft Blood Rites Told."[16]

Full panic over Satanism began in the 1980s. In 1988, Geraldo Rivera hosted a special entitled "Exposing Satan's Underground." The special featured cult experts, who explained that teenagers were the most likely to be seduced by Satanism and that heavy metal music indoctrinated young people through "back masking" or subliminal messages that are discernible when a song is played backward. There was also a panic over "ritual abuse" that was allegedly being inflicted on children by Satanists. This led to the infamous McMartin Preschool Trial, in which day care providers in California were accused of abusing children during satanic ceremonies. Despite the total lack of evidence, the investigation and trial lasted more than six years, costing the public over $15 million. The defendants were finally acquitted.

Satanic panic was empowered by a vision of evil as a transcendent, otherworldly force that found its physical manifestation at the margins of society. Advocates of the Three claim that the docket number assigned to the West Memphis Three case originally ended in 555 and was changed to 666 by one of the detectives, subtly framing the murders in supernatural terms.[17] This same equation of supernatural evil with otherness was present in the witch-hunts at Salem and other American colonies, where Satan was always believed to be conspiring with someone marginalized by the community.[18] Like Damien Echols, the targets of satanic panic often have connections to new religious movements such as Wicca or deviant subcultures such heavy as metal culture. They are also typically too poor to hire adequate legal counsel. Finally, teenagers—already a sort of liminal being—are frequently understood in terms transcendent forces, either demonic or angelic.[19] For the community of West Memphis, an idea of evil as an invading force anchored in the outer edges of society provided a way of thinking about a horrifying and senseless crime that rendered it meaningful. Belief in satanic cults allowed them to process the horror of these crimes and transition from fear to righteous anger.

IMMANENT EVIL

There is another view of evil, also well established in American culture, which sees evil not in the other but in how the other is treated. Nathaniel Hawthorne's *The Scarlet Letter* (1850) became a classic text of this immanent vision of evil. Hawthorne was born in Salem and was a descendent of John Hathorne, one of the judges during the witch trials. Unlike his Puritan ancestors, Hawthorne saw evil not in the supernatural agency of Satan and his allies, but in human nature. In one of his notebooks, he wrote, "There is evil in every human heart, which may remain latent through the whole of life, but certain circumstances may rouse it into activity."[20] In this view, evil always comes from within and arises through a complex web of social relationships. Intolerance and oppression of the socially marginalized were for Hawthorne, typically the result of our inability to face our own moral failings.

Hawthorne's vision of immanent evil is echoed by modern American artists. Horror author Brian Hodge wrote of the West Memphis Three case, "If there is such a palpable force as Evil, its triumphs come not in the guise of the faces that leer from stained glass and the landscapes of Bosch, but from beneath bland everyday anonymity and from bureaucracies that can paralyze otherwise good people by urging them, in the words of Edmund Burke, to do nothing."[21] Metallica expresses a similar understanding of evil. For prosecutors, the music of Metallica was associated with Satanism. In *Paradise Lost*, Metallica's sinister tones are indeed used to signal the presence of evil. But for Metallica, evil is not found in the supernatural but in the hypocrisy of religious and legal institutions. These themes are explored in songs such as "Leper Messiah," "Holier than Thou," and "And Justice for All." This view of evil takes a critical approach to those claiming to be righteous while expressing sympathy with the marginalized.

For advocates of the Three, evil exists both on an institutional scale and within our own hearts. In *The Last Pentacle of the Sun*, a collection of essays and fiction written in support of the Three, numerous authors draw parallels between the situation in West Memphis and the invasion of Iraq in 2003. Both events, they argue, amount to massive human suffering arising from fear and ignorance. But advocates of the Three also identify the seeds of evil within themselves. Margaret Cho explains that Echols represents "the parts of ourselves we send to the gallows, the freedom we often forfeit, the injustice we commit against the greatest of all enemies, the self."[22] Henry Rollins frames his support for the West Memphis Three as part of his struggle against "the forces of injustice," suggesting a unified phenomenon that may be internal and external.

THE EVIL OF THE ALFORD PLEA

The evidence suggests that the Three are innocent, and yet, in the eyes of the state they are guilty of murdering three children. The strange resolution of the West Memphis Three case through an Alford Plea, which seems illogical and satisfies no one, symbolizes a sort of uneasy truce between two rival realities. While the 2011 trial was held for Echols, Baldwin, and Misskelley, in a sense, the state was also on trial. If the Three are not satanic murderers, then it is the state of Arkansas that has nearly killed an innocent by lethal injection. By paradoxically declaring the Three both innocent and guilty, the Alford Plea exonerated the state as much as the accused. (Indeed, part of the impetus for the Alford Plea may have been to protect the state from a tort claim that might have awarded the Three with millions in compensation.) The situation seems to echo the lyrics of Metallica's James Hetfield, "Justice is lost. Justice is raped. Justice is gone." This compromise also ensures that the larger cultural dissonance arising from immanent and transcendent visions of evil will never be openly addressed, suggesting that justice—as a universal rather than a local reality—might truly be lost. It now seems that there are three evils in the case of the West Memphis Three: the evil that led someone to murder three children, the evil that led a jury to convict three innocent men, and finally the evil of two versions of the truth that will never be reconciled.

NOTES

1. Howard N. Snyder and Melissa Sickmund, *Juvenile Offenders and Victims: 2006 National Report* (Washington, DC: U.S. Department of Justice, Office of Justice Programs, Office of Juvenile Justice and Delinquency Prevention, 2006), 22.

2. Guy Reel, Marc Perrusquia, and Bartholomew Sullivan, *The Blood of Innocents* (New York: Pinnacle Books, 1995), 91.

3. Mara Leveritt, *Devil's Knot: The True Story of the West Memphis Three* (New York: Atria Books, 2002), 67–74.

4. Dan Stidham, "Dan Stidham's Case Synopsis," *Exonerate the West Memphis Three Support Fund*, http://www.wm3.org/CaseIntroduction/Page/DAN-STIDHAMS-CASE-SYNOPSIS (accessed February 12, 2012).

5. Bartholomew Sullivan, "Witnesses Call Boys Deaths Work of Group with Trappings of the Occult," *The Commercial Appeal*, March 9, 1994, http://www.commercialappeal.com/news/1994/mar/09/witnesses-call-boys-deaths-work-group-trappings-oc/?print=1 (accessed February 12, 2012).

6. Beth Warren, "Jury Foreman in West Memphis Three Trial of Damien Echols Accused of Misconduct," *The Commercial Appeal*, October 13, 2010, http://www.commercialappeal.com/news/2010/oct/13/echols-trial-juror-accused-of-misconduct/ (accessed February 12, 2012).

7. Margaret Cho, "Letter," in *The Last Pentacle of the Sun: Writings in Support of the West Memphis Three*, ed. M. W. Anderson and Brett A. Savory (Vancouver: Arsenal Pulp Press, 2004), 189.

8. Christopher D. Bader, Frederick C. Mencken, and Joseph Baker, *Paranormal America: Ghost Encounters, UFO Sightings, Bigfoot Hunts, and Other Curiosities in Religion and Culture* (New York: New York University Press, 2010), 175.

9. Joe Berlinger and Bruce Sinofsky, "Introduction," in *The Last Pentacle of the Sun: Writings in Support of the West Memphis Three*, ed. M. W. Anderson and Brett A. Savory (Vancouver: Arsenal Pulp Press, 2004), 12.

10. Burk Sauls, "California to West Memphis in Ten Years," in *The Last Pentacle of the Sun: Writings in Support of the West Memphis Three*, ed. M. W. Anderson and Brett A. Savory (Vancouver: Arsenal Pulp Press, 2004), 20.

11. Albert L. Winseman, "Eternal Destinations: Americans Believe in Heaven, Hell," *Gallup Poll News Service*, May 25, 2004, http://www.gallup.com/poll/11770/Eternal-Destinations-Americans-Believe-Heaven-Hell.aspx (accessed May 13, 2012).

12. Baylor University, *Baylor Religion Survey, Wave II* (Waco, TX: Baylor Institute for Studies of Religion, 2007).

13. Pew Forum on Religion & Public Life, *U.S. Religious Landscape Survey: Religious Beliefs and Practices: Diverse and Politically Relevant* (Washington, DC: 2008), 35.

14. Tom W. Rice, "Believe It or Not: Religious and Other Paranormal Beliefs in the United States," *Journal for the Scientific Study of Religion* 42, no. 1 (2003): 98.

15. William H. Swatos Jr. "Picketing Satan Enfleshed at 7-Eleven: A Research Note," *Review of Religious Research* 30, no. 1 (1988): 73–82.

16. Bill Ellis, *Raising the Devil: Satanism, New Religions, and the Media* (Lexington: University Press of Kentucky, 2000), 178.

17. Peg Aloi, "An It Harm None, Do What Ye Will," in *The Last Pentacle of the Sun: Writings in Support of the West Memphis Three*, ed. M. W. Anderson and Brett A. Savory (Vancouver: Arsenal Pulp Press, 2004), 89.

18. W. Scott Poole, *Satan in America: The Devil We Know* (Lanham, MD: Rowman & Littlefield, 2009), 21.

19. Sarah M. Pike, "Dark Teens and Born-Again Martyrs: Captivity Narratives after Columbine," *Journal of the American Academy of Religion* 77, no. 3 (2009): 648.

20. David S. Reynolds, *Beneath the American Renaissance: The Subversive Imagination in the Age of Emerson and Melville* (Cambridge, MA: Harvard University Press, 1988), 250.

21. Brian Hodge, "In Their Satanic Majesty's Service," in *The Last Pentacle of the Sun: Writings in Support of the West Memphis Three*, ed. M. W. Anderson and Brett A. Savory (Vancouver: Arsenal Pulp Press, 2004), 103.

22. Cho, "Letter," 191.

CHAPTER 28

Satan's Most Popular Pawn? Harry Potter and Modern Evangelical Cosmology

William H. Taylor and Kristi R. Humphreys

In 2006, the film *Jesus Camp* (Heidi Ewing and Rachel Grady) introduced the documentary-watching world to the Christian evangelist Becky Fischer. Near the depths of Devil's Lake in North Dakota, Fischer leveled a multitude of exhortations at the young audience attending her "Kids on Fire" summer camp in an attempt to better equip them for their lifelong battles with Satan. One such diatribe was a potent warning concerning the world renowned "boy who lived," Harry Potter: "Let me say something about Harry Potter. Warlocks are enemies of God, and I don't care what kind of hero they are; they're an enemy of God. And had it been in the Old Testament, Harry Potter would have been put to death!" Although the evangelist may have a unique approach to youth education, Fischer is not alone in her belief of the evils of Harry Potter. Within the ranks of American Christianity there are many who have decried Harry, and his author J. K. Rowling, as the tools of Satan and the harbingers of a satanic kingdom on earth. The language employed by these contemporary evangelical Christian sentinels resembles that from 17th-century Puritan New England, particularly the rhetoric concerning witchcraft. Borrowing the techniques of religious, social, and literary historians of the period, an examination of these condemnations of the *Harry Potter* series reveals more than an impassioned, and perhaps paranoid, reaction by evangelical Christian leaders. It is the contention of this study that these censures also illustrate the cries of a movement within evangelical Christianity that is seeking to reestablish a providential cosmos amongst Christians and their proper place therein.

Recent scholarship addressing modern American evangelicalism has revealed several characteristics of the movement. First, American evangelicals comprise an ever-changing group "marked by shifts in which groups, leaders, institutions, goals, concerns, opponents, and aspirations become more or less visible and more or less influential over time."[1] Second, although some aspects are in flux, there is consistency in the central tenets of the evangelicals: "conversionism (an emphasis on the 'new birth' as a life-changing religious experience), biblicism (a reliance on the Bible as ultimate religious authority), activism (a concern for sharing the faith), and crucicentrism (a focus on Christ's redeeming work on the cross)."[2] Finally, in extending the practices of the early 20th-century fundamentalists—who preferred literal interpretations of the Bible and simple approaches to faith—when confronting crises, modern evangelicals tend toward "over-simplification of issues and the substitution of inspiration and zeal for critical analysis and serious reflection."[3] Examining this tendency, a study of evangelical responses to the Harry Potter phenomenon sheds new light on the modern evangelical movement and its connections to a fundamentalist heritage. Instead of an approach mired solely in the anti-intellectualism of the fundamentalists, modern evangelicals also reflect the views and strategies of their Christian ancestors, dating as far back as the 17th century in Puritan New England, when confronting a crisis. Considering the *Harry Potter* series has been translated into 69 languages and has sold over 400 million copies worldwide,[4] many within the evangelical camp consider the popularity of these novels—novels involving plots steeped in historical and fictional witchcraft—quite the crisis.

The Puritans of New England and the witchcraft craze during the late 17th century offer invaluable insight into the modern evangelical's showdown with the young boy wizard, Harry Potter. For the Puritan communities, witchcraft represented an unholy reversal of the natural order—their cosmology—because it placed the Devil, instead of the triune God, as the focal point around which their lives were to revolve and to which their hopes should aspire. Accused witches were largely women and were considered dangerous because they communed with the Devil and acted on his behalf, both through the spoken and written word. Although scholars disagree on the full spectrum of factors that resulted in the New England witch hunts of 1692, one point of consensus is that Puritan leaders felt that their authority within the community was being diabolically challenged. For the Puritans, all misfortunes, such as the devastating events of King Philip's War and the revocation of New England colonial charters by the English government, were indications that God was allowing the Devil to launch an offensive against their community of saints. In an effort to combat these forces and reassert their God-given authority, they attacked what was in their minds the most obvious source of evil: witchcraft. In a similar fashion, many Christians within modern evangelical churches in America have latched onto what is, in their minds, Satan's most popular pawn—Harry Potter. By examining the Harry Potter protests through a Puritanical lens, the idea that modern evangelicals could be influenced by movements other than the fundamentalists comes into focus. In particular, the Harry Potter protestors reveal the following characteristics shared by the Puritans and the modern evangelical: A preoccupation with their role in providential history, a reverence for the spoken and written word as divine tools, and a belief in the innate spiritual weaknesses of women.[5]

Few people have devoted as much time or ink to counteract the evil influence of the boy wizard as Richard Abanes. Within evangelical circles, Abanes is touted as one of the most knowledgeable popular experts in occult studies. In 2001, taking full advantage of the printed word, Abanes began his assault on J. K. Rowling's novels with his work, *Harry Potter and the Bible: The Menace behind the Magick.* In the preface, Denver Seminary professor of philosophy Douglas Groothuis attempted to prepare the reader for his journey with Abanes. Groothuis wrote, "Spiritual discernment may be at an all-time low in both the Church and in the world." This predicament, the professor continued, existed because "far too many Christians have failed to develop their critical faculties concerning the enticements of a Post-Christian culture."[6] With this exhortation and call to action, Richard Abanes was primed to enlighten.

After a cursory glance at the harrowing success of the *Harry Potter* novels, Abanes calls out the "evangelical leaders who sadly have failed to understand the insidious nature of their message." The main offenders were Alan Jacobs of Wheaton College, Chuck Colson, the founder of Prison Fellowship, and the editorial staff of *Christianity Today.* Frustrated but focused, Abanes then takes aim at the novels to correct this collective oversight: "Is the success behind Rowling's books just a result of good writing and media hype? Or is there an unseen spiritual force of darkness possibly driving the craze?" Eventually, Abanes, like many evangelicals, answers the leading question, and claims the success of the novels was the result "of spiritual forces of darkness seeking to overshadow Christian values and virtues with occult myths, practices and morals. But this should come as no surprise." These dark forces worked subtly through the novels to implant in the audience, within children in particular, a sense of familiarity and comfort with the occult. Abanes writes, "Perhaps Satan's cleverest tool has been false religions, especially those religious belief systems that make adherents feel as if they have control over the world around them. One such belief system, nearly as old as humanity itself, is occultism— which . . . is the foundation of J. K. Rowling's Harry Potter series." With too many leading evangelicals supporting the novels, Abanes portrayed himself as a member of a small but stalwart group who recognized and were fighting what evangelical novelist Frank Peretti termed, "this present darkness."[7] However, as is clear through his numerous books, articles, and interviews, Abanes is not abandoning his role as an evangelical sentinel tirelessly trying to warn those duped by Satan.

Many evangelicals are frustrated partly because they believe that the United States was once better. "Welcome to Post-Christian America," Abanes writes. Perhaps Americans still claim to be religious, but that did not mean they were Christian. "Literature endorsing occultism used to be a rare thing in 'Judeo-Christian' America," but today, the author laments, "occult books are no longer confined to the dirty back shelves of libraries and occult curiosity shops." The printed word, a tool seen as valuable not only to modern evangelicals spreading Christianity, but also to their Puritan ancestors, has been tainted. Abanes elaborates on this topic in his 2005 follow-up book, *Harry Potter, Narnia, and the Lord of the Rings*. He fondly recalls the golden age of American history, and ironically notes the fairy-tale quality of the belief when he writes, "Once upon a time, children's literature was carefully chosen and published by editors whose main goal was to inspire and elevate young minds." Today, he regretfully adds, "consumerism is driving the children's book industry," but that is not the full extent of the problem. Abanes states that "book producers, with the help of well-meaning librarians and teachers, began painting a frightful portrait of millions of illiterate youths glued to the TV or video games—all because they had not developed good reading habits. Fear soon replaced critical thinking about children's literature, which in turn caused many adults to no longer care about *what* kids were reading." No longer are children being edified by Christian literature written by authors such as J.R.R. Tolkien and C.S. Lewis, they are increasingly enamored with books on the occult, such as the *Harry Potter* novels.[8]

As terrible as it is that the printed word, a tool used by American Christians since the colonial period, has been abused due to the fascination of publishers and the public alike, the spread of evil goes even further. "In addition to books and magazines, the television and film industry has undoubtedly persuaded countless young people to delve into occultism." The spoken word has also been abused and is not confined to living rooms or the movie theater; it has invaded the evangelical's turf—the church. Over several pages, Abanes reports the spread of occult within American churches and parachurch organizations, such as the United Methodist Church, the Presbyterian Church (USA), the Evangelical Lutheran Church in America, the National Council of Churches, and the World Council of Churches. One of the main offenses by these institutions, according to the author, is the sponsorship and participation in the "'Reimagining' Women's Conferences" (1993 and 1998) that hosted "twenty-seven speakers [which] included lesbians, radical feminists and neopagans." Unsurprisingly, the conferences "turned out to be an organized attempt to fit ('reimagine') Scripture, the church and theology into feminist/pagan ideals."[9] Harry Potter was just the tip of the iceberg; a way for the author to call attention to what he perceived as the encroaching fingers of the occult on the sly hand of Satan. And Satan was not content to make only subtle suggestions, through the printed and spoken word; the dark lord was now overtly drawing Christians, especially women and children, into his fold. The depth of the diabolic plot that Abanes perceives draws a parallel to the Puritan fathers' approach to the Salem witches in 1692.

Adding to the evangelical protest of the *Harry Potter* novels is Steve Wohlberg's book, *Hour of the Witch: Harry Potter, Wicca Witchcraft, and the Bible*. Although Wohlberg and Abanes are often in agreement, Wohlberg is much more aggressive in his pronouncements. Wicca, the largest division of neopagans and the religion of modern witches, was expected, according to one study, Wohlberg noted, to be the third largest religious group in the United States by 2012.[10] Time is not on the modern evangelical's side and Wohlberg points to disturbing youth trends as an indicator: "In the last few years both children and adults have been exposed to a vast array of pleasantly designed books, supernaturally charged TV programs, and magical movies portraying witchcraft as safe, exciting, and spiritually empowering."[11] However, not everyone will be affected equally, as Wohlberg specifically emphasizes the danger "for teenage girls." The author, like many evangelicals, is channeling his inner-Puritan. For the 17th-century New Englanders, all souls were feminine and therefore possessing certain inherent weaknesses. The combination of a feminine soul in a female body meant that women, more so than men, were prone to fall prey to the Devil's snares. For Wohlberg, as it had been with the Puritans and is for many evangelicals, Christian women need protection. However, the author further laments, the immediate future is not promising as "it seems a sorcery-filled tsunami is forming—with no stopping it." For Wohlberg there is no doubt as to "the sequence of books and films that tower above all others" in this approaching storm. "They're loved and hated, praised and feared, considered innocuous or full of subtle dangers. You know the name: *Harry Potter.*"[12]

Yet this ungodly development signifies more than a present discomfort for many modern evangelicals; the rise of witchcraft on the back of Harry Potter is an important indicator that end times are near at hand. Wohlberg calls to his aid the Biblical book of Revelation, noting that "it warns of real sorcery deceiving 'the nations'—the same nations filled with kids who love *Harry Potter* (those books are being read in over

200 countries), and who are being desensitized to the occult by J.K. Rowling's subtle witchcraft-made-funny novels. In these end-times, *prophecies are in conflict.*" Although a fascination with eschatology is seen as a common characteristic among the early 20th-century fundamentalists, the Puritans had long paved the way for such end-time postulation. Although Wohlberg believes that the Harry Potter books, and perhaps even their author J.K. Rowling, are evil, they allow him and evangelicals like him to know their place in providential history—their role in the cosmic conflict between God and Satan. In this way, Harry Potter affords Wohlberg a way to pose his most important and concluding question: "Whose side are we on?"[13] The end is at hand and several evangelical sentries are scrambling to rouse the masses of befuddled Christians who are following Harry Potter toward the enemy's camp.

As they delve into the depths of the past, historians have made clear the importance of literacy to the individual American Christian. For many, from the Puritans to modern evangelicals, becoming a Christian means first acquiring the ability to read the Bible. Among Christian communities, this reliance on literacy as a key to salvation has resulted in a unique respect for the written word, which in turn largely influences the Christian's approach to "dangerous" texts. When Christians encounter the written word being used in ways that present or promote non-Christian ideals, they often respond by engaging in an activity that seeks to "eradicate their ideas and also to punish the author": they burn books. For Christians, the act of book burning is largely founded upon a Biblical mandate found in Acts 19:18–20, which reports of a group of new believers confessing their sins and throwing their pagan texts into a fire. Books have been burned for a multitude of reasons, whether they threaten to diminish power or to corrupt humankind. Regardless of the reason, book burners seem to share the fear that "once ideas are let free, they will be impossible to restrain." The *Harry Potter* series has certainly received its fair share of attention with regard to committing pages to purifying flames. Led by Pastor and Founder Jack Brock, members of the congregation of Christ Community Church in Alamogordo, New Mexico, set out to burn *Harry Potter* books, which they considered to be "a masterpiece of satanic deception." Whereas Pastor Brock admits that he has not read any of the novels or seen the movies, he believes, "These books teach children how they can get into witchcraft and become a witch, wizard or warlock . . . behind that innocent face is the power of satanic darkness. Harry Potter is the devil and he is destroying people." Just as the Puritans sought to identify and eradicate the source of evil in their communities, some modern evangelicals such as Jack Brock, also drawing on their fundamentalist roots of literal interpretations of texts, take a perhaps oversimplified approach to the Harry Potter plots of wizardry by burning the novels without reading them because they could possibly "keep them from Jesus."[14] Whereas the motivations for destroying texts may be largely fundamentalist in nature, the technique of burning books reflects more the influences of their earlier Christian ancestors.

Additionally, this activity speaks of Christians' high regard for the power of the written word. Jack Brock's determination not to read *Harry Potter* could be interpreted as a desire to avoid being sucked into a world, willing or not, that in his mind promotes evil and corrupts its readers. In engaging this highly corruptible evil, modern evangelical book burners face a challenge their ancestors did not: in most places, staging a ceremonial burning of "ungodly" texts, where flame upon flame engulfs the offensive tomes and eradicates the evil therein, requires a city permit. This is not always an easy item to acquire. Reverend Doug Taylor motivated his Jesus Party congregation to combat the unholy forces of the Harry Potter phenomenon and engage in a collective book burning: "We're Bible believers. We're Christians. We believe these books are dangerous." No doubt Reverend Taylor was disappointed when his book burning plans were derailed by the city's refusal to grant him a burn permit. To circumvent this problem, the congregation staged a "book cutting" instead: "Everybody's going to have scissors, and we're going to cut those four [Harry Potter] books up right into the trash." This complication points to a more significant challenge encountered by modern evangelical book burners. Perhaps more than ever, many find the activity of book burning extreme and the motivations contradictory. As historian Hans J. Hillerbrand states, "Book burnings thus are but another instance in history where the destructive is clad in the language of virtue," and many may perceive that "evil is camouflaged as a good."[15] Although there were fewer restrictions regarding the eradication of evil texts for their Christian forefathers, these modern evangelicals are performing the same act (sometimes only in their imaginations) and often acting on similar principles, yet working within a system that is constantly redefining what is acceptable and what is unacceptable.

Whereas book burning still functions within modern society as a way to express discontent or to eradicate a known evil, many find they can be much more effective in reaching large numbers of people if they employ another tool of communication: the Internet. Information and opinions about the *Harry Potter* series, from plot summaries to thematic discussions, are certainly alive and well on the World Wide Web. For modern evangelicals who disapprove of these plots of wizardry, the Internet has functioned as a convenient way to warn the masses of the dangers of Harry Potter. The far-reaching abilities of the Internet have given popular culture a much grander stage on which to perform; worldwide, fans and critics alike can read information and post opinions, which gives a series such as *Harry Potter* the ability to achieve unparalleled popularity. For modern evangelicals like Dr. Paul Jehle, as the popularity of Harry Potter strengthens in America, the Christian movement weakens: "Throughout the Bible and history, evil gains momentum when Christianity is weak. Never has Christianity been so weak in America as it is today. . . . The success of the Harry Potter books and movies . . . indicates a weakness in the depth of the Christianity lived out by the average believer in America."[16] In the same way, the Puritans regarded tribulation as proof that God was allowing the Devil to work and that evil was pervading their communities, modern evangelicals regard the growing popularity of Harry Potter fan sites and blogs as proof that the Devil is doing similar work on a much larger scale, thus further weakening the Christian movement. That said, modern evangelicals have also embraced the Internet as an extension of the printed word to combat what they consider to be the evil forces of Harry Potter. For example, on opentheword.org, Dr. Tom Snyder and Dr. Ted Baeher warn of the dangers of the "boy who lived" in "Don't Be Fooled—The Final Harry Potter Book Still Teaches Witchcraft"; Chuck Colson takes a balanced approach in his article, "Witches and Wizards: The Harry Potter Phenomenon" on breakpoint.org, by offering suggestions to help kids be discerning about what they read; on seekgod.ca, Vicky Dillen rebuts the idea that Harry Potter is harmless to modern Christians in "Harry Potter: Christian Icons and Bad Advice"; and Dr. James Dobson denounces Harry Potter on christianpost.com. Whereas these are just a few of many possible examples, they represent a movement within the Christian community to warn the masses of the ways in which the Devil is working in popular culture.

Interestingly, these aforementioned sites, and many others like them, suggest the Christian movement has only been losing this battle with Satan in popular culture for a short while. They, too, advocate returning to a "golden age" of American history, one that had lasted uninterrupted, since the establishment of Plymouth colony, but which has recently been lost. These modern evangelicals seek to recover that time, which still seems just within reach, which embraced the popular, and thoroughly Christian, works of C. S. Lewis and J.R.R. Tolkien. Although there are some evangelicals who claim Christians should avoid worlds of fantasy altogether, most of the modern evangelicals examined here encourage others to explore the worlds of Narnia and Middle Earth. One of Harry Potter's cautious supporters, Chuck Colson, suggests hopefully, "Children will see Harry Potter, so show them deeper meanings and also point them to more obviously Christian books like Tolkien's and Lewis's." The unequivocally anti-Potter authors, Snyder and Baeher claim, "The story in Harry Potter occurs after Jesus Christ's death and resurrection, but the stories in Tolkien's universe occur before Jesus Christ's first coming. As such, the religious ideas in Tolkien's universe are based on the language and mythology of the elves and hobbits in Tolkien's world." They continue, "Consequently, the worldview of the elves and hobbits reflects a primitive form of ethical monotheism that looks forward to the first coming of the Messiah, Jesus Christ, and the afterlife." Similarly, Dillen argues, "Since people say fables like this can also have positive spiritual meaning, like Tolkien's Lord of the Rings, or Lewis' Narnia, we should be able to evaluate this from a Biblical perspective, since it is recommended as good for Christians."[17] For many modern evangelicals, the glorious days of Christian America are within reach through the pages of Lewis and Tolkien. Within the comfort of their own world of fantasy, it is much easier for these evangelicals to imagine reclamation of the American soul, but only, of course, if the likes of Harry Potter are renounced.

For many modern American evangelicals, addressing the "evil" in the *Harry Potter* series is a clear necessity. As Stephen Dollins exhorts, "According to the Word of God, the only good witch is a dead witch." It is tempting to treat evangelicals as one dimensionally as it appears they treat the rest of the world. However, as the Harry Potter protestors illustrate, there is more depth to modern evangelicals than meets the eye. Although this study focuses on the Puritan connection, the evidence examined reveals links to other periods and groups in American history. For instance, it is nothing new for members of society to fear fiction, based on a belief that truth and fantasy may not be as oppositional as they seem—that fictional evil can become real evil. Americans expressed similar sentiments regarding the rise of novels in the late 18th century. Novels were abused on the grounds that they induced fanciful thoughts and unrealistic expectations. According to historian Michael Warner, "Americans endlessly avowed a fear that fiction would detach readers' sentiments from the social world of the polity, substituting a private drama of fancy . . . no figure of the period seems to have been exempt from the anxiety (or at least from the discourse of anxiety)—including the novelists themselves." The novels were viewed, in short, as tools of seduction. This conviction is shared by many modern evangelicals, as indicated by the numerous Harry Potter protestors. Connections to periods and groups other than early 20th-century fundamentalism suggest avenues for further study that might uncover a more robust understanding of the evangelical. Even though it may be difficult, the Christian mandate to "do to others as you would have them do to you"[18] serves well the scholar who examines the potentially abrasive modern American evangelical.

NOTES

1. Mark A. Noll, *The Scandal of the Evangelical Mind* (Grand Rapids, MI: W. B. Eerdmans, 1994), 8.

2. Mark A. Yarhouse and Stephen R. Russell, "Evangelicalism," in *He Psychologies in Religion: Working with the Religious Client*, ed. E. Thomas Dowd and Stevan Lars Nielsen (New York: Springer, 2006), 111–25.

3. Noll, *The Scandal of the Evangelical Mind*, 12.

4. For more on evangelical historiography, see Randall H. Balmer, *The Making of Evangelicalism: From Revivalism to Politics, and Beyond* (Waco, TX: Baylor University Press, 2010); N. K. Clifford, "His Dominion: A Vision in Crisis," *Studies in Religion/Sciences Religieuses* 2, no. 4 (1973): 315–26; Richard Hofstadter, *Anti-Intellectualism in American Life* (New York: Knopf, 1963); George M. Marsden, *Evangelicalism and Modern America* (Grand Rapids, MI: W. B. Eerdmans, 1984); George M. Marsden, *Understanding Fundamentalism and Evangelicalism* (Grand Rapids, MI: W. B. Eerdmans, 1991); Mark A. Noll, *The Scandal of the Evangelical Mind* (Grand Rapids, MI: W. B. Eerdmans, 1994); Mark A. Noll, D. W. Bebbington, and George A. Rawlyk, *Evangelicalism: Comparative Studies of Popular Protestantism in North America, the British Isles, and Beyond, 1700–1990*, Religion in America Series (New York: Oxford University Press, 1994); Randall J. Stephens and Karl Giberson, *The Anointed: Evangelical Truth in a Secular Age* (Cambridge, MA: Belknap Press of Harvard University Press, 2011); Carl R. Trueman, *The Real Scandal of the Evangelical Mind* (Chicago: Moody, 2011); Noll, *The Scandal of the Evangelical Mind*, 8. Clifford, "His Dominion: A Vision in Crisis," 323; J. K. Rowling's Official Web site, http://www.jkrowling.com/en_GB/ (accessed February 13, 2012).

5. For more on the Puritans, see Gretchen A. Adams, *The Specter of Salem: Remembering the Witch Trials in Nineteenth-Century America* (Chicago: University of Chicago Press, 2008); Ruth H. Bloch, *Visionary Republic: Millennial Themes in American Thought 1756–1800* (Cambridge: Cambridge University Press, 1985); James West Davidson, *The Logic of Millennial Thought: Eighteenth-Century New England*, Yale Historical Publications: Miscellany (New Haven, CT: Yale University Press, 1977); John Demos, *Entertaining Satan: Witchcraft and the Culture of Early New England* (New York: Oxford University Press, 1982); Richard Godbeer, *The Devil's Dominion: Magic and Religion in Early New England* (Cambridge: Cambridge University Press, 1992); David D. Hall, *Worlds of Wonder, Days of Judgment: Popular Religious Belief in Early New England* (Cambridge, MA: Harvard University Press, 1989); Carol F. Karlsen, *The Devil in the Shape of a Woman: Witchcraft in Colonial New England* (New York: Vintage Books, 1989); Elizabeth Reis, "The Devil, the Body, and the Feminine Soul in Puritan New England," *The Journal of American History* 82, no. 1 (1995): 15–36.

6. Richard Abanes, *Harry Potter and the Bible: The Menace behind the Magick*, And the Bible Series (Camp Hill, PA: Horizon Books, 2001), xi.

7. Abanes, *Harry Potter and the Bible: The Menace behind the Magick*, ix, 6. For another source that mirrors many of the concerns and conclusions of Abanes, see Caryl Matrisciana and Robert S. McGee's, *Harry Potter: Witchcraft Repackaged*

(Jeremiah Films, 2001). Abanes, *Harry Potter and the Bible: The Menace behind the Magick*, 273, 154; Frank E. Peretti, *This Present Darkness* (Westchester, IL: Crossway Books, 1986).

8. Abanes, *Harry Potter and the Bible: The Menace behind the Magick*, 09, 205; See also Clete Hux, "Harry Potter vs. Aslan: Distinguishing Their Worldviews" (lecture, 34th General Assembly of the Presbyterian Church in America, Atlanta, Georgia, June 20–23, 2006). Richard Abanes, *Harry Potter, Narnia, and the Lord of the Rings* (Eugene, OR: Harvest House, 2005), 21, 22; C. S. Lewis and J.R.R. Tolkien are popular but Steve Wohlberg eschews any fantasy and recommends the Puritan John Bunyan's *Pilgrim's Progress*. Steve Wohlberg, *Hour of the Witch: Harry Potter, Wicca, Witchcraft, and the Bible* (Shippensburg, PA Destiny Image, 2005), 190.

9. Abanes, *Harry Potter and the Bible: The Menace behind the Magick*, 213. The offending women: Francis Wood (NCC) Elizabeth Bettenhausen (Evangelical Lutheran Church in America), Virginia Mollenkott (NCC), Aruna Gnanadson (WCC), Dolores Williams (Union Theological Seminary), Kwok Pui-Lan (WCC); Abanes, *Harry Potter and the Bible: The Menace behind the Magick*, 218. Hux, "Harry Potter vs. Alsan."

10. Wohlberg, *Hour of the Witch: Harry Potter, Wicca, Witchcraft, and the Bible*, 14.

11. Wohlberg, *Hour of the Witch: Harry Potter, Wicca, Witchcraft, and the Bible*, 15.

12. Hux, "Harry Potter vs. Aslan." Wohlberg, *Hour of the Witch: Harry Potter, Wicca, Witchcraft, and the Bible*, 18, 19.

13. Wohlberg, *Hour of the Witch: Harry Potter, Wicca, Witchcraft, and the Bible*, 70, 182. For another evangelical commentary on cosmologies, see Alison Lentini, "Harry Potter: Occult Cosmology and the Corrupted Imagination," *Spiritual Counterfeits Projects Journal* 23 (2000): 4–24. Wohlberg, *Hour of the Witch: Harry Potter, Wicca, Witchcraft, and the Bible*, 216.

14. Jill Lepore, "Dead Men Tell No Tales: John Sassamon and the Fatal Consequences of Literacy," *American Quarterly* 46, no. 4 (1994): 492; Hans J. Hillerbrand, "On Book Burnings and Book Burners: Reflections on the Power (and Powerlessness) of Ideas," *Journal of the American Academy of Religion* 74, no. 3 (2006): 593, 596, 608; "Burning Harry Potter or a Good, Old Fashion Book Burning," *Horrorfind*, http://wolfstone.halloweenhost.com/Hatred/brnhry_Burning HarryPotter.html (accessed February 13, 2012).

15. There may be another reason individuals such as Jack Brock choose not to read the novels. Book burnings of Harry Potter books tend to garnish a great deal of attention, which may be helpful to start-up churches. Found in "Burning Harry Potter." Andie Hannon, "Jesus Party Rips 'Harry Potter' on Eve of New Movie," *Lewiston-Auburn Sun Journal*, July 15, 2009, http://www.sunjournal.com/node/35087 (accessed February 13, 2012); Hillerbrand, "On Book Burnings and Book Burners: Reflections on the Power (and Powerlessness) of Ideas," 607.

16. Paul Jehle, "Harry Potter and the Deathly Hallows: Part 2: A Rebuttal to the *World Magazine* Review by Rebecca Cusey," *MovieGuide*, August 2, 2011, http://www.movieguide.org/articles/main/harry-potter-and-the-deathly-hallows-part-2.html (accessed July 30, 2011).

17. Chuck Colson, "Witches and Wizards: The Harry Potter Phenomenon," *BreakPoint*, November 2, 1999, http://www.breakpoint.org/commentaries/4635-witches-and-wizards (accessed February 14, 2012); Tom Snyder and Ted Baeher, "Don't Be Fooled—the Final Harry Potter Book Still Teaches Witchcraft," *OpentheWord.org*, September 5, 2007, http://www.opentheword.org/index.php?option=com_content&view=article&id=359:dont-be-fooled-the-final-harry-potter-book-still-teaches-witchcraft&catid=28:christian-news&Itemid=123 (accessed February 13, 2012); Vicky Dillen, "Harry Potter: Christian Icons and Bad Advice," http://www.seekgod.ca/imagination1.htm (accessed February 14, 2012).

18. Stephen Dollins, *Under the Spell of Harry Potter* (Topeka, KS: Prophecy Club, 2001), 9; Michael Warner, *The Letters of the Republic: Publication and the Public Sphere in Eighteenth-Century America* (Cambridge, MA: Harvard University Press, 1990), 175; Luke 6:31 (NIV).

About the Contributors

Aalya Ahmad lives in Gatineau, Quebec, Canada, and specializes in horror fiction and comparative literature. An Adjunct Research Professor at Carleton University in the Department of Film Studies, she teaches courses on gender, horror, and monstrosity at Carleton University, Ottawa, and has also taught courses on introductory women's and gender studies, activism, and gender and diaspora in the Pauline Jewett Institute for Women's and Gender Studies at Carleton. By day, she works for a national union and is a proud labour and feminist activist. She is a founding member of the "Radical Handmaids," a Margaret Atwood *Handmaid's Tale*–inspired group supporting women's reproductive rights, and she was recently nominated by grassroots groups in her region for "Femmy Award" for outstanding contributions to women's equality. Dr. Ahmad also writes and publishes short horror fiction under a pseudonym, and co-edits *Postscripts to Darkness*, a small press horror anthology.

"Blood in the Bush Garden: Gender, Indigenization and Unsettling." In *Terror of the Soul: Essays on Canadian Horror Cinema*, University of Toronto Press, 2013.
Fear and Learning: Essays on the Pedagogy of Horror with Sean Moreland, Jefferson, NC, McFarland, 2013.
"Gray Is the New Black: Race, Class and Zombies." In *Generation Zombie*, McFarland, 2011.
"When the Women Think: Teaching Horror in Women's and Gender Studies." In *Whispers in the Classroom: Essays on the pedagogy of horror*, McFarland, 2013.

My love for all things macabre began at a very early age and I have been fascinated by horror's paradoxes and formal features ever since. I am particularly interested in women's authorship, reception, and spectatorship of horror, and intrigued by cross-cultural comparisons of horror fiction and film, and the cultural politics underlying remakes and adaptations, as well as the horror of diasporic experiences. Horror is a rich field with endless possibilities for research and exploration.

Michael Butterfield is a writer and a lifelong student of the true crime genre. He is a recognized expert on the unsolved "Zodiac" murders in California and has served as a media source and consultant for news reports, articles, and television documentaries. He has been a guest on radio programs such as *Coast to Coast* with George Noory and *The Sean Moncrieff Show* in Ireland. He has appeared in the television documentary *Case Reopened* and the History Channel series *MysteryQuest*, and he served as a consultant for director David Fincher's feature film *Zodiac*.

I have always been terrified and fascinated by a world of murder that seems to dominate daily news yet is largely ignored in daily life, and I am drawn to the drama of true stories. The horror and bloodshed of these gruesome chapters in history are only a part of the story. The real people, the real victims, survivors, heroes, and even the villains make the "true crime" genre a unique window into the human condition. I struggled to understand human evil as I grew up in an age that combined true crime stories and modern pop culture into a phenomenon previously unknown in our world, the TV-movie of the week. News reports of various unfolding crime dramas were followed by the subsequent nonfiction accounts that regularly appeared at my local bookstore. Then came the made-for-television dramatization or the occasional big-budget Hollywood film version. Inevitably, I discovered that the public perception of these stories was often very different from the reality and disturbing facts were ignored in favor of more entertaining fiction. Society is eager to celebrate and exploit its horrors, but we seem unwilling to recognize our evil reflection and the monster in the mirror.

Jennifer S. Carlberg is a lecturer of English at Peking University. Experienced, too, as a lecturer of biology, she concerns herself with the ways in which the cognitive sciences intersect with popular culture, at times even impacting upon how the individual views herself or himself moving through the world. Thus, she often takes the interstices of the sciences and the humanities as her province of enquiry.

A native Midwesterner, Jennifer completed graduate work at the University of Chicago, before venturing to Beijing, China, to interrogate the transnational circulation of cultural forms. Unmoored from the shapes that evil commonly assumes within American pop culture, certain of its "stateside" contours have emerged to her again in stark relief.

This chapter on the works of Joyce Carol Oates is her first printed publication. As such, she is both daunted and excited to be included amongst her fellow authors.

Since my days as an undergraduate, Joyce Carol Oates's short story, "Where Are You Going, Where Have You Been?" (1966), has fascinated me. In particular, the ways in which Oates used the formal properties of her narrator's language to reveal certain underlying developmental, psychological, and cognitive traits of her main character intrigued me, as did the considerable role that she assigned to popular music—that is to say, one that was much more than simply "atmospheric"—in her neo-Gothic, postmodern fairy tale. Upon reading "Pumpkin-Head" (2009), its similarities to her earlier tale struck me, and I immediately seized upon these two nightmarish stories in light of one another and they might speak to the evolving nature of fear in America. I trust that readers might find these topics as titillating as I did and so might form their own responses to what it is that truly frightens them and–better yet—why it does so!

Carol Colatrella is Professor of Literature, Codirector of the Center for the Study of Women, Science, and Technology, and associate dean for graduate studies in the Ivan Allen College of Liberal Arts at Georgia Institute of Technology. Her scholarly interests focus on the cultural study of 19th- and 20th-century American and European literary, historical, and scientific narratives, particularly those emphasizing moral transgression and social marginality. Since 1993, she has served as the Executive Director of the Society for Literature, Science, and the Arts.

Colatrella has received fellowships from the Rockefeller Foundation, the Mellon Foundation, Northeast Modern Language Association, the Oregon Humanities Center, and the National Endowment for the Humanities. In 2000 and in 2005–2006, she held Fulbright fellowships based in Denmark. Recent grants include those from the Georgia Tech European Union Center, 2010–2011, and Zentrum für Literatur- und Kulturforschung, Berlin, June 2008. She won the Georgia Tech Faculty Outstanding Service Award in 2005, and the Geoffrey G. Eicholz Faculty Teaching Award, 2007–2010.

Cohesion and Dissent in America. Eds. Carol Colatrella and Joseph Alkana. Albany: State University of New York Press, 1994.

Literature and Moral Reform: Melville and the Discipline of Reading. Gainesville: University Press of Florida, 2002.

Technology and Humanity. Ed. Carol Colatrella. Salem Press/EBSCO, 2012.

Toys and Tools in Pink: Cultural Narratives of Gender, Science, and Technology. Columbus: Ohio State University Press. 2011. Listed in "*Choice*'s Compilation of Significant University Titles for Undergraduates, 2011–2012." *Journal of Scholarly Publishing*, October 2012.

Evolution, Sacrifice, and Narrative: Balzac, Zola, and Faulkner. New York: Garland, 1990.

My interests in literary depictions of transgression and marginality date to when I was a teenager. I wrote my college application essay on Herman Melville's *Billy Budd* because I was (and still I am) fascinated by the tension between law and ethics depicted in the narrative.

Mathias Clasen teaches English in the Department of Aesthetics and Communication at Aarhus University, Denmark. He specializes in scary entertainment, particularly American horror fiction from the 20th to 21st centuries, and uses a biocultural framework to make sense of the appeal and the functions of horror across media. He has published in humanities and social science journals on such topics as vampires, zombies, and scary clowns, and can be found online at www.horror.dk/mathias.

"Attention, Counterintuition, Predation: Why Dracula Won't Die." *Style* 46, no. 3 (2012): 378–98.
"The Horror! The Horror!." *The Evolutionary Review* 1, no. 1 (2010): 112–19.
"Monsters Evolve: A Biocultural Approach to Horror Stories." *Review of General Psychology* 16, no. 2 (2012): 222–29.
"Primal Fear: A Darwinian Perspective on Dan Simmons' *Song of Kali.*" *Horror Studies* 2, no. 1 (2011): 89–104.
"Vampire Apocalypse: A Biocultural Critique of Richard Matheson's *I Am Legend.*" *Philosophy and Literature* 34, no. 2 (2010): 313–28.

My professional interest in horror fiction grows out of personal fascination and a desire to understand the truly strange appeal of scary entertainment. Why do so many people willingly seek out media presentations that are designed to make them feel bad? Why do we even react to those illusions that are produced by ink on paper or pixels on a screen? What quirks of human neurocognitive hardwiring make us susceptible to and attracted to horror fiction, whether it is in literature, film, computer games, or another medium? To get a fix on those questions, I employ research on the evolution of human psychology and the construction of human cognitive architecture. As it turns out, humans evolved to be hypervigilant in the face of natural dangers, and horror entertainment is designed to exploit precautionary psychological adaptations. Thus, horror stories give us low-cost experience with danger and the horrifying.

Laura Colmenero-Chilberg is an Associate Professor of Sociology at Black Hills State University. Her scholarship has focused predominantly on gender inequality as represented in popular culture. Her most recent research focuses on the analysis of the witchcraft trials in late 17th-century New England.

"Displaced Homemakers Self-Sufficiency Assistance Act." In *American Women's History: An Encyclopedia*, edited by Hasia R. Diner. 2013.

"Gender in Pop Culture: 'Reading' the Power in Popular Fiction." *The Great Plains Sociologist*. 2008.

"Voters Reframe the Abortion Policy Debate: A Theoretical Analysis of Abortion Attitudes in South Dakota." *The Great Plains Sociologist*. 2010.

"Women Sociological Faculty and Scholarship Success in the Heartland." *Forum on Public Policy*, vol. 2010, no. 2.

My fascination with the Salem witch trials began when I read Elizabeth George Speare's novel *The Witch of Blackbird Pond* in elementary school. This early interest was later fed by other literature including Arthur Miller's *The Crucible*. What began as a literary curiosity has since been fed by my studies of early modern history as well as the work I've done on gender inequality. Why is it that even though both men and women pursued activity in the healing and occult arts, a community's negative social sanctioning primarily affected its women? To try to figure this, out I'm examining primary documents like the Salem witchcraft trial transcripts to help me understand the social context of what happened in Salem, and to try and figure out why it didn't happen elsewhere in the colonies.

Li Cornfeld lives in Montreal where she is a McGill University doctoral student in the Department of Art History and Communication Studies. She has lectured publicly on fairy tales and feminism in New York at the Brooklyn Museum and in Montreal through the Institute for Gender, Sexuality, and Feminism and Studio XX. In 2011, her short film, *3 Fairytales* was screened at The Brooklyn Academy of Music in conjunction with the Brooklyn Arts Council.

"ADHD: Empowerment in Soft Focus." In *Click: When We Knew We Were Feminists*, edited by J. Courtney Sullivan and Courtney E. Martin. Berkeley, CA: Seal Press, 2010.

"How to Do Things with Magic Words: the Scandal of the Spell-Casting Body." In *Hermione Granger Saves the World: Essays on the Feminist Heroine of Hogwarts*, edited by Christopher Bell. Jefferson, NC: McFarland, 2012.

"Shooting Heroines: On Dina Goldstein's 'Fallen Princesses Series'." In *Fallen Princesses*, edited by Dina Goldstein. Vancouver, BC: Blurb, 2011.

When I saw *Snow White on Ice* as a child, I asked to be taken to the bathroom during the last act, because I was afraid of watching the evil queen transform into a hag. Consequently, I missed the end of the production, and so did not see Snow White awaken to the prince's kiss. Around the same time, I refused to stay for the end of *The King and I*, because I had been told the king would die, which I found horrifying. I don't know why my parents continued to take me to the theater, but today my primary scholarly interests are fairy tales, death, and dramatic criticism.

Adam W. Darlage is an instructor in the Humanities and Philosophy Department at Oakton Community College (Des Plaines, Illinois), and Head Upper Elementary Teacher at DuPage Montessori School (Naperville, Illinois). He received his PhD in the History of Christianity from the University of Chicago Divinity School, specializing in 16th-century Reformations, Christian communalism, and polemical literature. His travel grant to study the Communal Studies Collection at University of Southern Indiana's David L. Rice Library spearheaded his research into George Rapp's Harmony Society.

"Double Honor: Elite Hutterite Women in the Sixteenth Century." *Church History: Studies in Christianity and Culture* 79, no. 4 (December 2010).

"The Feast of Corpus Christi in Mikulov, Moravia: Strategies of Roman Catholic Counter-Reform (1579–1586)." *Catholic Historical Review* 96, no. 4 (October 2010).

"Heaven on Earth: George Rapp on the Destiny of Man." *Nineteenth-Century Prose* 39, no. 1/2 (Spring/Fall 2012).

"'Qui tacet consentire videtur': Christoph Andreas Fischer's Polemical Exchange with the Hutterite 'King' Klaus Braidl (1603–1604)." *Renaissance et Réforme* 32, no. 3 (July 2009).

"'They are to be pitied and wept over, not envied': Hutterite Responses to Persecution in the *Chronicle*." *Mennonite Quarterly Review* 83, no. 3 (July 2009).

Evil clowns and serial killers always fascinated me. I vividly recall the first time my twin brother and I tried to watch the movie adaptation of Stephen King's *It*. It did not go so well, especially for my brother, who hates clowns to this day. Yet it wasn't until I began teaching about ancient and contemporary trickster characters for my course on World Mythologies that I became interested in the ever-evolving meme of the evil clown and its historical and cultural connection to John Wayne Gacy. Although early modern Christianity remains my base of research, I am excited about doing more academic work in the field of American pop culture.

George R. "Bob" Dekle Sr. became a legal skills professor at the University of Florida after retiring from the State Attorney's Office of the Third Judicial Circuit of Florida, where he served as an assistant state attorney from 1975 through 2005. The Florida Prosecuting Attorneys Association awarded him the Gene Barry Memorial Award as the outstanding prosecutor in the state (1986); two distinguished faculty awards (1996 and 2003); and a lifetime achievement award for his efforts in continuing education for prosecutors (2005). Professor Dekle served as faculty at the National Advocacy Center in Columbia, South Carolina, and has lectured to prosecutor's associations across the nation. Before becoming a prosecutor, he served from 1973 to 1975 as an Assistant Public Defender.

"Arguing Circumstantial Evidence in Murder Cases." In *Successful Trial Strategies for Prosecutors*. National District Attorneys Association, 2005.
The Case against Christ: A Critique of the Prosecution of Jesus. Cambridge Scholars, 2012.
Coauthor, *Cross Examination Handbook: Persuasion, Strategies, and Techniques.* Wolters-Kluwer, 2011.
The Last Murder: The Investigation, Prosecution, and Execution of Ted Bundy. Praeger, 2010.
Prosecution Principles: A Clinical Handbook. Thomson-West, 2007.

When I was in the seventh grade, I skipped school and went to watch a murder trial. That experience led to a lecture from the principal and a 32-year career in criminal law. During that time I handled hundreds of homicide cases including some against men capable of dimensions of evil I never dreamed existed—from the serial killer who bragged that he had his "own private graveyard" to Ted Bundy. Although I enjoyed trying cases, I also enjoyed serving as "flight instructor" for rookie prosecutors trying their first jury cases. Mentoring young lawyers gave me a passion for legal education, which I continue as director of the Prosecution Clinic at the University of Florida, Levin College of Law.

Ryan P. Doom is a tenured instructor of creative writing and composition at Cowley County Community College. Beyond his studies in fiction, he specializes in genre film, specifically horror, science fiction, and crime. He has written film reviews and columns for the last 10 years. He was awarded the Carol and Elton Holman award for screenwriting and founded Cowley College's first literary magazine, *Mile Marker Review*.

The Brothers Coen: Unique Characters of Violence. Santa Barbara, CA: Praeger, 2009.

I've been a lifelong film fanatic and have found ways to incorporate it in my teaching, my writing, and my studies. I find genre film perhaps the most interesting to explore because I feel it's often overlooked as something lesser even though it tackles more subjects about humanity and social issues than most dramatic features.

Glen M. E. Duerr serves as Assistant Professor of International Studies at Cedarville University in Cedarville, Ohio, USA. He was born in Chatham (southeast England) to an American father and an English mother. He was educated—and resided—in the United Kingdom, United States, and Canada, and conducted extensive research in Belgium. His academic interests include nationalism, international relations theory, and the relationship between Christianity and politics.

Specific publications on issues related to my chapter include:

"The Christian Right." In *Encyclopedia of American Populism,* edited by Alexandra Kindell and Elizabeth Demers. Santa Barbara, CA: ABC-CLIO.

"Faith in Foreign Policy: Evangelical Realism, Not Neo-conservatism in the Presidency of George W. Bush." In *Perspectives on the Legacy of George W. Bush,* edited by Grossman, Michael Orlov, and Ronald Eric Matthews Jr., 120–36. Newcastle upon Tyne: Cambridge Scholars Publishing.

"Non-Denominational Churches." In *Encyclopedia of Religion and Politics in America,* edited by Philip DiMare. Santa Barbara, CA: ABC-CLIO.

"Protestant Vote." In *Encyclopedia of U.S. Campaigns, Elections and Electoral Behavior,* edited by Kenneth F. Warren. Thousand Oaks, CA: SAGE Publishing.

My interest in the question of evil is connected with my faith as a Christian. Most of my political views fall on center-right of the political spectrum in countries of the west. I am interested in both theological and secular interpretations of evil and I am working on a project involving Just War theory, which examines the notion of a "just" governmental response to aggression in the world in light of recent developments in 21st-century warfare. I believe that "evil" is a real and viable concept, especially in light of a major foreign policy speech, but should be approached cautiously because of its potential ramifications. I think that students, academics, politicians, and laypersons alike should ruminate on the concepts of good and evil and their ramifications for both foreign policy and conflict.

Shawn Edrei is currently pursuing PhD at Tel-Aviv University where he also teaches a course in the Department of English and American Studies. While his primary field of research is narratology and new media, Shawn is also fascinated with postmodern literature and the genres of the fantastic (i.e., science fiction, horror, fantasy), and takes every opportunity that he can to conduct academic studies of the latest literary trends.

"For We Are Many: Decentralized Authorship and Reciprocal Readership in Internet-based Fan Fiction." In *Immersive Worlds and Transmedia Narratives.* eds. Shawn Edrei and Natalie Krikowa. Interdisciplinary.net, 2013.

"Once and Future: Representations of Camelot in Non-Arthurian Series." In *Camelot on the Small Screen.* eds. Tara Foster and Jon Sherman. Boydell and Brewer, 2013.

"Press Start to Continue: The Effects of Pseudo-Authorial Control on Video Game Narratives." In *Ctrl-Alt-Play: Essays on Control in Video Gaming.* ed. Matthew Wysocki. McFarland & Company, 2012.

My sudden and immediate obsession with narratology during my BA studies came as no surprise; I've always been interested in storytelling, and here was a field that offered insight into how stories were constructed. Over time, I came to recognize that basic narrative patterns existed in other media as well, though each platform had its own rules and formulae. So I decided to spend this portion of my academic career studying and analyzing "new media" such as the Internet and video games, in which the building blocks of fiction have taken new and surprising forms.

Kristi R. Humphreys is Assistant Professor of Critical Studies and Artistic Practice at Texas Tech University and teaches within the Fine Arts doctoral program. She earned her PhD in the Humanities, Aesthetic Studies at the University of Texas at Dallas, specializing in popular culture, musical theater, and novelist William Faulkner. As a working actress, she performed in over 40 stage productions. Whereas she aspires to earn numerous awards and fellowships for her research, her greatest award to date is the Perfect Attendance award she earned from the Lorena Independent School District for never missing a day of school for 12 years, from 1st through 12th grade.

"Elements of Discontinuity Editing and Film Montage in William Faulkner's *Absalom, Absalom!*." Hawaii International Conference on Arts and Humanities published conference papers, January 2005.

"Supernatural Housework: Magic and Domesticity in 1960s Television." In *Home Sweat Home*, edited by Mimi Choi and Elizabeth Patton. Scarecrow Press, 2013.

My interest in popular culture stems from my wonderfully conservative upbringing on a ranch in the one-stoplight town of Lorena, Texas. Having been reared on classic film musicals and books like *Amelia Bedelia*, I later developed an interest in "forbidden" texts—texts ranging from the works of William Faulkner to the more recent *Harry Potter* series—and in societal responses to these texts. I recognized the benefit of interdisciplinary approaches to my research, whether by understanding Faulkner's prose through film editing or by examining the *Harry Potter* series from a religious perspective. As a college professor, I take the same approach to my instruction, and hope to inspire students to go beyond the standard reading of a text and to consider the possibilities involved in examining it through the lens of another discipline.

Micah Issitt trained in biology and journalism at the University of Missouri and worked as a researcher in animal behavior before transitioning to science writing and journalism as a career. Issitt now works as a freelance writer and journalist and has contributed articles to numerous newspapers, magazines, and educational publications on subjects including science and technology, sociology, and politics. Issitt is the author of two books on deviant social behavior, and is currently working on a third dealing with the symbolism of religions around the world.

Goths. Santa Barbara, CA: ABC-CLIO, 2011.
Hippies. Santa Barbara, CA: ABC-CLIO, 2010.

I have been fanatically interested in animals since I was a child and animal behavior is the one core interest that has remained with me through my adult life. As I have come to focus on human behavior and culture in my writing, I have developed a keen interest in the intersections between human and nonhuman life. The way that humans view animals and the role that animals play in religion, culture, and mythology reflects a rich, often subconscious, host of primordial fears, drives, and desires that, in many ways, reflect the animal nature of humanity and reveal how, though we may wish to imagine ourselves as life of an entirely different order, we are still inextricably linked to the larger biosphere that surrounds us.

Michael D. Kelleher is the internationally acclaimed author of *Profiling the Lethal Employee, Murder Most Rare: The Female Serial Killer, When Good Kids Kill,* and *This Is the Zodiac Speaking.* His long list of publishing credits includes work for such venerable houses as Random House, Dell, and the Greenwood Publishing Group. Kelleher's work has appeared in many of the country's major dailies, including the *Washington Post,* the *New York Times* and the *San Francisco Examiner.* He is a frequent guest on both radio and television, and has appeared on the national news program 20/20. Kelleher has been a guest lecturer in the California State University system and consults to organizations in both the private and public sector.

Flash Point: The American Mass Murderer. Santa Barbara, CA: Praeger, 1997.
Murder Most Rare: The Female Serial Killer. Santa Barbara, CA: Praeger, 1998.
New Arenas for Violence. Santa Barbara, CA: Praeger, 1996.
Profiling the Lethal Employee. Santa Barbara, CA: Praeger, 1997.
This Is the Zodiac Speaking. Santa Barbara, CA: Praeger, 2001.
When Good Kids Kill. Santa Barbara, CA: Praeger, 1998.

Kelleher lives in the Pacific Northwest. He is the father of four grown children. Kelleher specializes in strategic management, threat assessment, and crisis resolution in both the public and private sectors.

Monika Keska is a postdoctoral fellow at the University of Granada. She obtained her European PhD in History of Art from the same University in 2009 with a thesis dedicated to the cinema of Peter Greenaway. In 2011, she received a mobility fellowship from the Spanish Ministry of Education for her project on the influence of the painting of Francis Bacon on visual and narrative systems in film and literature. She has also participated in the Bacon's Books project at the Hugh Lane Gallery and Trinity College, Dublin, where she catalogued the private library of the artist. Her current research interests are centered on the relations between 20th-century painting and cinema.

"Blue de Derek Jarman: Crónica de una muerte anunciada." In *Arte, Individuo y Sociedad* no. 22, 2010.
"Crucifixions and Popes: Religious Imagery in the Works of Francis Bacon." In *The Challenge of the Object/Die Herausforderung des Objekt.* Nuremberg, 2013.
"Las referencias a Francis Bacon en la obra de Peter Greenaway." In *Docta Minerva*, Jaén, Universidad de Jaén, 2011.
"The sonority of the Painting of Francis Bacon, 'The Shout' by Jerzy Skolimowski." In *Art Margins*, 2012.

I began my research on the relationship between Francis Bacon and cinema while working on my thesis. I found numerous references to Ba'con's art in the works of Peter Greenaway. I later found images from Greenway's films in Francis artist's studio while working on the Bacon's Books project in the Hugh Lane Gallery. The painter, who described his triptychs as *a way of making a film*, often sought inspiration in books on cinema and films stills, which he employed as source material for his own works. While Bacon's interest in cinema has been already thoroughly analyzed, the presence of his work in cinema is a subject yet to be studied.

Joseph Laycock currently teaches for University of Virginia's Semester at Sea Program and is an adjunct at Piedmont Virginia Community College. He taught for the Experimental College at Tufts University, specializing in American religious history as well as sociological approaches to religion and new religious movements. He received the Thomas Robbins Award for Excellence in the Study of New Religious Movements and the Angela J. and James J. Rallis Memorial Award/Alice M. Brennan Humanities Award for Outstanding Teaching Fellow in Religious and Theological Studies, both from Boston University.

"Carnal Knowledge: The Epistemology of Sexual Trauma in Witches' Sabbath, Satanic Ritual Abuse, and Alien Abduction Narratives." *Preternature* 1, 1 (2012): 100–129.

"Levitating the Pentagon: Exorcism as Politics, Politics as Exorcism." *Implicit Religion* 14, 3 (2011): 295–318.
"Review Essay: Paranormal Belief: A New Frontier?" *Nova Religio* 15, 5 (2011): 92–97.
Vampires Today: The Truth about Modern Vampirism. Westport: Praeger, 2009.
"'We Are Spirits of Another Sort': Ontological Rebellion and Religious Dimensions of the Otherkin Community." *Nova Religio* 15, 3 (2012): 65–90.

Like so many people interested in the West Memphis Three, I watched the documentary *Paradise Lost* and was profoundly disturbed, being roughly the same age as Damian Echols. What happened to him could have easily happened to me as a teenager. Fortunately, I was able to go to college and graduate school where I learned how to think about moral panic as a sociologist. It is important that we study causes of moral panic rather than villanizing the people of West Memphis or congratulating ourselves on the eventual release of the West Memphis Three. There are almost certainly other individuals whom the justice system has failed and who will never receive the support of filmmakers and celebrities. Only by studying history and promoting critical thinking can tragedies such as this be avoided in the future.

Martin J. Manning is a research librarian in the Bureau of International Information Programs, U.S. Department of State, Washington, D.C., on the Publications Team and archivist of the Public Diplomacy Historical Collection, a position he held with the bureau's predecessor, the U.S. Information Agency, 1978–1999. He has also been a researcher at the National Portrait Gallery, Smithsonian Institution, Washington, D.C., where he worked on exhibitions with the senior historian. His areas of research and expertise include U.S. diplomatic history, popular culture, world's fairs, propaganda, and library history. He has a BS from Boston College and an MSLS from Catholic University of America.

Encyclopedia of Herbs, Spices, and Botanicals, coauthored with Frank W. Hoffmann. Binghamton, NY: Haworth Press, 2002.
Historical Dictionary of American Propaganda; with Herbert Romerstein Westport, CT: Greenwood Press, 2004.
Media and Propaganda in Wartime America, coedited with Clarence Wyatt. Santa Barbara, CA: ABC-CLIO, 2010.
"Reading in the Era of Discovery and Exploration: Prior to 1700." In *Cultural History of Reading,* vol. 2. American Literature, edited by Sara E. Quay. Westport, CT: Greenwood Press, 2009.

I first became interested in Walt Disney through the Sunday night presentations, on black and white television no less, of his "Wonderful

World of Color" but I got to know his dark side, especially his role as an FBI informant, through my study of McCarthyism and the "red scare" throughout the United States. Disney's multifaceted personality continually fascinates and I think this came out in many of his films!

Gregory K. Moffatt, PhD, is Professor of Psychology at Point University, near Atlanta, Georgia, and Chair of the Department of Counseling and Human Services. He is a published author, licensed counselor, newspaper columnist, and public speaker who has presented to audiences in over 25 countries. Dr. Moffatt has served as a regular lecturer at the FBI Academy, a profiler with the Atlanta Cold Case Squad, and consultant to numerous airlines, businesses, and schools. He has appeared on ABC, NBC, CBS, and FOX news, as well as America's Most Wanted.

Blind-Sided: Homicide Where It Is Least Expected. Westport, CT: Praeger, 2000.
"Childhood Exposure to Conjugal Violence: Developmental Considerations and Consequences for Behavior and Neural Development." *DePaul Law Review* 56 (2007): 879–94.
Handcuffed: A Friendship of Endurance. New York: Publish America, 2007.
Stone Cold Souls: History's Most Vicious Killers. Westport, CT: Praeger, 2010.
Survivors: What We Can Learn from How They Cope with Horrific Tragedy. Westport, CT: Praeger, 2010.
"Typical and Atypical Homicide: Investigative Differences and Cold Case Profiling." *The Forensic Examiner* 19, no.1 (2010): 40–46 (with Nick Hersey).
A Violent Heart: Understanding Aggressive Individuals. Westport, CT: Praeger, 2002.
Wounded Innocents and Fallen Angels. Westport, CT: Praeger, 2003.

My interest in violent behavior began in my graduate school days in the 1980s when workplace and school shootings monopolized the news. I wanted to know why people went to such extreme measures and how seemingly ordinary people could transition to homicidal behavior. I have since learned that these were *not* ordinary people and that when one knows what to look for, signs of such behaviors can be seen in advance. This has led me to a career of violence risk assessment as well as a fascinating career assisting in the investigation of homicide, rape, and other violent crimes.

Sharon Packer, MD, is a physician, psychiatrist, and psychopharmacologist in private practice in Soho (NYC) and Woodstock and an Assistant Clinical Professor of Psychiatry and Behavioral Sciences at Albert Einstein College of Medicine. She authored many award-winning academic books, book chapters, and journal articles on psychiatry and film, psychiatry and religion, psychopharmacological side effects, psychiatric medicine, and the history of medicine. She is a regular columnist for both medical and trade magazines. She previously taught online college and graduate level classes in media studies and psychology and researched race and gender issues in online learning. Prior to completing her BA and MD at University of Illinois in Chicago, she earned certification in Orthodox Jewish Education. Her paintings showed at galleries and museums across the country.

Cinema's Sinister Psychiatrists. Jefferson, NC: McFarland, 2012.
Dreams in Myth, Medicine & Movies. Westport, CT: Praeger, 2002.
Movies & the Modern Psyche. Westport, CT: Praeger, 2007.
Superheroes and Superegos. Santa Barbara, CA: ABC-CLIO, 2010.

Dr. Packer was surprised to be asked to coedit this series on *Evil in Pop Culture*. She suspects that her query about *Cinemas' Sinister Psychiatrists* stirred the editor's imagination. Admittedly, decades ago, early in her career, she was promoted to Acting Medical Director of NYC's Department of Correction, where she designed and developed a health service for correction officers of the world's largest penal system. She proceeded to research correction officers' excessive use of force, thereby directly encountering evil daily. This foray into institutionalized evil was inadvertent, in that she was merely seeking a stable job that accommodated her evening art classes. She was relieved to return to regular psychiatric patient care and to pursue other research. In editing this series, she was surprised to see how much "evil" permeates mainstream pop culture and that "evil" is hardly confined to prisons.

Caleb Puckett is an academic librarian at Ottawa University, Kansas. Puckett directs the university's information literacy program and manages research technologies. Puckett published and presented on information literacy and is a member of several professional library associations, including Beta Phi Mu, the International Library and Information Studies Honor Society. Prior to becoming a librarian, Puckett taught writing and literature. He maintains his connection to the literary arts as a short story writer, poet, and scholar. He is an editor for *Nimrod International Journal* and a member of the Kansas Poet Laureate Advisory and Selection Committees.

Caleb Puckett & Friends—In Mixed Company. Neuville-les-Dames, France: mgv2> publishing, 2013.
Desertions. Alexandria, VA: Plan B Press, 2007.
"Ecopoetics." In *America Goes Green: An Encyclopedia of Eco-Friendly Culture in the United States*, edited by Kim Kennedy White, 75–77. Santa Barbara, CA: ABC-CLIO, 2012.
Market Street Exit. Rockhampton, Australia: Otoliths, 2011.

"Mina Loy." In *American Writers: A Collection of Literary Biographies, Supplement XXII*, edited by Jay Parini, 155–70. Farmington Hills, MI: Scribner's/ Gale Cengage Learning, 2011.

"Phillis Wheatley." In *American Writers: A Collection of Literary Biographies*, supplement XX, edited by Jay Parini, 277–91. Farmington Hills, MI: Scribner's/Gale Cengage Learning, 2010.

Tales from the Hinterland. Rockhampton, Australia: Otoliths, 2008.

No American writer has experienced a cultural afterlife as varied and all-pervading as the one accorded to Edgar Allan Poe. Puckett has an abiding interest in how the intersections between Poe's life and writing repeatedly manifest themselves in the products of our popular imagination. Indeed, whether we look at comic books, historical novels, or short films, we always find some element of Poe at play. Puckett is fascinated by the strange and oftentimes contradictory mythologies surrounding Poe and how those mythologies continue to provide us with opportunities to engage with the archetypes of outsider and artist.

Katherine Ramsland is a professor of forensic psychology and criminal justice at DeSales University in eastern Pennsylvania. She has published more than 1,000 articles and 47 books. She has researched and written about subjects as diverse as criminal psychology, forensics, paranormal practitioners, and the vampire subculture. She holds graduate degrees, respectively, in forensic psychology, clinical psychology, criminal justice, and philosophy, and in 2008, the John Jay College of Criminal Justice honored her as its outstanding alumna. Ramsland speaks internationally and has appeared on numerous documentaries, as well as on programs such as *The Today Show, 20/20, The Montel Williams Show*, NPR, *Larry King Live*, and *E! True Hollywood Story*. She also consulted for the popular TV series, *CSI* and *Bones*. Currently, she writes a regular blog for *Psychology Today*, called "Shadow Boxing."

Blood and Ghosts: Paranormal Forensic Investigators. Second Chance Publishing, 2012.

The Forensic Psychology of Criminal Minds. Berkley, 2010.

The Human Predator: A Historical Chronicle of Serial Murder and Forensic Investigation. Berkley, 2006.

Inside the Minds of Serial Killers. Praeger, 2006.

The Ivy League Killer. CrimeScape, 2012.

The Mind of a Murderer: Privileged Access to the Demons That Drive Extreme Violence. Praeger, 2011.

Piercing the Darkness: Undercover with Vampires in America Today. HarperCollins, 1998.

Psychopath. CrimeScape, 2011.

The Science of Vampires. Berkley, 2002.

Snap: Seizing Your aha! Moments. Prometheus, 2012.

As I have searched for "characters" for writing projects, I have interviewed demonologists, self-professed vampires, necrophiliacs, murderers, death fetishists, gravediggers, and many other unique individuals. Mostly, I find the dark side of human nature intriguing. Sometimes, it's disturbing, and in some cases, it's evil. As an explorer of dark psychology, I believe it's important to learn what we can about evil in all its manifestations, whether symbolic, literary, or real. My associates call me fearless; I just think I'm curious.

Eric Sandberg is a lecturer in literature at Miyazaki International College, in Miyzaki, Japan. He completed his PhD in English Literature at the University of Edinburgh, where he worked on modernist literature and issues of characterization. He received a Languages and Culture Scholarship from the University of Edinburgh. His MA thesis on Virginia Woolf won the Thesis and Project of the Year Competition at California State University, Dominguez Hills.

"A Certain Phantom: Virginia Woolf's Early Journalism, Censorship, and the Angel in the House." *Virginia Woolf Miscellany* 76 (2009).
"'Even the Faintest Imprint': Intertextualities in Philip Roth's *The Prague Orgy*". *Philip Roth: Transatlantic Perspectives*. Ed. Velichka Ivanova. Amherst: Cambria Press, 2013.
"A Floating Carnival: P. G. Wodehouse and the Atlantic Crossing." *The Atlantic: Tourists' Experiences in the 20th Century*. Ed. Claudia Andrea Müller and Brigit Braasch. Berlin: Lit-Verlag, 2013.
"To Want and Not to Have": Desire and Form in Virginia Woolf's *To the Lighthouse*." *Affirmations: of the Modern* 2 (2013).
"Virgil's Aeneid and the Ambivalence of Aeneas' Heroic Quest." *Critical Insights: The Hero's Quest*. Ed. Bernard Schweizer and Robert A. Segal. Ipswich: Salem House Publishing, 2012.
"Virginia Woolf." *The Year's Work in English Studies* 91 (2012).

I have been reading mystery, crime, and detective novels for much of my life, but my academic interest in the hard-boiled novel began when I realized that it is one of the most persistently popular forms of genre fiction. I began to ask myself why this particular type of narrative has resonated so powerfully with so many readers from so many parts of the world for so many years. My contribution to this volume attempts to understand part of this attraction. The classic work of Hammett, Chandler, and others demands rereading to help us understand the peculiar and powerful attraction of this bleakly expressive form.

Christoph Schiessl received an MA and a BA in history and political science from the Katholische Universitaet Eichstaett-Ingolstadt in Germany. During his fellowship at the Museum, he was a PhD candidate in history at Wayne State University and taught world and American history at Cranbrook/Kingswood Upper Schools in Michigan. For his Center for Advanced Holocaust Studies fellowship, Mr. Schiessl conducted research on "The Search for Eastern European Nazi Collaborators in the United States."

"An Element of Genocide: Rape, Total War and International Law in the Twentieth Century." *Journal of Genocide Research* 4 (2002).
"Nazi Collaborators from Eastern Europe as Immigrants and the Displaced Persons Act." *Michigan Academician* 35, no. 3 (Fall 2003).

Among Mr. Schiessl's honors include the Alfred H. Kelly Award and the Thomas C. Rumble Fellowship from Wayne State University. During his tenure at the Museum, Mr. Schiessl examined the efforts to locate and prosecute Eastern European Nazi collaborators in the United States of which approximately 10,000 were permitted entry through the Displaced Persons Acts of 1948 and 1950. Mr. Schiessl's historical overview addressed why so many collaborators were able to gain entry and why the search for collaborators in the United States did not begin until the 1970s.

Hans C. Schmidt is an assistant professor of communications at the Pennsylvania State University, Brandywine. He earned his PhD in Mass Media and Communication at Temple University in Philadelphia, Pennsylvania, and currently teaches courses in mass media and communication, public speaking, journalism, and public relations. His research interests include political communication, media literacy, and journalism education. He serves on the executive committee of the Pennsylvania Communication Association, and is also involved with the Eastern Communication Association, National Communication Association, and Popular Culture Association/American Culture Association.

"Addressing Media Literacy within Higher Education: A Comparison of Faculty and Student Perceptions." *Northwest Journal of Communication* 4, no. 1 (2013): 161–87.
"Communication Patterns and the University-Level Tutor." *Journal of College Reading and Learning* 42, no. 1 (2011): 45–60.
"Essential but Problematic: Faculty Perceptions of Media Literacy Education at the University Level." *Qualitative Research Reports in Communication* 13, no. 1 (2012): 10–20.
"The Flag Raising on Iwo Jima: The Importance of Presenting Photographs in Context." *Mid-Atlantic Popular/American Culture Association Gazette* (2011).
"Propaganda." In *Encyclopedia of Military Science*, edited by G. Kurt Piehler. Thousand Oaks, CA: Sage, in press.

"Television Variety Shows." In *Music in American Life: An Encyclopedia of the Songs, Styles, Stars, and Stories that Shaped Our Culture*, edited by Jacqueline Edmondson. Santa Barbara, CA: ABC-CLIO, in press.

My interest in political communication developed early in my career while working as a newspaper journalist and covering political and government stories. Today, I continue to follow the intersection of political communication, popular culture, and the dynamic relationship between media and society. In the modern age of media convergence, the importance of understanding this complex relationship between individuals, society, and the media we all both create and consume cannot be overstated.

Andrea Siegel, PhD, is an Adjunct Assistant Professor at the City University of New York (CUNY) and Coordinator of the Permanent Collection of Art at Hudson County Community College in New Jersey, where her work is to turn all the public areas of the college into an educational art museum. She has won numerous grants, most recently a CUNY adjunct development grant to study Art Crime in Italy.

"The James Bond/Woody Allen Dialectic." In *James Bond in World and Popular Culture*, edited by Rob Weiner, Jack Becker, and Lynn Whitefield. Cambridge Scholars Press, 2010.
Open and Clothed. Woodside, NY: Agapanthus Books, 1999.
Splash! A Handbook for Parents to Teach Kids Who Fear Water to Swim (forthcoming).
Women in Aikido. Berkeley, CA: North Atlantic Books, 1993.

My interest in vampire literature began when an otherwise-rational old friend with whom I'd worked in the 1990s at Lucasfilm, drove me to a bookstore, thrust a copy of *Twilight* into my hands and insisted I look at the lead vampire, Edward, as the perfect man. As I read through Meyer's works, I was "hooked" without understanding why, and not remotely embarrassed about it (a gift of middle age). Then I voraciously read on in contemporary vampire literature through the *True Blood* series and then read "backward" in time in vampire literature to *Dracula*, and into the earlier vampire myths. As these stories, contradictory and congruent in unexpected ways, bubbled in my mind one morning in bed, a pattern emerged that I explored through writing this essay. Ideas emerge in unexpected ways, and in unexpected places. The pleasure I encourage you to pursue, is to play with ideas and pursue them.

Joseph W. Slade is Professor of Media Arts and Studies and Co-director of the Central Region Humanities Center at Ohio University. A cultural historian of technology, he explores the ways that messages move through back channels of communication such as gossip, espionage, and outlaw forms of discourse, and also studies the displacement of thermodynamic metaphors by organic ones as keys to understanding how cultures stabilize themselves. He has been a Fellow in Technology and Culture at the National Humanities Institute at the University of Chicago, and has held the Bicentennial Chair of American Studies at the University of Helsinki. He has won two "Best Reference Work" awards from *Library Journal*.

Beyond the Two Cultures: Essays on Science, Technology, and Literature, edited by Slade and Judith Yaross Lee. Ames, IA: Iowa State University Press, 1990.

The Midwest, edited by Slade and Judith Yaross Lee, a volume of The Greenwood Encyclopedia of American Regional Cultures. Westport, CT: Greenwood, 2004.

Pornography in America: A Reference Handbook. Los Angeles: ABC-CLIO, 2000.

Pornography and Sexual Representation: A Reference Guide. 3 vols. Westport, CT: Greenwood Press, 2001.

Thomas Lake Harris and the Brotherhood of the New Life. New York: Microfilm Corporation of America (*The New York Times*), 1974.

Thomas Pynchon. New York: Warner Paperback Library, 1974; second edition. New York: Peter Lang, 1990.

Pornography has been one of my research interests for many years because sexual representations embody both socially constructed and sociobiological tropes and images, and because such representations refresh a culture as they move from margins to mainstream. However one might think of pornography, and it presents both positive and negative aspects, it tells us a great deal about what it means to be human.

William H. Taylor is an Assistant Professor of History at one of the oldest Historically Black College and Universities (HBCUs) in the United States, Alabama State University, which is located in Montgomery, Alabama. He specializes in Anglo-American religious and cultural history and has presented his research to academic and nonacademic audiences across the United States. Much of his of work has examined the 18th-century American Presbyterians, but it has also included the 17th-century New England Congregationalists, the Bloomsbury Group of Central London, C.S. Lewis, 20th-century American Fundamentalism, and *Harry Potter*. In 2012, Dr. Taylor received the Alabama State University Research Award. He has published within his fields and is currently working on two book-length projects.

"'All Things Respecting Us Are Loudly Alarming': The French and Indian War and the Origin of Presbyterian Interdenominationalism." In *Culture, Power, and Security: New Directions in the History of National and International Security*, edited by Mary Kathryn Barbier and Richard V. Damms. Cambridge Scholars Publishing, November 2012.

"Samuel Davies and the Curse of Cowardice." In *Defining Documents in American History: The American Revolution 1754–1805*, edited by Peter Kratzke. Pasadena: Salem Press, December 2012.

"Unintended Consequences: Southern Presbyterians and Interdenominationalism in the late Eighteenth Century." *Journal of Southern Religion*, XII (September 2010).

I was introduced to the *Harry Potter* novels as a freshman in college, but I readily dismissed them because I believed myself far too mature for such juvenile literature. During graduate school, where healthy doses of humility waited around every corner, I finally read J. K. Rowling's novels and was quickly enthralled. As much as I enjoyed the novels, however, there were increasing numbers of Americans who were outraged by their success. The myriad responses to the books provided me the excuse to reread them for academic purposes.

Brenda Gardenour Walter holds a PhD in medieval history from Boston University, specializing in the history of medieval medicine and hagiography. She was a Fulbright scholar in Madrid, an Evelyn Nation research fellow at the Huntington Library in California, and a National Endowment for the Humanities fellow at the Wellcome Institute for the History of Medicine (London). She is currently Assistant Professor of History at the Saint Louis College of Pharmacy.

"Beyond the Gothic: The Horror of Connectivity and the Transnational Flow of Fear." In *Transnational Horror across Visual Media: Fragmented Bodies*. New York: Routledge Press, 2014.

"The Biology of Blood-Lust: Medieval Physiognomy, Physiology, and the Vampire Jew in Twentieth Century Cinema," *Film and History* 41, no. 2 (2011).

"The Compassionate Country Doctor and Cold-Blooded Biomedicine: Bones, Spock, and Medicine beyond the Machine." In *Star Trek and History*. New York: Wiley and Sons, 2013.

"Corrupt Air, Poisonous Places, and the Toxic Breath of Witches in Late-Medieval Medicine and Theology." In *Toxic Airs: Chemical and Environmental Histories of the Atmosphere*. Pittsburgh: University of Pittsburgh Press, 2013.

Parasites, Worms, and the Human Body in Religion and Culture. New York: Peter Lang, 2012.

"*Silent Hill* and *Fatal Frame*: Finding Transcendent Horror in and beyond the Haunted Magic Circle." In *Finding Religion in Digital Gaming*. Bloomington: Indiana University Press, 2014.

"*Theorica et Practica:* Historical Epistemology and the Re-Visioning of Thirteenth and Fourteenth-Century Medicine." In *Teorie vědy* (Theory of Science). Prague: Academy of Sciences of the Czech Republic, 2011.

My next book is *Monster Flesh: The Bodies of Old Monsters from Medieval Theology and Medicine to the Horror Film.* My fascination with medicine, science, and mysterious creatures began with a childhood love of Creature Double Features. Now, as an adult, my work routinely comes back to ideas of monstrous embodiment and disembodiment, and the relationship between spirit and flesh.

Index